Making Men

Making Men

The Male Coming-of-Age Theme in the Hebrew Bible

STEPHEN M. WILSON

OXFORD
UNIVERSITY PRESS

OXFORD
UNIVERSITY PRESS

Oxford University Press is a department of the University of Oxford.
It furthers the University's objective of excellence in research, scholarship,
and education by publishing worldwide. Oxford is a registered trade mark
of Oxford University Press in the UK and in certain other countries.

Published in the United States of America by
Oxford University Press
198 Madison Avenue, New York, NY 10016,
United States of America

Library of Congress Cataloging-in-Publication Data
Wilson, Stephan M., author.
  Making men : the male coming-of-age theme in the Hebrew Bible / Stephen M. Wilson.
     p.   cm.
  Includes bibliographical references and index.
  Summary: "This book identifies seven narratives of male maturation in the Hebrew Bible,
and shows how this theme is employed by biblical redactors and narrators to highlight
transitions in the historical prose of the Hebrew Bible. It also considers how these stories
provide insight into the varying representations of biblical masculinity"— Provided by
publisher.
  ISBN 978–0–19–022282–6 (alk. paper) — ISBN 978–0–19–022283–3 (e-book) 1. Masculinity
in the Bible. 2. Maturation (Psychology)—Biblical teaching. 3. Bible. Old Testament—
Criticism, interpretation, etc. I. Title.
  BS1199.M34W55 2015
  221.8'30531—dc23
                              2015009157

9 8 7 6 5 4 3 2 1

Printed on acid-free paper

Printed by Edwards Brothers, US

To Blair, with gratitude and love

Contents

SECTION I: *The Depiction of Manhood and Boyhood in the Hebrew Bible*

Acknowledgments

IT HAS OFTEN occurred to me in the course of writing this book on coming of age that completing the book—my first—to a great extent marks my own maturation as a scholar (and yes, perhaps in some ways as a man). And as with most initiation rites, a host of venerable elders has guided me through the often harrowing process. At the outset of this study, I would like to acknowledge their contributions to its completion.

I would first like to express my sincere thanks to Carol Meyers, who was this project's primary adviser when it was a doctoral dissertation at Duke University. Carol's clarity of thought, attention to detail, and ability to provide practical solutions to convoluted theoretical problems helped me to streamline and discipline my thoughts during the writing process, and without this assistance the project could have followed a number of unproductive and time-consuming tangents. I am most thankful to Carol, however, for her high standards for me and my writing, her patience with me when I fell short of these expectations, and her belief that I could live up to them even when I worried that I could not. She demanded and eventually brought forth my best work.

This book represents the culmination of an education in the Bible that began as a child. My parents, Robert and Barbara Wilson, instilled in me a commitment to hard work that they modeled daily on our family farm, as well as a fascination with learning, and a profound respect for the Scriptures. I am immeasurably indebted to them and to my sisters and brothers: Deborah Carlton, Dr. Robert Wilson, Jr., Rev. Timothy Wilson, and Wendy Haddock. I am also grateful for the humility that comes with the awareness that, despite my degrees in biblical studies, I still am not the most knowledgeable student of the Bible in my family.

The initial interest in the Bible I inherited from my family would not have become my life's work were it not for the inspiration of Tod Linafelt: master of reality, martial artist, and professor of biblical literature at Georgetown University. Tod introduced me to an entirely new way of reading the Bible, encouraged me to trust my exegetical instincts, and convinced me to become a biblical scholar. His influence is evident in all of my work, including this book, which he helped foster from its early stages and through to its publication. Mark George also had an important impact on this project since it began as a half-baked eight-page paper written in an all-night Denver diner for his Judges seminar at Iliff School of Theology. Mark saw the potential in these nascent ideas—and in me—and has remained a trusted mentor.

My thanks also go out to the scholars who read this work in its dissertation phase and provided invaluable comments for its improvement: Ellen Davis, Eric Meyers, Stephen Chapman, and Susan Niditch. Ellen's unwavering encouragement and generosity with her time have buoyed my spirits again and again over the past few years, and she has done more than anyone else to motivate my study of the Hebrew language—and to show me why this is so vital to my future as a biblical scholar. Eric's interest in me and my approach to biblical scholarship was a deciding factor in my decision to attend Duke, and he was consistently a helpful and informative presence during my years there. Stephen kindly offered to teach a seminar on the Deuteronomistic History with my interests in mind, and the final paper for that course laid important foundations for this book. Susan Niditch's work on Samson inspired my initial reflections on this heroic figure, and with her expertise in folklore studies, she brought important sources on coming of age in traditional literature to my attention.

I would also like to thank Dr. Kevin Moore sincerely for his patient, careful, and erudite editing of many of the chapters in this book. Knowing that my work would pass before him prior to reaching a broader audience freed me to let my ideas take shape without stopping after every sentence to ensure that each "i" was dotted and every "t" crossed. I owe him much more than just coffee.

And of course I am also deeply thankful to Steve Wiggins and Oxford University Press for publishing this work.

These "elders" who have guided me through the academic-maturation rite of researching and writing my first book certainly deserve their credit, but completing this project would have been much more difficult were it not for the support and counsel of a cohort of fellow "initiates," some young academics like me, others on different paths with their own unique challenges and milestones. My thanks to Ben Gordon (who also provided helpful editing assistance), Julianne and Corey Kalbaugh, Kate Bowler, Toban Penner, Hans Arneson, Jessica Wong, Robert Moses, Joshua Vis, Erin Darby, P. J. "Russell" Wright, Jeffrey Scholes, Gregory Boylan (O. J. B.), Nas Gallina, Grant S. C. Gieseke, and Tina L. Wilson.

Finally, to my best friend and strongest supporter, the long-suffering Blair Wilson: my most heartfelt thanks and love for sharing all the joys, frustrations, failures, and successes of the last several years while I was writing this book. I could never have completed it without you. The least I could do to express my gratitude is to dedicate this book to you.

Introduction: Masculinity Studies, Rites of Passage, and the Absence of an Extended Treatment of Male Coming of Age in Biblical Scholarship

ONE OF THE most significant social and physiological transitions in a man's life is the change from childhood to adulthood. However, identifying and describing this transition in a particular culture is often difficult because the age or developmental stage at which a boy is considered a man, as well as the way that change is socially recognized, differs considerably among cultures. As a result of the imprecise border between boyhood and manhood, many cultures stage elaborate and occasionally traumatic public rituals for groups of boys to announce their transition into manhood, thereby providing proof of maturation independent of any observable physiological evidence.[1] These rituals are often accompanied by myths that are concerned with the theme of male coming of age and that feature boy protagonists whose maturation in the story reflects that of the young male initiates. Such coming-of-age stories, however, are not only told as myths in connection with maturation rituals. Indeed, in the modern West, where formal coming-of-age rites for boys have all but vanished—the noteworthy exception being the Jewish ritual of bar mitzvah—the enduring popularity of stories that incorporate this theme is unmistakable, with such "initiatory boy heroes" as young Werther, David Copperfield, and Luke Skywalker among the most memorable characters in modern literature and film.

In light of the prevalence of the narrative theme of male coming of age—even in societies lacking a system of maturation rites—it is worth asking whether this theme is attested in the literature of ancient Israel found in the Hebrew Bible (HB). Considering that many of the most recognizable male

heroes in the HB are initially introduced into the narrative as boys, the potential for locating male coming-of-age narratives is high. Therefore it is curious
that, with a few exceptions noted below, scholars of the HB have not previously undertaken a study of biblical depictions of maturation from boyhood
into manhood.

This lacuna in biblical scholarship is especially noteworthy because of the
comparatively large amount of attention scholars have paid to two closely related topics. The first is the growing field of HB masculinity studies, which
attempts to illuminate the tacit assumptions about manhood found in the
biblical text. Yet despite this increased interest in biblical manhood, *how* a
character becomes a man after previously being considered only a potential
man (i.e., a boy) has not been addressed. In addition, as I will argue below,
any discussion of manhood is incomplete unless accompanied by a consideration of boyhood and how a boy transitions into manhood.

The second topic concerns rites of passage. Even though this concept has
informed biblical narrative exegesis for decades, a review of the history of research into rites of passage indicates that anthropologists' original application of this concept predominantly focused on coming-of-age rituals.
Regrettably, by applying the concept of rites of passage to biblical texts without also discussing coming of age, biblical scholarship has heretofore missed
the opportunity to apply this concept to a uniquely appropriate subject.

This book is an attempt to fill these lacunae in biblical scholarship. The
primary objective is to read a select group of biblical narratives in light of the
coming-of-age theme. In pursuit of this goal, the Introduction begins by providing a more detailed look at the two subjects closely related to coming of age
just discussed: masculinity in the HB, and the exegetical application of the
rites-of-passage schema to biblical narratives. The review of these two subjects includes a discussion of their roots in fields external to the discipline of
biblical studies: masculinity studies and anthropology. It also clarifies the
application of these concepts (and occasionally their misapplication) in biblical studies and introduces how each respective subject provides important
foundational work for an investigation of the coming-of-age theme. The next
section of this Introduction begins with a discussion of previous attempts by
HB scholars to identify the coming-of-age theme in various biblical narratives. After highlighting the strengths and weaknesses of these attempts,
four methodological principles are presented, which guide the identification
of this theme in the present project and distinguish this study from previous
scholarship. The Introduction concludes by detailing the scope and goals of
the book, including an outline of the argument in the subsequent chapters.

The Impact of Masculinity Studies on Biblical Scholarship and This Project

The interdisciplinary field of masculinity studies gained momentum in the last quarter of the twentieth century as an inheritor of first- and second-wave feminism's critique of gender essentialism and patriarchal rule. It continues feminism's examination of gender's importance in shaping social life by discussing the impact of a society's construction of masculinity on the experiences of its men. Scholars in this field therefore attempt to reveal the often implicit assumptions about masculinity that perpetuate adult male domination and oppression of women and children. The following section outlines the history of this field of inquiry and identifies the major contributions of masculinity studies to research on manhood in the HB. Additionally, it demonstrates how this research frames my investigation of the male coming-of-age theme in the HB.

When reviewing the history of masculinity studies, most specialists in the field begin with Freud and the advent of psychoanalysis in the early twentieth century.[2] Freud believed that a mixture of femininity and masculinity is found in every person. During childhood, as gender development takes place, one of the two gender identities (i.e., femininity or masculinity) is encouraged while the other is suppressed but never entirely absent.[3] This revolutionary thought challenged the reigning notions of pure masculinity or pure femininity as well as the belief that there was something biologically natural and essential about the differences between men and women. Freud thereby cleared the way for the discussion of the cultural construction of gender in feminist theory and masculinity studies in the next century.[4]

The next significant precursor to modern masculinity studies is sex-role theory, which dominated sociological reflection on gender in the mid-twentieth century. The major tenet of this theory is that both the masculine and feminine genders are internalized through socialization and are performed as roles on the social stage. Performing these roles through enacting prescribed behaviors and attitudes results in a smoothly functioning society and psychologically well-adjusted individuals within that society, just as an actor's proper role-playing ensures the smooth functioning of a theatrical performance.[5] Modern masculinity studies is indebted to the notion of gender as performance so central to sex-role theory, although scholars like Judith Butler have provided necessary correctives and nuance to it by destabilizing the clear distinction between the biological sexes presumed by sex-role theorists.[6] However, the greatest impact of sex-role theory on masculinity studies in its current iteration is that it provides a theory against which to react. Indeed, the criticism of sex-role theory seems to be one of the few uniting concepts in the diverse field of masculinity studies.

Scholars of masculinity find several reasons to critique sex-role theory. First, by stressing how male and female roles complement each other for the sake of society, sex-role theorists neglect the importance of power in defining these roles and in perpetuating inequalities between men and women, as well as among men.[7] Furthermore, sex-role theory fails to account for the fact that few men within a given society actually live up to the society's ideal masculine role. Since masculinity is better viewed as a broad range or spectrum rather than a singular definitive type, many varieties exist within a society at a given time, some of which radically depart from the oversimplified and unitary "masculine role" that sex-role theorists posit.[8] Similarly, since sex-role theory is premised on a male/female binary, it does not account for the wide spectrum of biological sexuality, which includes eunuchs and intersex and transgender individuals.[9] Finally, sex-role theory does not sufficiently recognize the historical variability of masculinity—that is, that the characteristics and actions expected of a man can radically change over time within a society.[10]

In response to these weaknesses in classic sex-role theory, modern masculinity studies sought to create a theory of masculinity that acknowledges: (1) the role of power in establishing and perpetuating the cultural performance of masculinity; (2) the multiple articulations of masculinity within a society at any time; and (3) diachronic changes in masculinity. The notion of "hegemonic masculinity," formulated initially by Carrigan, offered scholars a corrective to these deficiencies of sex-role theory.

According to Carrigan, societies invariably create a "culturally exalted form of masculinity" that he dubs "hegemonic masculinity," which comes to dominate that society's view of what it means to be a man to the detriment of other possible articulations of masculinity.[11] Moreover, this hegemonic form of masculinity is a product of a particular historical moment and therefore can change over time.[12] Despite the fact that only a few men at any given time embody this hegemonic ideal, most men are complicit in sustaining it for reasons that include "gratification through fantasy, compensation through displaced aggression" or the benefit of the perpetuation of male dominance over women, a feature of nearly every example of hegemonic masculinity in history.[13]

Hegemonic masculinity naturally generates these "complicit" forms of masculinity. However, it also brings about a social order where subordinate and marginalized masculinities exist in relationship to the hegemonic ideal, as noted by Connell.[14] The former include types of masculinity that are actively oppressed and "expelled from the circle of legitimacy."[15] The latter consist of masculinities that are not viewed as normative because they are associated with a marginalized race, ethnic affiliation, or economic class.[16]

Recent work has challenged and refined elements of the original formulation of the concept of hegemonic masculinity, but it remains the dominant theory in contemporary masculinity studies.[17] Given its importance, it is not surprising that the notion of hegemonic masculinity has been central to the discussion of masculinity in the Bible. The initial applications of masculinity studies to the texts of the HB were most characterized by the attempt to identify the features of Israelite hegemonic masculinity.[18] The most influential example of this approach is Clines's "David the Man: The Construction of Masculinity in the Hebrew Bible." In this article Clines demonstrates that a succinct summary of biblical hegemonic masculinity (one characterized by strength, wisdom, beauty, and the avoidance of women) is present in the description of David in 1 Sam 16:18.[19] As Chapter 1 will show, Clines's article was followed by a number of studies that attempted to locate these same characteristics in different texts throughout the HB or to correct Clines's original list of characteristics by addition or subtraction.

Scholars of biblical masculinity have also shown interest recently in investigating how hegemonic masculinity in the biblical world interacted with alternative suppressed masculinities. This interpretative approach claims that certain biblical texts attempt to subvert the hegemonic form of masculinity prevalent in the ancient Near East. For instance, Haddox argues that the masculinity embodied in the ancestral narratives in Genesis is actually a *subordinate* masculinity that is much more submissive than the hegemonic masculinity prevalent in the ancient Near East.[20] Lipka's study of the masculinity advocated by Proverbs similarly shows how an alternative to hegemonic masculinity can outlast and eventually replace the original hegemonic masculinity to which it was responding.[21] Finally, Boer's work on Chronicles shows how the hegemonic ideal can be destabilized even by authors who wish to perpetuate it, which demonstrates the fundamental instability of hegemonic masculinity.[22]

The Interaction of Biblical Masculinity Studies and Biblical Male Maturation

The increased attention to the characteristics of biblical hegemonic masculinity and alternatives to it that has resulted from the impact of masculinity studies on biblical scholarship provides essential groundwork to a study of male coming of age. It is impossible to determine whether a biblical story describes a boy's maturation to manhood unless the reader knows what is expected of an adult man in the world that produced the text—that is, what qualities a boy must develop in order to be viewed as a man by his society. For this reason, Chapter 1 will examine in greater depth the scholarly consensus of the last two decades on what general features define the performance of masculinity in biblical texts.

As much as the following study of the male coming-of-age theme in the HB is *informed by* the important work on biblical masculinity, it also provides an essential *contribution to* that scholarship. The analysis of the construction and "cultural performance" of masculinity that has occupied biblical scholars is incomplete without a sustained treatment of how that performance repeats itself over generations—that is, how boys come to embody and reify that performance.[23]

The likely reason that biblical scholars have not yet investigated how men are made from boys is that much of their attention has been devoted to showing how masculinity is constructed in contrast to femininity.[24] Indeed, the concept of masculinity as a performance characterized by opposition to what is perceived as feminine has become a central tenet of the study of biblical masculinity.[25] Regrettably, biblical scholars have failed to ask the question *why* masculinity in general, and specifically biblical masculinity, is constructed primarily as a negation and avoidance of femininity. This formulation is simply assumed to be the case without further reflection. Probing further into this assumption helps to demonstrate the importance of male maturation to the discussion of the construction and performance of masculinity.

The question of why masculinity is so often constructed as a negation of femininity has been the subject of speculation among psychologists and anthropologists associated with gender studies, especially in the last decades of the twentieth century. It is significant that scholars who address the idea that masculinity entails the avoidance of femininity most frequently connect this avoidance to maturation and individuation processes in boys. Sociologist and psychoanalyst Nancy Chodorow's illuminating work on masculine development is representative of this scholarship.[26] She argues that every newborn, both male and female, first establishes a primary psychological identity and strong social bond with his or her mother. Later, after further growth, a time eventually comes when the child begins to think of itself as a psychological entity separate and independent from the mother.[27] For boys, this process entails a growing awareness of gender difference from the mother.[28] To achieve an identity independent from his mother, a boy must therefore reject her gender identity. This begins the pattern of rejecting the feminine as a way of demonstrating masculine maturation. As Chodorow states:

> A boy, in his attempt to gain an elusive masculine identification, often comes to define his masculinity in largely negative terms, as that which is not feminine or involved with women. There is an internal and external aspect to this. Internally, the boy tries to reject his mother and deny his attachment to her and the strong dependency on her that he still feels. He also tries to deny the deep personal identification with her that has developed during his early years. He does this by repressing whatever he takes to be feminine inside himself, and, importantly, by denigrating whatever he considers to be feminine in the outside world.[29]

Therefore, although the display of masculinity in adult men manifests itself as an avoidance of feminization, *it may ultimately stem from the maturation and individuation process*. Masculinity therefore can be defined as an avoidance of infantilization—a "revolt against boyishness [and] regression," according to this view.[30]

Anthropological research has both relied upon and expanded these views. Herdt's famous investigation of the Sambia people of New Guinea argues that their elaborate and violent maturation rituals for boys are designed to remove boys from the feminine world in which they had been living and to expunge feminine influence from them.[31] Here again the rejection of the feminine is tied directly to male maturation—a ritual reenactment of the psychological process of gender individuation. In fact, Herdt (with Robert Stoller) states that these rituals arise from "extreme symbiosis anxiety": the fear that boys who do not have the feminine influence removed will remain helpless children symbiotically connected to their mothers.[32] Gilmore's study of masculinity in multiple cultures around the world similarly argues that, from the perspective of a society, the regression of men to boyhood is a great danger, because society needs participating contributing adults to function properly. As a result, cultures construct their manhood imagery in stark opposition to boyhood. Moreover, the rituals that are employed to transition boys to manhood are designed to destroy remnants of femininity and therefore childishness in the boys.[33]

Whether or not this anthropological and psychological research is to be believed, it does suggest the need to reevaluate the common tendency of biblical scholars to define biblical manhood solely as a contrast to femininity. If masculinity entails avoiding feminization *and infantilization*, then as much attention should be given to how manhood is constructed vis-à-vis boyhood as has been given in recent years to distinguishing masculinity from femininity.

For that reason the investigation of biblical narratives that describe how a boy becomes a man, with a special emphasis on how this difference is displayed, will serve to broaden scholarly research into masculinity in the HB.

In sum, the notion of hegemonic masculinity, a central one in the field of masculinity studies, has informed and shaped research on the representations of masculinity in the HB. Biblical scholars inspired by masculinity studies have often attempted to specify the primary characteristics of biblical hegemonic masculinity as well as to search for alternative and subordinate masculinities in the HB. These attempts lay important foundations for the investigation of male maturation, and they will be discussed in greater detail in Chapter 1.

An oversight of this research in biblical masculinity is evident, however. Recent anthropological and psychological research has emphasized that the fear of infantalization may be an underlying motivation for the strong contrast between masculinity and femininity so characteristic of hegemonic masculinity. This connection has gone largely unexplored by scholars of biblical masculinity, which perhaps explains the absence of a scholarly discussion on the topic of the present book: how the maturation from boyhood to manhood is narrated in the HB. The suggestion that manhood is constructed vis-à-vis *boyhood* just as much as *womanhood* emphasizes the necessity of an investigation of male coming of age for any interrogation of masculinities, biblical or otherwise.

Rites of Passage: History, Application in Biblical Studies, and Relevance to a Study of Biblical Coming of Age

Like masculinity studies, the concept of rites of passage originated in a field external to biblical studies—namely, anthropology—but has been applied frequently to the HB by biblical scholars and is a valuable exegetical tool for the present project. This section provides a brief overview of the history of research on rites of passage and how the concept has been employed by biblical scholars, and then outlines the principles guiding the use of the rite-of-passage schema in this book. The section also highlights a relevant insight from rites-of-passage research that grounds the discussion in the ensuing chapters—namely, that the content of a society's male coming-of-age rites communicates important information about manhood in that society.

Anthropologist Arnold van Gennep first described rites of passage in the early twentieth century.[34] According to van Gennep, rites of passage are rituals performed at major social transition points in a person's life and are designed to facilitate these transitions, both for the individual and for the society recognizing the individual's change of status. His research identified a number of transition points with which rites of passage are associated, including pregnancy, childbirth, betrothal, marriage, and death. However, no social transition drew more of van Gennep's attention than the change from childhood to adulthood.[35] Van Gennep's discussion of rites involving the transition of a child into adulthood takes up almost a third of his original work on rites of passage.[36] Arguably this extra attention to puberty rites is due to the fact that these rites mark a more elusive moment than those associated with other social transition points. Although the event that engenders the accompanying rite of passage is clear in the case of birth, marriage, and death, it is more difficult to identify in the case of initiation into adulthood. The rite itself, therefore, functions as the primary evidence for the transition to manhood, which lends it a special significance that warranted van Gennep's extra attention.[37]

Van Gennep's contribution to the study of rites of passage goes beyond his recognition that across cultures humans use rituals to mark and facilitate social transitions. Significantly, he also discerned a remarkable consistency in the structure of the rites of passage that he studied, which included examples of rites from cultures on five continents. Each rite of passage, according to van Gennep, consisted of three phases: an initial period of separation, an intermediate marginal or "liminal" stage, and a concluding reintegration into society.[38] For example, in the case of a typical rite of initiation from boyhood into manhood, a boy, or more commonly a group of boys, is removed both spatially and socially from his community in the separation phase. The marginal/liminal phase follows, during which the initiates—who are not yet considered men, but who are also no longer viewed as boys—are kept separate from society and are often subject to ordeals or are imparted with special knowledge. After this liminal phase concludes, the boys—or, rather, newly formed men—return to their society and are celebrated for transitioning successfully to manhood.[39]

The apparent ubiquity of rites of passage and the elegance of van Gennep's tripartite schema for describing their structure led to a century of anthropologists adopting his model.[40] However, van Gennep's research would likely have not impacted biblical studies if it were not for the work of mid-to-late-twentieth-century anthropologist Victor Turner, who was the first to apply the rite-of-passage schema to narrative criticism.

In his work among the Ndembu tribe of Zambia, Turner recognized how van Gennep's rites-of-passage schema could be used to explain the structure of the tribe's rituals.[41] His later application of this schema to illuminate *narrative* is rooted in further reflection on these rituals. Specifically, Turner argues that rituals serve an important communicative function within societies by transmitting "traditional knowledge" and lessons that the society considers "axiomatic."[42] In other words, Turner was convinced that ritual "does not simply do something but says something."[43] This conviction led him to compare the communicative function of ritual to other ways in which Ndembu and other tribal societies transmit axiomatic information, including through traditional narratives like myths, sagas, epics, and legends. Since ritual shared its communicative role with such narratives, Turner argued that the same rite-of-passage schema that had proven useful in his analysis of ritual could also be applied to these narratives, even if they had no connection to actual rituals.[44] Over time his application of the rite-of-passage schema even expanded to include narratives that lacked a mythic, traditional, or folkloric origin. This allowed him, for example, to compare Dante's *Purgatorio* to Ndembu ritual, which he justified by claiming that all narratives and rituals share the same "dominant symbols"[45] and arise from within the same "experiential matrix."[46]

Turner's appropriation of van Gennep's tripartite rite-of-passage schema to the study of both ritual and narrative is especially characterized by his interest in the stage of that schema that had heretofore received the least amount of attention: the liminal stage. In particular, Turner's research on the liminal phase of Ndembu rituals added significantly more detail to the description of this stage than that originally provided by van Gennep's work. For example, Turner recognized that a typical feature of this "betwixt and between" ritual stage was the inversion of society's typical norms. As a result, in the liminal stage of ritual a radical leveling of social hierarchies, which Turner refers to as *communitas*, took place among those participating in the ritual.[47] Additional characteristics of individuals going through this ritual phase included minimization of sexual difference/asexuality, simplicity, acceptance of pain and suffering, sacredness, and the display of behavior considered "foolish" in normal society.[48]

Turner applied this research on *ritual* liminality to his reading of *narrative*, again reflecting his conviction that ritual processes and structures can illuminate literature. Specifically, he sought to identify liminal characters, spaces, and situations in oral and written narrative. Liminal characters/spaces are caught between two worlds or states of being. They are an amalgam that ambiguously mixes elements of both states, and they reflect a reversal of societal norms. Turner identified liminal themes and characters not only in myth and folklore (e.g., his identification of creation myths and trickster characters as liminal)[49] but also in modern literary works such as *King Lear, Crime and Punishment,* and *Don Quixote.*[50]

As mentioned above, Turner's application of the rite-of-passage schema to literature helped to introduce the concept to biblical scholars. Specifically, Turner's work prompted HB scholars to search for the tripartite structure of rites of passage in biblical texts, including those with no explicit reference to specific rituals.[51] In some cases—most notably in the work of Ackerman and Mobley—the application of the concept of rites of passage focuses on identifying and discussing liminality, as Turner's work on narrative had done. Mobley, for instance, views Samson as a figure "defined by contradiction, alienation, and hybridity," the kind of "neither here nor there" qualities commonly associated with liminality.[52] Similarly, Ackerman's reading of the History of David's Rise (1 Sam 16–2 Sam 5) is premised on viewing David and Jonathan as liminal characters throughout that narrative.[53]

Other scholars provide a more expansive application of the rite-of-passage schema—that is, one not focused solely on the liminal phase. For example, Hutton demonstrates that the story of David's escape from Jerusalem during Absalom's revolt, his exile east of the Jordan during that revolt, and his return to Jerusalem (2 Sam 15–19) precisely follows the tripartite structure of a rite of passage (separation, liminality, and reintegration).[54] Similarly, other scholars employ the rite-of-passage schema in their exegesis of important episodes in the lives of biblical characters, such as Jacob's struggle with his mysterious antagonist at the Jabbok (Gen 32:22–33), Moses in Midan (Exod 2:15–4:29), Joseph's early years in Egypt (Gen 39–41), and the escape by Lot and his family from Sodom (Gen 19:15–38).[55] Additionally, Hendel, Cohn, Talmon, and Propp apply the schema to the corporate experience of Israel in Egypt and in the wilderness.[56] In their view, the Israelites undergo a rite of passage by first separating themselves from Egypt through the symbolic act of crossing the Red Sea (alternatively, the separation phase can be identified as beginning when Jacob's family originally leaves Canaan for Egypt). Next, they spend forty years in the liminal wilderness, caught between their old status as slaves and their new status as inheritors of the land of Canaan. The Israelites complete their rite of passage when they enter into Canaan, a "reincorporation" that is also marked by a symbolic water-crossing, this time of the Jordan River.

Biblical scholars, therefore, have applied the concept of rites of passage to a range of biblical texts with edifying results. However, few scholars have employed the rite-of-passage schema to identify an individual narrative as a coming-of-age story.[57] Instead, many scholars typically discuss the tripartite rite-of-passage structures in light of other rituals or transitions such as pilgrimage,[58] purification,[59] royal installation,[60] or spiritual transformation.[61]

The almost complete absence of studies that apply a rite-of-passage reading to coming-of-age stories is especially noteworthy given that puberty rites were the most analyzed rituals in van Gennep's original work on rites of passage. Furthermore, for decades classicists and scholars of the ancient Near East have been locating coming-of-age themes in ancient texts with the help of the concepts of rites of passage and liminality.[62]

Consequently, this book is an attempt to fill a significant gap in biblical studies by reconnecting the rites-of-passage schema to the coming-of-age motif, the subject with which it was originally most associated.[63] As such, this endeavor identifies and analyzes HB narratives that make use of the structure of a rite of passage as they describe a boy's transition from boyhood to manhood.

Methodology: Applying Rites of Passage to Biblical Coming-of-Age Stories

Two principles direct how the tripartite schema of a rite of passage is applied to biblical coming-of-age stories in the following chapters. These principles provide an exegetical frame and are designed to prevent, or at least minimize, misuse of the schema. The first principle is: *while the presence of a rite-of-passage schema can help identify a narrative as a coming-of-age story, it does not provide sufficient evidence to make this case on its own.*

Based on extensive evidence, anthropologists assert a nearly universal connection between the tripartite structure of separation-liminality-reintegration and coming-of-age rituals throughout the world. If the connection between *rituals* associated with coming of age and the tripartite structure of a rite of passage is valid, it stands to reason that the rite-of-passage structure should be viewed as a clear marker of coming-of-age *narratives*. This conclusion is even more convincing if one follows Turner's claim that ritual and narrative arise from the same wellspring of human experience and therefore can be expected to share structural similarities.

However, even though the presence of a rite-of-passage schema is *suggestive* of the coming-of-age theme in narrative, it is not, in and of itself, conclusive evidence for this identification. Besides the presence of a rite-of-passage schema, additional corroborating evidence is needed to establish that a given narrative entails a coming of age. One reason for this caution is due to the fact that not all rites of passage are coming-of-age rites. To put it differently, a narrativized rite of passage may reflect a number of other social or psychological transitions. Furthermore, the presence of a rite-of-passage schema is insufficient evidence to identify a coming-of-age story because this argument ultimately relies upon unverifiable assumptions and universal claims about the similarities of ritual and narrative (for example, that an author can structure a narrative according to a ritual completely unknown to him or her because the ritual's structure corresponds to a universal human psychological pattern). To be sure, Turner's use of ritual structures to interpret literature is compelling and has produced insightful biblical exegesis. Nevertheless, it is not sensible to build a thesis upon such speculative and ultimately unknowable assertions. In short, a rite-of-passage schema merely aids in the identification of a narrative as a coming-of-age story.

The second principle concerning the application of the rite-of-passage structure to coming-of-age narratives is: *in order to identify a rite-of-passage structure in a text, each of the three phases of a rite of passage must be clearly visible and must take place in one pericope.* The aim of this principle is to prevent the rite-of-passage template from being forced or improperly overlaid onto a text.[64] Indeed, especially if the reader is willing to consider large blocks of narrative together (as opposed to just one pericope), practically any narrative with a beginning, middle, and end can be artificially subjected to a rite-of-passage analysis.[65] Moreover, liminality may be too easily read into any moment of discomfort or challenge in a character's story, resulting in a pan-liminalism that spans the majority of a character's life—an undesirable expansion of a phase that is intended to be viewed as a temporary inversion of society's rules. By limiting the analysis to single episodes and insisting that each phase of the tripartite structure is equally apparent to the reader, this second principle guards against the danger of pan-liminalism and the over-application of the rite-of-passage schema.

In sum, the presence of a rite-of-passage schema is viewed as only suggestive of the coming-of-age theme in this study. Where it is present it can aid in identifying this theme, but without supporting evidence it cannot definitively prove this case. Moreover, the rite-of-passage schema can be completely absent from a coming-of-age narrative, as it is in four of the seven case studies of the coming-of-age theme identified in this study.[66] Finally, in order to prevent the over-application of the rite-of-passage template in this study, it will only be discussed in cases where each of the three phases can be identified within one pericope.

Male Maturation Rites as Communicators of a Society's Masculine Ideal

The preceding discussion traced research on the concept of rites of passage and its application in biblical studies and identified two principles guiding its use in this study. However, before proceeding to the next section of this Introduction, an additional tenet of anthropological research into rites of passage requires attention. Anthropologists who focus on coming-of-age rites of passage for boys have observed a strong connection between rites of passage that facilitate the transition from boyhood into manhood and the features of normative masculinity in the society that performs the rituals.

For example, in his research among the Nuer people of Sudan, Evans-Pritchard noted that an important moment in the male maturation ritual is the presentation of two gifts to the initiate: a spear and an ox. These objects symbolize the two primary roles that the Nuer society expects a man to perform: warrior and herdsman.[67] A comparable example of the overlap between coming-of-age rites and the expectations for a man in a society is found among the Kabre people of Togo. Piot cites reports describing the initiation of boys into manhood among the Kabre in the 1950s when Kabre men often earned their living working on road projects funded by European colonialists. During this time a portion of the Kabre maturation rite involved mimicking actions common to road construction work, such as erecting mock telephone poles and building makeshift bridges—a fascinating and unexpected association that linked modern construction practices with a coming-of-age ritual.[68]

Besides indicating adult male roles, the connection between what a society values in an ideal man and the rituals for coming of age also explains many of the ordeals common to these rituals. Such ordeals range from the benign (such as a boy being called to read and interpret the Torah before his community during his bar mitzvah ceremony) to the traumatic (e.g., the Gisu practice of circumcising adolescent boys who must not flinch or show pain during the ceremony).[69] The function of these ordeals is to test the boy's "cultural fitness" to take on his role as a man.[70] In the case of the bar mitzvah, the qualities tested are erudition and commitment to Torah study, both highly valued traits in traditional Jewish communities. The Gisu ritual tests a boy's ability to endure pain, which is an important part of being a man in this warrior culture.

Just as coming-of-age *rituals* reflect the values attached to masculinity in a culture, so too do the *stories* of a boy's coming of age. Indeed, the purpose for rehearsing the story of a boy's transition into manhood is lost unless the manhood displayed by the boy at the story's conclusion is recognizable in that culture. A Gisu tale of coming of age that ends with a boy displaying his ability to engage in Torah study, for instance, would be incoherent. In short, coming-of-age stories provide a glimpse into the "culturally acceptable standards" for men and boys in a society.[71]

This point is central for two reasons. First, it reinforces the claim that male coming-of-age stories provide a window into a culture's assumptions about manhood. This again demonstrates the applicability of the present study to the ongoing discussion of HB masculinity. Second, the connection between rituals and stories of male coming-of-age and a culture's view of ideal masculinity provides a valuable tool for recognizing the coming-of-age theme in narratives. That is, if the values a society ascribes to manhood are clearly identified, it is possible to know what characteristics are expected of a boy as evidence of his newly minted manhood in a coming-of-age story. For example, if a given society values horticultural skills above all other traits for a man, a story from that culture in which a boy plants his first crop could be read as the boy's coming of age.

For this reason, Chapter 1 begins with an analysis of constructions of masculinity in the HB. By singling out the defining qualities of biblical manhood, it becomes easier to identify when a boy begins to display characteristic signs of manhood in a narrative, which in turn facilitates the identification of the coming-of-age theme.

Identifying the Coming-of-Age Theme in the Hebrew Bible: Previous Attempts, the Present Methodology, and an Outline of the Argument

The previous two sections have provided an overview of two fields of research external to biblical studies but with significance to this project. The present section departs from this discussion of the assumptions that underlie the investigation of coming of age in the HB in order to elaborate more directly on the purpose, goals, and scope of the following chapters. The section begins by surveying the scholarship on male coming of age in the HB, and then the criteria used in this study for identifying the coming-of-age theme are set forth. It ends with a statement of the project's goals and includes an outline of the subsequent chapters.

Previous Attempts to Define the Coming-of-Age Theme in the Hebrew Bible: White, Propp, and Bechtel

As indicated above, the coming-of-age theme in the HB has received very little scholarly attention. This is especially true with regard to male coming of age—as opposed to female coming of age or the collective and figurative coming of age of a group of people.[72] In fact, only three scholars, Hugh White and—on a less detailed level—William Propp, and Lyn Bechtel, have treated this topic at length.[73] Below I summarize their research on male coming of age, which will serve by way of contrast as an introduction to outlining my proposal for identifying this theme in biblical literature.

Hugh White

In two articles published in the 1970s, Hugh White offered the first and, until this study, the only extended treatment of male coming of age in the HB.[74] White argues in these articles that form critics have failed to recognize the genre of the "initiation legend" in HB literature. To address this oversight, he identifies two examples of this initiation genre: (1) the story of Hagar and Ishmael in the wilderness of Beersheba in Gen 21:9–21; and (2) the binding of Isaac in Gen 22. In White's opinion, these stories narrate Ishmael's and Isaac's coming of age, respectively.

In his study of Hagar and Ishmael in Beersheba, White shows how the motif of a mother abandoning her child found in this narrative is also present in many Greek myths, which some classicists claim were originally told in connection with ancient initiation rites for boys.[75] White argues for a similar ritual context for the story of Hagar and Ishmael. He notes that Hagar's casting of her son beneath a bush (Gen 21:15), departing from him so as not to witness his death (v. 16), and their eventual reunion (v. 19) follow the tripartite structure of an initiatory rite of passage where a boy experiences a separation from his mother, a "ritual death" during the liminal phase, and a reintegration into society.[76] The association of this legend with a specific geographical location (the wilderness of Beersheba; v. 14) demonstrates for White that the legend was associated with male puberty rites performed at a specific cultic center in that area by Ishmaelite tribes.[77] Finally, the report of Ishmael's future as a skilled bowman and of his marriage at the story's conclusion (vv. 20–21) signifies for White that the preceding narrative should be viewed as the story of the boy's coming of age.[78]

White's reading of Gen 22 as Isaac's initiation legend similarly relies on parallels in Greek myths that originally may have had initiatory contexts, especially the myth of Athamas and Phrixus.[79] White claims that the motif of a father nearly sacrificing his son found in both Gen 22 and the Greek myth— like the motif of a mother abandoning her son—is connected to coming-of-age rituals and the stories told about them. He further asserts that the presence of two servants/boys (נְעָרִים; Gen 22:3, 5, 19) with Abraham and Isaac as they travel to Moriah points to an initiatory ritual context because in his judgment the term נַעַר can describe "recently initiated young men."[80] In this view, the reference to Isaac as a נַעַר at the story's conclusion (v. 12) shows that he too has now transitioned into this new state—that is, he has ceased to be a boy and has become a "recently initiated young man."[81] White also notes that the next time Isaac appears in Genesis he is shown doing distinctly manly things like getting married (Gen 24:67) and having children (Gen 25:19–26), which again may highlight a transition made in Gen 22. Finally, White connects this legend with a particular place—in this case, the mountains of Seir—and claims that tribal initiatory rites may have taken place in this location and provide the original context of the story in Gen 22.[82]

White's work is admirable for drawing attention to the subject of male coming of age for the first time. Even so, a number of flaws in his argumentation cast doubt on his conclusions. To begin with, his attempt to describe the stories of Ishmael in Gen 21 and Isaac in Gen 22 as etiologies for tribal initiation rites relies on unsubstantiated speculation. In fact, as I show below, several pieces of evidence argue *against* the presence of such rites among ancient and proto-Israelites. Furthermore, White's appeal to Greek mythic parallels as examples of similar stories associated with initiation rites relies on a connection between these Greek initiation myths and puberty rites that is far from certain.[83]

Another weakness in his argument is that Ishmael's story does not ultimately resemble a rite of passage. Although the tripartite schema of separation/liminality/reintegration is loosely present, thorough scrutiny of the Hagar and Ishmael story reveals important disparities between this story and typical male coming-of-age rituals. For instance, Hagar's actions do not reflect the characteristic actions of an initiate's mother. In Gen 21, Hagar actively separates her son from herself, whereas in an initiation ritual boys are *taken away* from their mothers by men, or separate themselves.[84] Moreover, in Gen 21 Hagar is the agent who effects the reunion between herself and Ishmael by approaching him to give him water (v. 19). However, in tribal coming-of-age rites the boys are the active agents of their reintegration with their awaiting mothers and other female kin.[85] Finally, Ishmael's age in this story would appear to be far too young for coming-of-age rites that typically take place in the early teen years.[86]

Additionally, White's claim that the use of the term נַעַר to describe Isaac in Gen 22 implies that he has transitioned out of boyhood lacks evidence. As Chapter 2 demonstrates, this term describes boys from a broad range of ages, including infants (e.g., Moses in Exod 2:6). Therefore it is not a term reserved for older boys and young men who have transitioned beyond adolescence, as White argues.[87]

White's contention that Gen 21 and Gen 22 mark the beginnings of Ishmael's and Isaac's manhood because the two characters are depicted as men the next time they appear in the narrative after these stories is also question-able. For this argument to be persuasive both stories should immediately pre-cede the recognition of the boy as a man, but in neither instance is this the case. Isaac's next appearance in Genesis (24:62) occurs after two lengthy in-tervening narratives that describe Abraham's purchase of Sarah's grave (Gen 23) and the introduction of Rebekah (Gen 24:1–61). Similarly, although the summarizing report of Ishmael's maturation (Gen 21:20–21) may directly follow after the story of his rescue in the wilderness, it is temporally removed from this scene by a significant amount. This detail is suggested by the nar-rator's note about Ishmael's growth (גדל; v.20), which is mentioned before any evidence of his manhood is provided, specifically his marriage and mastery of the bow.

Finally, if the Ishmael and Isaac narratives do in fact relate a boy's coming of age, the boy heroes ought to display signs of maturation and act like men. However, Ishmael's and Isaac's actions in Gen 21 and Gen 22 are anything but manlike. In fact they are depicted as completely passive characters who are marked by helplessness (e.g., Ishmael's impotent cry from beneath the bush in Gen 21:17) and submission (e.g., Isaac's apparent willingness to be bound and sacrificed in Gen 22:9). These qualities, which are characteristic of *children* in the Bible, are certainly not those of men.[88] Since neither Ish-mael nor Isaac show evidence of any maturation towards manhood, these narratives should not be considered as coming-of-age stories.

William Propp

William Propp is another scholar who recognizes the presence of the male coming-of-age theme in biblical narrative and discusses it in some detail. He briefly argues that Moses's sojourn in Midian (Exod 2:15–4:29) should be read as the story of his transition to manhood. Like White, Propp premises his claim on the recognition of a rite-of-passage schema in these chapters, where Moses is separated from his people (Exod 2:15), experiences a liminal period of his life during which he is imparted with special knowledge (i.e., Yhwh's name; Exod 3:15), and then returns to his people as a man (Exod 4:29).[89]

Since Propp's reading is less extensive than White's, it can be analyzed succinctly. Like White, Propp is to be commended for highlighting this over-looked theme. However, his reading of Moses in Midian as a coming-of-age story contains a crucial flaw. Specifically, Propp's logic requires the accept-ance of Moses as somehow less than an adult man until his rite of passage is completed with his reintegration into the society of his fellow Hebrews in Exod 4:29. However, by every standard of manhood in the HB, Moses is con-sidered an adult man by the end of Exod 2 when he gets married, begets a male heir, and is referred to for the first time as a "man" (אִישׁ; Exod 2:19).[90] Moses certainly transitions to a leadership role upon his return to Egypt, but his maturation from boy to man is already complete well before this time.

Lyn Bechtel

The last example of a scholar who attempts to identify the coming-of-age theme in a biblical narrative is Lyn Bechtel, who reads the J creation account in Gen 2:4b-3:24 in light of this theme. For Bechtel, the actions of the man and woman in Eden symbolize the maturation of a human being from childhood to adulthood. She maintains that in this story the man and woman move from the carefree world of youth where death and struggle are unknown into the adult world of toil and the awareness of death's inevitability.[91] Moreover, this transition is achieved through a rite of passage when the man and woman eat the fruit of the tree of the knowledge of good and evil, since this action entails a "symbolic death" (Gen 3:3) that recalls the death imagery frequently found in puberty rites.[92]

While Bechtel's article does offer a novel reading of a well-known tale that is somewhat convincing—the claim that the ability to discern good and evil is characteristic of adulthood, for example, is one that I also make in Chapter 4—still her exegesis can be challenged on some points. First, Bechtel's argument relies on an image of childhood as an innocent and blissful period free of the concerns of adulthood that in general only fits a modern Western context. While the review of biblical boyhood in Chapter 2 shows that childhood is occasionally viewed in such an idealized way, this period is more frequently viewed in the HB as a time of great danger and vulnerability for the child.[93] The transition out of this dangerous period would therefore be something to be celebrated, and not viewed as a negative development as Bechtel's reading implies. Furthermore, the realization of mortality would likely come quickly for an ancient Israelite child growing up in a world of high childhood death rates and short life expectancy—especially if that child grew up in an agricultural village context, in which the cycles of life and death are a daily reality—and thus it would likely not be a significant marker of maturation into adulthood. Next, since none of the three stages of a rite of passage (separation-marginality-reintegration) are evident in Gen 3, Bechtel's argument for locating one in this story is indefensible. Finally, given that the main characters in this story are referred to as a man (אִישׁ) and woman (אִשָּׁה) before their expulsion from the garden (Gen 2:23, 24), their status as adults is already acknowledged well before the story's conclusion.

Although they deserve credit for highlighting a little-discussed topic, each of these three attempts to identify the male coming-of-age theme in the HB is premised on problematic assumptions and biases. The present study attempts to build upon these attempts and to advance scholarship in this area by avoiding the weaknesses outlined above.

Recognizing the Coming-of-Age Theme

In order to recognize the coming-of-age theme, this book employs four principles that distinguish it from previous studies. These principles are also designed to correct the problematic assumptions of prior research.

Before listing these principles, however, it is important to discuss a feature of this study that most distinguishes it from previous approaches, especially White's. In contrast to White, my purpose is not to argue for the existence of a complex of puberty rites in ancient Israel. Therefore, my identification of the coming-of-age theme makes no attempt to connect that theme with puberty rituals irrespective of their location, whether the location is in the distant historical background of the narrative or contemporary with the narrative's composition.

I avoid linking coming-of-age narratives with rituals for two reasons. First, no evidence exists for the presence of puberty rites in ancient Israel.[94] Hypothetically, such rites could have existed because ancient Israel appears to have been a society defined by high levels of adult male solidarity. Anthropologists have demonstrated that this trait is a typical one in societies that have maturation rituals for young men.[95] In fact, some scholars have argued that circumcision may not have always been a ritual for infants, but may have originally been a puberty or betrothal rite announcing a young man's final transition to adulthood.[96] Even so, other evidence from anthropological research suggests that such rituals would likely not have existed. Schlegel and Barry, for instance, show that in subsistence cultures (like ancient Israel), puberty rites are uncommon.[97] Kimmel further argues that these rites only arise in cultures with a high degree of gender inequality, which does not adequately describe ancient Israel.[98] In short, any attempt to identify a complex of maturation rites in ancient Israel is highly speculative. Therefore, it is ill-advised to attempt to connect the coming-of-age theme to such rites.

The second reason I do not argue for a ritual context for coming-of-age narratives is simple: it is unnecessary, since coming-of-age stories can exist independently of puberty rites. No scholar of nineteenth-century British literature, for example, would argue that *David Copperfield* requires a ritual context in order to be read as a coming-of-age tale, and indeed a tale that can inform the reader a great deal about Victorian England's conceptions of boyhood and manhood. Even in the ancient world, stories like the *Epic of Gilgamesh* and the *Hymn to Hermes*, both of which contain coming-of-age themes, were told in societies that appear to lack puberty rites.[99]

Arguably, societies lacking puberty rites are *even more likely* to have coming-of-age narratives. For instance, Gilmore demonstrates persuasively that societies without puberty rites produce adult men who are fundamentally insecure in their manhood because they have no clearly identifiable evidence of their transition out of boyhood.[100] In these societies stories of male coming of age could be quite popular because they help address male insecurity about the status of their adult manhood by providing a model for the transition between boyhood and manhood with which men can compare themselves and their experiences.

Setting these concerns aside, the primary goal of this book is *to argue for the presence of a literary theme of male coming of age in the HB*.[101] The following chapters identify five narratives in which the transition of the protagonist from boyhood to manhood is a key concern. Of special interest are two additional narratives that offer an alternative approach to this theme—that is, these stories describe the failure to come of age.

As noted above, four methodological principles guide the effort to locate and subsequently analyze the coming-of-age theme. These principles are designed to add specificity to the search for the coming-of-age theme and to limit the tendency to force the theme on other stories where it is not present.

The first principle is that *terminology is an important indicator of the status of a character as a boy or a man*. In other words, when terms denoting the status of "boy" are used of a character (such as נַעַר or יֶלֶד), the text views this character as a boy; similarly, when terms that denote manhood are employed (i.e., גִּבּוֹר חַיִל, גֶּבֶר, אִישׁ), the character the term describes is considered a man. Therefore, noting when the terminology used to describe a character changes from boy-vocabulary to man-vocabulary helps identify a story as a maturation tale, especially if this switch takes place within a single narrative. Therefore, Propp's identification of Moses's return to his people in Exod 4:29 as the completion of his coming-of-age tale violates this principle, as does Bechtel's claim that Adam and Eve only mature upon their expulsion from Eden, because Moses has already been referred to as a man (אִישׁ) in Exod 2:19, 20, and 4:10, and Adam and Eve are called man and woman (אִישׁ and אִשָּׁה) in Gen 2:23, 24.

The second principle holds that *a coming-of-age narrative features a boy protagonist acquiring and/or displaying qualities associated with manhood*. An important part of a story that details a boy's maturation is to show evidence of that maturation through some coherent display of masculinity. Any story, therefore, that depicts a character who has previously only been described as a boy performing characteristically manly deeds is a good candidate for consideration as a coming-of-age story. Conversely, a story like that of the helpless Ishmael in Gen 21:9–21 or the passive Isaac in Gen 22 should not be considered a coming-of-age narrative because powerlessness and passivity are viewed as unmanly in the HB, as I show in the following chapters.

Given the ubiquitous association between coming-of-age rituals and the tripartite structure of a rite of passage—as well as Turner's argument that ritual structures can be fruitfully applied to narrative exegesis—the third principle is that *if this tripartite structure can be identified in a biblical narrative, it may signify that it is a coming-of-age story*. Of course, the caveats mentioned above that guard against the overuse of the rite-of-passage schema serve to guide its application to the narratives examined in this study.

The fourth principle, which is closely related to the first and second, stipulates that *the changes that take place in a boy character signifying his maturation must happen within the borders of a narrative for that narrative to be viewed as a coming-of-age story*. Put differently, one cannot label a narrative a coming-of-age story simply because it precedes the moment when the text starts to describe the character as a man. The tale of Isaac's binding in Gen 22, for example, cannot be viewed as a coming-of-age story merely on the basis of some later maturation, which in this case is not reported by the narrator until two chapters later. A significant and recognizable transition within the easily recognized borders of the pericope itself (Gen 22: 1–19) is required for the passage to be recognized as Isaac's coming of age.[102]

Project Goals and Outline of the Argument

The primary goal of this investigation is to identify and explore the coming-of-age theme in key biblical narratives. However, this is not the only objective of this book. A secondary objective is to consider how the coming-of-age theme is employed by narrators or redactors to highlight broader thematic messages in the historical narratives of the HB. For example, the analysis shows that the coming-of-age theme is often found at crucial junctures in the narrative in which an old era is passing away and a new one is beginning. Similarly, the *failure*-to-come-of-age theme is used in the book of Judges to indicate symbolically Israel's national predicament as a fragmented and immature political/religious entity.

As discussed above, coming-of-age stories also provide insight into the conceptions of masculinity within a society. Therefore, another secondary goal of this study is to analyze each coming-of-age story in light of the image of masculinity that it presents. This analysis will reveal that certain narratives—specifically the maturation tales of Samuel (1 Sam 3) and Solomon (1 Kgs 3)—evidence a view of masculinity that differs from that found in the HB as a whole and in the other maturation tales identified below. The implications of these observations are explored primarily in the book's concluding chapter, in which I argue that the Deuteronomistic Historian uses these two coming-of-age stories to advocate for a new kind of manhood for a new historical context.

The book is structured according to the following outline:

The first section explores the characteristics of manhood and boyhood in the HB, and consists of two chapters. This section is foundational because only after recognizing how boys and men are described in the HB can we locate the narratives where a transition is made from childhood to manhood.

Chapter 1 presents a critical summary of recent research into biblical masculinity. It specifies the particular qualities associated with manhood in the majority of the HB. These include strength, wisdom, an avoidance of excessive association with women, self-control, fertility, honor, and kinship solidarity. The chapter also expands upon the discussion found in this Introduction of the predominant opinion among scholars that biblical masculinity is constructed primarily in opposition to femininity, and shows that it is just as important to recognize the distinction of biblical masculinity from boyhood.

Chapter 2 broadens the purview of the first by detailing the characteristics of biblical boyhood. It does so by examining the Hebrew terminology used to describe male youths in the Bible. After discussing the characteristics commonly associated with boys in the HB, the chapter concludes with a section comparing the description of boys with that of men. This comparison establishes essential foundations for the investigation of the coming-of-age theme in the following chapters.

The book's second section consists of three chapters that discuss specific examples of male maturation in the HB. The first two chapters in this section present case studies of successful maturation, while the third demonstrates that the coming-of-age theme also includes tales of failing to mature. The case studies of successful maturation are considered in canonical order.

Chapter 3 makes the case for reading Exod 2 and 1 Sam 3 as the coming-of-age stories of Moses and Samuel, respectively. Structural features of both narratives and the repetition of certain *Leitworte* combine to emphasize the centrality of the maturation theme to each narrative. In both stories the male protagonist is initially depicted as youthful, but by the tale's conclusion, he is described as a man. The chapter ends with a discussion of how the Samuel maturation narrative presents an intentionally alternative vision of coming of age to that found in Exod 2.

Chapter 4 identifies the coming-of-age theme in the stories of two royal figures: David and Solomon. However, despite the fact that two characters are considered, this chapter actually discusses three separate narratives. The exegesis of Solomon's youth in 1 Kgs 1–3 reveals two separate coming-of-age narratives for him: one in 1 Kgs 1–2 and the other in 1 Kgs 3. Solomon's maturation stories are considered together in this chapter with David's coming of age in 1 Sam 17. The purpose is not only because both David and Solomon are royal figures, but also because the first story of Solomon's maturation in 1 Kgs 1–2 reflects many of the views about maturation found in 1 Sam 17, while the other story in 1 Kgs 3 contrasts starkly with both. I conclude the chapter by showing that this contrast is intentional, and is used by the narrator both to mark a new era in Israel's history and to recommend a new conception of manhood.

Chapter 5 examines the brief story of Jether in Judg 8 and the longer Samson cycle in Judg 13–16. These two narratives provide examples of the converse of the coming-of-age theme—that is, they tell the story of youths who fail to transition to adulthood. This chapter includes a discussion of why cultures would tell stories in which a boy fails to mature, and it shows how Samson's failure to come of age is used to draw attention to broader themes in Judges.

The concluding chapter summarizes the major points presented in the book. It also addresses more directly the depiction of biblical masculinity as it changes *over time*. It does so by comparing each of the case studies examined in chapters 3–5, and finding that of the seven, five reflect the views of manhood shared by most of the texts in the Hebrew Bible and detailed in Chapter 1 of this study. Two case studies, however, differ markedly in their understanding of how a boy comes of age, and therefore in their view of what makes a man. Interestingly, these two maturation tales (1 Sam 3 and 1 Kgs 3) de-emphasize the importance of violence in becoming a man and in displaying manliness. Moreover, as this chapter shows, these two stories can arguably be attributed to the same hand: the so-called Deuteronomistic Historian (DtrH). The chapter therefore closes with a discussion of the social and historical forces that could have inspired DtrH's less bellicose views of masculinity.

The book also contains an Appendix addressing biblical narratives that appear to have elements of the coming-of-age theme, but are not considered in chapters 3–5. Jacob, Joseph, Saul, Jeremiah, and Daniel are briefly discussed here, and I explain their exclusion from consideration in the main body of the text. This exclusion in some cases is the result of the absence of any readily apparent coming-of-age story for the character, and in other cases it results from there being insufficient indications in the text that undoubtedly point to the presence of the coming-of-age theme.

The Depiction of Manhood and Boyhood in the Hebrew Bible

1

The Defining Characteristics
of Manhood in the Hebrew Bible

IN ORDER TO discuss the theme of a boy's coming of age in the HB, it is necessary first to have a clear understanding of what is meant by the designations "man" and "boy" in biblical literature. Without a detailed knowledge of the characteristics of boyhood and manhood, it is impossible to identify narratives in which a boy leaves childhood behind and is described as a man for the first time.

This chapter begins to lay these essential foundations for a discussion of the male coming-of-age theme by examining biblical manhood. As discussed in the Introduction, recent years have witnessed a heightened interest among biblical scholars in identifying the characteristic features of manhood in the HB, likely due to the influence on the humanities in general of the burgeoning field of masculinity studies. In this chapter, I offer a critical summary of the recent scholarship on biblical masculinity,

As already noted, one of the first works devoted to manhood in the HB was David Clines's 1995 article, "David the Man," in which Clines examines the narratives about this biblical hero and king in 1 and 2 Samuel in an attempt to identify the texts' assumptions about masculinity.[1] Clines draws particular attention to 1 Sam 16:18, in which a servant of King Saul describes the young David to the king: "One of the young men answered, 'I have seen a son of Jesse the Bethlehemite who is skillful in playing, a man of valor, a warrior, prudent in speech, and a man of good presence; and the LORD is with him."[2] Clines argues that this description, while not a "definitive summary of the characteristics of Israelite masculinity,"[3] is a helpful place to start when discussing the topic in that it succinctly highlights three major features of an idealized view of masculinity in the HB: (1) a man must have the strength and potential for violence that is incumbent upon a warrior; (2) he must possess intelligence and wisdom, which is actualized in his "prudent speech" (נְבוֹן דָּבָר); and (3) he is physically "beautiful" (which 1 Sam 16:18 expresses with the phrase "a man of good presence" [אִישׁ תֹּאַר]).[4] Later in this article, Clines adds to this list that the ideal biblical man is a "womanless male," a man who prefers the company of other men to that of women.[5]

In the years following Clines's groundbreaking article, practically every scholar taking up the question of biblical masculinity has looked to the characteristics highlighted in that article as their starting point, with the sole exception of male beauty, which has received comparatively little attention.[6] Indeed, the most recent volumes on the subject (2010's *Men and Masculinity in the Hebrew Bible and Beyond* and 2014's *Biblical Masculinities Foregrounded*) feature a collection of essays by a variety of scholars, few of whom significantly challenge Clines's characterization of biblical masculinity and many of whom simply apply his observations to texts other than those previously addressed by him. Clines's impact is summarized by Măcerlau's claim in *Biblical Masculinities Foregrounded* that scholars should "consider Clines's description of masculinity as a norm with regard to the Hebrew Bible and therefore use it as the rod against which biblical portrayals of masculinity can be measured."[7]

Given the influence of Clines's article, the four characteristics of biblical manhood that he identified are treated first in the following discussion. As that discussion shows, despite scholars' frequent emulation of Clines's work, not all of his conclusions stand up to closer scrutiny. Next, other important features of biblical masculinity that scholars have identified in the years since Clines' article are outlined. In so doing, a portrait of biblical masculinity emerges that is essential for comparing biblical manhood with boyhood and ultimately for identifying coming-of-age narratives.

It should be noted at the outset that the masculinity outlined below is idealized and consists of a general conglomeration of "culturally exalted" features; in other words, to use the terminology from the introduction to this study, it is a *hegemonic* masculinity.[8] As with any ideal, we should not expect any male character to embody all of these features consistently. Even David, whose characterization provides the basis for Clines's original description of the biblical masculine ideal, occasionally fails to live up to this ideal, as Clines notes.[9] Moreover, this outline of the features of idealized biblical masculinity does not reveal what it meant to be a man in ancient Israel as a whole. The final form of the text of the HB is largely a product of urban adult males, therefore it only provides an adequate reflection of the views shared among this group as to what constituted normative manhood.[10] Finally, it must also be kept in mind that this hegemonic ideal had the capacity to evolve over time through changing historical circumstances and/or by continued negotiation with alternate masculinities (i.e., subordinate, complicit, and marginalized masculinities).

Strength

The first characteristic of hegemonic masculinity in the HB that Clines high-lights is the ability to prevail on the battlefield: the biblical male is "the fight-ing male."[11] Clines finds ample evidence of the importance of this trait in the narratives about David, pointing to the shockingly high "body count" attrib-uted to David both in his role as king (approximately 140,000 enemy soldiers fall to armies that he commands) and through his individual actions (the deaths of fifteen different people are connected to him) to highlight its impor-tance. Furthermore, two of the descriptors used by Saul's servant to introduce David to the king in 1 Sam 16:18 stress this warrior capacity: David, the king is told, is a "man of war" (אִישׁ מִלְחָמָה) and a "mighty man of valor" (גִּבּוֹר חַיִל).

Clines stresses that this quality is not only the property of David, but that it defines what it means to be a man for every other male character in 1 and 2 Samuel. The "language of strength," specifically the strength to fight and kill another man, is found throughout the text as the touchstone of manliness.[12] This is perhaps nowhere better stated than in 1 Sam 4:9. Here the Philistine army is stricken by a sudden fear after having seen the ark of the covenant enter the camp of their Israelite enemies. Believing that their chances of over-coming and enslaving their enemies had now diminished considerably be-cause of the presence of a divine ally fighting with and for the Israelites, the Philistines nevertheless attempt to motivate and encourage themselves to go bravely into battle. They do so, significantly, by calling to one another: "Strengthen yourselves and be(come) men!" (הִתְחַזְּקוּ וִהְיוּ לַאֲנָשִׁים), and "be(come) men and fight!" (וִהְיִיתֶם לַאֲנָשִׁים וְנִלְחַמְתֶּם).[13] According to this text, being or becom-ing a man is equated with being strong and specifically with fighting on the battlefield. It is further marked by strength of will and courage, the opposite of which is fear (1 Sam 4:7; cf. Judg 8:20).

In defining a man by his physical strength, evidenced through his fearless warrior's performance in battle, this text reflects its broader ancient Near Eastern context. Hoffner's article on the symbols of masculinity and femi-ninity in the ancient Near East convincingly shows through the investigation of magic rituals that the symbols utilized in ancient Near Eastern society to represent masculinity are invariably military symbols, particularly the bow. Indeed, at times the equation of manhood and military prowess is quite ex-plicitly drawn: the Hittite noun LÚ-*natar*, for example, denotes "masculinity" both in the sense of "male genitalia" and "military exploit."[14] Hoffner finds the connection between the bow and masculinity in texts from all corners of the ancient world, including Greece (where the ability to string Odysseus's bow is the ultimate test of the masculinity of Penelope's suitors); Ugarit

(Aqat's rejection of the goddess Anat's request for his bow is based on his conviction that the bow is for men only [4 *CAT* 1.17: VI:39–41]); and also in Israel, where he sees this relationship at work in several texts (2 Sam 1:22; 22:35; 2 Kgs 13:15; Hos 1:5; Ps 127:4–5).[15]

Hoffner's arguments for identifying the connection between military symbolism and masculinity are expanded by Chapman's *The Gendered Language of War in the Israelite–Assyrian Encounter.* Chapman's examination of Assyrian royal inscriptions and palace reliefs, with their frequent depiction of the king victorious on the battlefield, leads her to the conclusion that "the battleground was the performance venue for achieving masculinity, a place where [a man] fought and sparred in a contest of masculinity."[16] The triumphant Assyrian monarchs frequently ascribe to themselves titles that stress their might—Chapman notes that *zikaru dannu* "strong/mighty man" and *eṭlu qardu* "valiant man/warrior" are commonly used to identify kings.[17] In contrast, defeated monarchs and armies are depicted as non-men, whose women are taken away by the more powerful and manly Assyrians,[18] and whose bows are frequently shown broken and abandoned on the battlefield.[19]

Finally, the connection between physical power and masculinity is also evident in Sumerian inscriptions and texts. Asher-Greve notes that among the most frequently employed titles for Sumerian monarchs was "strong man" (nita kala-ga), while the word for young man (guruš) was written with the sign for "strong" (kala).[20]

In the years since Clines's 1995 article, the relationship of masculinity to strength, fearlessness, and military prowess in the HB, as in other ancient Near Eastern literature, has been emphasized by other biblical scholars. Clines himself has recognized it outside of DtrH's tales about David that were the subject of his initial article: in prophetic texts that emphasize Yhwh's strength and the prophet's own power,[21] and in Exod 32–34.[22] Haddox evaluates the men in Genesis based on, among other things, their embodiment of this strength-ideal,[23] while Creangă's reading of the Joshua texts emphasizes the importance of the image of the "autocratic-warrior" to the construction of Joshua's masculinity.[24]

Frequently the significance of warrior-like strength to biblical masculinity is mistakenly equated with "violence." For example, Harold Washington writes that in the Bible "manhood entails the capacity to exert *violence*" both against men and against women.[25] However, to the extent that "violence" is understood to mean "unbridled bellicosity" or "bloodlust," it is inappropriate to equate the biblical ideal of masculine strength with this term. Doing so ignores the fact that self-control is also a frequent characteristic of the hegemonic masculinity found in the HB, as shown below. Furthermore, it disregards the fact that often disproportionate application of violence by men in the Bible is met with criticism (e.g., Yhwh's condemnation of the unjust shedding of Abel's blood by Cain in Gen 4:10–12 [see also Gen 9:6], the prohibition against murder in the Ten Commandments [Exod 20:13], and the legal establishment of cities of refuge to prevent the escalation of violence after an accidental death [Num 35; Josh 20]).

Considering the problems with connecting the warrior ideal that characterizes biblical masculinity with violence, it is best to think more generally about this aspect of masculinity. Its true core is the quality necessary for every warrior, that of *strength*, both *physical* and *psychological* (i.e., courage).[26] Certainly this strength is often displayed in battle with other men, and yes, in the committing of violent acts against them. But the HB is far too condemnatory of wanton acts of violence to assume that unbridled aggression would be a feature of hegemonic biblical masculinity.

Wisdom and Persuasive Speech

The second characteristic feature of biblical masculinity that Clines identifies is persuasiveness and intelligence.[27] These qualities figure into the description of David by Saul's servant in 1 Sam 16:18, where David is called "prudent in speech" (נְבוֹן דָּבָר). This "prudent speech" arises from a discerning and wise mind—the term NRSV translates as "prudent" here (נָבוֹן) is derived from the root בין, a root closely connected with the concept of intelligence and discernment.[28] Thus Clines argues that this quality be understood not simply as rhetorical flair but also as wisdom. David's wisdom and effective communication skills are evident throughout the David narratives.[29] Moreover, since these qualities are highlighted long before David becomes king, Clines argues that they belong to the description of his masculinity and are therefore not merely a part of the standard portrayal of kingship.[30]

Following Whybray's assertion that wisdom is an important theme in the Succession Narrative of 2 Sam and 1 Kgs, Clines asserts that wisdom and persuasiveness also define the masculinity of other male characters in the story. By way of example, he cites Absalom (whose words "stole the hearts of the men in Israel" 2 Sam 15:1–6), Joab (viz., his use of the wise woman of Tekoa in 2 Sam 14 to achieve his ends), and the paragon of biblical wisdom, Solomon.[31]

Few have challenged Clines on the assertion that wisdom and persuasive speech belong to the hegemonic view of masculinity in the Bible.[32] Indeed, it seems to be applicable to other texts outside of the David narratives. That wisdom comes with maturation and the attainment of adulthood is a

fundamental tenet of the culture that produced Proverbs: white hair is the
crown of glory according to Prov 16:31, a crown that gets identified with
wisdom in 14:24; moreover, the conceit of much of the collection is the imparting of wisdom from an adult to the young. Scholars provide other examples: in a later article, Clines reads Moses's negotiations with Yhwh on Sinai
in Exod 32–34 as highlighting this feature of idealized masculinity;[33] Di-
Palma expands this to include Moses's ability to get concessions from Yhwh
in the burning bush scene of Exod 3–4;[34] Măcerlau shows how Saul's masculinity is consistently undermined by examining his ineffective use of rhetoric;[35] Haddox views wisdom as an important part of the representation of the
Genesis patriarchs' masculinity;[36] and Creangă emphasizes the centrality to
Joshua's masculinity of his role as a "student of Moses," able to articulate
"well constructed arguments" in his interactions with the people he leads.[37]
Thus, wisdom and its corollary in persuasive speech appear to be essential
characteristics of manhood in the HB.

Beauty

Physical beauty is the next characteristic that Clines claims is an essential
aspect of hegemonic masculinity in the HB. Again, his claim begins with an
examination of what he believes to be the pithy encapsulation of biblical views
on masculinity in 1 Sam 16:18, where David is referred to as a "man of good
presence" (אִישׁ תֹּאַר). Elsewhere, David is described as "beautiful of appearance" (עִם־יְפֵה מַרְאֶה; 1 Sam 17:42) and having "beautiful eyes" (עִם־יְפֵה עֵינַיִם; 1 Sam
16:12). Noting that Saul (1 Sam 9:2), Absalom (2 Sam 14:25), Adonijah (1 Kgs
1:6), and—outside of the David narratives—Joseph (Gen 39:6) are all similarly complimented by the biblical narrator for their good looks, Clines adds
this to his checklist of essential features defining hegemonic masculinity in
the HB.[38] Unlike with the other three features of manhood Clines identifies,
however, few scholars have followed Clines in affirming the significance of
male beauty to the characterization of the ideal biblical man.[39] In fact, some
have challenged Clines on this point: Creangă notes that "most men's physical appearance . . . is not noticed by the biblical writers,"[40] while Lipka claims
that Clines builds this generalization "from only a few pieces of evidence for
beauty as a quality associated with the hegemonic masculine ideal."[41]

A closer look at the concept of male beauty in biblical texts reveals that this
challenge is warranted. First, it is not entirely certain that Saul is praised by
the text for being beautiful; his "goodness" (טוֹב) in 1 Sam 9:2 is connected
with his height: "from his shoulders up taller than all the people." Thus *imposing* might be a better understanding of what is meant by the term טוֹב, and

this could highlight the significant aspect of biblical manhood noted above: the man's strength.[42] Adonijah's attractiveness may well be the intended meaning for the claim that he was a man of "very good form" (טֽוֹב־תֹּ֫אַר מְאֹד֒), but this is mentioned only once in passing, not emphasized as it is for David, Absalom, and Joseph. For these three men, the text lingers over their beauty, significantly using the adjective יָפֶה (which undeniably connotes beauty, unlike טֽוֹב) in their description, and always adding further praise of their aesthetic appeal than a simple passing mention.[43] Thus, if one wishes to investigate conceptions of masculine beauty in the HB, these three characters must be the centerpiece of that discussion.

MacWilliam's work on male beauty recognizes this in his focus on these three characters.[44] Interestingly, his conclusions on the significance of their beauty differ significantly from Clines's argument that it is a vital feature of robust masculinity. Joseph's beauty, MacWilliam insightfully notes, puts him in harm's way in Potiphar's house and is a signal of his vulnerability. David's is cast in contrast to the hyper-masculine strength of those around him, like Saul and Goliath (e.g., 1 Sam 17:42), and thus it undercuts the equation of male beauty with muscle. His argument on the significance of Absalom's beauty is less persuasive, asserting without concrete evidence that his beauty "signifies tragedy" in that it "marks him out as a suitable sacrifice to expiate David's sin."[45]

Despite the flaws in part of his study, MacWilliam's conclusions put Clines's equation of masculinity with beauty into serious question. Vulnerability is not a trait of hegemonic masculinity. Nor can opposition to the idealizing of strength be said to exemplify masculinity. In fact, these are traits associated with *children* in the Bible—*as is beauty*. A closer inspection of each of these instances of the use of יָפֶה to describe a man reveals that his *youthfulness* is in view in the text: Joseph is still quite young at the time his beauty is discussed, perhaps still a נַעַר of seventeen (Gen 37:2); David's beauty is mentioned alongside his "ruddiness" (1 Sam 16:12; 17:42), a description that may carry the connotations of youthfulness, as is argued in the next chapter, and is directly connected with his youth in 1 Sam 17:42. The description of Absalom's beauty in terms that hearken to youthfulness reflects a consistent effort throughout the text to cast Absalom's rebellion as a youthful indiscretion.[46]

Male beauty in the HB, then, is more a sign of youthfulness than of robust masculinity, as explained further in the next chapter's discussion of biblical boyhood. In associating beauty with youth, the HB is closer to the conception of beauty found in classical Greece and Rome. New Testament scholar Stephen Moore, writing in response to Clines's work, notes that in these cultures "male beauty tends to be the province of youths—youths who are looked at,

desired, acted upon, mentored and formed by 'real' men who themselves are
not ordinarily said to be beautiful."[47] Unfortunately, Moore uncritically accepts this as a genuine difference between the two cultures. Closer analysis
shows, however, that Clines's position is deserving of critique in this
instance.

Avoidance of Association with Women

Clines's final feature of biblical hegemonic masculinity is "womanlessness";
that is, that the ideal man in biblical literature minimizes his contact with
women, instead forming strong relationships only with men. Clines sees this
operating in the David narratives in a number of ways: while David may have
had many wives throughout his life, he claims in 2 Sam 1:26 that he has never
experienced a love as wonderful as that of his male companion, Jonathan;
David takes pride in the separation of himself and his retinue from women
when on any military expedition (1 Sam 21:5 [MT 21:6]); and the sexual contact
between men and women in the David story—such as that between Amnon
and Tamar, Absalom and his father's concubines, and David and Bathsheba—
generally leads to strife. Clines summarizes:

> the image of masculinity in the David story . . . says loud and clear . . .
> that a real man can get along fine without women; he can have several
> women in a casual kind of way, but he has nothing to gain from them
> except children, and he owes them nothing. . . . A man does well to
> steer clear of women, a man does not need women, a man is not con-
> stituted by his relationship with women.[48]

Similarly, the womanlessness of the normative biblical man appears to reflect
the conception of masculinity in the broader ancient Near East. As Mobley
shows, women in this culture were commonly viewed as a taming and accul-
turating force on men, taking them out of the uniquely masculine world of
the "field," whether the wilderness or the battlefield.[49]

Though Clines's claim is that womanlessness entails a physical and emotional separation from entangling relationships with women, most biblical
scholars—borrowing a concept prevalent in some major works of masculinity studies—extend the idea to include the avoidance of being feminized or
perceived as feminine.[50] Moore is representative of this group when he writes
that "[t]he fundamental logic of biblical masculinity . . . is a binary logic: To
be a man is not to be a woman. . . . In particular this means not being identified *as* a woman. . . . But neither should a man be identified *with* women."[51]

There appears to be a fair amount of support for the view articulated by Moore—namely, that biblical masculinity is defined by the avoidance of feminization (or the perception of feminization) as much as the avoidance of contact with females—when one considers certain biblical and ancient Near Eastern evidence. This is particularly true of battlefield imagery, where a common trope is the ultimate humiliation associated with feminization of male warriors. Hoffner mentions two Hittite texts that express this notion. One is a prayer to Ishtar of Nineveh that asks the goddess to take away the masculinity of the enemy's warriors and force them to wear characteristically feminine clothes and headdresses while carrying a spindle and mirror, objects associated with women. The other is a self-maledictory oath sworn by Hittite soldiers; it states that, if they betray their warrior's duties, they should be changed from men into women and should be made to wear women's clothes and carry the characteristically female objects of the distaff and mirror.[52] Chapman's examination of Assyrian reliefs shows that defeated enemy soldiers are frequently pictured naked and penetrated by weapons; she suggests that this is a visual representation of feminization curses like those discussed by Hoffner.[53] Additionally, van der Toorn notes that in Akkadian reliefs, defeated male enemies are shown carrying mortars and pestles, a mark of their "complete effeminacy."[54]

The trope of the feminized and humiliated warrior is also found in the HB (e.g., Isa 19:16; Jer 50:37; 51:30; and Nah 3:13). A graphic and detailed representation of such feminization is seen in the fate of the warrior Samson after he falls into the hands of his Philistine enemies. Susan Niditch shows that the hero's shaving functions as a symbolic castration.[55] Also, being forced to grind grain (Judg 16:21) feminizes Samson in two ways. It does so first by making him do traditionally women's work.[56] Second, given the possible sexual overtones of the term "to grind," he is feminized by becoming the subject of forced penetration.[57]

Thus, in at least some cases, to be a man necessitates not being feminized or perceived as having feminine qualities. It should be noted, however, that in each of these instances from both ancient Near Eastern and Israelite literature, the men in question are warriors who have suffered defeat at the hands of their enemies or have been derelict in their military duties. Given that war was in general a distinctly male activity in the ancient world, to feminize a warrior through rhetoric, propaganda, or certain actions serves to insult him in that he is equated with the complete opposite of a warrior: a woman.

However, to assume based on these examples that all men at all times and in all situations must avoid any identification with feminine qualities is a leap too far. Indeed, it is not clear that when feminine imagery is applied to warriors the result is *always* to humiliate them. Bergmann has convincingly argued, for instance, that the motif of comparing a warrior to a woman *in labor* (eg., Jer 6:24; 30:6; 49:22, 24; 50:43; Psalm 48:7) is actually a "badge of honor" for the warrior, as it elevates his suffering to the level of a "crisis like no other" at "the threshold of life and death."[58] Furthermore, the quality of wisdom, which is undeniably a feature of the hegemonic masculinity in the HB, is also frequently associated with women, such as the wise woman of Tekoa in 2 Sam 4. Indeed, wisdom itself is famously feminized throughout Proverbs.[59] Most damaging for this argument, however, is the realization that the ultimate alpha male in biblical masculinity, Yhwh himself,[60] is occasionally described metaphorically with feminine imagery.[61] It is highly unlikely that a top priority of biblical masculinity would be to avoid all traits or tasks associated with women if such metaphorical imagery is freely associated with the mightiest warrior (Exod 15:3) and most powerful king (Isa 33:22), Yhwh.

The "womanlessness" of biblical hegemonic masculinity, then, should not be reduced simply to Moore's definition of a man as one who avoids identification *with* and *as* a woman. More evidence exists for the former proposition (that men in the HB generally seem to prefer the company of men to women, as Clines shows with his study of David) than the latter (that being a man entails avoiding feminization, no matter how subtle). Indeed, the latter only seems relevant in a certain very limited sphere (the battlefield), and even there it is not entirely the case that the warrior must not be associated with women.

The question naturally arises, then, why biblical hegemonic masculinity would entail a general avoidance of women. The view represented by Moore would hold that to associate with women is to court feminization in the eyes of other men, but this view has been contested above. In light of the work of scholars like Chodorow, Gilmore, and Herdt discussed in the Introduction, a different possibility emerges—namely, that the separation of hegemonic "real men" from women in the HB is a function of the need to avoid infantilization. As seen later, children are frequently associated with women in biblical texts. For a man to spend a great deal of time with women, then, implies that he is not yet a mature man. Given the probable absence in ancient Israel of a system of maturation rites that prove to society that one is a man, the young Israelite man must be even more forceful in asserting his transition to robust masculinity on his own, and an important way of doing so would have been to avoid the society of women, an avoidance which would be reflected in Israel's literature. This need for men to avoid infantilization could be the motivation behind the common shaming practice of shaving the beard of a defeated enemy (e.g., Jer 41:5; 2 Sam 10:4) and is almost certainly the cause for shaving the head (Judg 16:17), or the head and pubic region of a conquered foe (Isa 7:20).

Characteristics of Biblical Masculinity Not Recognized by Clines in "David the Man"

In the years since Clines published his study of David, other investigations of biblical masculinity have emerged that highlight features Clines does not mention in his article, and have added further detail to the portrait of biblical masculinity. These features are self-control, fertility (specifically the production of legitimate heirs), marriage, honor, and kinship solidarity.

Self-control

The value placed on self-control in biblical masculinity has already been mentioned in the refutation of the importance of the pejorative "violence" to biblical conceptions of manhood. It has frequently been noted that self-mastery is a central characteristic of Greco-Roman masculinity[62] and is significant in early rabbinic texts;[63] but it was not thought to be an important part of the masculine ethos of the HB until Mark George's convincing study of the "regimentation" of masculinity in the legal texts of Deuteronomy.[64] In George's view, the legal code of Deuteronomy sets up a regimented classificatory system that strictly regulates the social world of its audience and therefore is an invaluable source of information for the Deuteronomic views of masculinity.

For George, having "a name in Israel" (Deut 25:6, 7; 29:20 [MT 29:19]; see also 9:14; 26:19) is the central tenet of masculinity according to Deuteronomy's social vision. In Deut 29:16–20 (MT 29:15–19), the main task incumbent upon a man is to ensure that his name is not blotted out and forgotten. To ensure against this, a man must faithfully observe the regulations found in Deuteronomy itself. A basic feature of these regulations is that they limit excesses and recommend austerity and self-control. For example, the stipulations of Deut 14 restrict the foods one may eat; Deut 21:20 discourages gluttonous consumption of permitted food and drink; the sexual statutes found primarily in Deut 22 and 24 outline a system for keeping wanton sexual appetites in check; and the warfare laws of Deut 20 outline rules of engagement that limit gratuitous violence and, through the laws of the ban (Deut 20:16–18), the desire for plunder.

George's study is limited to the book of Deuteronomy, but his conclusions on the importance of self-control are applicable to biblical masculinity as a whole.[65] Other legal materials outside of Deuteronomy, for example, similarly prohibit certain sexual acts (e.g., Lev 18), excessive violence (Exod 21:12–27), and eating certain foods (e.g., Lev 11). Likewise, the Deuteronomistic History condemns unbridled violence (Judg 19–21), the violation of the laws of holy war (Josh 7), and illicit sexual contact (2 Sam 11). Wisdom literature, especially Proverbs, repeatedly recommends a life of sober self-control (e.g., Prov 6:24–35; 20:1; 23:20–21); and the prophetic books contain frequent proclamations against violence (e.g., Amos 1; Nah 3) and the unchecked desire for wealth (Amos 4:1; 5:11–12). Therefore, it is appropriate to consider self-control among the fundamental characteristics of ideal biblical masculinity.

Fertility and Marriage

George's emphasis on the importance of "having a name in Israel" leads to the next major characteristic of biblical masculinity, one also recognized by other biblical and ancient Near Eastern scholars: virility and the production of offspring. George notes that the laws of levirate marriage (Deut 25:5–10) speak to this concern, as the purpose of a deceased man's brother producing offspring with his widow is to ensure that his name is not "blotted out from Israel" (25:6).[66] Thus, having children is an essential feature of "having a name in Israel" and therefore of being a man. Other scholars have noted the importance of fertility to biblical masculinity: Stone identifies acquiring women and siring sons as important "signifiers of masculinity;"[67] Lipka cites Prov 31:3, Deut 21:17 and Gen 49:3 to support her argument that "a man who successfully performed the hegemonic ideal was supposed to produce many children as evidence of his potency;"[68] and Jacobs shows that for the Priestly source fertility is central to the construction of masculinity.[69] Additionally, Hoffner's study of the symbols of masculinity in the ancient Near East stresses the "double reference" evident in the meaning of the use of weaponry, particularly the bow, to symbolize masculinity. He argues that weaponry is a potent symbol for ancient Near Eastern masculinity because it represents two significant criteria for manhood, battlefield valor and fertility.[70] Pointing to Ps 127:4–5a ("Like arrows in the hand of a warrior are the sons of one's youth/ Happy is the man who has a quiver full of them"), Hoffner demonstrates that the equation between weaponry and fertility was present in ancient Israel as well.

This emphasis on fertility requires qualification. Heedlessly fathering many children by random women is not advocated in the HB; rather, the goal of manly virility was the production of legitimate male heirs. Thus a man's fertility should be expressed within the framework of marriage. Illegitimate children of Israelite men are excluded from the assembly of Yhwh in Deut 23:2 (MT 23:3) and therefore cannot inherit the paternal נַחֲלָה ("inheritance"). George therefore argues that marriage is "the basic social situation in which

Deuteronomy understands men to live."[71] This is also the case outside of the Deuteronomic literature: marriage is the first, foundational social institution in Gen 2:24, and the ubiquity of marriage in the HB is emphasized by the fact that of the many Israelite men in the HB, only Jeremiah is explicitly identified as unmarried throughout his life. Furthermore, while exogamy is not totally prohibited, the HB generally discourages marriage to—and consequently reproduction with—foreign women.[72] Therefore an ideal biblical man is expected not only to be fertile, but also to be legitimately *married*, preferably to an Israelite woman.

Lastly, the importance of marriage and fertility in biblical constructions of masculinity gives rise to a significant question: does an individual need to be married and to have children in order to be considered a man? The relevance of this question for a study of coming of age in biblical literature is obvious. If marriage and children are required in order to be considered an adult man, then one would expect maturation narratives to include reference to their protagonist's marriage, or at least to his betrothal. The question is even more pressing considering the recent claim by Steinberg in her informative study of biblical childhood that having children, particularly a male heir, was the only way an ancient Israelite male could transition from the social category of childhood to adulthood.[73]

Responding to this claim begins with examining Steinberg's argument more closely. It appears as a rather tentative afterthought to a compelling section on when childhood *begins*—that is, when an Israelite baby was considered a person—and the stages of early childhood development.[74] Her assertion that childhood only *ends* with marriage and having children, however, is not as convincing. Indeed, this argument is primarily based on van der Toorn's work on the *female* life cycle in ancient Israel, as well as a questionable interpretation of Ruth 1:5.[75] In this verse, the noun יֶלֶד, typically used for young boys, is employed to describe Naomi's sons Mahlon and Chilion in Ruth 1:5. Since these two young men are married but childless, the application of this noun to describe them suggests for Steinberg that it is only the reproduction of children that changes a person's status from child to adult.[76] However, in basing her claims on evidence from Ruth 1:5, Steinberg neglects the arguments by commentators that see the use of יֶלֶד in this verse as a narrative device designed to emphasize the redress of Naomi's loss by the end of the book.[77]

Moreover, the argument that adulthood only begins with marriage and children for a biblical man overlooks evidence of certain characters who clearly are identified and described as men even before they have had children or married. For example, even though Abraham does not reproduce until Gen 16, he is still depicted as a man before this time, engaging in the manly pursuit of war (Gen 14), exerting authority over his extended family and servants (Gen 12:5), and demonstrating wisdom by deciding to prevent conflict between his herdsmen and Lot's by separating from his nephew (Gen 13). Similarly, Joseph is called a man (אִישׁ; Gen 39:2, 14) well before his marriage (Gen 41:45), while Jeremiah never marries and remains childless, but is still considered a "man" (אִישׁ; e.g., Jer 15:10; 26:11).[78]

In sum, as aspects of the hegemonic ideal of masculinity, marriage and children certainly *enhance* one's masculinity—that is, the married and fertile man is "more of a man" than an unmarried and infertile man—but their absence does not mean that one has not attained adult manhood. Marriage and children, therefore, are sufficient conditions for biblical manhood, but not necessary ones.

Honor

Another characteristic of biblical masculinity highlighted by scholars in recent years is honor. One of the earliest studies to draw attention to the importance of honor to masculinity in the HB was Stone's *Sex, Honor, and Power in the Deuteronomistic History*, which examines how men in the Deuteronomistic History use sexual relations with women as a way to attain and defend their honor.[79] Other examples include the work of Haddox and Chapman, who separately discuss how honor provides the ideological foundation for the prophetic metaphors of Yhwh as a cuckolded husband avenging the insult to his honor against his unfaithful wife.[80] Clines, in an article published after "David the Man," stresses the importance of honor language in the prophetic literature, and connects this to "male values" and "male ideology."[81] Most recently, Lazarewicz-Wyrzykowska demonstrates that the struggle to gain honor is a central concern of the Samson narratives,[82] and Lipka asserts that communally recognized honor was the goal of an individual man's "successful performance of masculinity" in the biblical world.[83]

In arguing for the importance of honor to HB masculinity, these scholars often draw on research into honor (and its counterpart, shame) in cultural anthropology, the field in which the initial study of the concept was undertaken.[84] According to its original description by anthropologists in the mid-twentieth century, honor is a quality that in certain societies determines a man's reputation and self-worth.[85] Honor can be both *ascribed* to a man by the circumstances of his birth or his office/occupation, or it can be *acquired* by taking it from other men through competition. This competition can take several forms (e.g., athletic, martial, economic, verbal); however, it is most commonly sexual in nature.[86] A man increases his honor by protecting the chastity of the women in his family (mother, wife, sisters, daughters) while through his own sexual conquests simultaneously violating the chastity and fidelity of the women under the protection of another man. Female sexual fidelity/chastity therefore becomes the "currency and measurement" of honor among men.[87] The result of this incessant competition for honor among men is the creation of what Peristiany refers to as an "agonistic culture," wherein individual men feel obligated to assert and defend their precarious masculinity against other men with the same goal.[88]

Scholars of biblical masculinity have focused on this "agonistic" aspect of honor that creates a culture of endless and divisive male competition, particularly sexual competition. For example, Stone's work, together with that of Chapman and Haddox, emphasizes the importance of sex to the pursuit and defense of honor, while Lazarewicz-Wyrzykowska emphasizes the "strong link" between honor and male sexual competition.[89] However, the emphasis on sexual rivalry common to the initial anthropological research on manly honor in the mid-twentieth century has been balanced out by more recent work on the subject by cultural anthropologists. Scholars like Gilmore and Herzfeld argue for the inclusion of values such as hospitality and cooperation into the overall description of honor because they recognize that the kind of intensely agonistic society envisioned by earlier scholars of honor and shame could not be sustained without other values that stress societal cohesion.[90] Moreover, decades after editing the initial volume on honor and shame in the mid-twentieth century, Peristiany returned to the subject of honor and significantly reformulated his original position to include "grace" (i.e., honor as virtue) in his understanding of masculine honor.[91] Scholars of masculinity in the HB, however, generally have shown little interest in the more positive and socially constructive values associated with honor.[92]

Another issue in the appropriation of anthropological research on honor and shame scholarship by scholars of HB masculinity is that much of the work by biblical scholars on the role of honor and shame in the construction of masculinity focuses on individual men in the HB. The attention to the individual overlooks the fact that honor and shame systems typically belong to societies that are not premised on individualism, but instead on families, clans, and lineages. The importance of kinship in these societies was recognized from the inception of study of honor and shame. Zayid's essay in the original volume on the subject, for instance, noted that among the Bedouin of Egypt "it can be said that the study of honor and shame . . . is to a great extent a study of the bonds and values of kinship."[93]

Despite these oversights in the application of anthropological research on masculine honor, scholars of biblical masculinity are still right to consider honor an important feature of biblical masculinity. The frequency with which the term כָּבוֹד (which Clines considers the most significant term for describing honor in the HB)[94] is associated with other characteristically manly features strongly suggests that it is be considered together with them as constituent of hegemonic biblical masculinity. For example, it is paralleled with manly strength (גְּבוּרָה) in Ps 145:11 and with weaponry in Job 29:20 and Ps 3:3 (MT 3:4), and it is equated with military might in Isa 21:16.

For the purposes of this study, therefore, honor is considered a feature of biblical hegemonic masculinity.[95] However, the broader definition of honor informed by more recent anthropological research is employed. This means that while an idealized biblical man may engage in sexual competition with other men to gain honor, he is just as likely to acquire honor through values that promote social cohesion such as hospitality or grace. Moreover, he is not only concerned with his own individual honor but also with the honor of his kin. In the case of the Israelite culture that produced the HB, this kinship can be reckoned on the small scale (one's individual family unit or בֵּית אָב) or on the large scale (the entire people of Israel, whose unity is frequently described in kinship terms).[96]

Kinship Solidarity

The next characteristic of biblical masculinity that scholars have identified since Clines's original discussion of the subject is closely related to the characteristic of honor just mentioned. The biblical man stands in close solidarity with his fellow kinsmen.

Clines, in fact, recognized the importance of male solidarity in "David the Man" since he briefly mentions "male bonding" there as a characteristic feature of masculinity.[97] He develops this theme in greater detail in a later article on the Book of the Covenant in Exodus (Exod 20:22–23:1), a legal text which he claims envisions a unified society of closely allied men, referred to as neighbors (רֵעִים), who value the needs of the corporate whole above their individual desires.[98] However, in both of these articles Clines asserts that this "bonding" is unconnected to kinship.[99]

This separation of male solidarity and kinship is called into question when considering the growing scholarly consensus on the significance of kinship and kinship language in the world of the HB. Perdue, for example, argues that kinship solidarity is a fundamental value in the society that produced the biblical texts, and that this solidarity extended beyond the individual family unit:

". . . the ethics of solidarity shaped a network of understanding and care that moved beyond the immediate compound family to include clans, tribes, and the totality of the 'children of Israel.'"[100] This emphasis on kinship solidarity is the motivating force behind several distinctive features of biblical law, such as levirate marriage or the responsibility to redeem a kinsman's land, property, or person (i.e., the responsibility of the גֹּאֵל; e.g., Lev 25:25–55). Furthermore, Cross shows that kinship language is central to the notion of the covenant between Yhwh and his people.[101]

Steinberg's study of children in the biblical world also strengthens the connection between manhood and solidarity. She shows that the goal of children's socialization in the biblical world was not to develop them as individuals, as it is in the modern West. Instead the goal for the child was "learning to think like the group and to put group interests before individual ones," a "group" that consisted of "the family household and patrilineage."[102]

Therefore, the ideal biblical man stands in solidarity with his fellow kinsmen, first and foremost at the family and tribal level, but also more broadly with all Israelites. While this solidarity certainly extends to women and children, given the general avoidance of association with women described above, as well as the androcentric bias of the HB, this solidarity is most often displayed in the HB as solidarity among men.

Legal Manhood

Finally, it should be noted that, regardless of whether a man embodies the ideals of hegemonic masculinity outlined above (including marriage and children), he is legally considered a man at age twenty according to several biblical legal texts. At this age of legal majority, a man is eligible for military service (Num 1:3, 18; 26:2; 2 Chr 25:5) and taxation (Exod 30:14), and can be considered guilty of immoral choices and actions (Num 14:29; 32:11).[103] The valuation tables of Lev 27 similarly distinguish the twentieth birthday as the border between childhood and adulthood for both men and women in that the value of an individual at that age changes from twenty shekels (a person's value between the ages of five and twenty) to thirty shekels. The same tables put the upper limit to adult manhood at age sixty, after which the man is only valued at fifteen shekels. After age sixty, according to Eng, a man would be considered old and would be described with the term זָקֵן as opposed to terms more associated with adult manhood like אִישׁ, אָדָם, or גֶּבֶר.[104]

In sum, certain specific characteristics define normative or "hegemonic" masculinity in the HB (i.e., what it means to be a "man's man"). First and foremost, the biblical adult male must be physically strong and courageous, a quality that is most frequently and appropriately expressed on the battlefield. The idealized adult male must also have wisdom, evidenced by his persuasive words and prudent deeds. He avoids excessive socialization with women, as this is associated with childhood and therefore suggests that the man lacks maturity. He is further to embody self-control and self-mastery, keeping to a regimented life with strict guidelines for food consumption, sex, and war, among other things. He has ensured his legacy through his fertility, spawning legitimate heirs that will inherit from him. The concern for his heirs' legitimacy means that he expresses his fertility within the confines of marriage, preferably an endogamous marriage. He defends the honor of his kin—whether on the level of his close relatives or on the level of all Israel—and he stands in solidarity with them. Finally, although the male ideal is not connected explicitly with a particular age, it is worth noting that several biblical legal texts consider twenty the age of legal majority.

With a general description of the contours of biblical masculinity in place, the next task is to explore the characteristics of boyhood in the HB. Chapter 2 therefore provides a review of biblical boyhood and contrasts the features of the depiction of boyhood with that of manhood, in order to facilitate the recognition of male coming-of-age stories.

2

The Depiction of Boyhood in the Hebrew Bible

THE PRECEDING CHAPTER provided an overview of normative biblical masculinity in order to facilitate the study of male coming of age in the HB. That chapter identified certain qualities defining what it means to be a man in the HB, and therefore identified the characteristics that a boy can be expected to acquire in the course of a biblical coming-of-age story. This discussion can now be complemented by considering the HB's depiction of boyhood—the social and physiological starting point for a protagonist in a male coming-of-age narrative. To this end, the terms used to describe boys and young men in the HB are examined below.

The age range of biblical boyhood roughly spans from birth to age twenty, the age of legal majority (as demonstrated in the preceding chapter).[1] It therefore encompasses several developmental stages, including what in modern terminology is referred to as infancy, adolescence, puberty, and young adulthood. This diversity of age and development is reflected in the terms used to describe boyhood in the HB. These terms can be separated into two groups: one relating to younger boys (approximately from birth to age twelve) and the other to older boys/young men (approximately from age thirteen to twenty). The term נַעַר is noteworthy because it is the only term for boyhood that seems to describe boys in both groups; however, the investigation below shows that the description of the biblical נַעַר more resembles the former group of younger boys and it therefore will be considered together with the terms describing this group.

The discussion below first examines the terms employed to describe young boys, in order of their frequency of use.[2] The analysis shows that the characteristics associated with these terms are very similar. The terms describing older boys/young men are examined next, and their similarities are also noted. The chapter then summarizes the characteristic features of the respective groups (i.e., boys and young men) resulting in a more refined definition of male childhood in the HB. It concludes by offering a comparison between biblical boyhood and manhood, a necessary precursor to the case studies of male maturation found in the following chapters.

Terms for Young Boys (from Approximately Birth to Age Twelve)

נַעַר

Of the wide array of biblical Hebrew terms that connote "youth," none has been subjected to closer scholarly scrutiny than נַעַר, likely because of its frequency within the HB (239 attestations in the masculine form, 61 in the feminine) and because the title of נַעַר is given to individuals in considerably different social locations and of varying age groups.[3] While many of the significant scholarly treatments of the term in recent decades—two monographs on the term by Hans Peter Stähli[4] and Carolyn Leeb;[5] an article by John Mac-Donald;[6] and a discussion of the term by Lawrence Stager in a larger article on the family in ancient Israel[7]—argue for different understandings of the term in its social context in ancient Israel, they all tend to elevate newer arguments about the word's nuances at the expense of its obvious connection with the notion of youth.[8] Below, after briefly summarizing each of these scholars' conclusions, the case is made for the word's use to signify "youth" or "boy" (in its masculine form) and it will be shown that the term, when used in this context, provides useful data about male childhood in the Bible.

MacDonald's 1976 article "The Status and Role of the Naʿar in Israelite Society" was the first significant modern study of נַעַר. Influenced by the work of Cyrus Gordon[9] and Anson Rainey[10] on Ugaritic *nʿr*, a term that both believed carried military overtones and was applied to warriors,[11] MacDonald asserted that the "best known role" of the נַעַר in ancient Israel was that of an "elite military officer."[12] Of course, this was only the "best known" of the potential occupations for one dubbed a נַעַר in the biblical text, and MacDonald acknowledges that in some instances other non-military meanings are to be preferred, especially when the word is used of personal attendants.[13] In each instance, however, MacDonald believes that the term describes a "young male of high birth."[14] He therefore concludes that the English word that best captures the nuances of the Hebrew נַעַר is "squire," as this term was employed in the medieval era to designate a young man "of good birth" in both a military role and in the role of a personal assistant.[15]

Stähli's 1978 monograph, *Knabe-Jüngling-Knecht: Untersuchungen zum Begriff* נַעַר *im Alten Testament*, represents an even more thoroughgoing attempt than MacDonald's at creating an overarching definition of נַעַר that would adequately explain each of its attestations in the Bible. MacDonald argues that the term alternatively implied either a service or a military context, in contrast to Stähli, who asserts that a greater commonality unites all the instances of the term: all people identified as נַעַר or נַעֲרָה share the characteristic of *dependence* upon someone more socially authoritative than them.[16] Having emphasized this foundational commonality, he proceeds to separate the biblical נְעָרִים/נְעָרוֹת into two smaller groups: those who are dependent because they are unmarried and thus not yet the heads of their own households, and those who are grouped together as "servants"—this latter group including slaves, soldiers, or administrators of the king. Most importantly for the current discussion, Stähli moves even further away from the connotations of "youth" typically associated with נַעַר than does MacDonald, arguing that the term had more to do with "(Rechts-) status"[17] than with any determinable "Lebensphase."[18]

Stager's article, in contrast to the other studies mentioned here, pays closer attention to the social and familial forces that underlie the term נַעַר. For Stager, the increased demand for land that characterized the period after the establishment of the Israelite monarchy (a demand brought about by the closing of the frontier and increased royal gifts of land to the king's servants and allies) created a situation where equal division of land among male heirs could no longer provide each with sufficient plots. Primogeniture laws therefore were enforced with greater stringency, and younger males in any land-holding family would have found themselves unable to earn a livelihood on inherited land. This group of younger sons searching for occupation, wealth, and adventure comprised the ranks of the biblical נְעָרִים in Stager's view. The vocational options open to such נְעָרִים were threefold: becoming a steward for a wealthy or powerful individual; choosing a military life of knight-errantry; or joining the levitical priesthood.[19] For Stager, this is why most individuals called נְעָרִים in the HB are found in service, military, or cultic/priestly roles.[20] Furthermore, while it is the case that many of the נְעָרִים are young, the term נַעַר is not primarily one concerned with describing a phase of the life cycle, being only "indirectly related to age."[21]

The most thorough English-language treatment of נַעַר in the HB, Carolyn Leeb's monograph *Away from the Father's House: The Social Location of na'ar and na'arah in Ancient Israel*, attempts to articulate an all-encompassing definition of the term that can account for almost every one of its biblical attestations. For Leeb, former treatments of the term that emphasize a commonality of age, marital status (Stähli), or class and occupation (Stager, MacDonald) among individuals termed נְעָרִים/נְעָרוֹת are misguided. Instead, she locates the commonality in their shared social location as individuals located "away from the father's house," that is, "beyond the protection and control of their fathers, while not yet master or mistress of their own households."[22]

Leeb argues more forcefully for the separation of נַעַר from the connotation of youth than do the other scholars.[23] This is because of the specificity of her definition—which stresses the sociological meaning of the term, with no room for alternatives like those taken from the semantic realm of age/life cycle—and her claim to its near-complete applicability to every instance of the term in the Bible. The rift she posits between the term and a meaning signifying youthfulness, however, is ultimately based on questionable assumptions. Since Leeb's work is the most outspoken in contesting the usefulness of a word study of נַעַר for a discussion of boyhood in the Bible, it must be critiqued further.

In order to support her thesis, Leeb must explain why the LXX translators consistently translate נַעַר, when not used to describe a servant, with Greek terms for youth such as παιδάριον, which is used 140 times. Furthermore, for the rabbis, נַעַר (and its abstract form נְעוּרֹת) were "precise terms for youth, with the particular connotation of vigor and strength."[24] Leeb dismisses this seemingly decisive evidence against her argument by claiming that over time the society that created the institution of נַעַר-ship (one defined by the social centrality of the בֵּית אָב) changed so drastically that the original meaning of the term was lost. This resulted in a "semantic drift" over time, whereby a pars pro toto mechanism operated to elevate one quite incidental aspect of certain biblical נְעָרִים—their youth—to prominence at the cost of its original sociological meaning.[25] Moreover, Leeb contends that "no obvious pattern" obtains in the LXX translation of the term, thus conclusions about its meaning should not rely on this evidence.[26]

Leeb's argument is subject to critique on a number of levels. First, it is unlikely that a social institution as ubiquitous as that of the נַעַר/נַעֲרָה, so prevalent that the term describing it occurs over 200 times in the HB, would be so completely eradicated from the memory of a people that they would understand and translate its meaning incorrectly forever after. This is even more problematic given that over half of the occurrences of the term are found in the Deuteronomistic History,[27] which even by the most conservative estimates reached its final form in the sixth century B.C.E. It is highly unlikely that only three centuries later, when the LXX was translated, such a significant institution—if Leeb's thesis is to be believed—would be completely forgotten, its name misunderstood, and it would leave no trace in any similar or derivative institution (were post-exilic young people never in the dependent position of being away from their father's house?).

Also, while the LXX may use a variety of words to translate נַעַר, it is not the case that no "obvious pattern" is recognizable, as Leeb argues. As noted above, over half of the instances of the word are translated as παιδάριον, while the next most frequent Greek words employed are παιδίον (27 occurrences), νεανίσκος (25), and νέος (19).[28] Certainly a pattern is evident here, namely, that each of these terms signifies youth, a fact that Leeb ignores. Moreover, by claiming that an incidental feature of biblical נְעָרִים—their youth—later came to cloud the meaning of the original word, she neglects her own argument that "[b]iblical נְעָרִים are very rarely children" and that given the life expectancy of ancient Israelites, "a majority of [biblical] נְעָרִים were probably middle aged."[29] Leeb thus cannot claim that a "pars pro toto" mechanism brought about the eventual dominance of the meaning "youth" for נַעַר if she does not believe that the word in earlier sources had a strong connection with youth.

Finally, the critiques of Leeb's work offered by Eng and, separately, Gruber, point out the greatest flaw in her methodology. Leeb's attempt to unify every occurrence of נַעַר under one definition, according to Eng, "flies in the face of the universal linguistic principle called *polysemy*," which recognizes that almost every lexeme in every language has multiple meanings.[30] Gruber concurs, writing in his review of Leeb's work that the attempt "to find a social matrix that would account for the use of *na'ar* to describe both the infant Moses and Abraham's two servants (Gen 22:5)," is "quashed by common sense."[31]

This discussion of Leeb's monograph emphasizes that her study of נַעַר, like the work of any scholar who attempts to articulate an all-inclusive definition of the term, encounters unavoidable difficulties. In short, the multivalence of the term precludes a universal definition. Certainly the insights of MacDonald, Stähli, Stager, and Leeb have their place: the semantic range of the term is sufficiently broad that there are a number of instances of נְעָרִים in military contexts (MacDonald, Stager), disconnected from paternal patronage (Leeb), as personal attendants (Stähli, Stager), in the priesthood (Stager), or unmarried (Stähli). Still, the neglect of the term's connotation of youth—of which each of these scholars is guilty to some degree—is unfortunate, given the many biblical passages in which this meaning is implied.[32] Indeed, no discussion of the characterization of the male child in the Bible is complete without a thorough treatment of what the biblical text says about נְעָרִים. In recognition of the multivalence of the term, however, the discussion below focuses only on instances of the term that can be argued with reasonable certainty to refer to נְעָרִים with the youthful connotation in mind. Thus, it excludes instances where נַעַר refers to a man's role as a servant or a member of the military.[33]

Age range

As with each of the other terms for the young in biblical Hebrew examined below, no *strictly specific* age range is implied when an individual is referred to as a נַעַר.[34] However, the age range of נַעַר (when used as a life-cycle term) is significantly smaller than many scholars presume, provided one eliminates references to older men like Gehazi and Ziba, who are termed נְעָרִים because of their status as servants. Indeed, some scholars too quickly eliminate age from the semantic field of the term. Leeb, for instance, lists the named characters referred to as נְעָרִים, noting that their age range spans from unborn child (Samson in Judg 13:5, 7, 8, 12) to mature, if not elderly adult (Ziba throughout 2 Samuel). She thus concludes that age cannot be a "determinative criterion" for the word.[35] However, clearly Ziba is termed נַעַר throughout his life because of his servant status as the chief steward of Saul's house.

Other instances of the term's ascription to a mature man, commonly referenced by those who deny the term's connection with youth, are easily explained. Absalom, who appears to have attained adulthood by the time of his revolt, is famously called a נַעַר by David (2 Sam 18:5, 29, 32). [36] According to Fuhs, this is likely because David wishes to "play down [Absalom's] revolt and make it out to be a foolish escapade of youth," and therefore is not a declaration of Absalom's actual age.[37] Similarly, Joseph—who is called a נַעַר עִבְרִי by Pharaoh's cupbearer in Gen 41:12—is thirty years old when term is applied to him (Gen 41:46).[38] The cupbearer, however, is alluding to Joseph's servile status in the jail where they were both confined. Significantly, the cupbearer further elaborates on precisely this servile status in his next words about Joseph, when he identifies him as a servant (עֶבֶד) of the chief prison guard.[39]

Accounting for the multivalence of נַעַר as a term that includes servants, military men, and priestly functionaries, and for the two cases just mentioned that seem to skew the age-span of the word, one is left with a much narrower age range for the term in reference to youths. As already shown, the case of Samson—referred to as a נַעַר even before his birth—provides the lowest age on the spectrum. The oldest נַעַר whose age is mentioned is Joseph, who is seventeen (Gen 37:2). While this spectrum provides no rigid borders on its upper limit, and keeping in mind that biblical life-cycle terminology does not seem to be precise, the evidence suggests that individuals referred to with this word were youths in the first two decades of their lives, were unmarried (viz. Stähli), and had not yet had children.[40]

Feminine form

Evidence from the feminine form נַעֲרָה for the most part confirms the conclusions reached above. As with נְעָרִים, female characters called נְעָרוֹת are either servants/attendants (e.g., Gen 24:61; Exod 2:5; Ruth 2:8) or girls/young women (1 Kgs 1:2–4; Gen 24:14; Esth 2:4). The age range for נְעָרוֹת, however, is smaller than that of נְעָרִים, since the former term is reserved usually for older girls of marriageable age while the latter includes both very young boys and those of marriageable age.[41] Moreover, unlike נְעָרִים, occasionally girls referred to as נְעָרוֹת are married (Judg 19:3–9; Deut 22:13–21; Esth 2:20); however, Fuhs notes that this terminology is only applied to a married woman "when the text addresses her continuing relationship with her former family or her father."[42] Finally, unlike with the masculine form (e.g., 2 Sam 2:12–17), there are understandably no equivalent uses of the feminine form in a military context.

Characteristics of נְעָרִים

POWERLESSNESS

Turning to the specific characteristics ascribed to individuals referred to as נְעָרִים with respect to their youth reveals that the most frequently attested attribute is a lack of power. Biblical נְעָרִים are those *acted upon*, not the *actors*. Often this impotence is understood as an absence of *physical* strength.[43] The young Ishmael of Gen 21 (referred to as a נַעַר in v. 12, 17 [twice], 18, 19, 20) is consistently depicted as powerless: he is cast under a bush and left by his mother to die (v. 15), has no energy to do anything to remedy this situation but call out (v. 17), and must be lifted up (v. 18) and given water (v. 19) by his mother.[44] Joseph (a נַעַר according to Gen 37:2) lacks the strength to put up any resistance to the malicious actions of his brothers. The infant Moses, called a נַעַר in Exod 2:6, is the picture of helplessness when he is set adrift in a basket upon the Nile. Isaiah's famous utopian imagery of a young boy (נַעַר קָטֹן) leading fierce beasts (wolf, lion, and leopard [11:6]) draws its force from the expectation that under normal circumstances no one, but *especially not a powerless boy*, would be able to accomplish such a feat.

Frequently this physical powerlessness associated with the נַעַר is discussed in a military context and is connected with a crippling fear to enter battle. Jether's fear to draw his sword in battle (Judg 8:21) is recognized as a lack of strength. Saul's warning to David not to challenge Goliath (1 Sam 17:33) hinges on the claim that a נַעַר would have no chance to defeat a man of war (אִישׁ מִלְחָמָה), presumably because of the difference in battlefield experience and the ability to exert power. Solomon's claim that he is but a young boy (נַעַר קָטֹן; 1 Kgs 3:7) is further qualified by adding that he does not know "going out and coming in"—language derived from a battlefield context.[45] Solomon's claim therefore is based on the assumption that a נַעַר is unfit for battle because of his helplessness and inexperience. Finally, David's assertion that Solomon is but a "tender" (רַךְ) boy in 1 Chr 22:5 and 29:1 can be read in light of Deut 20:8, where the same relatively rare adjective is used to describe the hearts of men who are too afraid to fight in war and should be allowed to leave the army.[46]

Just as often, however, the powerlessness ascribed to a נַעַר is better understood as a lack of socially legitimated power, or authority.[47] As such, נְעָרִים have little to no control over their fate, being culturally obligated to submit to the will of their superiors. In the famous aqedah in Gen 22, Isaac (a נַעַר according to vv. 5 and 12) would seem to possess the physical strength to resist being bound and placed upon an altar by his hundred-year-old father (see v. 9, where he is depicted as strong enough to carry wood for the burnt offering up the incline of Moriah), but he does not resist, presumably because of his acquiescence to the will of his authoritative father. Shechem, a נַעַר according to Gen 34:19, is unable to negotiate for the hand of Dinah without the assistance of his father, suggesting his inferior social power. Throughout the Joseph novella, the נַעַר Benjamin (see e.g., Gen 43:8; 44:22) is a pawn in the hands of his social superiors, that is, his father and older brothers. Joseph demands that his brothers bring Benjamin to Egypt (Gen 42:34), Jacob attempts to keep him beside him (42:36–38), and Judah negotiates with Jacob to allow the brothers to take Benjamin back with them (43:8–10). In all of these maneuvers Benjamin is given no say with regard to his fate and is beholden to the will of those more authoritative than he. The נְעָרִים Ephraim and Manasseh (Gen 48:16) similarly have no voice in the blessing scene at Jacob's bedside but must accept the seemingly random decision of the patriarch to assign a greater blessing to the younger of the two. Their silence is telling compared to the strong objections of their authoritative father Joseph on this matter (48:17–18). Finally, the fear of the social (and possibly physical) power of his master Eli causes the נַעַר Samuel (1 Sam 3:1, 8) to refrain initially from telling him about God's revelation to him of the judgment against Eli's house (3:15).

LACK OF WISDOM AND PREDILECTION FOR RASH AND VIOLENT ACTION

Another common trait ascribed to נְעָרִים in the HB, especially prominent in wisdom literature, is that they lack wisdom, which comes only with age (cf. Prov 14:24; 16:31). Thus Prov 22:15 states that folly (אִוֶּלֶת) is bound up in the heart of a נַעַר and is only removed by the rod of discipline.[48] Similarly, Prov 7:7 pairs a נַעַר with the "simple" (פְּתָאִים) and describes him as lacking in "heart," here better rendered as "understanding."[49] It is this characteristic of biblical children that Jeremiah refers to in his response to the divine call to prophecy: his objection to the call is that, as a נַעַר, he does not know how to speak (Jer 1:6). This is not a confession of an inability to articulate clearly, as in Moses's call narrative, but rather indicates a lack of assurance on the thoughts behind the words, an acknowledgment of a lack of wisdom.[50]

Related to the biblical characterization of children as lacking in wisdom is the recognition that they are prone to rash and occasionally violent actions.

Shechem's sexual violence against Dinah, in addition to his hasty decision to reveal to Jacob his willingness to pay any price for Dinah's hand (Gen 34:11–12)—a poor negotiating tactic if ever there was one!—displays this violence and impetuousness associated with a youth's lack of wisdom. The tale of Elisha's taunting by the boys of Bethel in 2 Kgs 2:23–24 provides more evidence of the tendency of the young towards unwise actions that can end in violence, as they do here when the disrespected and angered prophet curses the boys and a bear emerges from the forest to maul forty-two of them. David's frequent reference to Absalom as a נַעַר also relies upon the cultural assumption that "youthful indiscretions" are common and should not be punished as severely as those of an adult. Thus Absalom—even though a mature man by this point in the text—is still a boy in his father's eyes and thus not deserving of death because, to use a modern idiom, "boys will be boys." Finally, although it is not clear whether the נְעָרִים mentioned as working in Boaz's fields in Ruth 2 are servants or young boys,[51] Boaz's promise to Ruth in 2:9 that he has commanded the נְעָרִים not to touch her suggests that there was a very real danger that they could possibly harm her. Indeed, Carasik argues that Ruth was a victim of "sexual harassment" by these נְעָרִים when trying to fetch water for herself from the vessels near them.[52] Thus, the biblical portrait of young men/boys, as in the literature of other ancient societies,[53] is colored by their tendency towards impetuous and often violent behavior likely resulting from a lack of the foresight for the consequences of their actions.

[margin notes: Also Ammon? How much are Fathers (passively) complicit in their sons' rapes?]

BEAUTY

A less prominent, but recognizable, facet of the biblical portrayal of youths identified by the term נַעַר is that they are held up as an aesthetic ideal for the male body. The admiration of the beauty of the young male is particularly focused on the freshness of their complexion and their lack of the scars, worn lines, and toughness that come with advancing years. Thus in the story of Naaman's healing by Elisha in 2 Kgs 5, the drastic change in the leper's skin after his bathing in the Jordan is emphasized by comparing it to the aesthetic ideal: the skin of a young boy (v. 14). This idealization of youthful complexion is similarly found in Job 33:25, where those whom God has chosen to deliver are given skin fresher than that of a youth (רֻטֲפַשׁ בְּשָׂרוֹ מִנֹּעַר) as a sign of God's favor. Furthermore, two of the three male characters[54] referred to in the Bible as beautiful, both with the phrase יְפֵה מַרְאֶה ("beautiful of sight;" i.e., "beautiful to behold"), are explicitly identified as נְעָרִים: Joseph (Gen 39:6) and David (1 Sam 17:42; see also 1 Sam 16:12 where he is said to have beautiful eyes and a good appearance).[55]

In the case of David, a significant aspect of his beauty is that he is אַדְמוֹנִי (1 Sam 16:12; 17:42), an adjective NRSV translates in these two cases as "ruddy."

The only other use of this term is applied to Esau; significantly it is only applied to him as a *newborn child* (Gen 25:25). Certainly Esau's hairiness at his birth is not characteristic of a newborn, but the fact that this term is associated with him at his birth, alongside the evidence from 1 Samuel that being "ruddy" was perceived as beautiful and that the skin of the young was the gold standard for the complexion, it is likely that this ruddiness is so attractive because it is characteristic of youth—a relationship that is also attested in the common practice in modern English of attributing a "rosy complexion" to the young. Thus, as in cultures both ancient and modern, the HB frequently associates beauty with youth. [56]

Summary

Summarizing the evidence of this study of נַעַר reveals features of the conception of male youth in the HB. When נַעַר is used in the context of the life cycle, the term's age range is from before birth to around twenty years old (the oldest named נַעַר being seventeen). Boys and young men who are called נַעַר are unmarried and childless. The most commonly noted attribute of the נַעַר is his powerlessness, lacking both physical strength (though not necessarily physical *energy*) and social authority. Young males are also characterized by their lack of wisdom, a trait that can be remedied through discipline and education. This lack of wisdom and disregard for the consequences of one's actions often result in rash and occasionally violent actions against others, often those with even less power and authority, such as young women. Finally, the נַעַר, especially his youthful complexion, is idealized as a paragon of physical male beauty in the HB.

יֶלֶד

Another common term for young boyhood in the HB is יֶלֶד, with eighty-nine occurrences. Analyzing the nuances of this term and naming the characteristics common to יְלָדִים adds further detail to the discussion of biblical boyhood.

Age range

The first issue to discuss is the age range of biblical יְלָדִים. Determining this presents many of the same difficulties as in the analysis of נַעַר. Again, a wide spectrum of ages at first glance seems to be encompassed by the term. Individuals called יְלָדִים include an unborn child (of indeterminate sex) in Exod 21:22; male infants in Exod 1:17–18 and 2:3, 2 Sam 12:15, and 1 Kgs 3:25; a newly weaned toddler in Gen 21:8; older boys capable of going to work with their father (2 Kgs 4:18, but note that the boy in that verse is still small enough to be lifted by his mother in 4:36–37) or congregating independently outside of town (2 Kgs 2:24); a seventeen-year-old (Gen 37:30); youths old enough to be trained as administrators and counselors in the Babylonian government (Daniel 1); and even married men (Naomi's deceased sons in Ruth 1:5) or the age-contemporaries of the forty-one-year-old king Rehoboam (2 Kgs 12:8, 10, 14). The frequency with which יֶלֶד is used to describe those who are also referred to as נְעָרִים further confuses the matter, suggesting that the two words may be interchangeable—that is, describing boys within the same age range.[57]

Again it is important to emphasize the inexact nature of life-cycle terminology in the HB, and that no specific age range will fit the data exactly. Still, as with נַעַר, the age range of יֶלֶד is smaller than an initial examination would suggest. Most significantly, Abraham Malamat has convincingly shown in his study of the יְלָדִים of 1 Kgs 12 that the term is used in that passage as a "literary device" for rhetorical effect, thus 1 Kgs 12 should not be included in attempts to specify the age range of individuals referred to with this word.[58] Next, the use of the term to describe deceased married men in Ruth 1:5—the only time the word is applied to a person known to be married—is typically explained by commentators as a counterpart to the mention of the word again at the conclusion of the book in 4:16.[59] The literary technique is employed to highlight the redress at the story's conclusion of the tragedy that befell Naomi at its beginning: whereas Naomi once lost her two יְלָדִים, Ruth's righteous deeds restored to her a יֶלֶד. Alternatively, the use of יֶלֶד in Ruth 1:5 may be rhetorical, where the audience is invited to view Naomi's loss from her perspective: she is now left without her husband and her "boys" (יְלָדֶיהָ).[60] The term's application to the seventeen-year-old Joseph (Gen 37:30) also is not compelling evidence to include in identifying the term's age range: it is possible that, as with David's affectionate use of נַעַר to describe Absalom, Reuben's distressed cry to his brothers ("the יֶלֶד is gone; and I, where can I turn?") may similarly employ a diminutive term to emphasize his pity for his youngest brother. The verse identifying Joseph as a יֶלֶד may also come from a different tradition than the one that gives his age as seventeen earlier in Gen 37:2.[61] Thus the three instances where the term is applied to older men or older boys should not be reckoned as evidence in the attempt to specify the age range of יֶלֶד, as the text employs the term in these instances for literary effect, or possibly due to source confusion in the case of Gen 37.

Having narrowed the age range somewhat by removing these three "outliers," it is important to examine the relationship between נַעַר and יֶלֶד and to reject the notion that they are exact synonyms. Looking more closely at the six instances where יֶלֶד is used in parallel with נַעַר (other than that in Gen 37), it is clear that half of the boys named are very young or infants (Moses in Exod 2, Ishmael in Gen 21, and David and Bathsheba's baby in 2 Sam 12), while the other half are of indeterminate age but seem quite young. For example, the taunting boys of Bethel in 2 Kgs 2:23 are specifically referred to as נְעָרִים קְטַנִּים or "young boys." The ages of Jeroboam's son (2 Kgs 14) and of Benjamin (Gen 43–44) are more difficult to identify, but their actions do not suggest the vigor and growing independence that comes with later adolescence. It appears, then, that יֶלֶד is primarily used in parallel with נַעַר in instances where the boy referred to with both terms is quite young. Thus, despite the apparent broad spread of ages denoted by יֶלֶד, upon closer inspection the range narrows significantly, encompassing instead infancy to prepubescent childhood, roughly birth to twelve years old.[62] The analysis of the characteristics ascribed to יְלָדִים strengthens this assertion.

Characteristics of יְלָדִים

POWERLESSNESS

As with נְעָרִים, the primary characteristic associated with יְלָדִים is their weakness and vulnerability to those who are more socially and physically powerful. This has already been shown with Ishmael, Moses, Joseph, and Benjamin, each of whom are simultaneously referred to as נַעַר and יֶלֶד (see n. 33). As with נַעַר, the adjective רַךְ ("tender") is used to describe this characteristic of יְלָדִים in Gen 33:13, where Jacob asks Esau if he can move his family at a slower pace than Esau's group of men because of his children's "tenderness." While both terms have the nuance of weakness, יְלָדִים more frequently than נְעָרִים are depicted as gravely endangered in some way, likely because of their younger age. For example, the Hebrew יְלָדִים of Exod 1 are in danger of being slaughtered on the order of Pharaoh; the יֶלֶד of 1 Kgs 3:25 comes close to being cleaved in two; the widow of Zarephath's young son dies (1 Kgs 17:17), although he is later resurrected by Elijah. Moreover, יְלָדִים can be seized and enslaved by creditors to pay back their parents' loans (2 Kgs 4:1), can be struck down by fatal ailments or injury during routine daily activities (2 Kgs 4:18–19), may be offered in sacrifice to idols (Isa 57:5), traded for prostitutes (Joel 3:3), or, horrifically, may be eaten by their mothers during times of starvation (Lam 4:10). In all these situations, יְלָדִים are depicted as helpless to defend themselves.

IMPETUOSITY AND LACK OF WISDOM

The portrayal of יְלָדִים is similar to that of נְעָרִים with regard to another feature: the actions of יְלָדִים are often depicted as impetuous and unwise. The case of the youths taunting the prophet Elisha outside of Bethel (2 Kgs 2:23–24), which has already been mentioned, exemplifies this characteristic: the disrespectful and violent actions of the boys emphasize their ignorance and they receive a disproportionate and violent comeuppance (being assaulted by a mother bear). The example of Rehoboam's folly at accepting the advice of the יְלָדִים with whom he grew up (1 Kgs 12) displays this characteristic as well. Whereas the king's council of elders advise him to answer the discontented and overburdened assembly of Israel with conciliatory language (v. 7), the brash יְלָדִים suggest a harsh and vulgar response (vv. 10–11) that Rehoboam ultimately opts for, resulting in the dissolution of the united kingdom. I have already shown that these יְלָדִים should not be taken literally as young children, given that they are said to have grown up with the forty-one-year-old Rehoboam (1 Kgs 12:8; cf. 14:21). Recalling Malamat's argument that the term is applied to this group pejoratively to stress their "hot-headed" nature and "political short-sightedness," it bears emphasizing that the pejorative use of this term relies on the audience's understanding that יְלָדִים are by nature prone to foolish and potentially destructive behavior.[63]

POSITIVE FEATURES OF יְלָדִים

Still, the depiction of יְלָדִים in the HB is not only pitiful (focusing on their weakness and vulnerability) and negative (drawing attention to their foolish, impetuous actions). Indeed, the intense emotional connection between a youthful boy and his doting parent is displayed in Jer 31:20: "Is Ephraim my dear son? Is he the child I delight in (יֶלֶד שַׁעֲשֻׁעִים)? As often as I speak against him, I still remember him. Therefore I am deeply moved for him; I will surely have mercy on him, says the Lord." Zechariah's vision of the new Zion anticipates streets filled with youths at play (8:5), demonstrating that the image of children at play is as associated with idyllic imagery in ancient Israel as it is today. Qoheleth (11:9–10) stresses that youth (here defined by the abstract noun יַלְדוּת) should be a time of rejoicing (שָׂמֵחַ), and that worry and vexation (כַּעַס) should be far from the heart during this time. He also emphasizes youth as a time of great potentiality, declaring in Qoh 4:13–14 that it is better to be a poor but wise יֶלֶד than an old and foolish king, because the fortunes of the youth can change radically for the better.

Feminine form

There are three occurrences of the feminine form יַלְדָּה. Of these, two are found in parallel with the masculine form, and therefore do not contribute new data on the characteristics of יְלָדִים beyond that already considered: Zechariah's vision of the new Zion (8:5) depicts both יְלָדִים and יְלָדוֹת playing in the streets; Joel's description of the endangered and powerless יֶלֶד sold for a prostitute (4:3) is paralleled with a similar יַלְדָּה who is traded for wine.

Special mention should be given to the third occurrence, where יַלְדָּה describes Dinah in Gen 34. This is the only instance of a female character who is simultaneously dubbed a יַלְדָּה and a נַעֲרָה. Both the narrator (34:3) and Shechem (34:11) refer to Dinah as a נַעֲרָה, however Shechem also calls her a יַלְדָּה in 34:4. Still, this does not equate these terms. Alter notes that Shechem uses the term יַלְדָּה when speaking to his father to convince him to negotiate with Jacob for Dinah's hand, and is likely using a diminutive to express tender affection. When the actual negotiations are proceeding, Shechem uses the more appropriate נַעֲרָה, as this term is more often used of older girls of marriageable age like Dinah.[64]

Summary

The data from this discussion of the term יֶלֶד provides further information about male youth in the HB. Many of the characteristics of the נַעַר also pertain to the יֶלֶד, thereby adding emphasis to their significance in the biblical view of boyhood. Most important is the repeated depiction of the יֶלֶד as weak, helpless, and vulnerable—indeed even more emphasis is put on the endangered nature of יְלָדִים than נְעָרִים, likely because the former are generally younger than the latter. Additionally, the actions of boys referred to by both terms are typically shown to be rash and resulting in unintended and tragic consequences. However, alongside these negative or pitiful characteristics, יְלָדִים are also described positively as full of potential and as (ideally) carefree. Moreover, the affection of a parent for the יֶלֶד is emphasized.

עוּל

Four distinct nouns are derived from the root עול and are considered together here: עוֹלָל, עֲוִיל, עוּל, and עֹ(ו)לֵל.[65] The age range reflected by these nouns becomes apparent when noting the meaning of the root עול, which means "to suckle." The participial form of the verb is found frequently in the HB to refer to animals who are not yet weaned from their mothers: calves in 1 Sam 6:7, 10; lambs in Isa 40:11 and Ps 78:71; and a mixed group in Gen 33:13. Evidence from cognate Semitic languages supports the connection of this root to suckling: the Ugaritic ʿl denotes a suckling animal, and the Arabic ġwl means "suckling" and the related ʿwl connotes "nurturing."[66] The use in Lam 2:11; 4:4; Joel 2:16; and Ps 8:2 of nouns derived from this root in parallel with the term יוֹנֵק—which denotes young children who have not yet been weaned (see below)—provides another important clue to the age range of עוּל.[67]

In all, it is apparent that the words refer to very young children that have not yet been weaned. However, because the age of weaning in ancient Israel is not certain (although three years old has been suggested),[68] it is impossible to give a specific age range for these terms. Still, it is important to note that actions attributed to certain children referred to by a derivative of עוּל, such as skipping about (Job 21:11), or being found outside of their homes on the streets (Jer 6:11; 9:20; Lam 2:11) suggest that toddlers (to use the modern terminology), not just infants, can be included in the age range the terms reflect.

It is also important to note that, unlike with נַעַר and יֶלֶד, the terms derived from עוּל do not specifically indicate gender. In other words, it is unclear whether the child referred to by these words is actually a young boy or a girl. Children of this age are essentially "pre-gender," being too young to be distinguished as boys or girls (cf. נַעַר and יֶלֶד, both of which have masculine and feminine forms).[69]

Characteristics

POWERLESSNESS

The characteristic most ascribed to children referred to by these terms, like the pattern shown for other terms describing children, is their vulnerability and weakness. They are often depicted as endangered by or the victims of violence. Sæbø, recognizing the frequency with which this vulnerability is displayed, notes that the nouns עוֹ(וֹ)לֵל and עוֹלָל "occur overwhelmingly in portrayals of war and profound distress."[70] It is no surprise, then, that the terms are frequently employed in that bleakest of biblical dirges, the book of Lamentations. Here children referred to with these nouns are depicted fainting from hunger in the streets (2:11, 19), begging for food (4:4), and being eaten by their starving mothers (2:20).The horrific image of עֹלְלִים being dashed against stones or walls is employed so frequently (2 Kgs 8:12; Isa 13:16; Hos 13:16 [MT 14:1]; Nahum 3:10; Ps 137:9) that it is practically the standard death description for young children in wartime. The precariousness of the life of a young child is highlighted in Isa 65:20, where it is prophesied that in the new heavens and new earth there will be no more of the all-too-common phenomenon of infant death.[71] Furthermore, such children are powerless to resist being taken as pledge for a loan in Job 24:9.[72] Finally, the psalmist lauds Yhwh in Ps 8:2 (MT 8:3) for establishing strength from the mouths of עוֹלְלִים and יוֹנְקִים, a feat that is worthy of praise only because under normal circumstances such children would never be associated with strength.

POSITIVE FEATURES OF עוֹלְלִים

While tragic images stressing the vulnerability and endangered state of children dominate these terms, positive imagery is sometimes present. The עֲוִילִים in Job 21:11 are compared to blithe sheep, and the parallel in the second half of the verse has them gamboling about (רקד).[73] Job also expresses dismay that even (גַּם) the young עֲוִילִים reject and despise him (19:18), a forceful complaint because young children typically do not do such a thing, but rather are normally trusting, affectionate, and accepting.

ASSOCIATION WITH WOMEN

The last important characteristic of the nouns derived from עול is that in many instances the children are associated with women. The intimate natural bond between mother and infant is displayed in Isa 49:15, where Yhwh declares that his loyalty to Zion is even greater than this strongest of human bonds. The association in the biblical text of women and children is often based on their similarities as the disenfranchised and powerless of society: in Mic 2:9, women and their children (עֹלְלֶיהָ) are grouped together as the innocent and powerless victims of the evildoers of Israel and Judah. Similarly, Isa 3:12 complains that the leaders of Judah are but women and children that mislead the people—a lament that resonates in the audience's collective ear only if it is assumed that these two groups are alike in their inappropriateness as leaders.

Summary

The infants and toddlers referred to by the four terms deriving from the root עול, then, are consistently characterized as powerless and fragile, like so many other young children described in the HB with different terms. These nouns in particular are frequently employed in graphic and tragic depictions of the horrors of war, where children's weakness and the precariousness of their life make them especially prone to danger. The picture is not completely bleak, however. The HB also depicts children called by these terms as playfully running about, and as fundamentally loving and trusting. Finally, these terms show the connection between women and children that arises from the natural bond between mother and child and their shared lack of social authority.

יוֹנֵק

As with the words derived from עול, the term יוֹנֵק is a participle from a root that carries the meaning of "to suck, nurse" (ינק) and denotes young children (both male and female) who have not yet been weaned. Indeed, of the eleven instances of the term, seven (1 Sam 15:3; 22:19; Jer 44:7; Joel 2:16; Ps 8:2; Lam 2:11; 4:4) use it in conjunction with a noun derived from עול, leading Domeris to state that there is no difference between the terms[74] and Ringgren to call them "near synonyms."[75]

As a result, many of the characteristics of children called by nouns derived from עוּל are also applicable to יוֹנְקִים. Thus יוֹנֵק, like עוּל, is a term with
no gender distinction, and therefore describes "pre-gender" youths. Furthermore, יוֹנְקִים are depicted as vulnerable, endangered, and helpless: in 1
Sam 15:3; 22:19 they are in danger of being killed in military action; Lam 2:11
has them swooning in the streets because of hunger and weakness; Lam
4:4 shows them begging for food; Ps 8:2 (MT 8:3), noted above, uses the
weakness of children to portray the strength of Yhwh; and Num 11:12 has
them too young to walk on their own. Similarly, positive imagery emphasizing the playfulness of youth is found: Isa 11:8 depicts a utopian future in
which the יוֹנֵק will be able to play happily and fearlessly (שִׁעֲשַׁע; cf. Jer 31:20)
over a snake pit. Finally, while there are no explicit instances where women
and יוֹנְקִים appear together (as was the case with the words derived from עוּל),
simply by describing them as "those who suckle," or "those who suckle
breasts" (יֹנְקֵי שָׁדָיִם; Joel 2:16), a maternal presence is implied. In short, the
characteristics of יוֹנְקִים overlap exactly with nursing children referred to
with words derived from עוּל, and for our purposes they can be considered as
synonymous.

גָּמוּל

Brief mention should be made of the term גָּמוּל, a rare passive participle (used
only three times) of the commonly attested root גמל, which means, among
other things, "to wean." The term thus technically means "a weaned child,"
which would probably put the child's age at approximately three, as suggested
above. Like the other terms for very young children, גָּמוּל is not a gender-spe-
cific term, and therefore can describe both young boys and girls. The term is
used in parallel with יוֹנֵק in Isa 11:8, reflecting the close relationship between
the two words: "The nursing child (יוֹנֵק) shall play over the hole of the asp, and
the weaned child (גָּמוּל) shall put its hand on the adder's den." The common
perception of a child as helpless and vulnerable makes the prophet's imagery
more striking. The normal reaction on the part of an adult to a child playing
or standing near a dangerous snake pit would be alarm, given the child's inability to assess danger and its limited capacity to escape. This anxious response is overturned in the prophet's idyllic vision.

In addition to the characterization of newly weaned children as helpless
and vulnerable, the גָּמוּל is also closely associated with its mother, as are the
other terms for infants. This association is found in Ps 131:2, the only other
verse to employ the term: "But I have calmed and quieted my soul, like a
weaned child with its mother; my soul is like the weaned child that is with

me."[76] The special bond between mother and child is evident here, with the exemplification of calm and peace being found in the image of a child with its mother.

טַף

With forty-two occurrences in the biblical text, the term טַף (a collective noun always in the singular) appears at first glance to be a significant part of the biblical vocabulary of childhood. However, upon closer examination, it becomes evident that this word's semantic range is not confined to describing childhood, and thus the amount of data that an analysis of the term can add to this discussion is diminished. Older studies of the term restrict טַף to its life cycle definition, glossing it as "children, little ones," and claiming that it derived from the hapax root טפף found in Isa 3:16, describing the "mincing" steps of jewelry-laden feet.[77] In this view, the term originally denoted the uncertain, stumbling gait of a very young child.[78]

In modern studies this consensus has crumbled. Locher's *TDOT* entry on the term represents the current opinion that translating the term consistently with this earlier limited meaning "does not do justice to the 42 occurrences of *ṭap*."[79] To begin with, Lee notes that over one-fourth of the instances of טַף are translated in the LXX with ἀποσκευή, a term which originally meant "movable property" or "baggage" but came to include the people brought along in military baggage trains with the army's material resources, specifically the soldiers' women and children.[80] Indeed, ἀποσκευή is used in the LXX itself with this understanding, as in Gen 15:14 and 2 Chr 20:25, where it translates רְכוּשׁ ("property, resources"). Lee thus shows, at least for the cases where ἀποσκευή translates טַף, that a more appropriate translation would be "dependents." Locher, although without closely considering the LXX evidence, independently concurs, suggesting that "the basic meaning is probably something like 'hangers-on,' i.e., those who are 'dependent,' the 'remainder.'"[81] This collective group would certainly include children and also women (Num 32:16–17) and at times the elderly (Exod 10:9–10). This realization has found its way into many modern English Bible translations, which choose to translate טַף as "dependents" instead of "children."[82]

It is debatable, then, given the broader meaning of טַף as a household's *dependents*, whether it is relevant to this examination of childhood in the HB. Eng's recent review of the literature on טַף concludes that the term is not relevant for this discussion. He states that "טַף would appear to have the sense of 'the members of a family (often nomadic) as dependents of a male head of household, often women and children but without specificity as to age or sex'" and thus that the term "is *not* a term belonging to the language of the life cycle."[83] Eng goes too far in this blanket disassociation of the term from the life cycle, however. Better is the recognition by O'Connor and Lee that the term has a "superordinate" meaning ("dependents") as well as a "hyponymous" meaning ("children"),[84] a duality of meaning that Locher also recognizes.[85] The LXX can be a helpful guide in recognizing when to consider טַף as a term referring solely to children, as it uses Greek terms denoting children to translate it in seventeen instances. This is certainly a significant decrease from the forty-two instances of the word in the HB, but is still a noteworthy body of data for consideration.

Age range and characteristics

Specifying an age window for the term, a difficult task with biblical Hebrew life cycle terminology, is made more difficult because of the limited relevant occurrences. Ezekiel 9:6 provides the only useful information in that it distinguishes children called טַף from בַּחוּרִים and בְּתוּלוֹת, terms for older youths (see below). Thus טַף should be understood as younger children, to be grouped with such terms as גָּמוּל, and יוֹנֵק, עוֹל, יֶלֶד.

A closer look at the characteristics of טַף supports grouping them with these terms for younger children because the features associated with these younger children are associated with טַף as well: vulnerability/endangerment and association with women. The endangered status of children dubbed טַף is best seen in Num 14:3, 31 and Deut 1:39, each of which depict the fear of the Israelites in the wilderness that, should enemies come upon them and defeat their warriors, their טַף would become booty (בַּז) for the avaricious plunderers. Association with women is also apparent: of the seventeen occurrences under consideration, seven (Gen 45:19; Num 14:3; Deut 3:19; 29:10; Josh 1:14; 8:35; 2 Chr 31:18) group טַף together with נָשִׁים.[86] Moreover, Num 14:3 specifically groups them together because they are all in danger of becoming spoils of war.

Terms for Older Boys/Young Men (from Approximately Age Thirteen to Twenty)

בָּחוּר

With forty-five occurrences, בָּחוּר is the third most common term associated with male youth in the HB. While no exact ages are given to young men called בַּחוּרִים, determining the age range for such youths is simpler than with other life-cycle terms because of the consistency with which this term is employed in association with certain characteristics. The close relationship of this term with images of youthful vigor, attractiveness, sexuality, military exploits, and a man's physical "prime"—to be outlined below—mark this phase of youth as one clearly advanced beyond those denoted by the terms already considered. Indeed, the בָּחוּר would seem to represent the farthest stage of male youthful development prior to mature adulthood in the HB. A בָּחוּר is apparently a man in everything but name—with the exception being that the בָּחוּר is always depicted as one without a wife and children, and thus the בָּחוּר lacks a major defining characteristic of biblical manhood. An approximate age range from the mid- to late teens is therefore appropriate, with the upper border at twenty years old, as this age represents the border of legal manhood in the HB (see above).

Scholarly discussion about the term בָּחוּר has focused primarily on its etymology, particularly whether more than one root underlies each of the term's occurrences. An alternative root is possible for the instances of בָּחוּר in a military context, such as in 1 Kgs 12:21, 2 Chr 11:1, and 2 Sam 6:1.[87] Yet all scholars recognize the relationship between most of the occurrences of the term and the root בחר, "to choose." The term is a passive participial form of the root, literally meaning "one chosen or selected." This use of the root to describe the "choicest" or "best" from among a group of things (see the related term מִבְחַר in, e.g., Gen 23:6; Deut 12:11; Isa 22:7) suggests the high value placed upon this period of life.[88]

Characteristics of בַּחוּרִים

STRENGTH AND MILITARY ASSOCIATIONS

One of the primary characteristics attributed to בַּחוּרִים, in contrast to the other terms for male youths examined thus far, is physical strength.[89] This is nowhere better exemplified than in Prov 20:29a: "The glory of youths [בַּחוּרִים] is their strength [כֹּחָם]." The frequent depiction of בַּחוּרִים in military contexts also suggests this physical strength, otherwise they would be ill-suited for the hardships of the battlefield.[90] The stereotyped description of the death of בַּחוּרִים by the sword (2 Kgs 8:12; Jer 11:22; 18:21; Ezek 30:17; Amos 4:10; Lam 2:21; 2 Chr 36:17) also suggests a military context, especially when juxtaposed with the stereotyped wartime death of infants by dashing (2 Kgs 8:12).

POSITIVE CONNOTATIONS

The positive evaluation of this virile period of the male life appears in all texts mentioning בַּחוּרִים. Qoheleth idealizes this period of youth, encouraging the בָּחוּר in 11:9 to rejoice (שְׂמַח) and be good to himself (וִיטִיבְךָ לִבְּךָ) in the period of his youth (בְחוּרוֹתֶךָ), following the designs of his heart and the desires of his eyes. The sage then contrasts the days of being a בָּחוּר with the "days of trouble" (יְמֵי הָרָעָה) without pleasure that come later on in life (Qoh 12:1). This period of youth is thus to be cherished: a time of levity, desire, and rejoicing.

The positive connotations of this period of youth also appear in the use of טוב ("good") with בָּחוּר: Samuel cautions the people of the many injustices endemic to monarchy by describing the king's penchant for taking the "good young men" (בַּחוּרֵיכֶם הַטּוֹבִים) and using them for his own purposes (1 Sam 8:16); and the only named בָּחוּר in the HB,[91] Saul in 1 Sam 9:2, is described as בָּחוּר וָטוֹב ("a young man and good").[92] Yhwh also appears to delight especially in בַּחוּרִים, as is apparent in Isa 9:17 (MT 9:16). Here the prophet announces that because of the people's iniquity, Yhwh will no longer rejoice (שׂמח) in their young men, nor will he have pity on their orphans and widows. The meaning of the prophecy is that the iniquity of the people has overturned the normal response of the deity to these groups: Yhwh is typically the champion of the orphan and widow (e.g., Hos 14:3 [MT 14:4]) and ordinarily rejoices in young men in this period of their lives.

SEXUAL MATURITY AND ABILITY TO MARRY

The quality perhaps most frequently associated with בַּחוּרִים is their attainment of the maturity necessary for sexual activity and marriage. This direct association with marriage is seen in two passages in particular. Judges 14:10 describes a banquet that Samson prepares prior to his nuptials with his Philistine bride, a banquet likely associated with the wedding ritual.[93] This celebration is said to be customary for בַּחוּרִים: ". . . Samson held a banquet there, for בַּחוּרִים do this."[94] A wedding-related celebration, a proto-bachelor party, is therefore explicitly connected with בַּחוּרִים. The connection with marriage also appears in Isa 62:5: "For as a young man [בָּחוּר] marries a young woman [בְּתוּלָה], so shall your builder marry you, and as the bridegroom rejoices over the bride, so shall your God rejoice over you."

There is no feminine form of בָּחוּר to add greater depth to the analysis of this term; however, as is seen in verse just quoted (Isa 62:5), the term בַּחוּרִים is frequently paired with בְּתוּלָה, "young woman."[95] Investigation of this common word pair further emphasizes the connection of בָּחוּר to marriage. The consensus among scholars who have studied the term בְּתוּלָה is that בְּתוּלוֹת are not necessarily virgins (otherwise there would be no need to add the phrase "who has not known a man" after the term in Gen 24:16; Judg 19:39; 21:12) but are certainly "girls of marriageable age."[96] The pairing of these terms supports the identification of בַּחוּרִים as "young men of a marriageable age."[97]

The sexual desirability accompanying the attainment of sexual maturity appears in Ezek 23:6, where Oholah's metaphorical Assyrian lovers are described as בָּחוּרֵי חֶמֶד ("desirable young men") and also in Ruth 3:10, where Boaz blesses Ruth for not "going after" the בַּחוּרִים, a noteworthy action only if pursuing these young men presents a temptation for Ruth.

Finally, the tragic image of Lam 5:13, in which the בַּחוּרִים of Jerusalem are forced by oppressors into the traditionally female occupation of grinding grain, achieves its force through an assumption of the already developed sexual maturity of these individuals. The depiction of a defeated enemy as emasculated is a common trope in ancient Near Eastern literary and visual texts, and this emasculation can often be achieved through the imagery of grinding grain (cf. Samson's forced labor in Judg 16:21).[98] The poet of Lamentations draws upon an image of emasculation, but it is noteworthy that for emasculation to have any rhetorical impact, the objects of emasculation must previously have been considered robustly masculine. To be sure, symbolically emasculating a male child who is embedded in the world of women, and is therefore already associated with them, would not achieve such an impact.

Summary

The בַּחוּרִים, then, are clearly removed from the characteristics of childhood that predominate in the nuances of the other terms applied to the young. The בָּחוּר is consistently depicted as physically strong, and he is often actively involved in military endeavors as a warrior (i.e., not as an aide or squire, as is often the case with the נַעַר). This period of life is valued highly in biblical texts, being viewed as the "prime" of the male life. Most significantly, the בָּחוּר is considered sexually mature and desirable, of a marriageable age, and possessing all the qualities of the fully developed masculine adult save for marriage and children.

עֶלֶם

The final term to consider is עֶלֶם. Unlike the other terms for male youth, this term occurs more often (seven times) in its feminine form, עַלְמָה, than in the masculine (twice).[99] Greater attention has probably been given to the feminine form because it is found in the Immanuel prophecy of Isa 7:14: "Look, the young woman [עַלְמָה] is with child and shall bear a son, and shall name him Immanuel." Given the significance of this verse to the Christian belief in Jesus's virgin birth (see Matt 1:23), Christian scholars throughout history have frequently attempted to define עַלְמָה as "virgin."[100] However, after examining every occurrence of עֶלֶם, עַלְמָה, and the related abstract noun עֲלוּמִים, in the HB—as well as evidence from cognate languages—most scholars now consider this connection with virginity indefensible.[101]

Far from representing "virginity," the terms עֶלֶם and עַלְמָה instead are closely associated with the ideas of *fecundity* and *virility* in biblical Hebrew and in cognate Semitic languages. Scholars contend that the two terms are related to Jewish Aramaic עֲלִימָא "strong," Arabic *galima* "to be or become filled with passionate desire,"[102] and even classical Hebrew חָלַם "to be vigorous/healthy" (Isa 38:16 and Job 39:4).[103] Walton argues that not only do later cognate terms stress the connotations of strength and virility associated with עֶלֶם and עַלְמָה, but these terms themselves as they are used in the HB "refer explicitly to childbearing interests and status."[104] To prove this point he looks to Cant 6:8, where עֲלָמוֹת are grouped together with concubines and queens, presumably in a stereotyped phrase that derives from the practices of the royal harem.[105] For Walton, *queens* are women married to kings for political/alliance purposes, *concubines* are sexual slaves, and עֲלָמוֹת are those whose main purpose in the harem is to bear children. Furthermore, he shows that childbearing is the "pivotal issue" with regard to the mention of עַלְמָה in Isa 7:4 (the Immanuel prophecy), as well as in the use of the abstract noun in Isa 54:4.[106] Similarly, two of the other three instances of the abstract noun (Ps 89:47 [MT 89:46]; Job 20:11) seem to refer to the virility and vigor of males: Ps 89:47 laments the shame of having youthful virility cut off, while the vigorous bones of youth are contrasted to dead bones in Job 20:11. With Walton, therefore, we can conclude that the "common ground" that unites all occurrences of the terms עֶלֶם and עַלְמָה is the "potential for procreative activity," suggesting that these terms and were applied to post-pubertal youths.[107]

Similarity to בָּחוּר

Since עֶלֶם describes older boys who have matured sexually and are of marriageable age, and since the term carries connotations of vigor and strength, it shares many features with בָּחוּר. In fact, just as with בָּחוּר, the period of life described with עֲלוּמִים (an abstract noun semantically related to עֶלֶם) is one that is idealized as a man's "prime." This is evident in Job 33:26, where a man's return to the days of his youth is depicted as a wondrous blessing from God, and even more so in Prov 30:18–19. Reading with the LXX, Syriac, Vulgate, and Arabic versions, the latter passage takes on a much different and more understandable meaning than in the MT. The NRSV of Prov 30:18–19, which translates from MT, reads: "Three things are too wonderful for me; four I do not understand: the way of an eagle in the sky, the way of a snake on a rock, the way of a ship on the high seas, and the way of a man with a girl." Following the other textual witnesses means altering only one word: the final בְּעַלְמָה "with a girl." It would appear that the *Vorlage* behind the alternative textual witnesses instead reads בַּעֲלָמָיו, "in his youth." Reading with versions clears up the confusion that the MT engenders,[108] with the relationship among the four events becoming much clearer: each portrays a creature or entity at their most majestic, doing the things for which they are most heralded (a soaring eagle, a snake somehow moving without legs or feet, a manmade ship defying the fearful sea, and a young man at the height of his virility).

The characteristics of the עֶלֶם (virility, advanced physical development, and the view of this time as a young man's "prime") suggest that the term is practically synonymous with בָּחוּר (a term that denotes strength, sexual maturity, and a young man's "prime"). This close association of עֶלֶם with בָּחוּר, however, faces a potential objection that must be addressed: each instance of the term עֶלֶם appears to be used as a synonym for נַעַר. If these two were synonymous, the age range covered by עֶלֶם would be skewed downward to include younger boys, and would therefore call into question the association between עֶלֶם and בָּחוּר—since the later term clearly describes older male youths.[109]

The first instance in which עֶלֶם seems to be equated with נַעַר is in 1 Sam 17, where Saul calls David an עֶלֶם in v. 56 but refers to him as a נַעַר in vv. 55 and 58. However, closer inspection reveals that it is not altogether clear that נַעַר and עֶלֶם are synonyms in this case. Indeed, as the discussion of the David and Goliath story in Chapter 4 shows, Saul's use of the term עֶלֶם in 1 Sam 17:56 likely represents a major change in his estimation of David, who moves from being referred to as a נַעַר to being labeled with a term that has more connotations of greater maturity: עֶלֶם.

The second and last instance where עֶלֶם appears to be synonymous with נַעַר is in 1 Sam 20. In v. 22, Jonathan refers to an עֶלֶם who seems to be the same person as the נַעַר mentioned twelve other times in the chapter (20:21, 35–41). However, these two characters may not be the same. Jonathan, at this stage in the narrative, is informing David of the details of his plan to communicate with him in the near future through a code that only they will know: David is to hide behind a stone while Jonathan feigns at target practice with his bow and arrow. If King Saul's anger towards David has cooled, Jonathan will call out to the young assistant with him fetching his arrows that they are to be found on one side of the stone, while if David is in danger, Jonathan will tell the assistant that they are beyond where he currently stands. The assistant Jonathan brings with him to participate in this feigned target practice is a נַעַר קָטֹן ("a small boy;" v. 35). However, when the עֶלֶם is mentioned in v. 22, the plan is still hypothetical, and Jonathan is unsure of the age of the assistant who will accompany him when he goes out to communicate with David. He thus wisely covers both options: *either* a younger boy will accompany him (v. 21), *or* an older youth (v. 22).[110] Therefore, because of the reasons outlined here, the claim that the noun עֶלֶם describes an older male youth is not weakened by the apparent association of the term with the noun נַעַר.

Summary

The term עֶלֶם describes young men who are at a stage of physical development more advanced than very young boys. They are sexually mature (i.e., post-pubertal) and ready for marriage. The term is not associated with virginity, but instead with virility and strength. This period in the male life cycle is often considered a man's "prime." Therefore, עֶלֶם appears to describe the same stage of male development as בָּחוּר.

Conclusions about Biblical Boyhood

Some conclusions can be reached on the approximately twenty-year time span prior to mature manhood in the HB that may be broadly labeled "biblical boyhood." The first is that the category of biblical boyhood can be divided into two groups: young boys (those younger than approximately twelve years old) and older boys/young men (from approximately thirteen years old to twenty years old).[111]

The first group consists of boys referred to by יֶלֶד, עוּל and its derivative terms יוֹנֵק, גָּמוּל, טַף, and, in many cases, נַעַר.[112] A clear similarity exists among the characteristics associated with the male youths for whom these terms are used: their vulnerability and endangerment, and their lack of both social authority and wisdom. However, even within this group of young boys (i.e., boys under the age of thirteen, approximately) some slight differences in characterization are evident. Certain of these terms which describe very young boys—עוּל, יוֹנֵק, גָּמוּל, and טַף, specifically—are frequently associated with women, an association that is not so evident for the slightly older boys called יֶלֶד or נַעַר.[113] Additionally, the four terms for very young children (גָּמוּל, יוֹנֵק, עוּל, and טַף) are not gendered beyond the grammatical gender given to every Hebrew noun. In other words, the children described by these terms are essentially "pre-gender," unlike the slightly older יְלָדִים and נְעָרִים (both words that have masculine and feminine forms) with which they are grouped. Another difference among the terms in this group of "young boys" is that a predilection for rash and violent actions is more common to the slightly older boys (יְלָדִים and נְעָרִים), and their fresh and youthful complexion is the frequent subject of praise. These slight differences, however, do not preclude the grouping of these terms together into a single group as "young boys," a group that contains prepubescent boys from birth until approximately age twelve.

The second group consists of older boys from approximately age thirteen to the age of "legal manhood" at twenty for whom the terms בָּחוּר and עֶלֶם are used. The description of young men in this group is characterized by their physical strength, and often this life cycle phase is understood as the physical "prime" of a man's life. Youths in this group are unmarried and childless, but their virile sexuality is emphasized. They are also old enough to engage in military exploits. These characteristics distinguish the older boys in this category from their younger counterparts in the first group and in fact associate them much more with fully adult males. They are not referred to as "men" in biblical literature, however, presumably because they have not yet reached the age of majority and lack wives and children. Instead, the label "older boys/young men" more appropriately fits this group, distinguishing it from "young boyhood," but also recognizing that it is not yet fully manhood.

With a more refined definition of "biblical boyhood" now in place, this investigation can turn to a comparison between boyhood and manhood in the HB.

Comparing Boyhood and Manhood in the Hebrew Bible

Identifying the coming-of-age theme in the HB requires familiarity with the characteristic features of biblical boyhood and manhood so that the exegete can recognize when an individual character puts aside boyishness and begins to act like a mature man. The investigation of boyhood and manhood above reveals fundamental differences between the two that are frequently emphasized in the coming-of-age narratives discussed in the following chapters.

The contrasts between idealized, hegemonic biblical masculinity and boys in the first group identified above ("young boys" referred to with the terms יֶלֶד, עוּל, יוֹנֵק, גָּמוּל, טַף, and often נַעַר) are especially stark. Young boys in the HB are vulnerable and endangered; biblical men are physically strong and self-sufficient. On the battlefield, a young boy is characterized by fear (Judg 8:20), whereas a man displays courage (1 Sam 4:9).[114] Authority within the society is in the hands of men, not boys. A man must be wise, but young boys exhibit a lack of wisdom. The youthful complexion is praised, whereas the physical appearance of men elicits comment mainly for its strength or imposing quality (1 Sam 9:2; 17:4–7). Men must exercise self-control, while boys are given to impetuous acts. Young boys live in the domestic space dominated by women and thus are more associated with them; men are found in the company of their fellow men with whom they stand in solidarity, and they eschew excessive contact with women. Finally, very young male children (those described with the terms עוֹל, יוֹנֵק, גָּמוּל, and טַף) are often not gendered in the terms used to describe them, while men in the HB are constantly measured against a hegemonic masculine ideal.

Comparing older boys/young men—the second group within the larger category of boyhood, for whom the terms בָּחוּר and עֶלֶם are used—with adult men in the HB reveals far fewer contrasts. Like men, older boys are praised for their strength, and are frequently depicted engaging in military exploits. To be sure, many of the other characteristics of biblical manhood (such as wisdom, self-control, or kinship solidarity) are not explicitly mentioned as belonging also to these older boys; however, nowhere are older boys and young men depicted displaying the opposite qualities (i.e., foolishness, impetuousness, etc.) as their counterparts in the group of "young boys" often are. Indeed, it appears that older boys/young men differ from adult men in only one major way: they are unmarried and childless.

Perhaps because of the comparatively minor differences between older boys/young men and adult men, none of the coming-of-age stories identified in the following chapters depict the transition of an עֶלֶם or a בָּחוּר into manhood. Biblical coming-of-age narratives instead depict a more dramatic and noticeable change than that between a young man and an adult man, since this would seemingly only entail a simple report of marriage and the birth of children. The coming-of-age narratives discussed in the following analysis depict boys who undergo a maturation in the course of the story that significantly alters them, in which they change from being described with characteristics similar to those of the group of younger boys analyzed above (such as powerlessness, association with women, etc.) to displaying the qualities associated with both men and older boys. In one case (David in 1 Sam 17), this maturation is described as a change from young boyhood (נַעַר; 1 Sam 17:33, 42) to older boyhood (עֶלֶם; v. 56); but more often the narratives end with the boy who was previously shown in very childish ways being recognized as a fully adult man.[115])

In the next chapter, the identification of coming-of-age narratives in the HB begins with the discussion of two stories of male maturation featuring protagonists from pre-monarchic Israel whose leadership positions in Israel share many similarities: the coming-of-age story of leader/prophet/lawgiver Moses in Exod 2, and that of leader/prophet/judge Samuel in 1 Sam 3.

Case Studies of Male Coming of Age in the Hebrew Bible

3

Moses and Samuel: Case Studies of Pre-Monarchic Maturation

THE FIRST TWO tales of successful male maturation in the HB canon are those of Moses in Exod 2 and Samuel in 1 Sam 3. The reason for considering these two narratives together, however, goes beyond the simple fact of their canonical location before the rise of the monarchy. A look at the leadership roles played by both characters reveals some remarkable similarities between them. Both Moses and Samuel hold authority over "all Israel" (כָּל־יִשְׂרָאֵל; e.g., Deut 1:1; 1 Sam 3:20), are referred to as prophets (נָבִיא; Deut 18:15; 1 Sam 3:20), and can effect military victory for Israel through intercession with Yhwh (Exod 17:8–13; 1 Sam 7:7–14). In addition, the two characters are associated with jurisprudence: Moses as the lawgiver par excellence (e.g., Exod 31:18), and Samuel as a lawgiver (1 Sam 10:25) and a legal interpreter (1 Sam 7:15–17). Moreover, as argued below, it is possible that the character of Samuel is intentionally cast in the mold of Moses and is meant to be viewed as his inheritor. Given these points of contact between the two figures, the respective stories of their maturation are appropriately read side-by-side in this chapter.

Below, the two narratives are first considered separately, with the primary goal of identifying the presence of the coming-of-age theme in both. This analysis will also detail how the coming-of-age theme can complement other narrative goals and themes, which is particularly the case with Samuel's maturation story. The chapter concludes by comparing the two stories, with an eye towards what this comparison means for the multiplicity and diachronic development of biblical masculinities.

"In Those Days, Moses Grew Up": Exodus 2 and the Maturation of Moses

Moses's coming of age is narrated in Exod 2. More specifically, the second "scene" in this chapter, Exod 2:11–22, is the central locus of the coming-of-age theme. However, some of the tactics employed by the narrator to draw attention to this theme only become evident when considering it alongside its counterpart in Exod 2:1–10, the story of Moses's birth and rescue by Pharaoh's daughter.[1] Therefore, an examination of Exod 2:11–22 within its broader context is required to identify and discuss the coming-of-age theme.

A close look at the structure of Exod 2 reveals the importance to the story of highlighting Moses's maturation into manhood. The literary structure can be represented as follows:

> *Tales of Moses's Youth: Exod 2:1–22*
> Scene I (Exod 2:1–10): Moses's Birth Narrative
> Scene II (Exod 2:11–22): Moses Comes of Age[2]
> >   *Episode 1 (vv. 11–12)*: Moses defends his Hebrew kinsman
> >   *Episode 2 (vv. 13–15a)*: Moses attempts to adjudicate among his fellow Hebrews
> >   *Episode 3 (vv. 15b–22)*: Moses rescues Reuel's daughters and marries.[3]

The transition from the first scene to the second scene in the larger narrative unit is marked by an obvious temporal gap, with the first scene depicting Moses as a helpless infant set adrift on the Nile and the second representing him as a more proactive young adult.[4] Additionally, the boundaries of the two scenes are set off by the repetition of a particular verb in the two verses at the juncture of the two scenes, vv. 10 and 11. Significantly, that verb is גדל ("to grow"). By repeating this verb at this prominent location in the story's overall structure, the text emphasizes Moses's growth, making it the literal center of the narrative. Moreover, while the first instance of גדל in v. 10 describes the growth of the infant until he can be weaned and brought to Pharaoh's court, the second instance is often understood by scholars to imply that Moses has fully "grown up" and become a man by this time, owing to the presumably large time gap separating the two scenes.[5]

The preceding assumption is rendered problematic by the subsequent text, in which Moses's adulthood is not so obvious as to be beyond debate (see the discussion of Exod 2:14 below) and where he is not definitively called a "man" (אִישׁ) until near the story's end (v. 19, 20). Still, it is possible to maintain the translation of גדל in v. 11 as meaning "to grow up to adulthood" by following Levy's reading of v. 11. Levy argues that the clause in which the verb גדל is used (וַיְהִי בַּיָּמִים הָהֵם וַיִּגְדַּל מֹשֶׁה) is a "descriptive heading for things to come" and not a "preliminary factual detail for the scene."[6] The effect is to provide a veritable title for the following scene that introduces its most important theme: "In those days Moses grew up."

By making use of this structure for Exod 2—that is, seeing vv. 10–11 as the hinge between the two scenes—another narrative technique that draws emphasis to the coming-of-age theme emerges. In the first scene (vv. 1–10), in which Moses is depicted as an infant, the noun יֶלֶד ("young boy") is repeated seven times, marking it as the critical *Leitwort* of this scene.[7] In fact, the word יֶלֶד is found in the exact center of the scene, with 70 words preceding it and 70 following it.[8] In contrast, the second scene (vv. 11–22) repeats the word אִישׁ ("man") seven times, with one instance of the plural אֲנָשִׁים.[9] Furthermore, this second scene's *Leitwort* is used to describe Moses by the scene's conclusion in 2:19, 20; notably Moses is never again referred to as a child after this point, having become "the man Moses" (הָאִישׁ מֹשֶׁה; Exod 11:3). By means of the sevenfold repetition of "boy" in the first scene and "man" in the second, the text highlights the shift within Moses from boy to man in Exod 2.

Accompanying this shift from the word יֶלֶד in the first scene to אִישׁ in the second scene is the movement by Moses out of the world of women and into the world of men. In the first scene, each major character other than the infant Moses is female: Moses's mother, his sister, Pharaoh's daughter and her maids. In contrast, Moses father is conspicuously absent from the action in this scene aside from a brief mention of his marriage to Moses's mother in 2:1. The second scene, however, is almost exclusively concerned with men. The women that are mentioned—Reuel's daughters—are not described in any great detail, especially in comparison to the attention paid to other women introduced in similar "meeting at the well" scenes in the HB (Rebekah in Gen 24; Rachel in Gen 29). Moreover, as Coats points out, the text of vv. 15–22 seems to focus less on describing Moses's relationship to his wife Zipporah than on his connection through marriage to her father Reuel.[10]

The transition in the story from the world of women to the world of men reflects the similar movement from female to male influence that marks the maturation of the male child in the biblical world, as noted in preceding chapters. As such, it is an appropriate narrative tactic for a coming-of-age story.

In sum, the pericope from Exod 2:1–22 draws attention to the coming-of-age theme structurally by repeating the verbal root גדל ("to grow") at the hinge between the two scenes that comprise the larger narrative (i.e., vv. 10–11). In so doing, it stresses growth as a significant aspect of the narrative, and the use of this verb in v. 11 perhaps also provides a title to the second scene: "In those days Moses grew up." Additionally, the first scene's sevenfold repetition of the *Leitwort* יֶלֶד and its prevalence of female characters, when viewed in contrast with the second scene's repetition of the *Leitwort* אִישׁ and dominance by male characters, mirrors Moses's transition from boy to man.

Describing Moses's Maturation in the Second Scene of Exodus 2

The tactics of repetition and narrative structure already suggest the importance of the coming-of-age theme in Exod 2, but it is in the chapter's second
scene (vv. 11–22) that this theme is fully realized with the detailed description
of Moses's maturation. As previously mentioned, this scene has three episodes, which together represent Moses's coming of age. However, since each
episode stresses different aspects of that maturation process, they are explored separately in order to demonstrate how they individually depict and
contribute to an understanding of Moses's transition to manhood.

Episode 1 (vv. 11–12): Moses defends his Hebrew kinsman

In the first episode of Exod 2 (vv. 11–12) Moses exhibits a fundamental characteristic of masculinity, strength, which is frequently demonstrated through
the use of violent force against another man. Here Moses encounters an
Egyptian beating (Hiphil of נכה) a Hebrew man, an act that symbolizes the
Hebrews' burdens under their oppressors. In an expression of proportional
retributive justice, Moses retaliates on behalf of the Hebrew, with whom
Moses identifies as a kinsman (אָח; v. 11), by slaying (נכה) the Egyptian. It is
also noteworthy that this act exemplifies the *solidarity* Moses shares with his
fellow kinsmen, a point previously identified as belonging to the description
of biblical masculinity. Despite having been reared among the Egyptians in
Pharaoh's court, Moses is here depicted as a Hebrew/Israelite man, willing to
act forcefully in defense of a kinsman.

This episode further underscores—albeit subtly—that Moses's retaliation
is indicative of his development as a man. Before striking down the Egyptian,
Moses looks around the area and sees that, according to v. 12, "there was no
man" (אֵין אִישׁ). While many have seen in this act Moses's desire to ensure that
his retaliation remains hidden, another compelling interpretation popular
among early rabbinic readings of this verse is possible.[11] According to this alternative interpretation, Moses's survey to see if there was a "man" in the area
is not motivated by a desire for secrecy but instead by a hope that someone else
nearby will aid the abused Hebrew by putting a stop to the Egyptian's violence. Midrashic sources cite Isa 59:16 to support this reading, where אֵין אִישׁ is
used to describe how no one is available to challenge injustice, therefore compelling Yhwh to do so personally.[12] Moreover, in *Pirkei Avot* 2.5, the declaration
that "there was no man" in Exod 2:12 is understood as the basis for Hillel's
maxim "Where there are no men, try to be a man," thereby indicating that at
least according to this interpretation what is more at stake in this verse is not
that there is no *person* present to act, but instead that no *man* is present.[13]

In light of this traditional interpretation, Exod 2:12 becomes a key verse in the coming-of-age reading of the larger story. When encountering violence against a fellow Hebrew, Moses finds to his dismay that there is no man who can counter this brutality with a masculine show of retaliatory strength. Thus the young Moses is himself forced to act as a man by overpowering and slaying the Egyptian.

Episode 1, therefore, contributes robustly to the depiction of Moses's transition from boy to man. Prior to this episode, the narrator depicts Moses as a boy (יֶלֶד). In episode 1, however, for the first time the youthful Moses demonstrates qualities of manhood: both his physical strength and his solidarity with a fellow adult kinsman. Furthermore, Moses acts courageously because no other *man* is present, a deed indicating that Moses is taking on that role and is himself becoming a man.[14]

Episode 2 (vv. 13–15a): Moses attempts to adjudicate among his fellow Hebrews

The second episode in the scene describing Moses's coming of age, like the first, depicts Moses exhibiting a quality typically associated with idealized masculinity in the HB: wisdom, specifically juridical wisdom. In v. 13, Moses mediates between two Hebrew men who are fighting, admonishing the guilty party (הָרָשָׁע) for striking his companion (רֵעַ). Moses's juridical wisdom is seen in his immediate recognition and criticism of the guilty party in the quarrel. The prevalence of words associated with biblical jurisprudence such as רָשָׁע and שָׁפַט calls further attention to the legal context.[15] Moreover, the guilty Hebrew's response to Moses (v. 14), which questions his right to serve as a judge (שֹׁפֵט), again indicates that Moses's ability to apply his wisdom to legal matters is at issue in this scene.

Episode 2 also provides another example of Moses's defense of solidarity among Hebrew/Israelite males, thereby continuing the development of this theme first introduced in the preceding episode. By mediating a quarrel between two kinsmen, Moses is portrayed as a defender of in-group cohesion. Moses's word choice in his attempt to adjudicate between the men, referring to the men as companions (רֵעַ), contributes to this portrayal. As Clines shows, the term רֵעַ is one frequently used in the description of the Israelite community of adult men.[16] By using this term, Moses positions himself as an Israelite man, committed to the manly solidarity that resides at the heart of the group's sense of masculinity.

The coming-of-age theme in this episode and in the scene as a whole also appears in the guilty Hebrew's objection to Moses's display of judicial authority: מִי שָׂמְךָ לְאִישׁ שַׂר וְשֹׁפֵט עָלֵינוּ (v. 14). Some commentators assume that the phrase אִישׁ שַׂר should be read together, with the word שַׂר in a relationship of apposition to אִישׁ. This reading results in a translation similar to that of NRSV: "Who made you a ruler and a judge over us?"[17] Other scholars propose an alternative translation in which אִישׁ is read as an independent term that is not in apposition to the following word שַׂר.[18] Seen from this perspective, the guilty Hebrew's objection is translated "Who set you as a man, ruler, and judge over us?" (so Propp).[19] This translation is preferable because it shows how Moses's authority is being challenged on three levels: his authority as a judge, as a leader, and, most significantly of all given its priority of placement at the head of the list, *as a man*.[20]

The significance of the guilty Hebrew's challenge to Moses for a coming-of-age reading of this text is readily apparent when this alternative translation is followed. The young man Moses's authority and status as a man is questioned by the guilty Hebrew's challenge, which suggests that Moses's authority and transition to manhood is a primary concern of the narrative. The text's position in response to this challenge is also evident: by placing the challenge in the mouth of a character who is called "guilty" (רָשָׁע) and who clearly prefigures the grumbling and insubordinate Israelites that Moses would lead in the wilderness, the text takes its stand in opposition to the challenge.[21] Moses, in other words, should be invested with the authority of a judge, a ruler, and, most importantly, a man.[22]

The second episode in the scene depicting Moses's coming of age (Exod 2:11–22) thus highlights his maturation in the same way as does the first episode: by ascribing to him qualities associated with masculinity. Here those qualities include wisdom (specifically juridical wisdom) and, as also seen in the preceding episode, a commitment to the solidarity of adult male Hebrews/Israelites. His demonstration of these qualities, however, is challenged by a fellow Hebrew "man" (אִישׁ; v. 13), who questions his status and authority as judge, ruler, and most significantly *as a man*. This challenge to Moses's budding manhood again emphasizes that his transition to manhood is a central concern in the larger narrative. The fact that this challenge is voiced by an unsympathetic "guilty" (רָשָׁע) character indicates the narrator's position on this vital question: the recalcitrant Hebrew is wrong to question Moses, who through his actions in scene II (Exod 2:11–22) shows that he has become a man.

Episode 3 (vv. 15b–22): Moses defends Reuel's daughters and marries
The third and final episode in Moses's coming-of-age story is found in vv. 15b–22. After challenging Moses's status as a man, the Hebrew antagonist reveals that he, and presumably others, knows that Moses has killed an Egyptian (v. 14). When Pharaoh too learns of this deed (v. 15a), Moses flees into the wilderness fearing for his life and eventually settles in Midian (v. 15b).

Before considering how this episode contributes to the description of Moses's maturation as a man, the "fear" that motivates him to leave Egypt (v. 14) raises a critical question that must be addressed.[23] Does Moses's fear—a quality typically associated with childhood—contradict the identification of Exod 2:11–22 as a coming-of-age narrative? A convincing solution to this query emerges as the result of the discussion in Chapter 2 of fear as a characteristic of boyhood. There I argued in light of the story of Jether in Judg 8 and of the frightened Philistines in 1 Sam 4 that the kind of fear identified as non-manly is the fear to act, specifically the fear of fighting and killing in battle.[24] On the other hand, the fear of *being killed* may not represent the manly ideal; however, it does not disqualify one from being considered as a man. For example, Gideon is frequently identified as fearful (e.g., Judg 6:27; 7:10), yet he is still considered a mighty man of valor (גִּבּוֹר; Judg 6:12).

Moses's fear is clearly of the latter variety—the fear of being killed rather than the fear of killing. Moses has shown the willingness to use deadly force in defense of his kinsmen (vv. 11–12). His fear is a response to the wrath of Pharaoh who seeks to kill him for this deed (v. 15a). Therefore, Moses's "fear" in v. 14 is not an expression of a childish emotion that would detract from the depiction of Moses performing manly deeds to demonstrate his transition to adulthood.

Following Moses's arrival in Midian, he performs two acts characteristic of biblical masculinity. First, he shows courage by "saving" (יֹּשַׁע) Reuel's daughters from the shepherds who are harassing them and who are driving the women away from a well.[25] Witnessing this injustice, Moses rises up, confronts the hostile shepherds, and intervenes on behalf of Reuel's daughters.[26] Following his courageous actions, in an extra act of kindness he waters the women's sheep (vv. 16–17).

After the daughters report Moses's noble deed to their father, Reuel invites Moses to dwell with him and his family. This invitation leads to Moses's second characteristically masculine deed in this episode: marriage, specifically to one of Reuel's daughters, Zipporah (v. 21). Following the report of his marriage, Moses's manly virility is exhibited with the birth of his first child, a male heir named Gershom (v. 22). Appropriately, after having displayed several defining features of biblical masculinity throughout the story, the narrator begins to refer to Moses unequivocally as a man in this episode (vv. 19, 20).

To summarize: The importance of the coming-of-age theme in Exod 2 is suggested by the presence of certain broad thematic and structural features of the narrative, and this impression is confirmed upon a detailed analysis of the three episodes that comprise the chapter's second scene (vv. 11–22). Each episode shows Moses engaging in acts characteristic of manhood in the HB.

In the first, Moses displays physical strength by defeating/slaying another man and shows his solidarity with his Hebrew brethren (אֶחָיו; v. 11). In the second episode, Moses displays both wisdom and, once again, solidarity with his fellow Hebrews/Israelites. Finally, Moses's maturation as a man (אִישׁ; see v. 19, 20) is completed in the third episode when Moses courageously defends Reuel's daughters, marries Zipporah, and fathers a son.

These characteristics of masculinity in Exod 2, moreover, are consistently viewed through the lens of the coming-of-age theme. Hints within the episodes as well as literary tactics and structural features establish the centrality of this theme. Moses undertakes his violent retribution against the Egyptian because "there was no man" present who could take this responsibility upon himself. Since there was no man, the narrator implies, Moses had to become that man. In addition, the guilty Hebrew's challenge of Moses's manhood draws attention to precisely the question of his status as a man, a question to which the scene from vv. 11–22 provides the definitive answer. Having transitioned from boyhood to manhood, Moses is now ready to receive his vocation from Yhwh in the prophetic call narrative in the next chapters, Exod 3–4.

"And the Boy Samuel Grew with Yhwh": The Coming of Age of Samuel in 1 Samuel 3

Uniquely among the coming-of-age tales in the HB examined in this book, 1 Sam 3—detailing Yhwh's revelation to Samuel at the Shiloh sanctuary—has previously been identified by scholars as a story of maturation. Brueggemann, for instance, contends that "by the end of the narrative, Samuel arrives at manhood."[27] McCarter similarly claims that the story in 1 Sam 3 serves as a conclusion to Samuel's childhood narrative in 1 Sam 1–3.[28] However, the recognition that this story entails Samuel's coming of age has not yet gone beyond brief and tentative summarizing claims. The analysis here, in contrast, elaborates on the literary devices used to focus the narrative on the coming-of-age theme. These narrative features include the repeated initial emphasis upon Samuel's youth and the use of narrative structure and threefold repetition to highlight Samuel's transition out of boyhood. Moreover, the discussion below reveals the significant ways in which the coming-of-age theme complements other central themes in the broader narrative found in 1 Sam 1–3.[29] The analysis of Samuel's coming-of-age story in this section concludes with a consideration of the changes that occur in Samuel by the end of 1 Sam 3.

Emphasis on Samuel's Youth

The first indication that 1 Sam 3 entails Samuel's coming of age is that until this point in the narrative Samuel is depicted as a child. Indeed, his youth is emphasized repeatedly throughout 1 Sam 1–3. To begin with, the term נַעַר is used for Samuel more than any other named character in the entire HB.[30] The extent of Samuel's association with the term נַעַר is further indicated by the anomalous way in which the word is occasionally applied to him. In contrast to every other character in the HB to whom נַעַר refers, only Samuel is identified with the designation הַנַּעַר immediately *preceding* his name (i.e., he is called הַנַּעַר שְׁמוּאֵל in 1 Sam 2:21, 26, and 3:1), while in every other instance in which a person is named and is identified as a נַעַר, the term will *follow* the person's name.[31] Referring to Samuel as הַנַּעַר שְׁמוּאֵל functions to provide a veritable title for the character: he is "the boy Samuel," just as, for example, David is "the king David." The placement of the title הַנַּעַר before Samuel's name is especially noteworthy because the Hebrew of the Deuteronomistic History tends not to vary in the placement of a character's titles. Kings are by far more frequently referred to as "the king PN" than "PN the king." David, for instance, is called "David the king" only once, in 2 Sam 13:39, with scores of other references to him as "the king David" (e.g., 2 Sam 6:12, 16; 8:8, 10, 11, etc.). Prophets are unanimously called "PN the prophet" rather than "the prophet PN" (e.g., Gad [1 Sam 22:5; 2 Sam 24:11]).[32] To alter the convention of placing הַנַּעַר after a character's name as is the case with Samuel, therefore, is a relatively rare occurrence that indicates the narrator's emphasis on Samuel's youth.

Perhaps nowhere is the emphasis on Samuel's youth more obvious than in 1 Sam 1:24. While the text of the MT may suffer from corruption here, this verse as it currently reads highlights Samuel's youth with an almost comic tenacity. Here Hannah brings Samuel to Eli at Shiloh for the first time, along with several items to be sacrificed at the shrine. The text refers to Samuel's presence alongside his mother with a curious tautology: "and the child was young" (וְהַנַּעַר נָעַר; literally "and the boy was a boy"), an expression that again draws special attention to Samuel's youth.[33]

Other indicators of Samuel's youth are apparent in 1 Sam 1–3. Repeated references to his weaning in 1 Sam 1 (vv. 22, 23, 24) as well as the mention of the "little robe" (מְעִיל קָטֹן) Hannah makes and gives to Samuel each year he is at Shiloh (2:19) are examples of the emphasis on his youth prior to the Shiloh theophany in 1 Sam 3. Even within 1 Sam 3 itself—the specific pericope I identify as Samuel's coming of age—subtle indicators of Samuel's youth are evident. For example, upon hearing Yhwh's judgment against Eli's house,

Samuel is afraid to report the pronouncement to Eli (3:15). Furthermore, he only reveals the message to Eli when the older priest exerts his authority, adjuring Samuel with an oath that forces him to disclose the prophecy (3:17). Samuel's reluctance to assert himself, together with his submission to the authority of his elder, reflects characteristics regularly associated with children in the HB.[34] Samuel's youth is further highlighted by his initial misidentification of Yhwh's voice, thinking it instead to be Eli's (vv. 5, 6, 8). According to Moberly, the mistake points to Samuel's youth because it reflects the early stages of a child's development, in which a parent or teacher stands *in loco Dei* until the child matures enough to distinguish God's "voice" from that of his or her elder.[35]

In sum, Samuel's youth is apparent throughout the "childhood narrative" in 1 Sam 1–3. He is referred to as a נַעַר until 3:8 and acts in a manner characteristic of children until 3:18 (where he is compelled to disclose Yhwh's revelation to Eli), suggesting that until this point in the narrative he is still reckoned as a boy.

Highlighting Samuel's Coming of Age through Narrative Structure and Repetition

Although 1 Sam 1–3 repeatedly portrays Samuel as a callow boy, several literary features point to the young boy's growth throughout his "childhood narrative." The first feature is the structure of the second half of the narrative—that is, that portion of the text following Hannah's prayer in 2:1–10 until the childhood narrative's conclusion in 4:1a.[36] This textual block contains distinct scenes separated by six parallel reports detailing Samuel's growth and service at Shiloh.[37] This structure can be represented as follows:

> **Report 1** (2:11b): "The boy (הַנַּעַר) ministered (מְשָׁרֵת) to Yhwh before Eli the priest"
> *Scene 1* (2:12–17): The sins of Eli's sons
> **Report 2** (2:18): "Samuel was ministering (מְשָׁרֵת) to Yhwh, a boy (נַעַר) clad in a linen ephod"
> *Scene 2* (2:19–21a): Hannah and Elkanah make regular visits to Samuel, and Eli blesses them
> **Report 3** (2:21b): "The boy Samuel (הַנַּעַר שְׁמוּאֵל) grew (גדל) with Yhwh"
> *Scene 3* (2:22–25): Eli confronts his sons
> **Report 4** (2:26): "The boy Samuel (הַנַּעַר שְׁמוּאֵל) kept growing (גדל) and was in favor with both Yhwh and men"
> *Scene 4* (2:27–36): A man of God pronounces judgment on Eli's house

Report 5 (3:1a): "And the boy Samuel (הַנַּעַר שְׁמוּאֵל) was ministering to (מְשָׁרֵת) Yhwh before Eli"

Scene 5 (3:2–18): Yhwh's theophany to Samuel at Shiloh

Report 6 (3:19): "And Samuel grew (גדל) and Yhwh was with him, and he did not let any of [Samuel's][38] words fall to the ground"

Scene 6 (3:20–4:1a): Summary of Samuel's recognition as a prophet and man

The shared traits of the six reports accentuate their structural importance in the narrative. Not only does a comparison reveal the careful literary artistry of the text's final form, but it also highlights the progression of the six reports that matches the development and maturation of Samuel.

First, and most important, each of the first five structuring reports describes Samuel as a boy/נַעַר: in the first he is only "the boy"; the second gives the name Samuel but adds the term נַעַר when providing more information about him; and the third through the fifth call him "the boy Samuel." However, in the sixth report following the Shiloh theophany, the term נַעַר is no longer used in conjunction with Samuel's name. Here he is no longer "the boy," or even "the boy Samuel," but is simply "Samuel." Moreover, this terminological transition is permanent in that Samuel is never referred to as a boy again after this point. This suggests that a significant change has taken place in Samuel in the scene that separates the fifth and the sixth report—the scene narrating Samuel's first prophetic revelation at Shiloh (1 Sam 3:2–18). This change renders the term נַעַר now inappropriate.

The importance of threefold repetition in these reports, a technique common in biblical literature to signify completion, is also significant.[39] Three times Samuel is said to have served Yhwh as a priest (מְשָׁרֵת), and three times he is described as growing (גדל). [40] The reports that reference Samuel's priestly ministry at Shiloh are reports 1, 2, and 5; those that emphasize his growth are reports 3, 4, and 6. If A represents reports of Samuel's ministry and B signifies his growth, an AABBAB structure emerges. Moreover, the third and final reports of Samuel's ministry and growth, in 3:1a and 3:19 respectively, bookend a pericope in which a threefold repetition is also present in the form of the three calls to Samuel before he is able to recognize Yhwh's voice (3:4, 6, 8).

The rhetorical strategy of threefold repetition in this section of the narrative signals the culmination of three separate acts. The third call of Yhwh in v. 8 finally alerts Eli to the presence of the deity beckoning Samuel. The third reports of both Samuel's ministry (3:1) and growth (3:19) that border this scene in Shiloh represent the final accomplishment of these respective processes.

Samuel's priestly service at Shiloh is mentioned in 3:1 and is completed when he is called to be a prophet in the ensuing narrative.[41] So too, the report of Samuel's growth in 3:19 marks the conclusion and culmination of his growth.[42] In other words, the rhetorical strategy of threefold repetition in these structuring reports functions to highlight both Samuel's inauguration as a prophet and—more importantly for our purposes—his transition to manhood.

Therefore, the most obvious structural feature of the second half of Samuel's childhood narrative (1 Sam 2:11–4:1a)—the presence of six similar narrative reports dividing the overall story into six scenes—serves to emphasize the theme of young Samuel's maturation. While each of the first five of these reports refers to Samuel as a boy, the sixth report no longer employs this terminology. Finally, in light of the significance of threefold repetition to the story, the fact that the third and culminating notice of Samuel's growth occurs in the final report indicates that by the story's end Samuel has completed his growth and is no longer properly referred to as a boy/נַעַר.

Samuel's Coming of Age in the Context of 1 Sam 1–3: A Comparison with Eli's Sons

A number of scholars have recognized the contrast between Samuel and Eli's wayward sons Hophni and Phinehas in 1 Sam 1–3.[43] For example, the narrative reports identified above serve this purpose by interjecting positive comments about Samuel between scenes detailing the iniquities and injustices perpetrated by Eli's sons. In so doing, these reports draw attention to the significant differences between Samuel and Eli's sons.

The contrast is more complex than a simple juxtaposition of the "good" Samuel versus the "evil" sons of Eli, however. Specific features of Hophni and Phinehas's characterization are brought into direct comparison with contrasting features of Samuel's portrayal. The sons of Eli, for instance, are criticized for not knowing (ידע) Yhwh in 1 Sam 2:12. In contrast, the narrative in 1 Sam 3 traces Samuel's progress beyond a similar lack of knowledge (ידע) of Yhwh (1 Sam 3:7) to the point when he becomes a prophet of Yhwh with special knowledge of the deity's ways and plans. Moreover, McCarter notes that the frequent mention of Samuel's priestly service (מְשָׁרֵת; 2:11, 18; 3:1) as well as his priestly vestments (i.e., the linen ephod mentioned in 2:18) are meant to identify Samuel as a righteous priest strikingly different from the corrupt and sinful priests Hophni and Phinehas (cf. 1 Sam 1:3).[44]

Scholars have failed to notice, however, the ways in which Samuel's growth and maturity factor into the critique of Eli's sons, and by extension the line of the Elides in general, through 1 Sam 1–3. Given that the six narrative reports emphasize both Samuel's priestly ministry *and* his growth, it stands to reason that the latter trait would comprise as significant a portion of the comparison between Samuel and Eli's sons as does the former. In particular, this comparison portrays Samuel as an example of successful manly maturation as opposed to Eli's sons, whose transition to manhood is questioned (see below). In this way the narrator further emphasizes the establishment of a new system of leadership under the prophet/priest/judge Samuel, and the atrophy and death of the old order under the Elides.

The incomplete and tenuous status of Hophni and Phinehas's maturation is seen in the tendency of the text to alternate qualities in depicting them, occasionally describing them in terms that imply manhood (e.g., they hold the office of priest [1:3] and are married [4:19–22]) but just as often attributing boyish qualities to them. Assuming with the majority of scholars that Hophni and Phinehas are the subject of condemnation in 2:17, this verse encapsulates the text's questioning of their adulthood.[45] Here the narrative summarizes the corrupt practices of the Shiloh priesthood as follows: "The sin of the young men (נְעָרִים) against the Lord was very great, for the men (אֲנָשִׁים) treated the Lord's offerings impiously" (NJPS). In two consecutive clauses in one verse Eli's sons are called both boys and men, a testament to the text's equivocal estimation of their status as men.[46]

The blurring of lines between boyhood and manhood is also evident in the description of Hophni and Phinehas's sins. They are criticized for two misdeeds in particular: (1) their violation of the standard sacrificial practices by which the priests' portion of the sacrificial meat would be selected (2:13–17);[47] and (2) their illicit sexual contact with female attendants assisting the sacrificial cult (2:22). The description of the former sin employs imagery that evokes childishness as depicted in the HB, particularly the impetuosity and potential for rash violence characteristic of boyhood. This is evident in 2:16, where the request by a sacrificing worshipper first to burn fat to Yhwh before the priests take their portion is met with a curt "No, you must give it now; if not I will take it by force."[48] The second sin involves the direction of sexual energies outside of their proper function: the siring of legitimate (especially male) offspring.[49] By demonstrating no self-control over their sexual appetites—a self-control that is a fundamental feature of biblical manhood—the sons of Eli are subject to critique for being less than men and more like boys unable to control their impetuous nature.

Samuel stands in sharp contrast to this depiction of Hophni and Phinehas, self-serving priests who act like boys rather than men. As previously demonstrated, once Samuel comes of age in 1 Sam 3 the text is unambiguous about referring to him as a man. Moreover, the emphasis on Samuel's growth, definitively achieved by 3:19, distinguishes him from the Elides whose maturation is questioned.

Therefore, alongside the evidence presented above for viewing 1 Sam 3 as a coming-of-age narrative, similarly convincing evidence can be identified by noting the complementary role of the coming-of-age theme in the narrator's extended critique of the Elides in 1 Sam 1–3. A full appreciation of the contrast between the ascendant Samuel and the declining Elides is only possible through a reading the childhood narrative in light of the coming-of-age theme.

Changes to Samuel Marking His Maturation

Thus far the case for viewing 1 Sam 3 as a coming-of-age story has been bolstered by three narrative features. First, Samuel is no longer referred to as a boy after 1 Sam 3. Second, the structural features of the narrative point to the importance of Samuel's growth. Third, the coming-of-age theme enhances the comparison between Samuel and Eli's sons. However, additional evidence must be mustered to show that 1 Sam 3 is a coming-of-age tale. Specifically, in a maturation story a noticeable change must take place in the boy in order to transform him into a man by the story's conclusion. For Samuel, two events contribute to his development in 1 Sam 3.

The most apparent difference between Samuel at the beginning of 1 Sam 3 and at the chapter's conclusion is that he has learned to recognize Yhwh's voice, or as it is called throughout the chapter, Yhwh's "word" (3:1, 7, 21). No longer does he mistake the call of the deity for that of his mentor Eli. In Moberly's view this signifies that Samuel has reached the point of spiritual maturation at which a youth is able to "perceive and respond to God as God and as distinct from the parent/teacher."[50] Discerning the word of Yhwh changes Samuel from one who did not "know the Lord" because that word had not yet been revealed to him (v. 7) to a "prophet of the Lord" (v. 20)—one to whom the word of Yhwh is revealed (v. 21).

Another change in Samuel in 1 Sam 3 is his transition from timidity to authority. Samuel's fear of disclosing Yhwh's word to the more authoritative Eli in 3:17 signals the character's boyishness, as I have noted. However, Samuel overcomes his fear when he proclaims the word of Yhwh, which serves as his inaugural act as a prophet. The text indicates Samuel's promotion to a position of authority by reporting in 3:19 that Yhwh let none of Samuel's words "fall to the ground." This statement highlights Samuel's religious authority as a prophet, since its likely meaning is that Samuel's predictions were never unfulfilled (so NJPS) and that he consequently passes the Deu-teronomic test for an authentic prophet of Yhwh (Deut 18:21–22).[51] The next verse (v. 20) continues to stress Samuel's religious authority, applying to him the title of a trustworthy (נֶאֱמָן) prophet of Yhwh. The story concludes with a note on the purview of Samuel's authority: his prophetic role is recognized from Dan to Beersheba (v. 20), and his "word" influences all of Israel (4:1a).

In narrating the progression of a male character from boyish fear to manly social power/authority, 1 Sam 3 functions as a typical coming-of-age story. Fear and lack of power (both physical and social) are characteristics of chil-dren in the HB as a whole, and Samuel's transition out of fear and powerless-ness in 1 Sam 3 effectively signals the end of his boyhood. However, the other major change to Samuel in this story—that is, his newfound ability to discern Yhwh's word—is distinctive from each of the other coming-of-age narratives considered in this book. No other boy character in biblical narrative changes in this way as a result of his maturation into manhood. Furthermore, the abil-ity to mediate Yhwh's speech to humanity is not characteristic of manhood in general in the HB, nor is the inability to do so regularly stressed as typical of biblical boyhood.[52]

The ability to discern Yhwh's voice as a feature of the maturation process is understandable because 1 Sam 3 functions not only as the story of Samuel's transition to manhood, but also as the story of his call to prophecy. In fact, 1 Sam 3 arguably can be identified as a prophetic call narrative, albeit one that also contains coming-of-age themes.[53] While the ability to discern and medi-ate the deity's voice is not an essential element of biblical manhood, it is *the* defining characteristic of a prophet. Thus, in 1 Sam 3 Samuel's change into one who is uniquely able to communicate with Yhwh has more to do with his taking on the role of a prophet than with his maturation as a man. In short, 1 Sam 3 serves a double-duty role, describing both a prophet's call and a boy's coming of age.

Therefore, 1 Sam 3 narrates the transition of the boy Samuel into the man Samuel, the prophet of Yhwh. The youthful imagery and terminology found throughout the "childhood narrative" (1 Sam 1–3) is no longer employed after this chapter. The six parallel reports following Hannah's song in the child-hood narrative (i.e., 1 Sam 2:11–4:1a) further highlight the importance of Sam-uel's growth in the story. In addition, the threefold repetition in the narrative reports signifies the culmination of Samuel's process of growth in the final report of v. 19. Finally, the dramatic change in Samuel from the timidity and powerlessness commonly associated with boyhood to a position of authority recognized by all Israel heralds Samuel's maturation and signifies that 1 Sam 3 is a coming-of-age story. The second change in Samuel in 1 Sam 3—Samuel's

movement from one who does not know Yhwh (3:7) to one who is able to discern Yhwh's voice—is unique to this story and does not rely upon the typical
depictions of boyhood and manhood in the HB. This change in Samuel is best
explained by the fact that 1 Sam 3 is also concerned with Samuel's inauguration as prophet.

Thematic Comparison of the Pre-Monarchic Coming-of-Age Narratives

Despite the notable similarities between Moses and Samuel—two figures
whose leadership roles over pre-monarchic Israel include prophetic, political,
and legal facets—a comparison of the two characters' coming-of-age stories
reveals many more differences than congruities. Regarding the latter, the
most obvious similarity between the two narratives is that they have a
common subject matter: the transition from boyhood to manhood of a future
prophet and leader. Beyond this broad thematic correspondence, the tactics
the respective narratives employ to draw attention to the maturation theme
are similar. Specifically, both Exod 2 and 1 Sam 1–3 use structural features
and the repetition of *Leitworte* to indicate that maturation is a central theme
of the narrative. In Exod 2, the narrative structure consists of two scenes that
feature different *Leitworte*: יֶלֶד is repeated seven times in the first scene, while
אִישׁ is repeated seven times in the second scene. Moreover, in the hinge between the two scenes in vv. 10–11, the verb גדל ("to grow") appears twice. The
change of *Leitwort* between the two scenes and the emphasis on growth at the
hinge point between the scenes highlights Moses's transition from boyhood
into manhood. Similarly, in 1 Sam 1–3, the narrative applies the term נַעַר repeatedly to describe Samuel in order to emphasize his initial youthfulness.[54]
However, the threefold repetition of the verb גדל in the narrative reports that
structure the narrative into shorter scenes—as well as the absence of the
term נַעַר in the sixth and final report—functions to indicate Samuel's transition out of his boyhood.

   The only other point of contact between the two narratives is that in both
the transition out of boyhood entails a shift from a childlike position of social
powerlessness to one of social power/authority. This theme is more pro-
nounced with Samuel, whose timidity is initially emphasized (1 Sam 3:15) and
then contrasted with his new authoritative status by the end of the narrative.
A series of clauses in 1 Sam 3:19–20 highlight this authority. He has grown
up (גדל; v. 19), hence he possesses the authority that comes with manhood.
Additionally, he is established as a trustworthy and bona fide (נֶאֱמָן; v. 20)
prophet whose religious authority extends throughout Israel.

While Samuel's authority as a man and prophet is explicitly proclaimed by the narrator in 1 Sam 3:19–20, for Moses the issue of authority is more implicit. When Moses's authority as a man, a political leader (שַׂר), and a judge (שֹׁפֵט) is challenged by the guilty Hebrew, the narrator never directly answers this critique. Nevertheless, the fact that this critique is voiced by a character whom the story's audience would view unsympathetically due to his "guilty" status (רָשָׁע) indicates that the narrator disapproves of this challenge. Moreover, Moses's display of distinctly manly qualities (e.g., strength, solidarity with adult Hebrew men, wisdom) in the second scene of Exod 2 undermines the critique of his manhood.[55]

The transition of a socially powerless boy to authoritative manhood along with narrative features that underscore the transformation process are shared by these two coming-of-age stories. Yet numerous differences appear in specific details of the two narratives. To begin with, Moses displays a number of qualities that are typically associated with biblical masculinity. These include the use of violent force against another man (Exod 2:11–12); a commitment to the in-group solidarity of adult Israelite/Hebrew males (2:11–12, 13–15a); the demonstration of wisdom (2:13–14); and finally marriage and procreation (2:21–22). In contrast, the primary change to Samuel in 1 Sam 3—aside from the emphasis on his increased authority—is that he is able to discern the word of Yhwh. This ability is nowhere articulated as a typical feature of biblical manhood, but instead primarily characterizes a legitimate prophet.

The manner in which maturation is accomplished is another notable difference between the two stories. In Exod 2:11–22, Moses is a proactive character who demonstrates and validates his manhood through his own bold actions, often in the face of antagonism by other men. Samuel, however, is a more passive figure who receives his status as man and prophet from Yhwh (a character conspicuously absent from Exod 2). Even in his most proactive moment, where he delivers his first prophetic oracle (1 Sam 3:17), Samuel acts only when compelled to by Eli. Additionally, while Moses's confrontations with other men prove his masculinity, Samuel's transition to manhood is peacefully facilitated by his older male mentor Eli. In short, Moses's coming of age reads as an *agon*, while Samuel's is an idyll.[56]

Thus, Exod 2 and 1 Sam 1–3 tell the story of a prophet/leader's coming of age in markedly different ways. It is worth considering why this is the case. Of course, one answer would emphasize that 1 Sam 3 functions as both a coming-of-age tale and a prophetic call narrative, as shown above. For this reason, Samuel's new prophetic abilities are highlighted just as much as his acquisition and display of the characteristics of manhood. Moreover, since prophecy is a gift from Yhwh and hence requires no competition or conflict with others in order to receive it, the idyllic setting is more appropriate. For Moses, the story of his prophetic vocation receives its own separate treatment in the call narrative in Exod 3–4; therefore Exod 2 can focus more on the features of his maturation as a man. The agonistic qualities of the story reflect the posturing and competition characteristic of hegemonic masculinity, where manhood is often displayed through struggle with other men.

Another answer to the question of why such differences exist between the maturation stories of these two similar characters begins with the suggestion that the depiction of Samuel in the HB is meant as an intentional echo of Moses. As already shown, both characters combine political, legal, and prophetic authority in a way unique in the HB. Moreover, the same terminology that is used to describe Moses's special position as the confidant of Yhwh is also used of Samuel. Moses—according to Num 12:7—is entrusted (נֶאֱמָן) with all of Yhwh's house and therefore can receive Yhwh's word in face-to-face conversation (Num 12:8); likewise, Samuel is confirmed (נֶאֱמָן; 1 Sam 3:20) as a prophet and has the same sort of immediate contact with the deity as did Moses, such as in their discussion over the Israelites demand for a king in 1 Sam 8.[57] These similarities suggest that one character's portrait has influenced the other's, and if the majority of scholars are correct about the editing and composition of the Deuteronomistic History, then that influence runs from Moses to Samuel, since Exod 2 is recognized by most scholars as an earlier text than 1 Sam 3.[58] Furthermore, Samuel's role as a Moses redivivus is emphasized by the fact that in replacing the corrupt Elides he inherits the mantle of leadership from the Mosaic line, since the Elides traced their lineage to Moses.[59]

It is possible then that the story of Samuel's maturation in 1 Sam 3 may have been intended as an alternative to that of Moses in Exod 2, composed likely by a neo-Babylonian DtrH and added as a part of a sixth-century edition of the Deuteronomistic History, if Römer's recent dating of 1 Sam 3 is to be believed.[60] Moreover, since the way a culture tells the story of a boy becoming a man is directly related to its views on manhood, the differences between the coming-of-age stories of Samuel and Moses likely also point to contrasting views of normative masculinity in the respective stories. The manhood advocated for in the later Samuel maturation story is one less rooted in competitive shows of strength and bellicose force than in the earlier Moses tale. The authority that comes with adulthood is not something that must be acquired through constant struggle with other men, according to this view, but is something passively received from Yhwh.[61]

As will be seen in the next chapter, a similar development can be tracked in the stories of royal coming of age. There I discuss the story of David's maturation in 1 Sam 17, and the two tales of Solomon's transition to manhood in 1 Kgs 1–2 and 1 Kgs 3. The latter tale, in ways similar to 1 Sam 3, sketches a less bellicose depiction of masculine development, and therefore of what it means to be a man, than in the former two stories. The implications for the discussion of biblical masculinity, as well as the possible motivations and historical *Sitz im Leben* for this less violent alternative vision of manhood, are elaborated further in the concluding chapter of this book.

4

David and Solomon: Case Studies of Royal Maturation

IN THE PRECEDING chapter, I examined the coming-of-age narratives of the pre-monarchic figures Moses and Samuel. This chapter focuses on both the story of David and Goliath (1 Sam 17) and that of the early years of Solomon's reign (1 Kgs 1–3). These narratives, like those in the preceding chapter, detail their protagonist's maturation from boyhood to manhood. They are considered together due to their canonical order (following the stories of Moses and Samuel), the fact that their respective protagonists eventually become kings of Israel, and David's significance to both stories.

My primary purpose is to identify and highlight the importance of the coming-of-age theme in 1 Sam 17 and 1 Kgs 1–3 and to show how this theme interacts with others in these texts. The final portion of the chapter compares the narratives of royal maturation and addresses the varying constructions of masculinity they display—a worthwhile endeavor given that male coming-of-age stories can provide a unique glimpse into this subject, as I argued in the Introduction.[1] The chapter ends with a brief discussion of how the evolution in the coming-of-age theme observed in these case studies points to a thematic shift in Israel's historical narrative and a change in the biblical construction of masculinity over time.

"Give Me a Man, That We May Fight Together": David's Coming of Age in 1 Samuel 17

The first example of royal coming of age is the famous story of David and Goliath in 1 Sam 17.[2] In this narrative David's characterization undergoes a crucial transformation. The narrator employs youthful imagery to portray David prior to this point in 1 Samuel, but this imagery is entirely absent after David's victory over Goliath. In fact, David is never referred to as a boy again in the HB after 1 Sam 17.[3] Drawing on that sharp literary demarcation, the section below will investigate how the narrator draws attention to the coming-of-age theme in 1 Sam 17 and will analyze how this particular story understands manhood, including what it takes to become a man.

Before arguing that 1 Sam 17 represents David's coming-of-age story, it is critical to consider and ultimately to dismiss a fundamental critique of my proposed reading. Simply stated, this critique claims that in 1 Sam 17 David is not a young and untested shepherd boy who is naïve to the brutal realities of war but instead is already depicted as a man.[4] If David is viewed as a man by the time of his duel with Goliath, then no coming-of-age theme is possible in 1 Sam 17.

Proponents of the view that David is characterized as a man in 1 Sam 17 typically argue that the preceding chapter also depicts him as a man. Specifically, 1 Sam 16:18 identifies him as both a גִּבּוֹר חַיִל (traditionally translated as "a mighty man of valor"; see, e.g., KJV, NAS) and an אִישׁ מִלְחָמָה (literally, "a man of war"). These titles are applied to David *prior to his duel with Goliath*, which suggests that David was far from being a callow boy when he fought the Philistine champion. Furthermore, in this view the references to David as a נַעַר throughout 1 Sam 17 (vv. 33, 42, 55, 58; cf. 16:11, 18) are best understood in light of the occasional military use of this multivalent term; David is therefore described here as a "squire," not as a "boy."[5] Even David's use of a slingshot when battling Goliath is not a choice indicative of his youthful lack of facility with more "manly weapons"; on the contrary, it is the sound tactical choice of a thoughtful and adept warrior.[6]

A closer examination of the text of 1 Sam 17, however, reveals significant deficiencies in the preceding argument and reinforces the traditional understanding of David as a boy—albeit a precocious one—when he battles Goliath. The first and most obvious indication of David's youth is that while "all the men of Israel" are bivouacked with Saul in the Elah valley at the beginning of the tale (1 Sam 17:19; cf.17:2), David is *not* among them but is instead with his father Jesse in Bethlehem. David is therefore not reckoned as a "man of Israel" at this point. Furthermore, according to vv. 13–14, only the three eldest of Jesse's eight sons are with the men of Israel in Saul's army. It would seem then that David is significantly younger than the age at which one could serve in the army among the "men of Israel," since even four of his *older* brothers are still too young to join Saul's force.[7]

Second, the scene in which David presents himself before Saul to persuade the king that he should be permitted to fight Goliath (vv. 32–40) contains several indicators of David's youth. To begin with, if David is a mighty man and fearsome warrior in 1 Sam 17, it is unlikely that he would need to argue for his suitability to duel with the Philistine, yet this is precisely what

David does here—making his case over Saul's strong objections (v. 33). Similarly, a warrior would not reference his experience fighting animals as his best qualification for the job of fighting Goliath (vv. 34–39), nor would he be unaccustomed to a soldier's armor (vv. 38–39). Finally, if a slingshot were such a tactically superior weapon against a heavily armored foe—as opposed to the meek weapon of a shepherd boy that just happened to be the best choice for the situation—it is curious that the veteran warrior Saul does not recognize this, and instead insists that David arm himself with a sword and heavy armor.

Third, the cold reception David receives from his eldest brother Eliab upon his arrival at the camp again supports the observation that David is characterized as youthful in the narrative of 1 Sam 17. Eliab's anger towards David hinges on his conviction that David does not belong with the army, but with the "few sheep in the wilderness" (v. 28) he has left behind. The message is clear that Eliab believes that the menial task of tending the sheep is more appropriate for the boy David than the "man's work" of fighting in war.

Finally, David's beauty and his ruddy complexion, referred to in v. 42, rely on the common association of youth with beauty.[8] In fact, the terms used to designate David's attractive appearance are rather rare and are used exclusively in the HB in reference to children. For example, David's ruddiness is described with the adjective אַדְמוֹנִי, a term that is only applied to one other character: Esau, in Gen 25:25. Significantly, the adjective is applied to Esau *as a newborn*. In addition, David is said to be "beautiful to behold"[9] (יְפֵה מַרְאֶה), an expression associated with only one other character: Joseph, in Gen 39:6, when he is still young and is referred to as a "boy" (נַעַר; Gen 37:2). Given the common practice of viewing the youthful body, and particularly the youthful complexion, as an aesthetic ideal throughout the HB, David's beauty and notably attractive skin mark him as a youth in biblical literature.

In sum, contrary to scholars who view David as an adult warrior in 1 Sam 17, the evidence shows that David is portrayed as a youth throughout the tale. Therefore, when the term נַעַר is employed in the David and Goliath narrative, it should be understood primarily as a life-cycle term denoting "boy."

Of course, this still leaves the problem of how David could be described as a "mighty man of valor" and a "man of war" in the previous chapter (16:18) when he is clearly a boy in 1 Sam 17. I discuss this issue in greater depth below in the section on the textual criticism of the David and Goliath story. At present, it is worth mentioning that the contradictions discussed above (that arise when reading 1 Sam 17 in light of David's description as a man in 16:14–23) suggest that 1 Sam 16:14–23 may represent a source or tradition unknown to the David and Goliath narrative.

Having identified the flaws with this potential critique of my interpretation of 1 Sam 17, the discussion can now turn to the evidence for reading this pericope as David's coming-of-age story. To argue for the centrality of the coming-of-age theme in the David and Goliath story requires more than simply showing that David is depicted as a boy in much of the narrative. Specifically, David must also make some clearly identifiable transition from boyhood to manhood in the story. The discussion below shows that such a transition takes place in 1 Sam 17. At times the tactics the narrator employs to illustrate this transition are recognizable through a straightforward close reading that is attentive to the maturation theme. At other times the coming-of-age theme is evident only when viewed against the broader narrative structure of the story—particularly how it imitates the tripartite structure of a rite of passage.

Explicit Narrative Evidence for David's Transition into Manhood in 1 Samuel 17

The narrator of the David and Goliath story explicitly draws attention to the coming-of-age theme in four ways. First, the theme's importance is demonstrated by the narrator's frequent use of life-cycle terminology in the story, as well as the presence of a significant terminological shift in describing David at the story's end. Next, David's transition to manhood is marked by his performance of two uniquely manly tasks: displaying strength on the battlefield and defending his and his nation's honor. Lastly, a significant marker of masculine maturation—that is, the act of marriage—is an important theme in the story.

Terminology in 1 Sam 17

The first category of evidence pointing to the coming-of-age theme in 1 Sam 17 is terminology. I have already argued that the prevalence of youthful imagery used to describe David in 1 Sam 17 strongly suggests that when the term נַעַר is applied to him, it connotes his boyhood and not his role as a squire or servant. More significantly, while David is frequently referred to as a נַעַר/boy in texts up to and including 1 Sam 17 (the term is used in reference to David by the narrator [17:42], by Samuel [16:11], by Saul's servant [16:18], and by Saul himself [17:33, 55, 58]), David is never again called a נַעַר in the text after 1 Sam 17. This indicates that David experiences a significant change in 1 Sam 17, which makes נַעַר no longer appropriate as an identifying term for him.

Similarly, attention to the text's use of the Hebrew words for boy (נַעַר) and man (אִישׁ) highlights the coming-of-age theme in the story. The text repeatedly acknowledges that only a "man" (אִישׁ) will be able to challenge Goliath: the giant demands that a "man" from the Israelites be sent out to fight him (vv. 8, 10); Israelite soldiers inform David about the reward for the "man" who kills Goliath (vv. 25, 27); Saul attempts to dissuade David from challenging Goliath because he is just a boy (נַעַר), implying that to kill Goliath—the "*man* of war" (אִישׁ מִלְחָמָה)—requires a man (v. 33); and David himself acknowledges that a "man" will kill the Philistine champion (v. 26).[10] The repetition and interplay between the words אִישׁ and נַעַר indicates that the relationship between boyhood and manhood is crucial to the story.[11] This dynamic compels the reader to ask along with the text: "What man will defeat the mighty Philistine champion? If the job requires a man—as every character in the narrative acknowledges—how could a boy be successful?" The answer, towards which the narrative leads the reader, is that a boy can be successful in this task only if in the process of performing it he becomes a man.

The next terminological indicator of David's transition to manhood is Saul's use of the rare term עֶלֶם to refer to David at the conclusion of the story (1 Sam 17:56). As the discussion of this noun in Chapter 2 showed, עֶלֶם is a term that, along with בָּחוּר, denotes a stage of male development that I labeled "older boyhood/young manhood." This stage is more advanced than young boyhood, which is more commonly denoted with terms like יֶלֶד or—in certain contexts—נַעַר.[12] Indeed, young men referred to with these two terms (עֶלֶם and בָּחוּר) seem to be men in almost every sense of the word, with the notable exception that they are unmarried. For Saul to switch at the end of the story from addressing David as a נַעַר (v. 33), a term more associated with inexperience, immaturity, and weakness, to a term with the connotations of virility and advanced physical development like עֶלֶם strongly suggests that in Saul's estimation, David has crossed a significant threshold by slaying the Philistine.[13]

However, if the terminological shift from נַעַר to עֶלֶם in 1 Sam 17:56 indicates Saul's recognition of David's maturation, the question remains why Saul would revert back to calling David a נַעַר in v. 58. At first glance this appears to equate the two terms and thus may undermine my argument that the term עֶלֶם signifies an advanced stage of development beyond boyhood. This problem is mitigated when considering that Saul uses the term עֶלֶם only when in private conversation with his adviser Abner. The king calls David a נַעַר, on the other hand, when David has returned to Saul in v. 58 and is directly addressed by the king. In each case, the context for Saul's speech dictates which term he uses. Within the protected space of a private communication with his ally Abner, Saul is able to let his guard down and speak what he truly believes (i.e., that David has made a significant transition out of boyhood by slaying the

Philistine). However, when David is before the king, holding in his hand the monstrous head of the giant (a silent indictment of the cowardice of Saul and his men), Saul is understandably intimidated. Thus he wishes to "put David in his place," pointedly referring to him in v. 58 as just a boy (נַעַר). Indeed, Saul's question itself in v. 58 ("whose son are you?") demeans David by only ascribing him worth in relation to older men. The awkward addition of the emphatic נַעַר at the end of Saul's question in v. 58 is a further unsubtle jab at the young man, in an attempt to downplay his accomplishment.

Battlefield displays of strength and feminization of the enemy in 1 Sam 17

In Chapter 1 I established that in the ancient Near East and in biblical literature the battlefield was the ideal stage for the "performance" of masculinity. It was there that the display of a man's bellicose strength vis-à-vis his enemy announced and established his manhood. Moreover, the exertion of power in battle over one's enemy frequently entailed the metaphorical (and at times literal) feminization of the defeated foe.[14] David's defeat of Goliath in battle, therefore, is a characteristically manly activity through which David shows his fellow Israelites that he has made the transition from boyhood to manhood. His development as a warrior—and therefore as a man—is further highlighted by the contrast between his inability to function in armor prior to the duel with the Philistine (vv. 38–39) and his appropriation after the battle of the defeated Goliath's armor as his own (v. 54).

David's defeat of Goliath also functions as a metaphorical emasculation of the Philistine. The contest of masculinity between enemies on the battlefield, as already mentioned, is a zero-sum game in the ancient Near East: the victor's reaffirmed manhood comes at the cost of the diminished manhood of the conquered foe.[15] Thus the description of Goliath's emasculation at David's hand functions to announce David's entry into manhood—and to burnish his masculine credentials—at the Philistine's expense.[16]

Goliath's emasculation is portrayed both as a feminization and as a metaphorical castration in 1 Sam 17. The brief retrospective summary of the duel in v. 50 reports David's victory over Goliath by declaring that he "overpowered the Philistine" (וַיֶּחֱזַק דָּוִד מִן־הַפְּלִשְׁתִּי).[17] Significantly, the verbal root חזק is also used with the preposition מִן indicating the verb's object in 2 Sam 13:14, where David's son Amnon rapes his half-sister Tamar (וַיֶּחֱזַק מִמֶּנָּה וַיְעַנֶּהָ וַיִּשְׁכַּב אֹתָהּ). The narrator's use of a verb–preposition combination such as this—given its association with the violent exertion of sexual dominance against a woman—may serve as rhetorical propaganda depicting Goliath as a feminized sexual victim of the newly minted man, David. Such erotically tinged rhetoric may also explain why David approaches Goliath with his "stick in his hand" and a pouch full of stones (v. 40). The apparently phallic description of David's weapons suggests an analogous relationship between them and his genitalia. Just as these weapons will literally overcome the giant, the masculine David's sexual dominance will metaphorically be asserted over the feminized Goliath.

In addition, Goliath's emasculation at David's hands takes the form of a metaphorical castration. In v. 49 David slings his stone towards what is typically interpreted to be the Philistine's forehead; however, it is not clear that this is the proper referent of מִצְחוֹ. Scholars often have speculated on alternative understandings of this term. For instance, Deem suggests that the greaves covering the Philistine's feet, which similarly are referred to with the term מִצְחָה (v. 6), are the target of David's missile.[18] Sasson, however, notes that מִצְחוֹ is in the singular, thus making it unlikely that the word would refer to two greaves. Instead, Sasson suggests that the "feet" covered by this מִצְחָה are in fact the giant's genitals, given the frequent use of רַגְלַיִם as a euphemism for this part of the body. The proper referent for מִצְחוֹ, in his view, is the giant's "codpiece" worn to protect his groin.[19] If Sasson is correct in identifying the target of David's slung stone as Goliath's testicles, then the act reflects the common "emasculation trope" in battlefield images and narrations. David successfully crushes the Philistine's masculinity as his stone sinks into his codpiece crushing his testicles.[20] Finally, David's dispatching of Goliath by using the Philistine's own oversized sword to decapitate him (v. 51) similarly relies upon the symbolic rhetoric of emasculation: Goliath's symbolic phallus (i.e., his sword) is removed by David and, adding harsh insult to injury, is used to kill him.

Defense of collective honor in 1 Sam 17

A repeated theme in 1 Sam 17 is the indignity that follows from not responding to Goliath's insults against Israel (vv. 25, 26), its ranks (מַעַרְכָה; vv. 10, 26, 36, 45), and, by extension, its god (v. 45). The root employed to express Goliath's challenge, חרף, clearly falls within the semantic field of honor and shame (note its use in parallel with בֹּשֶׁת ["shame"] in Isa 30:5 and in opposition to the root כבד ["to honor"] in Prov 14:31).[21] Goliath's insulting challenge therefore functions as a shaming of the men of Israel. For David in 1 Sam 17:26, the need to remove any reproach from such a shaming insult represents the primary casus belli that motivates his duel with the Philistine (see vv. 36, 45). When David defends the collective honor and reputation of Israel—or more specifically the nation's *men*—and its god, he clearly exhibits a central masculine trait to his fellow Israelites.[22] By doing so the boy of the early scenes of the story transforms into the young man of its conclusion.

Marriage in 1 Sam 17

The importance of marriage for manhood in biblical literature was examined in Chapter 1.[23] While it is true that he does not get married until 1 Sam 18:27, David initially secures his marriage into the Saulide royal family by killing Goliath in 1 Sam 17. The story stresses in 1 Sam 17:25 that one of the rewards that will go to the Israelite that kills Goliath is the hand of Saul's daughter. Thus, David's progression towards fully recognized manhood takes a significant step forward when he wins his betrothal to the king's daughter by slaying the Philistine giant.

It is possible, however, that Jonathan's covenant with David, reported immediately after David had finished speaking with Saul (18:1–4), could be viewed as a symbolic marriage. Certainly it is precisely at this point in the story that the reader would expect Saul's daughter to be introduced to David, since he has just completed the task required to win her hand and is in the presence of the person (Saul) who initially made the offer. Instead of the expected daughter, however, Jonathan is introduced to David at this point, suggesting that Jonathan may function as a metaphorical substitute for David's princess bride. Moreover, the language used to describe their meeting contains echoes of matrimony: Jonathan is said to love (אהב) David and their souls are bound together (קשר; 1 Sam 18:1). Jonathan also wraps David in his own cloak (18:4), an act associated with marriage elsewhere in the HB (Ruth 3:9; cf. Hos 2:2–3 [MT 2:4–5]).[24] The point of this language may be to advance the "erotic apologetic" that Ackerman has recognized as so vital to the David–Jonathan story, where the text hints at a sexual relationship between the two in order to belittle Jonathan (the feminized partner in the relationship) and by extension the Saulides.[25]

Whether one can argue for a symbolic marriage between Jonathan and David at the conclusion of the David and Goliath narrative is debatable. Despite this ambiguity, the marriage theme is a prominent one in the story and David's actions in securing his betrothal here represent a significant movement towards manhood.

David's Coming of Age as a Rite of Passage

The preceding evidence indicates that 1 Sam 17 should be read as a tale about David's maturation into manhood. The case for this reading is further strengthened in light of the fact that the structure of the story mimics the tripartite structure of a rite of passage (separation, liminality, and reincorporation).

As discussed in the Introduction, ever since Turner imported concepts from research into rites of passage to narrative criticism, scholars have applied the model of rites of passage in their analysis of certain biblical texts—even those with no recognizable connection to actual rituals in Israelite society. Indeed, portions of the David story have been the subject of such an analysis. Ackerman's *When Heroes Love*, for example, employs a rite-of-passage hermeneutic to large sections of the David narrative (1 Sam 16–2 Sam 5) and finds the concept of "liminality" useful for describing aspects of David's characterization, as well as the relationship between David and Jonathan.[26]

Unlike Ackerman, however, I will limit the scope of my rite-of-passage–informed exegesis to a smaller block of narrative, and one where liminality is not the only rite-of-passage stage that is emphasized, but is found alongside the other two stages in the tripartite schema (separation and reincorporation). Doing so prevents the potential for over-application of this schema, as discussed in the Introduction.

First Samuel 17–18:9 is a promising candidate for this rite-of-passage analysis not only because of its clear boundaries, comparative brevity, and the fact that all three stages of the schema can be recognized (as I will show below). Given that the concept of rites of passage was first applied to maturation and puberty rituals more than any other rite, a biblical text recounting a character's coming of age may be the most appropriate kind of text to which a rite-of-passage analysis can be applied.[27] Beyond that, the similarity of 1 Sam 17 to a traditional folktale—with its monstrous enemy, young hero, and princess bride—marks this story as appropriate for rite-of-passage exegesis.[28]

The relevance of this genre identification to my argument is simple: folk and fairy tales lend themselves well to an analysis informed by rites of passage. Eliade was among the first to argue that the folktale "takes up and continues 'initiation'" on a narrative plane.[29] Propp, who argues that all folktales contain a common morphological structure, identifies this structure as the same as that of an initiation rite.[30] More recently, Girardot has drawn the connection between the two by showing that "the narrative form of a fairy tale as a particular structural constellation of symbols basically reveals an initiatory pattern."[31] Therefore, since the David and Goliath story likely has a folkloric or fairy-tale background—and for the other reasons enumerated above—an exegesis informed by the rites-of-passage/initiation pattern should prove illuminating.

Turning back to the narrative in 1 Sam 17, a close reading reveals that the story's structure follows exactly the tripartite structure of a rite of passage (separation, liminality, and reincorporation). The separation phase of a rite of passage, as the name indicates, physically separates the individual undergoing the rite—that is, the "initiate"—from his or her community, placing him or her into a marginal social and geographical space. In 1 Sam 17, the separation that David experiences pushes him progressively outward from more to less familiar and intimate circles. Specifically in this case, he first leaves his father (v. 20), then his brothers (v. 28), and finally is separated from his countrymen as he enters the valley of Elah to fight Goliath (v. 40).

After David's initial separation, the narrative continues to follow the typical tripartite structure of a rite of passage by having David enter a liminal phase. As discussed in the Introduction, initiates in this liminal period are defined as being "betwixt and between" two different social positions,[32] and are typically located in marginal geographical space for the duration of this phase of the rite.[33] Furthermore, it is often during this liminal period that initiates endure the trying physical ordeals typically associated with maturation rites. Several features of the scene in which David and Goliath meet in battle (vv. 40–54) identify this moment as the liminal stage of David's narrative rite of passage. The battleground on which David and Goliath duel represents liminal space because it—like all battlefields—is located on land *between* two military encampments.[34] The valley of Elah, however, is recognizable as a liminal space for more than just this reason. Not only does the site of David's duel with Goliath fall between the Israelite and Philistine camps, but Elah itself was "an essential buffer zone lying between the heartland of Judah and the heartland of Philistia."[35] Furthermore, the duel is in a valley, a middle ground between the two hills on which the rival armies are encamped. Thus, the site of the duel can be identified as liminal ground on three levels: tactical (being the ground between the two armies); political (as a border between two states); and topographical (falling between two hills). A narrator would be hard-pressed to find a more quintessentially liminal space on which to set the middle phase of David's rite of passage.

Given the liminal imagery associated with the battleground on which David and Goliath fight, the meaning of the curious title applied to Goliath in 1 Sam 17:4 and 17:23 takes on special significance. In these verses the narrator refers to Goliath as an אִישׁ הַבֵּנַיִם, literally, "a man of the in-between-two."[36] This appellation appears nowhere else in the HB, and its precise meaning has long eluded scholars. Regardless of whether the term ultimately connotes a "champion" who fights between two rival army lines, a "skirmisher," or a chariot warrior—three suggestions scholars have proposed to define the term more specifically—the designation draws attention to the theme of liminality.[37] Goliath is a "man of the in-between," or perhaps better a "man of the liminal space."[38] In other words, he embodies this phase of David's rite of passage. Fighting and defeating the man of liminal space represents narratively the ordeals that so often must be overcome by initiates in coming-of-age rites.[39]

After stepping into the liminal space of the Elah valley and overcoming this liminal ordeal, symbolized by the "man of the liminal space" (i.e., Goliath), David completes his rite of passage signifying his masculine maturation via his reincorporation into his community. This reincorporation begins when David returns to the leaders of the "men of Israel," Saul and Abner (v. 57). David's full reincorporation into his society, now as a young man (עֶלֶם) instead of a boy, comes in 1 Sam 18:6–9, which functions as the natural conclusion to the David and Goliath narrative. Here David, returning from his battle with Goliath (v. 6), is greeted by the women of his people with songs lauding his martial prowess (v. 7). Such lavish public praise for the successful initiate is a very common feature of the reincorporation phase of a rite of passage; indeed initiates in male puberty rites are frequently greeted at the rite's conclusion by the women of their society, from whom they have been separated during the ritual.[40] Therefore, the celebration of David by the women of Israel at the conclusion of his coming-of-age story is fitting.

In sum, the narrative of David and Goliath in 1 Sam 17–18:9 exactly follows the tripartite structure of a rite of passage. The initiate David experiences in perfect sequence a period of separation from his people, a liminal stage on marginal ground where an ordeal must be endured successfully, and a reincorporation phase where the initiate is welcomed back into his community and celebrated.

While identifying the presence of a narrativized rite of passage is important, it is not an end in itself. More important for my exegesis is the recognition that the presence of a rite-of-passage structure in this narrative advances the case for viewing 1 Sam 17–18:9 as a coming-of-age tale. As clarified in the Introduction, the presence of a rite-of-passage schema in a narrative does not offer conclusive evidence for the coming-of-age theme; however, it is *suggestive* of it.[41] Therefore, considered alongside the other evidence for considering 1 Sam 17 a coming-of-age story, the presence of the tripartite rite-of-passage schema makes this case even more forcefully.

In sum, several factors demonstrate that 1 Sam 17 functions as a coming-of-age story. The story's terminology marks David's initial boyish characterization, and a shift in that terminology signals his transition out of boyhood. His display of bellicose strength and his defense of honor also announce his newly minted masculinity. The marriage he secures through his victory over Goliath (whether his actual marriage to Michal or his metaphorical marriage to Jonathan) represents an important act in his masculine maturation. Finally, all three phases of a rite of passage are present in the narrative, which strongly supports a coming-of-age reading.

It is also important to note that the contours of the coming-of-age theme articulated here point to the understanding of masculinity that informs and underlies this narrative. The kind of man that David becomes and the way he attains that manhood illustrates what the narrator views as characteristic of idealized manhood. To be sure, David is an exemplary figure upon whom the (likely elite, urban, and male) narrator projects his views on manhood, yet even though David may set an unattainable standard for male gender performance, his characterization in this story provides an invaluable window into the construction of biblical masculinity. Therefore, in this understanding of masculinity, a proper man can utilize violence effectively, especially on the battlefield—just as David does here. He also defends his personal honor and that of his nation by not allowing an insult to his people to go unpunished. Marriage too is an important part of his identity as a man. Finally, his manhood is an achievement that he has proactively attained, not something that is simply given to him.

Excursus: Text Criticism of 1 Samuel 17

Before turning to the next story of royal coming of age—that of Solomon in 1 Kgs 1–3—it is important to address the notoriously complicated text-critical issues associated with the MT of 1 Sam 17.[42] These issues include the apparent contradictions and repetitions of the MT: the two introductions of Goliath in v. 14 and v. 23; the report in v. 50 that "no sword" was in David's hand when he slew Goliath, which is immediately contradicted in the next verse where David decapitates the giant with a sword; and the fact that Saul does not appear to know David at the conclusion of the chapter (vv. 55–58), despite meeting him on at least two prior occasions (16:18–23; 17:32–39). While these issues are significant, the most vexing text critical problem is that large sections of 1 Sam 17 in the MT are absent from the Old Greek text of the Septuagint Vaticanus (henceforth LXXB), which corresponds only to the MT's 1 Sam 17:1–11, 32–40, 42–48a, 49, 51–54. Almost half of the MT text (1 Sam 17:12–31, 41, 48b, 50, 55–58), therefore, has no equivalence in the LXXB.[43]

Text critics have offered a number of detailed arguments to explain the development of the MT and LXXB texts of the David and Goliath tale, with new studies of the issue regularly appearing.[44] In spite of the large number of possible solutions to the text-critical problems of 1 Sam 17, most solutions fall into one of four broad categories.[45] I will briefly outline these four categories below in order to demonstrate that regardless of which strategy a scholar uses to analyze the textual-critical issues in 1 Sam 17, the coming-of-age theme in the story of David and Goliath remains evident.

The first explanation in the text-critical debate holds that the MT is a compositional unity. According to this position, the contradictions and repetitions within the MT are the result of the tale's oral/folkloric background, such repetition and apparent inconsistency being common in orally composed and transmitted tales.[46] Alternatively, some scholars in this group argue that the contradictions within the tale can in fact be reconciled through an attentive close reading of the text.[47] Scholars that support the compositional unity of the MT believe that the LXXB represents a later abridgment of the originally longer text by a translator who did not recognize the story's overall unity and therefore sought to remove what he thought were inconsistencies.

The second position also considers the LXXB to be an abridgment of the MT that attempted to eliminate what were perceived to be its contradictions. This harmonizing edit could have been the work of the Greek translator of the LXXB or that of the Hebrew editor who created the *Vorlage* for the LXXB. However, this position differs from the first in arguing that the MT was not a compositional unity to begin with but was a combination of at least two disparate sources that lacked significant inconsistencies before their combination. The LXXB translator, attempting to reconcile the MT's inconsistencies, produced a translation that roughly corresponds to one of the original internally consistent sources of the MT text.[48]

The third explanation represents the majority position. It holds that the LXXB was not a harmonizing emendation but faithfully translated the story that existed at the time. A second version of the story (corresponding to the MT's vv. 12–31, 41, 48b, 50, 55–58—the so-called "non-LXXB"), whose provenance was from a source unknown to the LXXB translator, was later added to the first story to form the current MT version.[49]

Finally, a few scholars claim that the MT text was created as a result of the addition of a theological layer onto an older popular folktale about David's defeat of the Philistine giant. This theological revision is responsible for portions of the text such as David's "mini-homily" in vv. 45–47, where he declares his faith in Yhwh and affirms that Yhwh will grant him victory. This theologically revised version of the story corresponds to the current MT and was the basis of the LXXB translation. However, the translator abridged it in order to iron out perceived inconsistencies that apparently did not trouble the earlier "theological editor" of the Hebrew text.[50]

Although these four explanations differ significantly, each is amenable to my claim of the centrality of the coming-of-age theme to 1 Sam 17. On the one hand, the first position—which sees the MT as a compositional unity—does not challenge my interpretation of 1 Sam 17, since my exegesis is also based on a reading of the MT as a unity. Similarly, the fourth position presents no obstacle to my claim that the original story was concerned primarily with David's coming of age, since almost none of my conclusions are derived from the theologically infused verses (e.g., vv. 45–47).[51] Instead, my argument is constructed primarily from portions of the narrative without a heavy theological bent, which scholars of this view would likely attribute to the original folktale behind the text. In short, the coming-of-age theme's presence is not seriously undermined by either the first or fourth explanation.

The situation is more complex with the second and third explanations. Because my case for the coming-of-age theme is based on the MT, positions like these that split the MT into two separate sources—the LXXB and non-LXXB—appear to weaken my thesis. This, however, is not the case. Even when the text is separated into two purported sources (i.e., LXXB and non-LXXB) *both* tales still contain coming-of-age themes, albeit with slight differences in emphasis. Both sources, for instance, depict David in 1 Sam 17 as a youth. In LXXB Saul warns David that because he is a נַעַר he is unfit to fight Goliath (v. 33). Here too David is unaccustomed to a warrior's armor and weapons (vv. 38–40). Similarly, Goliath is said to disdain David because he is a boy (נַעַר) who was ruddy and handsome (v. 42)—descriptors that I have shown to be characteristic of youth. In non-LXXB David is also described as a youth. Here the reader is told that only the three eldest of David's seven brothers are in the army (v. 13), which makes David appear quite young. This source also contains Eliab's belittling rebuke of David (v. 28)—a derogative that suggests David's youth.

Both the LXXB and non-LXXB sources follow the same plot line of a young hero performing the quintessentially masculine act of defeating an enemy on the battlefield.[52] They also stress the importance of David's defeat of Goliath as a defense of the honor of Israel (LXXB: vv. 10, 36, 45; non-LXXB: vv. 25, 26), reflecting another important feature of biblical masculinity. Given that David's public demonstration of his masculinity through victory in battle and the defense of Israel's honor—two signs of his transition to manhood—are found in LXXB and non-LXXB, the coming-of-age theme is evident in both sources.

Finally, both stories incorporate the tripartite structure of a rite of passage. In LXXB David separates from the men of his people (v. 40) to enter the liminal space in the valley to face the "man of the space between" (v. 4), and is reincorporated into his community with celebration and songs (1 Sam 18:6b). In non-LXXB David separates from his father (v. 20), brothers (v. 30), and countrymen (v. 48b); meets the "man of the space between" (v. 23) and defeats him in the liminal stage; and is reincorporated into the community of his fellow men, represented by Saul and Abner (vv. 57–59).

Nevertheless, two features of the coming-of-age theme are unique to the non-LXXB. The first is the theme of marriage (i.e., the betrothal to Saul's daughter [v. 25] and the possibly metaphorical marriage to Jonathan in 18:1–4). Second, only in the non-LXXB does Saul recognize David's maturation—referring to him at the end of the story as an עֶלֶם. These two variations strengthen the connection of this story to the coming-of-age theme, suggesting that this theme is more clearly articulated in the non-LXXB.[53]

Thus, even when 1 Sam 17–18:9 is viewed as a combination of two sources, the importance of the coming-of-age theme is still apparent, being found in both sources. There remains, however, one more significant challenge which comes to light when considering the relationship between 1 Sam 17–18:9 and the text that immediately precedes it: 1 Sam 16:14–23. This textual block, which is included in the LXXB, reports how Saul's servants introduced David to the king as one who could soothe his troubled spirit with music. In his description of David in v. 18, Saul's servant calls David both a "mighty man of valor" and a "man of war." Such terminology would obviously not be used in reference to a boy. Some scholars argue, therefore, that the depiction of David in 1 Sam 17 cannot be a youthful one, given that he has already been introduced as a man in 1 Sam 16:14–23.[54] A variant of this argument claims that since 16:14–23 is found in the LXXB, this source depicts David as a man throughout 1 Sam 17 as well, but the non-LXXB differs on this by viewing David as a youth in his duel with Goliath.[55]

I have already addressed much of this critique above. Still, it is important to emphasize again that *even in the LXXB text of 1 Sam 17*, despite evidence to the contrary (i.e., 1 Sam 16:14–23), David is clearly depicted as a youth. It is this source that reports that David had to convince Saul to be allowed to face Goliath over Saul's objection that as a נַעַר David is unfit to do so (vv. 33–37).[56] Furthermore, in the LXXB David makes his case for his suitability for the duel by describing his success when fighting animals and is unaccustomed to the typical armor and weapons of a warrior (vv. 34–39). Finally, David's beauty and complexion are emphasized in this source (v. 42), both of which are markers of youthfulness. David's depiction in the LXXB of 1 Sam 17, therefore, differs significantly from that of the mighty man of war described in 1 Sam 16:14–23.

At least two solutions can explain this discrepancy between 1 Sam 16:14–23 and what follows in 1 Sam 17. Given the tangle of sources and numerous internal inconsistencies throughout 1 Sam 16–18, it is possible that the report identifying David as a man to Saul in 16:14–23 comes from a source separate from the text of 1 Sam 17 (or its sources, if the MT is not a compositional unity). The argument for separate sources is supported by the fact that no irrefutable evidence proves 1 Sam 17 (and even the LXXB of 1 Sam 17) knows of or is dependent upon 16:14–23. Furthermore, the thematic plot points appearing in 16:14–23—such as the "evil spirit" tormenting Saul and David's attempts to soothe the king with music—do not reappear until after the David and Goliath tale concludes.[57] In sum, the narrative in 1 Sam 17 in no way logically follows from 1 Sam 16:14–23, therefore suggesting that the two tales ultimately derive from separate sources.

Another solution emerges when considering the conclusion of 1 Sam 17 in the LXXB source—the same source to which 1 Sam 16:14–23 belongs. The concluding verse of the LXXB account of the duel scene between David and Goliath (v. 54) claims that after defeating the giant, David took his head to Jerusalem, an obvious anachronism given that Jerusalem would not fall to David's forces until 2 Sam 5. Campbell's explanation for why such a glaring mistake found its way into the text is illuminating. He believes that the mention of Jerusalem here serves as a conscious foreshadowing of what is to come, writing that

> Perhaps rather than see David carrying the head [of Goliath] to Jerusalem, we should hear in this statement an awareness that it was victory over the Philistine that carried David to Jerusalem—and to kingship there.[58]

Since the LXXB source contains one such foreshadowing anachronism in this report of David carrying Goliath's head to Jerusalem, it is plausible that it contains yet another in 16:18. The servant's identification of David here as a "mighty man of valor" and a "man of war" is certainly anachronistic when considering it in light of David's obvious youth in the following chapter; however, it may serve to herald David's military accomplishments that are the subject of later treatment in 1–2 Samuel.

In summary, despite the complicated text-critical issues in 1 Sam 17, my contention that the coming-of-age theme is central to the narrative remains intact. Neither of the four most common scholarly explanations of the text's development contradict or diminish this thesis.

"Be Strong, and Become a Man": Solomon's Coming of Age in 1 Kings 1–3

The next case study of royal coming of age to consider is that of David's son and heir, Solomon. Upon initial consideration, Solomon may seem a curious

choice for such a study. A coming-of-age reading of a given biblical text requires that the character under consideration begin the story as a youth, yet
Solomon is most frequently associated with a quality characteristic of adult
manhood in the HB: wisdom.[59] One would therefore not expect a character
defined by this quality ever to appear boyish and immature.[60]

However, a closer look at the earliest interpretations and retellings of the
Solomon story in 1 Kgs 1–11 reveals that alongside the common characterization of Solomon as wise, early readers of this story also frequently highlighted
Solomon's youth at the time of his accession to the throne. For instance, on
two occasions in 1–2 Chronicles—the earliest extant retelling of the Solomon
story—David stresses Solomon's youth by referring to him as נַעַר וָרָךְ ("young
and inexperienced"; 1 Chr 22:5; 29:1).[61] The first-century Jewish historian Josephus is even more specific in describing Solomon's youth. In *Ant.* 8.211 he
reckons Solomon's age to be only fourteen when he takes over the kingship
after the death of David, which causes his subjects initially to mock him as a
mere boy (μειράκιον; 8.32) until they witness his precocious wisdom firsthand.
Similarly, other ancient rabbinic sources put Solomon's age at twelve or thirteen when he began to rule as king.[62]

These indications of a "youth theme" in the Solomon narrative of 1 Kgs
1–11 do not simply appear de novo in these early retellings and interpretations;
they appear in the source text itself, which contains several references to Solomon's boyishness. I will begin my analysis below by identifying these indications of Solomon's youth in 1 Kgs 1–3. This in turn supports the broader
claim that the early episodes of the Solomon narrative highlight the king's
youth in order to draw attention to the coming-of-age theme in 1 Kgs 1–3. Ultimately, I will argue that David's dying wish for Solomon to "be strong, and
become a man" [63] in 1 Kgs 2:2 articulates a crucial theme in the surrounding
narrative. In this text, the reader is provided with an informative glimpse into
what the text and the culture that produced it understood as necessary in ac-
complishing the transition from an "inexperienced" נַעַר (to use the Chroni-
cler's term) to a man.

However, the answer to the question of what makes a boy a man in these
chapters is by no means settled. Indeed, two different views of how one becomes a man, and, by extension, what characteristics most define a man,
seem to be at odds in this text. These two contrasting views of manhood and
how one becomes a man in 1 Kgs 1–3 do not intertwine in these chapters, re-
quiring minute and tedious analyses to tease out which view is predominant
in which verse. Instead, the two views of coming of age are each associated
with one of the two large textual units within these three chapters. One is
found in 1 Kgs 1–2, which details the political machinations and violent

purges that put Solomon on the throne. The other is set forth in 1 Kgs 3:1–15, the scene of Yhwh's dream revelation to Solomon at Gibeon.

Significantly, the separation of 1 Kgs 1–3 into two units reflects a long-standing scholarly practice that understands 1 Kgs 1–2 and 3:1–15 as originating from different sources. This source-critical division was first made by Rost, who proposed in the 1920s that 1 Kgs 1–2 provided the conclusion of the so-called Succession Narrative, a composition that runs through 2 Samuel (beginning in 2 Sam 9) and that is concerned thematically with the question of who will succeed David.[64] While scholars in recent decades have challenged elements of Rost's theory, the belief that the dream narrative of 1 Kgs 3 originally existed as a story deriving from a different traditional or historical source than that behind 1 Kgs 1–2 still dominates.[65]

Even though there is a consensus regarding the bifurcation of 1 Kgs 1–3 based on source criticism, no one as yet has investigated this narrative in light of the divergent views of masculinity and coming of age found in the two blocks of text. Such an investigation is offered below. I will consider each textual unit separately, showing first how youthful imagery defines Solomon's characterization in the beginning of the respective narratives, but that at their conclusion Solomon is described as a man. The different ways Solomon transitions to manhood in these parallel stories are then compared to each other and to David's coming-of-age narrative in 1 Sam 17. This comparison reveals how the coming-of-age theme highlights thematic shifts in Israel's historical narrative and can also be used to track the diachronic development of biblical masculinity.

Solomon's Coming of Age in 1 Kings 1–2

Solomon's youth

As in each of the previous case studies of the maturation theme, establishing the immaturity of a character is essential to a coming-of-age narrative, otherwise the readers have no foil against which to gauge how the character matures as the story unfolds. Therefore, identifying the coming-of-age motif in 1 Kgs 1–2 begins with the ways that the narrative *initially* emphasizes Solomon's youth. His youthfulness is first indicated by his passivity throughout 1 Kgs 1. Significantly, even though the chapter is largely devoted to the story of how Solomon, rather than his older and better-credentialed brother Adonijah, becomes David's successor, Solomon hardly speaks or acts independently in 1 Kgs 1.[66] His passivity stands in strong contrast to the whirl of activity in which practically everyone else in the chapter seems caught. For instance, Bathsheba and Nathan's court intrigues to ensure Solomon's succession are described in great detail, as is Adonijah's feast with his supporters and his subsequent retreat seeking sanctuary once informed of his younger brother's coronation. Meanwhile, from the narrator's perspective, Solomon remains passive and takes no active part in any of this action. Indeed, as a character he is consistently the one *acted upon*, not the actor. Throughout 1 Kgs 1:10–37, where his fate as future king is decided, he is completely absent from the action, and is only spoken about in the third person by others. Moreover, when he finally does appear in the story (1 Kgs 1:38–40, 51–,53), it is primarily as the object of verbs. He is made to ride David's mule (וַיַּרְכִּבוּ אֶת־שְׁלֹמֹה) and is led by others to Gihon (וַיֵּלְכוּ אֹתוֹ) in v. 38; he is anointed by Tsadok (וַיִּמְשַׁח אֶת־שְׁלֹמֹה) and acclaimed by "all the people" (כָּל־הָעָם) in v. 39; David is said to have "made him king" (הִמְלִיךְ אֶת־שְׁלֹמֹה) in v. 43; and he "is informed" (וַיֻּגַּד לִשְׁלֹמֹה) about the actions of his brother in v. 51.

In displaying such passivity in the face of events with tremendous impact on his life, Solomon exhibits a characteristic common to the description of children in the HB. As seen in Chapter 2, children are routinely portrayed as powerless to act on their own behalf, both in terms of their physical weakness and their lack of social power, or "influence."[67] Simply put, an ancient audience would recognize passivity and powerlessness as characteristic of the common portrayal of children. For Solomon to be consistently depicted as one acted upon in 1 Kgs 1, but not a potent actor, therefore suggests that he is a youth.

However, Solomon's inactivity in 1 Kgs 1–2 is not the only indicator of his youth. Another characteristic feature of children in the HB is their close association with women, particularly their mothers. For example, Isa 49:15 and Ps 131:2 rely on the intimate relationship between mother and child to symbolize peace, comfort, and compassion. Psychological data similarly demonstrate the ubiquity of this connection across cultures, as discussed in the Introduction.[68]

Solomon, in particular, strongly exhibits a close connection with his mother Bathsheba throughout 1 Kgs 1 and the first half of 1 Kgs 2. First, she is a major player in the machinations that bring him to power in 1 Kgs 1. Moreover, in 1 Kgs 2 everyone in the text (namely Adonijah, Bathsheba, and Solomon himself) assumes that Solomon would never refuse a request made by his mother—yet another indication of the strength of their bond. Similarly, Bathsheba occupies the position of honor in the royal court at her son the king's right hand.[69] Even more significant is the report in 1 Kgs 2:19 that when Bathsheba came before Solomon to make a request on behalf of Adonijah, Solomon bowed down to her. The verb employed to describe this act is the Hishtaphel verb חוה, which always describes an act of proper respect or worship due to one's superior, whether human or divine (see, for example, Bathsheba's own obeisance to King David in 1 Kgs 1:16).[70] Most importantly, this verb—which occurs 170 times in the HB—is never elsewhere used to describe a man bowing and doing obeisance before a woman.[71] Certainly a level of respect and intimacy is to be expected between a mother and son in any culture. Still, what is on display in 1 Kgs 1–2 is a unique example of extraordinary closeness between Bathsheba and Solomon. Since the close bond between children and mothers in the biblical text has been established above, these data describing Solomon's deferential and dependent relationship with Bathsheba contribute to the text's portrayal of the king, until this point in the narrative, as still very much a boy.

The evidence for Solomon's youth in 1 Kgs 1–2 is nowhere more obvious, however, than in the dying David's final words of counsel to his son that he "be strong, and become a man" (וְחָזַקְתָּ וְהָיִיתָ לְאִישׁ; 1 Kgs 2:2).[72] Some translations, like NRSV, render David's words here "be strong, be courageous"; however, this represents an indefensible alteration of the literal sense of the Hebrew. David literally tells Solomon to "be strong, and *become* a man."[73] Of special importance here is the use of the verb היה with the preposition לְ. According to Koehler and Baumgartner (using 1 Kgs 2:2 as their premier example), the force of the construction is not "to be," but instead "to become."[74] The implication is that David believes that Solomon at this point in the narrative is not yet a man, but that he must become one in order to rule the kingdom after his father's death.[75] When David's directive to his son to "become a man" is combined with Solomon's passivity in the early parts of the narrative and his close and dependent relationship with his mother, a detailed depiction of Solomon as a boy in the first half of 1 Kgs 1–2 emerges.

David's plan for Solomon's maturation

While Solomon is portrayed as a boy in the beginning of the narrative in 1 Kgs 1–2, this boyhood is left behind by the story's conclusion. The manner in which Solomon accomplishes his father's wish for him to become a man is described in the latter half of 1 Kgs 2. The path to manhood, however, is originally charted earlier in the chapter in David's last will and testament. His father's final decree functions to set out the precise steps that Solomon must take to mature into his manhood. The first step, according to David, is to "be strong" (וְחָזַקְתָּ; 1 Kgs 2:2)—the command that David places alongside his demand for Solomon to become a man. David's directive reflects the repeated connection between strength and manhood that is common to the HB. As demonstrated in Chapter 1 and earlier in this chapter, manly strength is often reckoned as the effective use of violent force against enemies, especially on the battlefield.[76] Here too, it seems, David's understanding of "being strong" entails the efficacious use of violence. This connection is palpable in David's final instructions, as he outlines the bloody revenge that Solomon is to take on those with whom David still has a score to settle—namely, Joab (David's former army commander) and Shimei ben Gera. David's message is clear: if you want to be a man, be strong; that is, be forceful and violent if necessary.

The next feature of masculinity that David's dying words to Solomon emphasize is wisdom. Twice, in vv. 6 and 9, David refers to Solomon's wisdom—the first time the term is associated with Solomon in the HB. As with the association of strength and masculinity, the relationship between wisdom and ideal biblical manhood is well established. However, the wisdom referred to here has what Fokkelman refers to as a "sinister undertone."[77] Just like the strength that Solomon must show is associated with his commission to take vengeance on those whom his father has marked for death, so too is his wisdom viewed in relation to this vengeance. After describing Joab's crimes to Solomon in v. 5, David tells Solomon in v. 6 to "act according to [his] wisdom" when dealing with the Joab. In case Solomon has not perceived David's meaning clearly, he adds the ominous addendum "but do not let his gray head go down to Sheol in peace." Similarly, in v. 9 David appeals to Solomon's wisdom while again calling on him to bring Shimei ben Gera's "gray head down with blood to Sheol."[78]

The "wisdom" (חָכְמָה) referenced here clearly seems more a political cunning or cleverness, and less the kind of judicial, engineering, or academic wisdom that is more often attributed to Solomon. Indeed, Müller compares this usage of wisdom with that of Jonadab in 2 Sam 13:3 or Pharaoh in Exod 1:10, both of whom use their "wisdom" to hatch Machiavellian or criminal schemes. Müller therefore defines this kind of חָכְמָה as "skill" or "tactical ability of . . . [an] ambiguous nature."[79] Alongside strength, therefore, David's understanding of what it takes for his heir to become a man includes "wisdom," or more accurately, "cleverness."

The other two requests that David makes of his son from his deathbed are: (1) Solomon is to keep Yhwh's commandments and statutes as written in the Torah of Moses (v. 3); and (2) he is to deal favorably with the sons of Barzillai the Gileadite in recompense for the loyalty their father showed David during Absalom's rebellion (v. 7). The first of these requests is related to the manly value of self-control through obedience to Yhwh's laws, as discussed in Chapter 1.[80] In Deuteronomy, this self-control ensures that a man will "have a name in Israel," thereby ensuring his memory and lineage (Deut 25:6, 7; 29:20 [MT 29:19]). The same motivation is attached to David's request in v. 4. David claims that if Solomon will obey Yhwh's precepts, then Yhwh would "establish the word that he spoke concerning [David]" (v. 4) and would guarantee that David's descendants would perpetually sit upon the throne of Israel. Therefore, the motivation for obeying Yhwh appears to be the solidifying of David's legacy through the perpetuation of his line, which of course also ensures Solomon's legacy.[81]

The second request in v. 7 (that Solomon reward Barzillai's sons for their father's loyalty to David) concerns issues of honor, another significant feature of biblical masculinity. David's reputation as an honorable and powerful man is at stake if Barzillai's loyalty goes unrewarded, hence his request that this oversight would be corrected.[82] Maintaining his father David's honor is essential to Solomon, given that the defense of family honor is as important as one's individual honor.[83] For Solomon to follow his father's command to "become a man," therefore, he must be honorable, which requires protecting his father's reputation.

In summation, then, David's final instructions to Solomon disclose how the narrative in 1 Kgs 1–2 depicts the key components of "becoming a man." First, strength as evidenced by the adept use of violent force is essential. Second, a clever mind that displays strategic political acumen is necessary. Third, displaying self-control by obeying the statutes of Yhwh plays a significant role in this articulation of the tenets of manhood, although it seems that its ultimate motive is to further ensure the lineage of both David and Solomon. Finally, David's advice to Solomon shows that the need to defend family honor is incumbent on one who would "become a man."

Solomon becomes a man

Thus far I have highlighted the ways that the text emphasizes Solomon's youth and identified the characteristics associated with manhood in 1 Kgs 1–2. My initial contention that 1 Kgs 1–2 should be read as coming-of-age narrative, however, is not established unless the boyish Solomon of 1 Kgs 1 and the opening verses of 1 Kgs 2 comes to embody those masculine characteristics outlined in David's farewell speech. The means by which Solomon fulfills his father's wish that he become a man is described in the remainder of 1 Kgs 2, following David's death in vv. 10–11. First, Solomon employs the violent strength his father recommended and has two of King David's foes, Joab and Shimei, executed.[84] In fact, Solomon goes even further when he disposes of a rival not on David's "hit list": his brother Adonijah, who Solomon feared was planning to usurp him. It is atypical that Solomon's acts of vengeance do not occur on the ideal stage for displaying bellicose manly strength (i.e., the battlefield) nor does Solomon himself bear the avenging sword in his own hand. However, the text is clear that Solomon's orders are behind each of these acts, which in its own way constitutes an effective use of force.[85]

Alongside his demonstration of the ability to exert violent strength, Solomon is shown demonstrating wisdom as that concept is understood in David's deathbed speech (i.e., tactical skill, cleverness, and political savvy). The young king discerns the potentially rebellious intentions of his older brother Adonijah that underpinned his seemingly innocuous request for marriage to David's former concubine Abishag. More impressively, he carries out the vengeance killings of Shimei and Joab by having them both condemn themselves with their own words or actions. Shimei brings his blood on his own head by breaking an oath he made to Solomon never to leave the veritable house arrest that the king imposed on him in Jerusalem (v. 37). Joab, too, speaks his own death sentence. In v. 30 he responds to the order by Solomon's henchman Benaiah that he is to leave the tent of Yhwh where he had sought sanctuary by saying "No, I will die here" (לֹא כִּי פֹה אָמוּת). Benaiah's reluctance to enter the holy place on a murderous mission sends him back to Solomon requesting new orders. Solomon's response is the height of morbid wit: "Do as he said, strike him down and bury him" (v. 31). In other words, "Joab said he would die there; he has condemned himself, so go make his words come true." Such cunning political maneuvers exemplify the kind of political "wisdom" David recommended to his son as essential to becoming a man.

The Torah obedience highlighted in David's deathbed instructions (1 Kgs 2:3–4) is not explicitly reflected in Solomon's actions in the remainder of his maturation tale in 1 Kgs 2. However, the motivation behind this Torah obedience, ensuring the Davidic lineage, is evident. For example, when commissioning Benaiah to execute Joab in v. 33, Solomon expresses his wish that this act will result in peace from Yhwh for *David, his* descendants, *his* house, and *his* throne. Solomon's final words in the narrative (v.46) similarly demonstrate the significance of issues of lineage—both David's and his own: "But King Solomon shall be blessed, and the throne of David shall be established before the Lord forever." Thus, while Solomon does not mention the Torah of Yhwh at all in the remainder of 1 Kgs 2, his repeated reference to his father's memory and legacy suggests that he is aware of the deeper motivation behind David's advice to keep Yhwh's commandments.

Finally, Solomon's defense of his father's honor—and by extension Solomon's own honor—provides the motive for his actions in the latter half of 1 Kgs 2. Solomon claims that the motivation for killing Joab is to remove (Hiphil of סור) the shameful stain of bloodguilt from both himself and his father's house (v. 31). Furthermore, before executing Shimei in v. 44, Solomon reminds him of his disloyal acts against his father David. As David's counsel and Solomon's actions show, an honorable man does not allow such disloyalty against himself or his family to go unpunished.

To be sure, Solomon personifies strength, wisdom/cleverness, and a concern with lineage and honor in the latter verses of 1 Kgs 2. These are the same traits that David's final words indicated were necessary if Solomon was to become a man, and they mark his transition from the boyish character at the beginning of the story to the powerful man and ruler at its end. However, along with these qualities there are three more hints in the text that highlight Solomon's maturation. The first is found in the related and corresponding verses (vv. 12, 46) that enclose most of the narrative in 1 Kgs 2. The first verse reports that "Solomon sat on the throne of his father David; and his kingdom was firmly established" (v. 12). This verse describes Solomon before he has acted on David's advice. In contrast, v. 46, which is found after Solomon's purge of the court, contains an important difference: "So the kingdom was established in the hand of Solomon." The latter verse is much clearer about Solomon's proactive role in the kingdom's security. The kingdom is not passively "firmly established" as in v. 12, but is established "in the hand of Solomon", a subtle, but significant contrast that highlights Solomon's transition from passive child to vigorous man and proactive ruler.[86]

The second hint is that, for the first time in the narrative, Solomon displays an independence from his mother; in fact, he criticizes her for failing to see Adonijah's intentions in requesting Abishag's hand (1 Kgs 2:22–24).[87] Given how close the relationship between Bathsheba and Solomon had been up to this point and how that relationship had been used by the narrator to stress Solomon's childishness, such an act of self-sufficiency by Solomon represents a significant move towards masculine maturation for the young king.

Finally, as both Montgomery and Šanda have each speculated, it is possible that the text block of 1 Kgs 1–2 does not end with the final verse of 1 Kgs 2 but instead includes 1 Kgs 3:1a, which reports that Solomon "made a marriage alliance with Pharaoh king of Egypt."[88] If Šanda and Montgomery are correct, this report of Solomon's marriage at the conclusion of the story once again draws attention to Solomon's maturation into manhood, since marriage is one of the definitive markers of manhood in the biblical text.

Before turning attention to the alternative tale of Solomon's coming of age in 1 Kgs 3, a review of the major themes of his maturation in 1 Kgs 1–2 is warranted. David's deathbed instructions in 1 Kgs 2:1–9 not only encourage his son to "become a man," but also specify how this transition is to be accomplished. Solomon—until this point in the narrative characterized by passivity and a close, dependent relationship to his mother—must learn to wield violence effectively, to display "cleverness," to perpetuate his father's lineage through Torah obedience, and he must settle his father's unfinished business to ensure David's image as an honorable man. Solomon follows the directions of his father exactly, and by the end of the story has shown himself a proactive man. His masculine development culminates in the announcement of his marriage in 3:1a, which functions as the natural ending to this tale of coming of age.

Solomon's Coming of Age in 1 Kings 3

A second version of Solomon's coming of age is found in 1 Kgs 3:4–15. This well-known tale of Solomon's dream vision of Yhwh at Gibeon presents a different understanding of how a young immature male transitions from boyhood to manhood. The story recounts how Solomon is given carte blanche by the deity to request anything he requires. In response, Solomon chooses wisdom, which he is granted by Yhwh together with riches, honor, and—if Solomon will follow Yhwh's commandments—a long life.

Solomon's youth

As was the case with 1 Kgs 1–2, it is necessary to establish that Solomon is initially described as a youth in this pericope. This is especially important because to the reader viewing 1 Kgs 1–3 as a unitary text, it appears that Solomon has already matured fully into a man by 1 Kgs 3:1, as I have just shown. Given the relative brevity of this tale vis-à-vis the larger block in 1 Kgs 1–2, the textual clues pointing to Solomon's youth are not as numerous, yet they are still evident. Indeed, the best indicator of his youth in 1 Kgs 3 is explicitly stated by the character himself with his response to Yhwh's open-ended offer. Before requesting wisdom, Solomon outlines how challenging it will be to rule Yhwh's people given that, in Solomon's words in v. 7, he is only a נַעַר קָטֹן (literally, "a little boy").[89]

In light of the brevity of this passage, this narrative detail should be sufficient to sustain the case for Solomon's youthfulness in 1 Kgs 3. Indeed, even in the longer narrative in 1 Kgs 1–2 Solomon's youth is never so plainly stated. Still, other indications of Solomon's boyishness appear in this passage. For example, Solomon follows his request for an "understanding mind" in v. 9 by adding that the motive for this request is not only to judge the people, but also "to discern between good and evil" (לְהָבִין בֵּין־טוֹב לְרָע). This phrase may also reveal Solomon's youth in light of Deut 1:39, where Moses declares that it is only the *children* of the exodus generation who will be permitted to occupy Canaan. In describing these children, Moses refers to them as those who "do not know good and evil" (לֹא יָדְעוּ הַיּוֹם טוֹב וָרָע). Clark argues that this description in Deuteronomy is the biblical Hebrew equivalent of the modern English term "minors"—that is, those whom the law does not consider fully responsible for their actions because of their youth. He further contends in light of other biblical legal material that this phrase likely indicates an age under twenty.[90] If the narrator is drawing upon Deuteronomy here—a proposition that is bolstered by the fact that much of the language of this short pericope reflects Deuteronomistic style and theology, a point that I will address below—Solomon's request to discern between good and evil indicates his youth. In other words, Solomon is, by his own admission, acknowledging that he has not reached the legal age of majority.

Next, Weitzman claims that the phrase immediately following Solomon's confession of immaturity and youthfulness in 1 Kgs 3:7 ("I do not know how to go out or come in") may likewise reveal the character's young age. While most scholars believe that the phrase "to go out and come in" refers to military endeavors, Weitzman claims that in this case it may be "an admission of sexual inexperience."[91] His argument is strengthened when considering that in the many examples of the phrase "going out and coming in" used in an obviously military context, no one is ever said to "know (ידע) going out and coming in"—the phrase Solomon employs here. Given the sexual undertones of the verb ידע, its anomalous use in this common construction may point to the sexual meaning proposed by Weitzman.[92] While the military meaning of the phrase is much more likely, it is possible that this is a case of double entendre, by which the narrator emphasizes Solomon's youth because of his lack of sexual experience.

An obvious problem with these claims of Solomon's youth is that he marries in 3:1. Since marriage is so closely associated with biblical manhood, it appears wrongheaded to consider him a boy in the following text. However, as already noted, at least two scholars (Šanda and Montgomery) argue that the report of Solomon's marriage to Pharaoh's daughter constitutes the conclusion to the narrative in 1 Kgs 1–2. If they are correct, this objection would be irrelevant. Solomon's marriage, in this case, would belong to the conclusion of a different maturation narrative (1 Kgs 1–2), and therefore his married status would not be assumed at the introduction of the maturation narrative in 1 Kgs 3.

However, even if Šanda and Montgomery are wrong, 3:1 should still not be considered the proper introduction to the tale of Solomon at Gibeon. Scholars are unanimous in their belief that 1 Kgs 3:1–3 represents a separate textual unit from the Gibeon dream narrative in 3:4–15.[93] The hand of the Deuteronomistic editor is obvious in vv. 2–3, as the vocabulary and style matches the summary royal notices that report the beginning and end of most reigns in

1–2 Kings and that serve as a structuring device throughout the books.[94]
Verse 1 does not contain such obvious indications of editorial composition;
however, its contextual dissonance with the surrounding narrative and its
total absence in the LXX (only to be added in the LXX together with the information in MT 9:16 after the current MT 5:14) have caused the majority of
commentators to consider it "a redactional note formed from notices in 1 Kgs
7:8, 9:16, and/or 9:24."[95] The indications of Solomon's youth in the Gibeon
dream narrative just discussed, therefore, are not discredited by the report of
Solomon's marriage in 1 Kgs 3:1, a verse that either represents the conclusion
of the previous independent narrative (1 Kgs 1–2) or is an editorial note likely
added quite late in the development of the biblical text.

Solomon becomes a man

Having established a valid case for seeing Solomon initially as a youth in 1
Kgs 3, the next step in arguing that this narrative is an alternative account of
Solomon's coming of age is to show how he transitions out of his former boyishness in the narrative. Solomon's departure from boyishness is marked
when Yhwh unconditionally grants him wisdom, riches, and honor at the
conclusion of his dream vision in vv. 12–13. I have already demonstrated that
both wisdom and honor (כָּבוֹד) are characteristic features of biblical masculinity. To be sure, riches are less closely associated with biblical masculinity and
the image of the man as the "breadwinner" is purely a modern construction.[96] Yet, riches are often a sign of God's favor in the Bible, and certainly
contribute to a man's status in comparison to his fellow men—indeed, Yhwh
explicitly values the riches he is giving to Solomon in comparison to the
wealth of other *men* (לֹא הָיָה כָמוֹךָ אִישׁ בַּמְּלָכִים; v. 13).[97]

Arguably, then, these three divine gifts to Solomon provide the necessary
changes in Solomon's character that will transform him from a נַעַר קָטֹן into a
man. Moreover, Yhwh does not promise to give Solomon these gifts in the
future. On the contrary, both appearances of the verb "to give" (נתן) in
vv. 12–13—where Yhwh announces his decision to grant Solomon gifts—are
in the perfect conjugation. This conjugation indicates that the action is completed and the wisdom, riches, and honor have been fully bequeathed at that
moment. Solomon need not look to the future for the moment when he can
be considered a man; he is already a man, having received these gifts from
Yhwh.[98]

The final indicator that this tale should be read as Solomon's coming of age
is the incorporation of the tripartite rite-of-passage structure, which is also
found in David's coming-of-age narrative in 1 Sam 17. As emphasized above,
the presence of a rite-of-passage structure highlights the coming-of-age theme

in a narrative, particularly if the main character begins the narrative as a youth and subsequently experiences an important change in the course of the story. Solomon's rite of passage begins with his *separation* from his home and family by leaving Jerusalem to go to Gibeon (1 Kgs 3:4). While in Gibeon, the young Solomon is afforded a vision of the divine and receives special knowledge and skill that will guide him in his adult life as king. According to Turner, a crucial part of the liminal phase of a rite of passage is the revelation of special gnosis by a divine figure (usually mediated through an older tribesman) to the young initiate.[99] Yhwh's revelation of unique wisdom to Solomon at Gibeon thus has typical features of the *liminal* stage of a rite of passage. Furthermore, Gibeon is uniquely suited to be the location for the liminal phase of Solomon's rite of passage because the town itself is defined by liminality.[100] Finally, Solomon in v. 15 is *reincorporated* into the community amid the feasting and sacrifices characteristic of this phase of a rite of passage.

Taken together with Solomon's youthful portrayal in the Gibeon dream narrative and the fact that by its end Yhwh has given to Solomon the very manly qualities of honor, wealth, and wisdom, the presence of the rite-of-passage structure serves to highlight the importance of the coming-of-age theme to this tale.

Summary

In sum, this examination of Solomon's coming of age in 1 Kings reveals that there are two contrasting versions of this story. Both 1 Kgs 1–2 and 1 Kgs 3 begin by describing Solomon with language unmistakably associated with boyhood in the HB. The narratives then proceed to detail how Solomon transitions out of this boyish state and becomes a man by the story's end. However, the ways in which Solomon accomplishes this transition and the kind of man that he becomes upon its completion differ considerably in the two narratives. A detailed discussion of these differences and their larger significance, as well as a comparison of both stories with David's coming of age in 1 Sam 17, is offered in the section below.

Thematic Comparison of the Royal Coming-of-Age Stories

The final section of this chapter compares how the three coming-of-age stories examined above narrate their main character's transition from boyhood to manhood. The purpose is not merely to point out subtle differences among the articulations of a literary theme in three different sources, however. As stated in the Introduction, my analysis of the coming-of-age theme also attempts to demonstrate: (1) how a narrator/redactor can use this theme to emphasize broader messages and transitions in the historical narratives in the HB; and (2) how these stories can provide unique insight into the conception of normative biblical masculinity.[101] I conclude my discussion in this chapter, therefore, with a brief discussion of how the coming-of-age theme highlights a transition in the narrative of Israel's history and a proposal for understanding the diachronic development of biblical views of normative masculinity as informed by royal coming-of-age stories.

The two tales of Solomon's coming of age provide a starting point for comparison. Certain differences between the two tales of maturation are evident upon a cursory glance. For instance, while Solomon takes a proactive role in his transition from boy to man in 1 Kgs 1–2 and the scene plays out on the political stage, in 1 Kgs 3 he is the recipient of his manhood from Yhwh and the story is set within sacred space (the "high place" or בָּמָה at Gibeon). In addition, the second story employs a rite-of-passage structure to highlight the coming-of-age theme, while the first does not.

Yet some of the most significant differences between the two versions of Solomon's coming-of-age story only come to light when considering the image of masculinity offered in the respective narratives. In other words, the qualities of manhood that the boy Solomon embodies by the conclusion of these two stories differ considerably. For example, Solomon receives and displays "wisdom" as part of his transition to manhood in both narratives but this attribute is portrayed in quite distinct ways. In 1 Kgs 1–2, "wisdom" is better understood as tactical savvy or cleverness—it is the ability to recognize a rebellion before it manifests itself and to use his political opponents' own words to condemn them. In contrast, Solomon's wisdom in 1 Kgs 3 is seen as the antidote for his fears about leading the nation of Israel; and it is associated with the verbs שפט ("to judge") and בין ("to discern"; see vv. 9, 11). This wisdom is therefore not the shrewd skill of 1 Kgs 1–2 but is instead the ability to rule the people justly. Appropriately, the story that immediately follows the Gibeon dream narrative showcases Solomon's unique *judicial* insights: the famous story of two prostitutes and the baby each claims as her own.

Another distinction is seen in Solomon's capacity for violence. This trait, which is so important to manhood in 1 Kgs 1–2, is rejected in the Gibeon tale of 1 Kgs 3, where Solomon's declaration of youth in v. 7 is further amplified by his confession that he does not know "how to go out or come in." While other meanings of this phrase may be possible—as discussed above—most scholars agree that "to go out and come in" means to lead a military force.[102] Thus

Solomon feels unready to lead Israel because he can neither effectively employ bellicose violence nor lead others in its use; this more than anything makes him a boy. Yhwh, however, does not share Solomon's belief that manhood and violence are intertwined. Yhwh mentions "the life of [Solomon's] enemies" as a potential blessing in v. 11 but pointedly does not give this to Solomon in the subsequent speech (vv. 12–14). This observation is even more noteworthy given that the subjugation of enemies is routinely mentioned as a gift of Yhwh to Israelite/Judahite kings—alongside riches and glory—in various royal coronation psalms.[103] Beyond that, at the beginning of his reign Solomon receives the riches, honor, and even conditionally the length of days referred to in these psalms but, significantly, not the defeat of his enemies. As a result, the message is clear: Solomon's manhood will not be defined by the violence that had so marked the narration of his coming of age in 1 Kgs 1–2.

Next, honor represents a feature of masculinity in both narratives; however, its importance in 1 Kgs 1–2 is greater than in 1 Kgs 3. In 1 Kgs 1–2, Solomon's actions are often motivated by his desire to settle his father's scores, which demonstrate his concern with defending familial honor. In contrast, honor (כָּבוֹד) is also a part of the story's construction of masculinity in 1 Kgs 3:4–15, but it is not valued as highly as in 1 Kgs 1–2. Yhwh does grant Solomon honor as a feature of the king's manhood in 1 Kgs 3 (v. 13) but only as an afterthought. Instead, "a wise and discerning mind" (v. 12) is clearly valued far more than honor, since Solomon's request for wisdom is looked upon with favor by Yhwh and leads the deity to grant the less-esteemed gifts of riches and honor as a reward for Solomon's choice. Moreover, the honor in 1 Kgs 3 is not associated with the need to defend it by force, as in 1 Kgs 1–2. In sum, maintaining honor is a component of masculinity articulated in 1 Kgs 3, but it is of secondary importance after wisdom and obedience to Yhwh and is disassociated with violent force.

Finally, while the self-control that comes with Torah obedience is mentioned in both narratives of Solomon's maturation, it is emphasized as essential to becoming a man in the first story, whereas in the second story it is mentioned after Yhwh has already bequeathed to Solomon the gifts that transform him from a boy into a man. Moreover, the reward for obedience to Yhwh's commandments is different in each story. Recall that in the first narrative David's pious wish that Solomon follow Yhwh's commandments (1 Kgs 2:3–4) is motivated and justified by the promise to continue David's lineage if his descendants will obey Yhwh. Torah obedience, therefore, is subsumed under considerations of lineage—that is, the wish that David (and by extension Solomon) would "have a name in Israel." In 1 Kgs 3:14, this direct connection between lineage and Torah obedience is not present; instead, Yhwh tells

Solomon that if he obeys the deity's statutes and commandments, then he will have a long life.

Comparing the two versions of Solomon's coming of age, therefore, reveals substantive differences in both the manner in which Solomon becomes a man and the qualities of manhood that he eventually embodies. In 1 Kgs 1–2, Solomon is initially presented as a boy, but through the proactive exertion of violent force on the political stage, the display of shrewd tactical "wisdom," and the defense of his father's honorable reputation and lineage, he becomes a man by the story's end. In 1 Kgs 3, the boy Solomon attains manhood in a less bellicose manner. The youthful and inexperienced Solomon does not proactively assert his manhood on the political stage via the adept use of violence, but instead is given everything he needs to be a man by Yhwh. Wisdom is understood as judicial or administrative acumen, not cleverness. Honor is not as significant a concern as in 1 Kgs 1–2, nor is the establishment of the Davidic lineage. And, finally, the structure of a rite of passage is found in this version of the story but not in 1 Kgs 1–2.

While comparing the two tales of Solomon's coming of age primarily highlights their differences, a look at the story of David's coming of age in 1 Sam 17 reveals its thematic similarities to the story of Solomon's maturation in 1 Kgs 1–2.[104] First, in both 1 Sam 17 and 1 Kgs 1–2 the expression of manly strength through violent force is important. Moreover, this force is employed in the defense of honor: David kills Goliath in order to protect the honor of Israel by removing (סור; 1 Sam 17:26) the shame and reproach of the Philistine's insult; Solomon executes Joab to remove (סור; 1 Kgs 2:31) the reproach of bloodguilt from David's good name and the reputation of his house.[105] Second, "wisdom" is viewed as craftiness in both stories: Solomon's wisdom is seen in his ability to sense incipient rebellion and in his use of his enemies' words against them; David's wisdom is indicated by his use of unconventional weapons and tactics to overcome his oversized Philistine foe. Third, if 1 Kgs 3:1a is viewed as the conclusion of Solomon's first coming-of-age tale, then marriage functions as the culmination of Solomon's manly deeds just as it serves as the ultimate reward for David's heroic victory over Goliath.

Arguably, the thematic similarities between these two coming-of-age stories indicate a close relationship between the textual block of 1 Kgs 1–2 and the preceding books of Samuel, in agreement with Rost's classic formulation of this relationship. Solomon's coming of age here has a retrospective quality that corresponds with the tone of the immediately preceding narrative, in which a major character—David—has died.[106] In contrast, the tale of David's maturation in 1 Sam 17 differs radically with the construction of masculinity and the means for attaining manhood presented in 1 Kgs 3.[107] Furthermore, as opposed to the retrospective tone of 1 Kgs 1–2, the Gibeon dream narrative presents a view of manhood that points forward to the Solomon of 1 Kgs 3–10: the wise and peaceful builder of a mighty empire. Therefore, while the coming-of-age theme is used in 1 Kgs 1–2 to emphasize continuity with the past, in 1 Kgs 3 it highlights an important transition in the historical narrative of Israel from a time of war to one of peace.

Finally, as suggested above, comparing the coming-of-age theme in these three stories may also provide insight into the diachronic development of the Israelite construction of masculinity. An important observation informing my reconstruction of this development is Carr's argument that the original folkloric *Vorlage* behind the Gibeon story in 1 Kgs 3 has received a heavy DtrH editing in the course of its textual history.[108] Carr shows the presence of stereotyped Deuteronomistic language hearkening back to the Torah throughout the story, attributing the following portions of the narrative to the Deuteronomistic editor: 3:3, 6aβb, 8, 9, 11aa4-b, 12bβ, 13b, 14a.[109] In contrast, the influence of DtrH's editing is far less evident in both 1 Kgs 1–2 and 1 Sam 17.[110] Assuming with most scholars that the historical narratives found in 1 Kgs 1–2 and 1 Sam 17 preceded the Deuteronomistic History, it is possible to argue that DtrH heavily edited an independent story about Solomon (the Gibeon story) and placed it immediately alongside the previous story of the king's maturation in 1 Kgs 1–2 in order to present an alternative articulation of manhood and coming of age.

In this view, DtrH's goal was to describe and advocate a new kind of man, and a new way of becoming such a man. In the new conception of masculinity offered by DtrH, the violence and vendettas characteristic of the older understanding of manhood found in 1 Kgs 1–2 (and earlier in 1 Sam 17) are de-emphasized. Similarly, the importance of honor is diminished, particularly honor that requires defense by force as in 1 Sam 17 and 1 Kgs 1–2. Wisdom in the service of personal advancement and unmoored from Yhwh's knowledge and justice, like the political savvy found in 1 Kgs 1–2, was minimized in favor of "the wisdom of God to execute justice" (1 Kgs 3:8). Finally, Torah obedience could no longer guarantee the continuation of royal lineage, an aspect of this new masculinity that would seem particularly appropriate to DtrH's exilic or post-exilic context because the Davidic monarchy no longer reigned in Jerusalem during this time. Instead, for DtrH, Torah obedience results in a long life. Therefore, by placing the narrative where he did and by using the same coming-of-age theme as the preceding narrative, DtrH gives an image of a new Israelite man for a new age.[111]

The five narratives analyzed in the previous two chapters constitute the total number of successful male coming-of-age stories in the HB. However, the coming-of-age theme is not only limited to these stories of successful coming of age. On the contrary, some narratives can be read as inversions of the coming-of-age theme—that is, as tales of *failing to come of age*. In the next chapter I identify two narratives of this sort and explain why societies might tell stories about a boy failing to transition to manhood. In addition, I consider the function of the failure-to-come-of-age theme within the broader Deuteronomistic History.

5

Failing to Come of Age
in the Hebrew Bible

THUS FAR THIS study has investigated the transition of several biblical figures from boyhood to manhood in order to demonstrate the significance of
the male coming-of-age theme in the HB. This theme, however, is not defined solely by these success stories. If it were, and if success in maturation
was inevitable for each male character making this transition, the stories
likely would not hold the interest of an audience. There must be a potential
for failure, otherwise the achievement of leaving boyhood behind and becoming a man—or any other accomplishment—is empty. The potential for failure does not merely exist in the implicit background of all coming-of-age
stories but also may be the explicit subject of a given narrative. These tales of
the failure to transition from boyhood to manhood are the topic of this
chapter.

Two biblical stories, both in Judges, invert the coming-of-age theme and
narrate the failure of a boy to mature into a man. The first is the rarely discussed tale of Gideon's son Jether in Judg 8:18–21, which illustrates the
theme directly and concisely. The second—the narrative of Samson in Judg
13–16—presents a more detailed, yet subtler, treatment of this theme. The
following analysis first investigates the presence and nuances of this "failure
to come of age" theme in both narratives. I then offer some suggestions inspired by folklore studies on the possible purpose of narratives describing
failure to come of age like these two (beyond simply offering a foil for successful tales of maturation), and their potential *Sitz im Leben* in an ancient
Israelite context at the time of their original composition. This chapter concludes with a discussion of the literary function of the Samson cycle specifically, paying special attention to how DtrH uses Samson's immaturity to
indicate broader themes in the book of Judges and the Deuteronomistic History as a whole.

Jether's Failure to Come of Age

Judges 8:18–21 functions as an odd coda to the narrative of Gideon's military exploits and rarely elicits comment from ancient or modern readers.[1] Up to this point in the Gideon cycle, the Israelite judge, called and empowered by Yhwh, has miraculously turned back the Midianite threat against Israel with a greatly outnumbered force and a clever battle plan (Judg 7:15–23). After executing the captains of the Midianite army, Oreb and Zeeb (7:25), Gideon pursues and eventually captures the Midianite kings Zebah and Zalmunna, while also punishing the Israelite cities of Penuel and Succoth for not supporting his weary troops during this mission (8:1–17). In Judg 8:18, however, the narrative takes an unanticipated turn. The reader learns for the first time here that Gideon's motive for capturing the Midianite kings is not the defense of Israel, but a personal vendetta. Zebah and Zalmunna were responsible for the deaths of Gideon's half-brothers, and he acts to avenge their blood.[2] Not only do new motives emerge in this brief textual unit, but so too does a previously unmentioned character: Gideon's firstborn son Jether. Although Jether's appearance is admittedly brief, these four verses reveal much about biblical conceptions of manhood and boyhood.[3] Moreover, they show how a boy's attempt to prove himself as a man can fail.

Jether enters the narrative when Gideon orders him to rise and kill the two captive Midianite kings (קוּם הֲרֹג אוֹתָם; Judg 8:20).[4] With this order, Jether is called to demonstrate a quintessential quality of biblical masculinity (strength, here both of body and will) on the stage most fit for its expression—the battlefield. Moreover, since the Midianite kings killed Jether's uncle, the boy's execution of the kings would function as an expression of kinship solidarity and a defense of family honor, both of which are features of manhood in the worldview of the HB. Instead of rising to this challenge and passing this test of masculinity, Jether is unable to draw his sword, "for he was afraid, because he was still a boy" (כִּי יָרֵא כִּי עוֹדֶנּוּ נָעַר; Judg 8:20). Seeing Jether's inability to act, Zebah and Zalmunna ask Gideon himself to kill them, supporting their request by quoting what appears to be a popular proverb: "As the man is, so too is his manly strength" (כָּאִישׁ גְּבוּרָתוֹ; 8:21).[5]

Several factors demonstrate that this brief tangent in the Gideon cycle narrates the failure to transition from boyhood to manhood. First, the proverb quoted by Zebah and Zalmunna draws a direct correlation between strength and manhood, with the effect of showing that Jether, in the words of Schneider, "was *not man enough* to carry out [Zebah and Zalmunna's execution]."[6] The proverb's use of the term גבורה (translated above as "manly strength") suggests even further that the difference between boyhood and manhood is in view here. Not only does the noun sonically recall the word for "man" (גֶּבֶר) and "mighty warrior/hero" (גִּבּוֹר) by employing the same root as these terms—comparable to the relationship between the Greek term for "courage" (ἀνδρεία) and "man" (ανήρ)—but this same word is used elsewhere in the HB to emphasize the difference between a boy (נַעַר) and a noble (חוֹר) adult (Qoh 10:16–17). The contention that Jether's diffidence may stem from a chivalric code of conduct that proscribed the killing of men of superior rank therefore fails to recognize the proverb's importance to the story's meaning.[7] Since the proverb clearly draws attention to the difference between boy and man with regard to "manly strength," its use in this story only makes sense if the Midianite kings are commenting on the frightened Jether's tender age in contrast to strong manhood.

The tale of Judg 8:18–21 strongly suggests a reading that highlights the failure to come of age for other reasons beyond the meaning and terminology of the proverb in Judg 8:21. For instance, Jether's fear specifically prohibits him from "drawing [his sword]" (לֹא־שָׁלַף; Judg 8:20). In the same chapter the phrase "men drawing the sword"(אִישׁ שֹׁלֵף חֶרֶב; Judg 8:10) is synonymous with "soldier." The implication is that if Jether cannot draw his sword, he is no soldier (i.e., he is no "man drawing the sword"); therefore, he is no *man* at all. Furthermore, scholars often note that Jether's fear in this section reflects the "fear theme" running through the Gideon cycle: namely, Gideon's fear at incurring his kinsmen's wrath for destroying their altar to Baal (Judg 6:27); his fear of entering the Midianite camp alone (Judg 7:10); and Yhwh's removal of Gideon's frightened soldiers from his army at the "Spring of Trembling" (עֵין חֲרֹד; Judg 7:1–2).[8] However, these scholars fail to distinguish the difference between the fear evidenced by Gideon earlier in the story and that of Jether here. Gideon's fear is the fear of being killed, while Jether's is the fear of killing. The former fear does not disqualify an individual from being considered a mighty warrior. Gideon, for example, is referred to as a mighty warrior (גִּבּוֹר; Judg 6:12), full of strength (כֹּחַ; Judg 6:14), despite his fears. Nor does such fear disqualify one from being considered a man—note that the fear of the enemy and defeat may lead to being dismissed from the army (Deut 20:3–8), but still these frightened soldiers are addressed as "men" (20:8).

In contrast, the fear of killing is a different matter entirely—one that is more at odds with the image of masculinity in the biblical text. Admittedly, since Jether provides the only example of this type of fear in the HB, any conclusion is limited and speculative. Even so, military leaders have long recognized that, in the words of World War II general George Marshall, "the fear of killing rather than the fear of being killed [is] the most common cause of battle failure."[9] As a result, while Gideon's fear of being killed may be incongruent with an idealized image of soldierly valor, Jether's fear of killing is more fundamentally incompatible with being a solider. Given the correlation between manhood and battlefield prowess in the biblical text (see Chapter 1), Jether's fear is recognized as distinctly unmanly.

Another indicator of the failure-to-come-of-age theme in this tale is the extent to which the story provides a negative foil to the successful battlefield coming of age of the נַעַר David in 1 Sam 17, which is discussed in Chapter 4.[10] A significant amount of evidence suggests that such a contrast exists. Whereas David boldly crosses over the threshold into manhood covered in the blood of the sentry protecting the gateway to maturity (i.e., Goliath), Jether is not yet ready to engage in the test of strength that must accompany the transition of an adolescent to manhood. David is shown as a master of fear (in contrast to the so-called "men of Israel" who are afraid to face Goliath [1 Sam 17:11, 24]), and Jether is defined by his fear (Judg 8:20). Jether cannot defend the honor of his close kinsmen, but David defends the honor of all the men of Israel. David demonstrates martial aptitude by unsheathing (שָׁלַף) the oversized sword of a giant (1 Sam 17:51), but Jether cannot even draw (שָׁלַף) his own sword. Jether is marked by his lack of manly strength (גְּבוּרָה; Judg 8:21), whereas David's new characterization in 1 Sam 17:56 employs a term replete with connotations of power and passion (עֶלֶם).[11] David walks away from the battlefield with the trophies of his successful transition in his hand (the giant's head and armor [1 Sam 17:54]); in contrast, Jether must watch while his father takes the trophies that should have been his (the crescents on the necks of the Midianite kings' camels [Judg 8:21]). In sum, David makes a significant transition towards manhood in 1 Sam 17, while the fearful Jether does not display "manly strength" and thus fails to pass the test that would establish his identity as a man.

Samson the Man-Child

While the failure to come of age is illustrated succinctly in the Jether story of Judg 8, the Samson cycle (Judg 13–16) demonstrates this theme with more subtlety and over the span of a much longer text, perhaps explaining why biblical scholars have not recognized it. However, Mobley's recent work arguing for the importance of *liminality* in the text's depiction of Samson lays the groundwork for examining Samson's failure to come of age.[12] By highlighting Samson's liminality, Mobley shows that the character's defining quality is not his famous hair or renowned strength, but rather his status as a character caught "betwixt and between" two different worlds or states of being. The "liminal hero" Samson straddles borders, at once occupying the ground on both sides, or moving unabated and carefree between them.[13]

Mobley's study is noteworthy for its thoroughgoing application of the concept of liminality to Samson's character, but Samson's transcending of social, political, and even gender borders did not escape earlier readers. For instance, Gunkel drew attention to Samson's perpetual location at the border of nature and culture—a "wild man" marked as much by animalistic traits (beastly ferocity, untamed hair) as by the trappings of human society.[14] Niditch anticipated certain features of Mobley's argument by showing that Samson not only straddles the border between nature and culture but also that between man and woman. Samson, the once masculine and mighty warrior, is effectively feminized by the Philistines when they capture him (Judg 16:21–25), but later this feminization is overturned by his reassertion of manly might in his final act of vengeance (16:29–30).[15] Mobley builds upon these early soundings of the liminality theme and provides many more examples of the theme at work. For example, he notes that even such minor details as Samson's status as a Danite—a member of a borderland tribe living adjacent to the enemy Philistines—functions to emphasize his liminality to an ancient Israelite audience.[16] For Mobley, however, Samson's liminality is most visible in his free movement across the borders between house and field,[17] agitation and rest,[18] and the social worlds of men and women.[19]

This emphasis on liminality common to recent scholarly readings of the Samson cycle provides a useful lens for interpretation. However, the concept has yet to be applied to one of the most significant facets of Samson's character. Among the many borders that Samson is unable to cross permanently is that separating boyhood and manhood.[20] Samson, in other words, is a perpetual man-child.

The oversight of this feature of Samson's liminality on the part of scholars is surprising given the history of the concept of liminality in scholarship. Liminality, as discussed in the Introduction, was originally a central idea in the anthropological work of Arnold van Gennep, and later inspired Victor Turner's thought. Only later was the notion of liminality imported into biblical studies via literary theory. It is worthwhile to note that van Gennep and Turner frequently employed the concept in their analyses of the coming-of-age rituals that many tribal cultures use to mark the transition from boyhood to manhood. The investigation below—which demonstrates Samson's liminality with regard to his maturity as a man—therefore reconnects the concept of liminality with its original context and emphasis on describing the transition from boyhood to manhood. Several indications within the text of the Samson cycle point to the hero's failure to make this transition.

At first glance it seems ridiculous to posit that Samson's depiction in the text of Judges is anything less than hyper-masculine. Samson is not just any man; he seems to be an Übermensch: the embodiment of idealized machismo. In some ways, this is true. Certainly, as studies of ancient Israelite masculinity show, one of the most important features of manhood in that culture, according to its texts, is physical strength. Moreover, this male ideal of physical strength is most appropriately displayed on the battlefield. When one instead displays weakness on that stage (viz., Jether), one's manhood is called into question. Given Samson's renowned might and the high number of Philistine enemy dead attributed to him throughout the narrative (such as the one thousand Philistine men that he slays with the jawbone of an ass in Judg 15:14–16), Samson clearly exemplifies this quality of masculine invincibility. Moreover, as Niditch argues, long hair like Samson's is an indicator of masculinity to an ancient Near Eastern audience, for whom a man's hair functioned to symbolize "manliness, maturity, and power."[21] Finally, Samson's facility with language—demonstrated by his affinity for word games/figures of speech (e.g., Judg 14:18), poetry (15:16), and riddles (14:14)—corresponds to another fundamental characteristic of hegemonic Israelite masculinity: intelligence, and particularly the mastery of the art of rhetoric and persuasion.[22]

Alongside Samson's manly traits (strength, long hair, rhetorical skill), however, are other features in the narrative that point to his immaturity and boyishness. These more boyish features of Samson's characterization, which are scrutinized below, demonstrate that Samson's recognized liminality extends to his failure to transition completely from boyhood to manhood. Before enumerating these boyish traits, however, two pieces of textual evidence that would seem at first to rule out an analysis of Samson as a case of arrested development must be addressed and dismissed.

The first is based on Judg 13:24, which states that the boy Samson "grew" (וַיִּגְדַּל). Some translations (e.g., NJPS, NAS) render the verb here as "grew up," a translational choice implying that Samson had matured completely and left childhood behind.[23] Since the text explicitly states that Samson "grew up," according to this argument, how then could he still be reckoned as a boy or young man? This objection, however, has a significant flaw. It misconstrues the meaning of the verb גדל by assuming that in every case the verb implies "growing up," when just as frequently it simply denotes "growing." For instance, in Gen 21:8 the baby Isaac is said first to have grown (וַיִּגְדַּל), and then to have been weaned. Since the verb here describes the growth of an infant from birth to the time of weaning at approximately age three, it clearly does not imply "growing up" in the sense of achieving mature adulthood.

The second objection draws attention to the fact that Samson appears to be sexually active, as his visit to the prostitute in Gaza (Judg 16:1–3) indicates.[24] If

Samson has crossed the significant border between virginity and sexual knowledge, the argument goes, characterizing him as a boy is a misreading of the text. This objection, too, is misguided. It is premised on modern views of the significance of sexual experience to a boy's coming of age. As I argue in Chapter 2, however, the boundary between virginity and sexual experience is more socially significant for girls and young women in the HB (viz., the importance of a female's intact virginity in such legal texts as Deut 22:13–21) than for young men.[25] Samson, then, can simultaneously be sexually active and still very much a boy in the estimation of both the biblical text and the society that produced it.

Having dismissed these two objections, the way is clear for a discussion of the characteristics that indicate Samson's immaturity and boyishness. When these boyish traits are viewed alongside Samson's masculine features, a portrait of Samson as perpetually liminal with regard to his masculine development emerges.

Evidence in the Text Indicating Samson's Immaturity

His lack of children and unmarried status

The first indicator of Samson's immaturity is that he remains childless throughout his life. The virile production of multiple offspring is a fundamental feature of biblical masculinity, just as much as the strength, intelligence, or hairiness mentioned above. For instance, when Absalom's equally famous head of hair is first mentioned in 2 Sam 14:26, the description is immediately followed in v. 27 by a report of his success in siring children: three sons and a daughter. According to Niditch, this is evidence that for the biblical writers, hair is understood as the physical sign of the quality of "fertility and manly fecundity."[26] Samson's possession of a telltale marker of the manly trait of fertility—that is, his long hair—while simultaneously showing no evidence of that fertility through offspring, already suggests the blurring of boundaries characteristic of liminality.

As argued in Chapter 2, the fertility so central to normative Israelite masculinity is not viewed as an end in itself. The goal of manly virility was not simply the fathering of many children, but rather the production of legitimate male heirs. This is especially true in the Deuteronomistic tradition to which the final form of the Samson cycle belongs, where legitimate male heirs are essential to "perpetuating a name in Israel" (Deut 25:6–7), a task this tradition considers vital to Israelite manhood.[27] In the Deuteronomic (Dtn) literature, a child is considered legitimate if he or she is the product of a legitimate marital union; otherwise the child would be excluded from the congregation of Yhwh (Deut 23:2).[28] Furthermore, while exogamy is not totally prohibited (note David's marriage to a Canaanite and an Aramaen in 2 Sam 3:3), the Dtn tradition generally discourages marriage to foreign women.[29] Therefore, if an Israelite man is to perform the important manly duty of perpetuating his name by producing male heirs, he is expected to be married and preferably that marriage is endogamous.

Therefore, Samson's failure to live up to the masculine ideal presented in the Dtn literature and the HB as a whole goes deeper than his lack of off-spring. Since this quality of virile fertility is only properly expressed within the bounds of a legitimate and ideally endogamous marital union, both Samson's unmarried status and his persistent attraction to foreign women further contribute to his characterization as a boy who has not completely matured into manhood.[30]

His impetuousness

A second sign of Samson's failure to mature is his tendency to engage in rash and disproportionately violent actions, which is frequently attested in the narrative. For example, Samson destroys the Philistine harvest in reaction to having his amorous intentions thwarted (Judg 15:4–5). He slaughters the Philistines as vengeance for the death of his betrothed (15:7–8). He obstinately insists on courting Philistine women in the face of his parents' objections (14:3)—a potentially treasonous act especially worthy of reproach in the early books of the Deuteronomistic History, in which the Philistines are depicted as Israel's archetypal enemy. His lack of impulse control results in a careless violation of his nazirite vows when he eats honey from a lion's carcass (14:8–9). In his final, suicidal act of massive destruction and death, Samson's predilection towards disproportionate violence reaches its culmination, considering that his stated motive is only to avenge his blinded eyes (16:30).

In expressing such impetuousness, Samson exhibits a characteristic often employed in the description of children, and boys in particular, in the HB, as discussed in Chapter 2. The ideal Israelite *man*, in contrast, is marked by self-restraint and impulse control, carefully keeping his desire towards gluttony, unbridled violence, and wanton sexuality in check.[31] The Samson cycle implicitly highlights this contrast between boyish and manly behavior. While the text does not necessarily condemn Samson's impetuousness outright, it does indicate that uncontrolled violence breeds more violence, in that the cycle of vengeance Samson perpetuates only concludes with his death and that of his Philistine enemies.[32] Moreover, the narrative shows the tragic results of heedlessly indulging one's appetites at the expense of fidelity to one's vows and loyalty to one's people. The effect is to emphasize the gap between Samson's inability to control his passions—and thus his immaturity—and an Israelite adult man's proper behavior.

His strong connection to his parents

A third sign of Samson's incomplete transition to manhood is his exceptionally close relationship with his parents. Crenshaw emphasizes this characteristic to the point of arguing that one of the chief tensions in Samson's character—as well as in the Samson cycle as a whole—is that between "filial devotion and erotic attachment."[33] This tension is evident in Judg 14:16, when Samson is pressed by his betrothed bride to reveal the answer to his riddle. His response, which is to ask incredulously how he could be expected to reveal the answer to her *when he has not yet even told his parents*, highlights Samson's devotion to his mother and father over his fiancée.

Judges 14:5–9 provides another example of Samson's close connection to his parents. Here Samson, having found honey in the carcass of the lion he had killed earlier, postpones his visit to his Timnite lover (and perhaps even turns back from visiting her entirely—the text is unclear) in order to share this treat with his parents. More than just providing evidence of a timid reluctance to set out independently into the world—and away from his parents—Samson's actions here take on special significance because it is the potentially sexual relationship with the Timnite woman that he is rejecting in favor of his parents. The symbolic importance of honey as a food often associated with fertility in folkloric narratives further highlights the sexual component of this scene's imagery.[34] Samson's choice to share his honey with his parents instead of with the Timnite woman is therefore comparable to a young man today purchasing roses and chocolates for a romantic rendezvous, and then promptly offering them to his parents![35] The scene implies that Samson has failed to reach the point of sexual maturity at which he can direct his erotic energies outward—that is, the point at which he can leave his father and mother and cling to his wife (Gen 2:24).

Samson's bond with his parents is also evident in the frequency with which his adventures into Philistine territory end with a childlike retreat to the safety of his parents.[36] For example, his first trip down to Timnah ends in the next verse with his return to his parents (Judg 14:1–2). His journey to visit the Timnite woman in the same chapter (14:8–9) is postponed in order that Samson may share his honey with his parents. Samson's ruined and unconsummated marriage is immediately followed by his slaughter of thirty Ashkelonites, but the story's culmination finds him returning to the safety of his father's house (14:19). The symbolism of Samson's return to his parents continues even after his death, since his corpse is brought from Gaza and placed in his father's tomb (16:31).

The primary significance of Samson's exceptionally strong bond to his parents is that he never achieves the emotional separation and individuation from one's parents that comes with maturation, which is a necessary prerequisite for sexuality and marriage (Gen 2:24). Given the importance of marriage and reproduction to Israelite manhood in the Hebrew Bible, a male who is not ready for these experiences is not yet fully considered a man in the society that produced these texts.

Terminological considerations

A fourth indicator of Samson's perpetual state of boyhood is the frequency with which Hebrew words for "boy" and "young man" are applied to him. The Hebrew נַעַר, or "boy," is employed to describe Samson five times in the cycle of narratives (Judg 13:5, 7, 8, 12, 24), while בָּחוּר, meaning "young man," is used once (Judg 14:10).[37] In contrast, terminology connoting adult manhood is generally not applied to Samson.[38] This is especially striking given the fact that the two major judges preceding him—Gideon and Jephthah—are not only referred to with the word אִישׁ (Gideon in 7:14; Jephthah in 10:18 [cf. 11:8]), but also with a term even more suggestive of robust masculinity: גִּבּוֹר חַיִל (in 6:12 and 11:1, respectively).[39]

Even when Samson offers three times to tell Delilah how she could weaken him (Judg 16:7, 11, 17), he claims that the effect of her actions would be to make him "like any other *human being*" (e.g., 16:7: וְהָיִיתִי כְּאַחַד הָאָדָם).[40] Significantly, the word used is אָדָם, a term that lacks a definitive gendered meaning and is often best translated as "person," "human being," or "mortal."[41] Samson therefore does not claim that he can be weakened like any other *man*, as some translations suggest (NJPS, KJV). If that had been the narrative's intention, a more specifically gendered term like אִישׁ would be more appropriate. Instead, the contrast depicted is that between Samson's superhuman strength and that of a mere human.[42] In sum, nowhere does the text speak of Samson unambiguously as a man, nor does the character self-identify as a man. Rather, the text depicts Samson as a boy (נַעַר), or at most as a young man who has yet to complete his maturation (בָּחוּר).

His age at death

The fifth indicator of Samson's immaturity concerns Samson's length of service as a judge. According to Judg 15:20 and 16:31, Samson judged Israel for twenty years. These twenty years immediately stand out as anomalous, because the paradigmatic length for a prominent judge to lead the tribes of

Israel in Judges is forty years, as with Othniel (Judg 3:11), Deborah (5:31), and Gideon (8:28).⁴³ This discrepancy of twenty years between the length of Samson's career as judge over Israel and the ideal forty years begins to draw attention to Samson's youth because it highlights an unnatural truncation of his judgeship at his early and untimely death. Indeed, the narrator does this emphatically by reporting Samson's twenty-year career as judge on two separate occasions (Judg 15:20; 16:21), which is a departure from the standard style employed in Judges for chronicling this information.⁴⁴

The text may be communicating more here than merely reporting a leader's premature death, however. A close reading of the narrative reveals that twenty is not only the number of years that Samson judged Israel, but also is his age at the time of his death. In other words, according to the narrator's chronology, Samson judged Israel from the time of his birth.

This is not an untenable claim. A repeated theme, appearing three times in the Samson narrative (Judg 13:5, 7; 16:17), is that the hero is set apart as a charismatic nazirite *from the day of his birth*.⁴⁵ Significantly, in Judg 13:5—the first verse where the theme appears in the Samson story—the child's nazirite status is placed immediately alongside the pronouncement that he will begin to save Israel (וְהוּא יָחֵל לְהוֹשִׁיעַ אֶת־יִשְׂרָאֵל). This strongly suggests that this nazirite status is intimately connected with delivering the people from their enemies, one of the characteristic actions of an Israelite judge.⁴⁶ Therefore, Samson's twenty-year reign as a judge of Israel corresponds with his time as a nazirite, because it is precisely this status that defines his saving role as judge. And as the text emphasizes, the length of Samson's nazirite status is from birth to death, a span of twenty years.

To be sure, the significance of Samson's death at age twenty is not immediately apparent but only comes to light when considered in view of the male life cycle in the HB. As I show in Chapter 1, reaching the age of twenty marks a pivotal milestone in the male life cycle, especially in HB legal texts.⁴⁷ For example, when a boy reaches age twenty he is eligible for military service (Num 1:3, 18; 26:2), is accountable for his actions and choices (Num 14:29; 32:11), and can be taxed (Exod 30:14). Reporting that Samson died at twenty, then, has the same resonance to the ancient Israelite ear as saying a boy died at eighteen or twenty-one in contemporary American society. In each case, the tragedy of the untimely death is compounded by the fact that death came just as the boy had become a man from the perspective of his society's laws. If an Israelite storyteller wished to highlight the theme of Samson's liminality between childhood and manhood, there is no more appropriate age for his death than twenty.

His lack of solidarity with adult men

The fifth and final indicator of Samson's liminality with regard to his maturation as a man is his lack of solidarity with his fellow Israelite men, an important characteristic of biblical masculinity. Samson is famously a loner, unique
among the judges of Israel in that he achieves his victories against his people's enemies without any cooperation with them.[48]

Nowhere is Samson's lack of solidarity with his fellow Israelite men more
evident than in Judg 15:10–14. Here, Samson has just completed the destruction of the Philistines' harvest and has massacred of a large number of them.
In spite of these daring actions against their most feared enemy, three thousand Judahite men *chide him* for his deeds against their Philistine subjuga-
tors, and bind him in order to deliver him into Philistine hands. This
collaboration with the Philistines and betrayal of Samson is a far cry from the
manly solidarity at the core of biblical masculinity. Tragically, until his kinsmen take his corpse back to his homeland (Judg 16:31), no group of men—
neither the men of his own people nor the men of the Philistine society to
which he is so compulsively drawn—claims him as one of their own and
celebrates his manly deeds.[49]

Summary

In sum, several factors indicate that the liminality so significant to Samson's
characterization extends to his inability to cross the border definitively from
boyhood to manhood. On the one hand, Samson's manly strength, long hair,
and facility with words speak to the more mature side of the hero. On the
other hand, Samson's unmarried and childless status, his predilection for
rash and impetuous action, the terminology used to describe him, his exces-
sively strong connection to his parents, and his lack of solidarity with fellow
Israelite men are all features that contribute to the thematic development of
Samson's boyish side. Moreover, by reporting Samson's death at age twenty,
the text succinctly portrays his liminal status between boyhood and manhood. Taken together, these manly and childlike attributes combine to create
the image of Samson as a liminal man-child.

The Function and Social Context of Narratives
Describing the Failure to Come of Age

The next issue to address in this discussion is the question of why stories that
feature a liminal character caught between boyhood and manhood like

Samson, or a character that fails in his transition to manhood like Jether, would exist at all. Stated differently, in what social context would stories like these *originally* arise, and what would their purpose be?

One explanation for both the purpose and context of the "failing to come of age" theme comes from folklore studies.[50] In the last century, scholars in this field began to recognize the recurring presence of oral traditions about young male characters who fail to overcome initiatory ordeals that, if passed, would confirm their status as adult men. For example, David Bynum's research among South Slavic storytellers identifies two adolescent novice characters—Mehmed Smailagić and Omer Hrnjica—who are frequent protagonists in stories that take up the theme of failing to come of age.[51] Margaret Beissinger finds a similar character in the Romanian epic cycle of the hero Novacs: the hero's son (or nephew, in some versions of the story) Gruia.[52] These characters over time have become so inseparably linked with the theme of failed transition to manhood that they rarely if ever appear as mature older characters in other tales from the respective cultures' oral tradition.[53] While each of these characters have attracted many tales in the storytelling traditions of these cultures, their stories typically follow a remarkably similar plotline: the young overconfident novice usually sets out to accomplish a heroic deed, often with the final goal of marriage in sight, yet he inevitably fails his ordeal and often requires the help of his father or other elder males to rescue him from his predicament.[54]

In an attempt to explain the ubiquity of the failure-to-come-of-age theme in folklore—which Bynum traces all the way back to Homer—both Bynum and Beissinger offer an interpretation that stresses the value of these tales to society.[55] They argue that this genre addresses intergenerational dynamics, specifically the succession of an older male generation by a younger generation.[56] From their perspective, rehearsing these stories and highlighting this theme allows the elder generation to give voice to their fears of becoming socially marginalized and weakened, as well as their uncertainties about the readiness of the younger generation to assume leadership in the culture.

The work of Bynum and Beissinger offers some insight into the Samson cycle and the Jether narrative even if these two stories do not perfectly correspond to the typical tale of a Balkan novice hero.[57] Their research is most helpful for the suggestion that tales of arrested development and failing to come of age are composed and retold in response to intergenerational tensions. The presence of similar tensions, typically reflecting a fear of the marginalization of the elderly and the unease over generational succession, is already recognizable in certain texts in the Hebrew Bible. One need look no further than the commandment to honor father and mother (Exod 20:12) for proof: why establish this rule unless dishonor and mistreatment of the elderly were a persistent problem?[58] Biblical narratives also reflect intergenerational conflict. For example, Meyers notes that the family narratives of Genesis offer abundant evidence of the "inevitable" tensions that result across generations living together in the village setting of ancient Israel.[59] Additionally, Berquist recognizes the presence of the theme of intergenerational tension in the story of Elisha and the taunting boys of Bethel (2 Kgs 2:23–24).[60]

If intergenerational concerns lie at the heart of certain biblical laws and narratives, perhaps also the original composition of the biblical failure-to-come-of-age narratives can be attributed to a similar motivation. For example, the Samson narratives could be understood as stories told among elders about the difficulties associated with rearing a boy properly: the need to channel his sexual urges into appropriate (endogamous) expressions; the dangers associated with adolescent willfulness and impetuosity; and so forth.[61] In complementary fashion, the Samson and Jether stories could also have originally functioned as cautionary tales told by adults to boys on the verge of manhood. In this case too intergenerational tensions would serve as the primary motivation for the stories' compositions, only here the audience is different. In this view, the Jether story could have been told to young men to stress the importance of valor and of obedience to both one's father and one's battlefield commander. Similarly, the Samson cycle's purpose would be to ensure a child's proper obedience to parental advice by warning the child of the dangers associated with disobedience.[62] The message of the stories to young men, then, is that to behave like Samson or Jether is to never become recognized as an Israelite man.

In contrast to the opinion shared by Bynum and Beissinger that these tales function as responses by the elder male generation to issues of intergenerational succession, another possible explanation suggests that stories of failing to come of age address common psychological concerns among the young. According to this theory, the difficulties and ambiguities associated with male coming of age provide the psychological subtext for tales about the failure to mature. For boys who are still navigating this time of transition, or young men not too far removed from this stage of their life, a story about a man-child like Samson or a failed attempt at maturation like Jether would have a natural appeal. These characters' struggles reflect young men's/boys' struggles, and in their ultimate failure to reach their goal of maturation other boys can find the embodiment of their own worst fears about the status of their newly minted manhood, or a negative foil against which to measure their own accomplishments.

Supporting this hypothesis is Niditch's claim that both the stories of Jether and of Samson originally found their oral-performative context (prior to their being written down) in what she calls the "epic bardic tradition."[63] This tradition of oral narratives concerns itself with tales of mighty warriors and heroes, chivalry, codes of military conduct, the division of spoil, and so forth.[64] While Niditch speculates that tales from this strain of oral narrative were eventually written down in the context of a royal court,[65] the obvious interest of these stories with martial matters suggests an original military context for the narratives in this tradition. In other words, narratives in the epic bardic tradition like those of Jether and Samson started out as "army stories," told by the young men who comprise Israel's army to other young men (or even boys serving as squires or retainers), in order to pass the time. If the identification of these stories as originally coming from an epic bardic tradition is correct, the *Sitz im Leben* better fits the psychological explanation just offered than the previous explanation offered by Bynum and Beissinger. These tales, then, would respond not to the social and psychological anxieties of the elder generation, but to the psychological anxieties of youths negotiating their own maturation.

To summarize, two convincing theories inspired by folklore studies help to explain the possible origins of "failure to come of age" stories like those of Jether and Samson. One theory suggests that these tales—that can be found in cultures as temporally removed from each other as ancient Greece and the modern Balkans—may have been composed originally to address the perpetual social problem of generational succession. Another theory finds the genesis of such folkloric tales in the mental and emotional concerns of older boys and young men in the process of maturing into full adult manhood in their society.

The Literary Function of Samson's Failure to Come of Age

Having discussed the possible social context and purpose of the failure-to-come-of-age theme, I will now treat the less speculative subject of the theme's narrative function in the context of Judges and the larger Deuteronomistic History. In this final section, I will treat only the Samson cycle, since its literary function in Judges is much more noteworthy than the brief Jether narrative.

The choice by DtrH to put a narrative like Samson's—with its deeply flawed hero—into the historical narrative demands explanation, as does the prominent position this story takes at the conclusion of the cycle of named judges. An analysis of the Samson cycle in light of the character's failure to come of age reveals solutions to these questions by highlighting how Samson's immaturity reflects broader themes in DtrH's assessment of Israel during the period of the judges.

An important insight for this discussion is that the character of Samson in many ways embodies Israel at this point in the historical narrative. A number of scholars make this observation, but few devote more detailed attention to this comparison than Dennis Olson and, separately, Edward Greenstein.[66] For Olson, Samson's submission to the Philistines and his tragic captivity in Gaza is used by DtrH to mirror the plight of Israel during the Babylonian exile.[67] Greenstein sees Samson's story as an "allegorical digest" of the preceding narrative in Judges, where Samson stands in for the Israelites in his time and his nazirite vows represent the covenant between Israel and Yhwh.[68]

Olson, Greenstein, and others are right to highlight how Samson epitomizes the plight of Israel at this point in the Dtr historical narrative. However, by not recognizing the significance for Samson's characterization of his failure to come of age, they limit the explanatory potential of their insights. It is precisely in his inability to cross the border into maturity once and for all that Samson most resembles Israel in the period of the judges. This first becomes evident when considering the cyclical pattern of Israelite history running through Judges, wherein Israel does evil in the eyes of Yhwh, is punished by being given into the hands of an enemy, and cries out to Yhwh who sends a deliverer to free the people and bring a period of peace.[69] The repetition of this pattern—recurring in six completed cycles in the textual block of Judg 3:7–16:31—illustrates Israel's inability to escape the destructive cycle of behaviors that keeps the nation stuck in a state of weakness and vulnerability to external powers. Samson's similar failure to transition out of his liminal status caught between boyhood and manhood metaphorically corresponds to Israel's repetition of this pattern that prevents the nation from maturing politically.

Moreover, the reasons that both Samson and Israel remain caught in their respective vicious cycles share similarities. For example, just as Samson's boyish impetuosity causes him to ignore his parents' advice that would guide him towards proper Israelite manhood (14:2), so too Israel repeatedly turns its back on the lessons of history and the instruction of the nation's symbolic parent, Yhwh. As a result of not heeding his parents' advice and instead choosing to court foreign women, Samson fails to accomplish the manly deed of producing legitimate heirs with an Israelite woman and thereby endangers the perpetuation of his paternal lineage. Israel, likewise, endangers their future on the land that is their inheritance due to a penchant for marriage with foreigners causing them to stray from Yhwh, their sustainer upon the land (Judg 3:6).

Samson's similarities with Israel are further illustrated by the fact that unlike each of the judges preceding him, his fatal flaw inhibiting his potential as a leader is ostensibly something within his control: his immaturity. In contrast, Ehud's left-handedness, Gideon's humble origins, and Jephthah's illegitimate birth—all of which are considered flaws that an ideal military and religious leader in the world of the text would not possess—fall outside of the individual judge's control.[70] In this sense too Samson resembles Israel. Both are given every advantage from the moment of their birth and both possess a special relationship with God (Samson through his oft-neglected nazirite vows and Israel through its covenant). Yet in spite of this, each consistently fails to live up to their potential and willfully strays from the proper path of development: masculine maturity in Samson's case, religious and consequently political rectitude in Israel's.

Still another way in which Samson's status as a liminal man-child typifies Israel at the time of the judges is his inability or unwillingness to form bonds with the adult men of Israel. This functions as a significant feature in Samson's characterization as someone less than a man in his society, as seen above. Here again a feature of Samson's liminality parallels the plight of the Israelites in Judges. Throughout the book the portrayal of Israel's own political immaturity is similarly defined by a failure to achieve internal cohesion among its constituent tribes, a situation that tragically culminates in the Israelite civil war described in Judg 19–21. Just as Samson's lack of solidarity with his fellow Israelites prevents his maturation, so also does Israel's own internal lack of solidarity prevent its political development.

Given these similarities between Samson's story and that of Israel, it is no wonder that DtrH chose to place the Samson story at the tragic endpoint of the process of deterioration that the historian traces throughout the cycle of major judges in Judg 3:17–16:31.[71] It is likely that DtrH wished to draw attention to the comparison between the man-child Samson and Israel, since Samson's immaturity so perfectly embodies the historian's understanding of Israel's predicament at that time in the narrative. He did so, therefore, primarily through his editorial choice to place the Samson cycle in a position of prominence within the larger narrative.

In summary, an important feature of Samson's epitomization of Israel in the time of the judges is his inability to transition to manhood. Just as Samson seems stuck in a liminal phase between boyhood and manhood, so too Israel cannot help but repeat a self-destructive cycle that keeps it vulnerable and weak. Samson's disobedience to his parents, his attraction to foreign women, and his failure to bond with Israelite men—each of which marks him as less than a man in Israelite society—parallels Israel's disobedience of Yhwh, intermarriage with Canaanites, and internal divisiveness. Moreover, both Samson and Israel have only themselves to blame for their failures, since they have squandered the immense potential resulting from their special relationships with Yhwh. To emphasize the notable similarities between Samson's failure to come of age and Israel's political immaturity, DtrH made the editorial decision to situate the Samson story prominently at the conclusion of the cycle of named judges.

Samson would die while still suspended in his liminal phase between boyhood and manhood. The troubled adolescence of Israel, however, did not last forever. Israel would experience its own transition into mature and well-formed nationhood in the Deuteronomistic History with the coming of the Davidic monarchy, whose eponymous founder, significantly, is associated with a narrative (1 Sam 17) full of coming-of-age tropes (see Chapter 4). Israel embodied in David (the boy who slays a giant and becomes a man) stands in bold contrast to the earlier Israel embodied in Samson (the man-child who is unable to mature).

In this chapter, therefore, I have completed the study of the male coming-of-age theme in the HB by demonstrating that this topic also encompasses stories of a boy's failure to come of age. The story of Jether in Judg 8 depicts a boy who is unable to do the grisly work of killing enemies in battle and avenging familial honor required of a man. The Samson cycle provides an example of arrested male development, with its liminal hero perpetually caught at the border between boyhood and manhood. I also showed that like coming-of-age tales, stories describing the failure to come of age are attested over time in many cultures and serve important social and/or psychological purposes. Finally, I demonstrated how the Deuteronomistic editor and redactor of the Samson cycle used Samson's failure to come of age to emphasize Israel's political immaturity at that point in its history.

6

Conclusion

THE PRIMARY OBJECTIVE of this book has been to identify male coming of age as a recurring theme in the HB. Four principles guided the effort to identify this theme in the preceding chapters: (1) terminology is a key indicator of a character's status as a boy or as a man; (2) a coming-of-age narrative will feature a boy acquiring and/or displaying qualities associated with manhood; (3) the presence of a rite-of-passage schema can help to identify a narrative as a coming-of-age story, although it is not necessary; and (4) the changes that signify a boy's coming of age must happen within the defined borders of an individual narrative for it to be considered a coming-of-age story. Additional groundwork essential to the project was provided by the summary in chapters 1 and 2 of the depiction of biblical hegemonic masculinity and how it differs from the depiction of boyhood in the HB. With these necessary methodological and contextual foundations in place, the project achieved its foremost purpose by locating five narratives that tell the story of a boy's successful transition to manhood and two examples of the failure to do so.

The book also had two secondary goals. The first was to consider how the coming-of-age theme is employed by biblical narrators and redactors to highlight important messages, themes, and transitions in the historical narratives of the HB. The Samson cycle provided the most obvious example of how the coming-of-age theme (more specifically, its inverse in the failure-to-come-of-age theme) was used in this way. Samson's status as a liminal man-child typifies the political predicament of Israel in the time of the judges in several ways, thereby justifying its placement by DtrH at a prominent position at the end of the cycle of major judges. Moreover, both the Jether and Samson stories function as counterpoints to the successful coming of age of David in 1 Sam 17. The relationship between these two tales of failing to come of age and David's successful maturation signifies the transition of Israel from immaturity to nationhood and political power.

The analysis revealed other examples in which the narrator calls attention to broader themes and transitions through coming-of-age stories. For example, Samuel's successful maturation functions as an important aspect of the extended comparison between him and Eli's sons, a comparison that heralds the establishment of a new system of leadership under Samuel and the death of the old order under the Elides. Finally, the two stories of Solomon's coming of age in 1 Kgs 1–2 and 1 Kgs 3 mark a significant transition in the history of Israel. The retrospective nature of 1 Kgs 2, in which Solomon matures like his father David, with displays of strength and cunning, signals its close connection with the David narratives and their militaristic ethos. The Gibeon story in 1 Kgs 3 instead looks forward to Solomon's peaceful reign, since here Solomon's maturation is not achieved through the exertion of his power and political machinations against other men but rather is accomplished by Yhwh bestowing certain manly qualities (judicial wisdom, riches, and honor) on the young man.

The other secondary objective of this project was to use coming-of-age stories as a window into biblical masculinity, a hermeneutical choice justified by the connection between the two subjects explored in the book's Introduction. To this point, the discussion of what maturation tales can tell us about biblical views of masculinity has remained peripheral, confined to occasional comments comparing the understanding of masculinity in one coming-of-age story with that of one or at most two other stories. In this concluding chapter, in contrast, this subject will receive more direct attention. First, a review of the characteristics of idealized manhood offered in each story is offered, and the contrast between the masculinity advocated in one set of stories with that of another set is discussed. Then, by way of conclusion, I offer a hypothesis for the possible source of this difference, and how it relates to the varying historical contexts in which these texts were composed.

Summary and Comparison of Images of Masculinity in Biblical Coming-of-Age Narratives

The male coming-of-age stories identified and examined in this book by definition tell the tale of a boy becoming a man, or failing to make that transition in two cases. The kind of man that the main characters of these stories become (or attempt to become), however, is not the same in each story. Two stories in particular—the maturation tales of Samuel at Shiloh in 1 Sam 3 and Solomon at Gibeon in 1 Kgs 3—seem to understand manhood, and what it takes to transition from boyhood to manhood, in very different ways from the other five, which themselves share a number of similarities in their description of idealized masculinity. A brief review of these narratives clarifies the similarities in the description of masculinity shared by the majority of these stories and the differences from this characterization of manhood present in the other two.

The first coming-of-age stories examined in this book (in chapter 3) also come first in the biblical canon: the stories of Moses and Samuel's maturation. Moses's transition to manhood is presented in Exod 2, and the coming-of-age theme is emphasized primarily through Moses's performance of a series of "manly" actions in the second scene of Exod 2 (vv. 11–22). These actions demonstrate the qualities of strength, wisdom, courage, and kinship solidarity. The story also tells of his marriage and the birth of his firstborn son. Samuel's coming of age is highlighted by the structure of his childhood narrative in 1 Sam 1–3 and by the repetition of certain *Leitworte* (e.g., the frequent use of נַעַר to describe Samuel prior to his first prophetic act and the threefold repetition of גדל signaling the completion of his growth). Samuel's transition from social timidity and powerlessness to a position of authority is the most significant change to the character signifying his maturation. The other major change to Samuel in 1 Sam 3—his ability to discern Yhwh's word—owes more to the genre of 1 Sam 3 as a call narrative than it does to the coming-of-age theme. Unlike in Moses's maturation story, Samuel's idyllic coming of age lacks any bold demonstration of valor or force, and is in fact facilitated by the authoritative mentor figures of Yhwh and Eli.

The coming-of-age stories of two royal figures—David and Solomon—were discussed in Chapter 4. David, who begins 1 Sam 17 described as a boy, transitions out of this boyishness through his display of strength and his defense of Israel's honor by defeating Goliath—a transition emphasized by the reference to David as an עֶלֶם at the story's end. Moreover, David ensures his final transition to manhood by securing a marriage for himself. The presence of the tripartite rite-of-passage schema (separation-marginality-reintegration) in this story further helps to identify 1 Sam 17 as David's coming of age.

Solomon's coming of age is narrated in two versions: one in 1 Kgs 1–2 (the conclusion of the Succession Narrative) and the other in 1 Kgs 3 (the scene at Gibeon in which Solomon asks for and receives wisdom from Yhwh). The former shares many features with David's maturation tale in 1 Sam 17. Both stress the display of strength through bellicose force as an important marker of masculinity, along with marriage, wisdom, the defense of honor, and kinship solidarity. In contrast, 1 Kgs 3 depicts Solomon's coming of age without violence. Moreover, in this version Solomon is not compelled to assert his masculine qualities to demonstrate maturation because the qualities of manhood (which in this narrative include wisdom as judicial acumen, riches, and honor) are given to him at once by Yhwh.

Chapter 5 demonstrates that the coming-of-age theme is not limited to stories of successful maturation to manhood but also includes narratives that can be read as inversions of the theme—that is, as tales of failing to come of age. Two examples were discussed: the brief Jether narrative in Judg 8, and in the longer Samson cycle in Judg 13–16. The former tells of Jether's failure to do the manly deeds of using violence against other men on the battlefield and defending family honor and solidarity. Similarly, Samson is depicted as a man-child: a figure who combines features of manhood with those of boy-hood, and who appears to be a perpetually liminal character caught at the border between these two statuses.

This review of the case studies at the center of this book shows that several of the stories concerned with male maturation share a common understand-ing of the essential features of manhood, an understanding that reflects the same views of hegemonic masculinity present in other texts in the HB, as outlined in Chapter 1. The tales of the successful maturation of Moses in Exod 2, David in 1 Sam 17, and Solomon in 1 Kgs 1–2 each stress strength, wisdom, honor, solidarity, fertility, and marriage as essential to ideal masculinity—as does the HB in general. Even the stories describing the fail-ure to come of age reflect this understanding of masculinity, as Jether's fail-ure to mature is marked by his inability to show bellicose strength and to defend his family's honor, both values generally associated with masculinity throughout the HB. Similarly, Samson's liminal status as a man-child is in-dicated by his possession of some of these masculine characteristics (most notably strength, but also rhetorical skill—a function of wisdom) but lack of others (self-control, kinship solidarity, marriage, and children).

In contrast, the image of masculinity offered in the maturation tales of Solomon in 1 Kgs 3 and Samuel in 1 Sam 3 differs from the standard hege-monic masculinity in the HB. Most significantly, the display of physical and often violent force is absent in these stories and the transition to man-hood is more a passive process. The status of both Samuel and Solomon as men is given to them by Yhwh, who guides Samuel's growth (1 Sam 2:21b) and ends his boyish social powerlessness by establishing and sustaining him in his office as prophet (3:19–20), just as the deity bestows Solomon's manly authority upon him in an instant at Gibeon (1 Kgs 3:12–14). Further-more, while values like honor, social authority, and wisdom are present (see 1 Kgs 3:13, 1 Sam 3:19–4:1a; 1 Kgs 9–12, respectively) they are not displayed by the boy protagonists as signs of maturation but rather are given to them by Yhwh. Thus, these narratives do not depict a boy's agonistic effort to prove his manhood, as do the other coming-of-age stories, and the men that Samuel and Solomon become by the conclusion of their maturation stories do not correspond to the model of idealized masculinity found in the other stories.

Explaining the Differing Portraits of Masculinity in Biblical Coming-of-Age Narratives: A Hypothesis

It is not at all surprising that the understanding of ideal manhood would be occasionally inconsistent throughout these tales of biblical male maturation. Indeed, as modern scholars of masculinity have repeatedly shown, hegemonic masculinity is ever-evolving, often in response to alternative understandings of manhood. What is unexpected, however, is that the two coming-of-age stories that evidence the most difference from the articulation of hegemonic masculinity found in general throughout the HB (Samuel's coming of age in 1 Sam 3 and Solomon's in 1 Kgs 3) would themselves be so similar in the ways that they diverge from the norm, as just demonstrated. This suggests the possibility that these two stories may be the work of the same hand. Postulating one author for both stories also explains the high amount of congruencies between the stories other than their similar views on manhood and maturation, such as their practically identical settings (both are nighttime revelations where their protagonist sleeps alone in a shrine) and their comparable plots (both feature a theophany to an individual that provides him with essential skills for his role as a leader in Israel).

I have briefly noted in the preceding chapters, based on the work of several scholars, that DtrH may be the author behind both 1 Sam 3 and 1 Kgs 3.[1] To be sure, source attribution of this kind is notoriously speculative work, and the debate on the existence and possible historical context of a Deuteronomistic Historian or Historians continues in earnest today just as it did when Noth initially proposed his theory.[2] Still, the similarities between 1 Sam 3 and 1 Kgs 3, together with the number of scholars who have separately ascribed these narratives to DtrH, make it well worth considering the possibility that DtrH has shaped both stories, and that therefore a profile of DtrH's views of masculinity may be created using 1 Sam 3 and 1 Kgs 3 as primary evidence.

My reconstruction of the *Sitz im Leben* for DtrH's composition of these two stories is based on Römer's recent synthesis of European and North American scholarship on the Deuteronomistic History. Römer envisions the growth of the Deuteronomistic History as a three-stage process: a first edition in the seventh century B.C.E. that served primarily as Josianic propaganda; a second edition compiled during the exilic period and functioning as "crisis literature" attempting to rationalize the catastrophe of Judah's collapse; and a third minor edition in the Persian Period adding only material pertaining to strict monotheism, segregation of Israelites from other peoples, and other Golah concerns such as the boundaries of the land of Israel and the centrality of public Torah reading and study.

To which of these three editions of the Deuteronomistic History would each of the narratives examined above belong? In my judgment, the long-standing scholarly consensus of viewing the History of David's Rise and the Succession Narrative as pre-Deuteronomistic sources argues for placing 1 Sam 17 and 1 Kgs 1–2 in Römer's earliest edition of the Deuteronomistic History. Next, the heavy folkloric coloring of the Samson and Jether narratives along with their concern with pre-exilic Israelite enemies like the Philistines and Midianites suggests that these also belong to this edition. Similarly, while not a part of the Deuteronomistic History proper, recent work summarized by Römer argues that Exod 2 belongs to a seventh-century *vita Mosis* that was influential for the original seventh-century Deuteronomists, and therefore it too is a pre-exilic source.[3]

In contrast to these older sources, the stories of Samuel and Solomon's maturation in 1 Sam 3 and 1 Kgs 3 would belong instead to the second, exilic edition of the Deuteronomistic History. Indeed, Römer concurs that 1 Sam 3 seems to demand an exilic context, given its concern with the "replacement of the temple by the prophetic word as a medium of access to the divine will."[4] Römer does not, however, place the composition/significant redaction of 1 Kgs 3 in this later edition, because he believes it bears many similarities to the "wise king" motif in ancient Near Eastern royal ideology. Römer neglects the congruencies noted above that would suggest the same authorship for both 1 Kgs 3 and 1 Sam 3, but also, by assigning 1 Kgs 3 to the earlier edition, he contradicts his own claim elsewhere in his chapter on the seventh-century edition that Assyrian influence accounts for most of the edition's militarism and nationalism.[5] Solomon's maturation in 1 Kgs 3 notably lacks these two qualities—recall that the life of Solomon's enemies is conspicuously absent from the list of things Yhwh will grant the new king—thus an Assyrian context seems unlikely.

If the DtrH who is behind both 1 Sam 3 and 1 Kgs 3 can be historically located in the exilic period, his views on masculinity—that differ to such a great extent from other earlier stories of coming of age and from the overall construction of masculinity in the majority of the HB—can arguably be traced to this unique social and historical context. An understanding of masculinity premised on qualities like strength through physical force and the combative defense of honor like that found in earlier maturation narratives would not be appropriate for elite Judean/Jewish men in an exilic context because their governance and the monopoly of force were no longer in their control. Instead, qualities like knowledge of and a relationship with Yhwh, wisdom reckoned more as legal or intellectual insight and less as tactical cunning, and honor disassociated from bellicosity became the prized qualities for manhood. This construction of masculinity sees manhood as something that comes from Yhwh only, and not something one achieves through one's own display of power or cunning in competition against other men. DtrH, therefore, uses the coming-of-age stories of Samuel at Shiloh and Solomon at Gibeon to argue for a reimagining of what it means to be a man in the context of exile.

In sum, by examining biblical coming-of-age narratives and the ways that they understand manhood and how one becomes a man, a diachronic change can be identified in Israelite views of masculinity. The exilic context of DtrH engendered a reconsideration of manhood that diminished certain qualities previously central to Israelite masculinity, most notably strength as expressed through bellicose force.[6]

This book, then, has shown that the male coming-of-age theme so prevalent in world literature throughout history is also present in the collected literature of ancient Israel. The names of David, Solomon, Moses, and Samuel, therefore, can be added to the list of famed initiatory heroes that includes, among many others, Gilgamesh, Candide, and Holden Caulfield. Whenever and wherever there are boys who grow to become men—or men who remember their own transition to maturity—it seems that there too will be stories about that experience.

Are There Other Stories of Biblical Male Maturation?

In this book I have limited my scope to narratives that, in my judgment, undoubtedly describe the transition of a boy to manhood. To guide this endeavor, I identified four principles that ensured that the preceding discussion did not become weighed down by multiple attempts to demonstrate the coming-of-age theme when evidence for its presence was not readily apparent. Due to the strictures imposed by these principles, certain narratives that may appear to contain some elements of the coming-of-age theme have not been considered. In this Appendix, therefore, I will briefly address these stories and will explain why they were not included among the seven case studies in the main body of this book.

JACOB

Although many individual narratives comprise the Jacob cycle of Gen 25–36, none can definitively be identified as a coming-of-age story. Among the most significant reasons that I did not seek to make the case in this book for the existence of a Jacob maturation story is that immediately after Jacob and Esau's birth is narrated in Gen 25:25–26, a report of the boys' growth (גדל) is given and they are referred to as men: Jacob as a "quiet man" (אִישׁ תָּם) and Esau as a "man of the field" (אִישׁ שָׂדֶה; Gen 25:27). Certainly, at this point in the cycle Jacob is still far from being representative of the hegemonic masculine ideal (for example, he is not yet married, has no children, and accomplishes his goals through trickery rather than through more conventionally "manly" means), but presumably he is referred to as a "man" from the beginning of his adventures because he has at least reached the age of full physical/mental development and legal majority.

One could argue that the description of Jacob in Gen 25:27 as a "quiet man" (אִישׁ תָּם) is more concerned with the overall assessment of Jacob in the stories to come as opposed to an accurate description of his age at this point, and therefore this is not a sufficient reason to disqualify any of the following pericopes as potential coming-of-age stories. This objection is potentially valid; however, one is at pains to identify *any* narrative in the Jacob cycle in which the protagonist enters the story as a boy, displays qualities associated with manhood, and emerges at the end of the story as a man.

Jacob does experience major transformative events in his life, such as in his dream vision at Bethel in Gen 28 and his struggle with the mysterious figure at the Jabbok in Gen 32, but neither of these stories views Jacob's resultant transformation through the lens of his development from boyhood to manhood. Instead, the Bethel story is concerned with the inauguration of Jacob's special relationship with Yhwh. No new qualities are acquired here that are associated with manhood and maturation, and in fact Jacob's more "unmanly" qualities, such as his tricksterism, do not change as a result of this encounter (see, e.g., his scheme a few chapters later to increase his flocks; Gen 30:31–43). The scene at the Jabbok, in contrast, *does* mark the end of Jacob's trickster ways, and after this point he more embodies normative masculinity. But by this point in his life, Jacob has reached an advanced age, is married, and has fathered several children, each of which militates against this story being considered Jacob's coming-of-age narrative.[1] Nor can Jacob's description prior to Gen 32 be viewed as an example of the failure-to-come-of-age theme, because there are simply too many indicators of his manhood in the preceding chapters. Indeed, Jacob changes significantly at the Jabbok, and this change brings him more in line with hegemonic biblical masculinity; however, he is still clearly reckoned a man before this time—but perhaps not an ideal one.

JOSEPH

When Joseph is introduced in Gen 37:2, his age is specified as seventeen. One might expect, then, that one of the early scenes in the Joseph novella (Gen 37–50) would describe the transition of this character from boyhood to manhood. The story that immediately follows the report of his age in Gen 37—that of his being overpowered by his older brothers and sold into slavery—does not, however, depict the maturation of Joseph. Instead, throughout the story he is described with *childlike* qualities. He rashly tells his brothers and father of his dreams that, in thinly veiled symbolism, depict them bowing to him (Gen 37:1–11). Furthermore, he seems powerless to defend himself against his brothers when they attack him (Gen 37:23–25).

A more likely candidate for Joseph's coming-of-age story would be that of his public display of the manly quality of insight (בין; Gen 41:33, 39) before Pharaoh, a story that additionally shows Pharaoh publically proclaiming Joseph as a "man"

(אִישׁ; Gen 41:38). Still, a key factor makes it difficult to consider Gen 41 as a maturation tale: by the time of this narrative, Joseph is thirty years old (Gen 41:46), which
simply makes him too old for such a story. Indeed, Joseph has even been referred to
as a man (אִישׁ) well before this time: in Gen 39:2, when he is a servant in Potiphar's
house. Joseph's maturation, therefore, is not recounted in the HB, but would seem
to occur "offstage" in the intervening time between when he is sold by his brothers
and when he enters Potiphar's service.

SAUL

The story of Saul's anointing as king by Samuel in 1 Sam 9–10 might at first glance
appear to be a good candidate for consideration as a biblical coming-of-age story. The
main argument in the story's favor is that Saul begins the narrative referred to as a
young man (בָּחוּר; 1 Sam 9:2), but the narrator makes a terminological switch in the
middle of the narrative and begins to refer to Saul as a man (אִישׁ; 1 Sam 9:16, 17). Such
a terminological shift is often the most apparent signal of the presence of the coming-
of-age theme in the HB. However, in Saul's case, this terminological shift is not preceded by any noticeable change in his character that justifies his new title. Saul has
not displayed any of the characteristics of manhood nor have any of these characteristics been bestowed on him by Yhwh between when the narrator refers to him as a
young man (v. 2) and when the shift to adult terminology takes place in v. 16. Just as
he appears naïve and overwhelmed by circumstances before this shift (e.g., vv. 4–6),
so too does he appear afterwards (v. 21)—indeed, this quality seems to define Saul's
characterization throughout the remainder of his life (e.g., 1 Sam 15:17, 24–25).

Moreover, it is not entirely clear that when the term בָּחוּר is applied to Saul in 1
Sam 9:2 it should be translated as "young man." Instead, the usage of the passive
participle of בחר here may be understood as adjectival (as in, for example, Judg
20:15), not substantival. In other words, this term could refer to Saul's impressive
physique (i.e., he is "choice"), a translational option supported by the term's placement alongside another adjective that highlights Saul's appearance, טוֹב. Indeed,
NAS chooses to translate this section of 9:2 as follows: "And he had a son named
Saul, a choice and handsome *man* . . ."

Thus, given the fact that no significant change takes place to Saul from the time
that he is referred to as a young man until when the narrator shifts to adult terminology to describe him—and that it is not entirely clear that when בָּחוּר is applied to
him the life-cycle meaning of the term is implied—insufficient evidence exists to
label 1 Sam 9–10:16 a coming-of-age tale.

JEREMIAH

Certain features of Jeremiah's call narrative in Jer 1 suggest that this story may be
viewed as a maturation story. First, Jeremiah self-identifies as a "boy" (נַעַר; Jer 1:6)

who does not know how to speak. Moreover, in the course of this pericope Jeremiah acquires rhetorical skill (v. 7), fearlessness (v. 8), and strength (v. 18) from the Lord, all qualities associated with manhood. In some ways, then, Jeremiah 1 seems to be a hybrid pericope, thematically concerned with both a prophet's call and a boy's coming of age—much like 1 Sam 3. The reason for its exclusion from consideration in the preceding chapters, however, is due to the fact that there is less evidence for Jeremiah's youth at the pericope's beginning than there was with any of the other stories that were considered in the main body of the book. In each of the seven main case studies of male coming of age, the youthfulness of the protagonist at the story's beginning was heavily emphasized in order to draw attention to his transformation into manhood throughout the story, but in Jer 1 the only indication we have of Jeremiah's youth is his self-identification. In fact, since Jeremiah is already considered both a priest (Jer 1:1) and a prophet (1:5) before this self-identification, it is likely that Jeremiah's claim that he is a נַעַר is a rhetorical device to emphasize his reluctance to take on the prophetic office, a standard trope in such call narratives.

DANIEL

The story of Daniel, his companions, and their preparation for service in Nebuchadnezzar's court in Dan 1 contains elements of the coming-of-age theme, but that theme is not fully fleshed out, therefore it was not considered in the preceding chapters. In this tale, Daniel and his fellow Judahite exiles Hananiah, Mishael, and Azariah—each referred to as boys (יְלָדִים; Dan 1:4, 10, 13, 15, 17)—refuse to eat from the king's ration of wine and meat given to the youths in training for the king's service, lest they "defile themselves" (Hithpael of גאל; Dan 1:8). Instead, they negotiate with the guard assigned to them to secretly allow them to eat only vegetables. The guard agrees, but only if it will not become evident to his superiors that these boys are eating different food than the others. After a ten-day test of eating these vegetarian rations, not only do Daniel and his friends show no sign of their comparatively meager rations, but they in fact seem more fit and healthy than their non-Judahite peers. The story concludes with Daniel and his friends being presented to Nebuchadnezzar, who appoints them among his advisers (i.e., his "magicians and enchanters;" Dan 1:20), and their exceptional wisdom (חָכְמָה) and insight (בִּינָה) is noted.

In the course of this narrative, therefore, a group of boys perform an act of resistance against their imperial overlords that culminates in their being recognized for their wisdom and insight, qualities closely associated with biblical masculinity. This would seem at first to be an appropriate case study for the main chapters of this book, and indeed one with interesting implications for the diachronic development of Jewish masculinity, showing a growing emphasis on secret acts of resistance as opposed to the former preference for open acts of force that demonstrate manliness.

The primary purpose for excluding it from consideration, however, is that the connection between their act of resistance and their eventual posting in the king's court is not so clearly drawn. In fact, a good deal of time passes—likely three years—between their act of resistance as boys and their presentation to Nebuchadnezzar (see Dan 1:5, 18). Moreover, the protagonists' youth is not as clearly emphasized at the story's beginning as in the case studies I considered in the book. They are referred to as יְלָדִים, but they do not display any qualities that are especially boyish, thus a clear contrast cannot be made between their depiction at the beginning of the story and its conclusion. Finally, there is no terminological shift evident within the story to clearly mark their transition to manhood. In fact, the first time Daniel is referred to explicitly as a "man" (גְּבַר) is much later, in Dan 2:25. For these reasons, and since my project was limited to only those cases where the coming-of-age theme could be identified without doubt, I ultimately excluded the narrative of Dan 1 from the discussion in the main body of the book.

Notes

INTRODUCTION

1. In contrast to these public rituals for groups of boys, the rites that accompany a girl's maturation in many societies are private and individual. See Bruce Lincoln, *Emerging from the Chrysalis: Rituals of Women's Initiation* (Oxford: Oxford University Press, 1991), 91–109.

2. See, e.g., R. W. Connell, *Masculinities* (Cambridge and Oxford: Polity Press, 1995), 7–9; Stephen M. Whitehead, *Men and Masculinities: Key Themes and New Directions* (Cambridge and Oxford: Polity Press, 2002), 23–26; and Rachel Adams and David Savran, *The Masculinity Studies Reader* (Malden, MA: Blackwell, 2002), 9–13.

3. This notion of the presence of both masculinity and femininity within every individual was also discussed by Jung, who argued that for men a balance exists between the masculine "persona" (the public self shaped by social interactions) and the female "anima" (the unconscious self). See Connell, *Masculinities*, 12–14.

4. The recognition of Freud as an important predecessor of masculinity studies is likely because of the indebtedness of scholars of masculinity to second-wave feminism, which took a much more positive view of Freudian thought than did first-wave feminism. See Whitehead, *Men and Masculinities*, 23–33.

5. Sex-role theory is most often viewed as an outgrowth of the work of Talcott Parsons, particularly his notions of functionalism and the socialization of individuals to serve society's needs. See the discussion of sex-role theory in Whitehead, *Men and Masculinities*, 19–23.

6. Butler argues that the biological sexual binary of male and female may itself be "the effect of the apparatus of cultural construction designated by *gender.*" See Judith Butler, *Gender Trouble: Feminism and the Subversion of Identity* (2d ed.; New York and London: Routledge, 1999), 11.

7. See Tim Carrigan, Bob Connell, and John Lee, "Toward a New Sociology of Masculinity," in Adams and Savran, *Masculinity Studies Reader*, 107; repr. from *Theory and Society* 14 (1985). See also Connell, *Masculinities*, 21–30.

8. See Carrigan, Connell, and Lee, "Toward a New Sociology," 107. See also Whitehead, *Men and Masculinities*, 22.

9. For a discussion of the spectrum of biological sexual features that fall between the poles of male and female, see Anne Fausto-Sterling, *Sexing the Body: Gender Politics and the Construction of Sexuality* (New York: Basic Books, 2000), 1–45.

10. See Arthur Brittan, *Masculinity and Power* (Oxford and New York: Blackwell, 1989), 19–24. See also Michael S. Kimmel, *The Gendered Society* (3d ed.; Oxford: Oxford University Press, 2008), 92–97.

11. Carrigan, Connell, and Lee, "Toward a New Sociology," 112.

12. See Connell, *Masculinities*, 185–203.

13. Carrigan, Connell, and Lee, "Toward a New Sociology," 113. Note that while there are similarities between hegemonic masculinity and patriarchy, the two are not to be equated. According to Whitehead (*Men and Masculinities*, 90): "hegemonic masculinity differs from patriarchy in that there is less of an essentialist assumption about the outcome or conditions under which this gender power play is experienced and enacted. For while the fundamental premise remains that male power is a 'hegemonic project' . . . embedded in ideological and material structures, there is space for ambiguity—and change."

14. So Connell, *Masculinities*, 76–86.

15. Ibid., 79. According to Connell, homosexual masculinities are the most obvious example of subordinated masculinity in modern Western society, however any other masculinity that is seen as too feminine is included, such as the "wimp, milksop, nerd . . . mother's boy . . . geek . . . and so on" (ibid.).

16. Ibid., 80–81. Presumably this list of the causes for marginalization of a particular articulation of masculinity could include any affiliation or identity that differs from the authoritative hegemonic ideal, such as one's religious affiliation. However, Connell does not specifically mention religion as a factor in marginalization.

17. An element of the original formulation of the concept of hegemonic masculinity that has received criticism is that a society only has one conception of hegemonic masculinity at a time. Both Margaret Wetherell and Nigel Edley ("Negotiating Hegemonic Masculinity: Imaginary Positions and Psycho-Discursive Practices," *Feminism and Psychology* 9 [1999]:335–56) and Tony Jefferson ("Subordinating Hegemonic Masculinity," *Theoretical Criminology* 6 [2002]: 63–88) argue that more than one idealized form of masculinity may be present within a society at a given time, thus it is more accurate to speak of plural hegemonic *masculinities* rather than a singular hegemonic masculinity. In response, Connell (together with James W. Messerschmidt, "Hegemonic

Masculinity: Rethinking the Concept," *Gender and Society* 19 [2005]: 845) has accepted that multiple varieties of masculinity may be competing for hegemony at a particular time, but he notes that it is important to remember that these varieties are competing for a position atop the masculine hierarchy that only has room for one dominant paradigm: "Whatever the empirical diversity of masculinities, the contestation for hegemony implies that gender hierarchy does not have multiple niches at the top."

Another common critique is that the relationship between hegemonic and subordinate/marginalized masculinities is more complex than simply one of oppression and submission. Demetrakis Z. Demetriou ("Connell's Concept of Hegemonic Masculinity: A Critique," *Theory and Society* 30 [2001]:346–47)asserts that, in fact, hegemonic masculinities can and often do incorporate elements of these other masculinities, which suggests the potential for subordinate and marginalized masculinities to influence the hegemonic form of masculinity in their culture. See also Connell and Messerschmidt, "Hegemonic Masculinity," 838–39.

18. For a summary of the impact of masculinity studies on New Testament scholarship, see Stephen D. Moore and Janice Capel Anderson, eds., *New Testament Masculinities* (SemeiaSt 45; Atlanta: Society of Biblical Literature, 2003), 4–16. For a more recent discussion of the question, see Brittany E. Wilson, *Unmanly Men: Refigurations of Masculinity in Luke-Acts* (Oxford: Oxford University Press, 2015).

19. David J. A. Clines, "David the Man: The Construction of Masculinity in the Hebrew Bible," in *Interested Parties: The Ideology of Writers and Readers of the Hebrew Bible* (ed. David Clines; JSOTSup 205; Sheffield: Sheffield Academic Press, 1995), 216–27.It should be noted that while Clines does not use the term "hegemonic masculinity" in this work, his description of the "components of masculinity" found in the David story that reflect the "cultural norms" of the story's author (ibid., 216) essentially function as a description of the hegemonic masculinity dominant at the time of the story's composition.

20. Susan E. Haddox, "Favoured Sons and Subordinate Masculinities," in *Men and Masculinity in the Hebrew Bible and Beyond* (ed. Ovidiu Creangă; The Bible in the Modern World 33; Sheffield: Sheffield Phoenix, 2010), 15–16. See also Brian Charles DiPalma, "De/Constructing Masculinity in Exodus 1–4," in Creangă, *Men and Masculinity,* 36–51.DiPalma argues that in the narratives of Moses's youth in Exod 2, the hegemonic masculinity represented by Pharaoh is undercut, and Moses's character deconstructs the values of this hegemonic masculinity by embodying opposite values.

21. Hilary Lipka, "Masculinities in Proverbs: An Alternative to the Hegemonic Ideal," in *Biblical Masculinities Foregrounded* (eds. Ovidiu Creangă and Peter-Ben Smit; Hebrew Bible Monographs 62; Sheffield: Sheffield Phoenix, 2014), 86–103.The manhood advocated by Proverbs, according to Lipka, prizes

wisdom and diplomacy over demonstrations of force and emerged as the hegemonic ideal in Israel in the historical context of colonization and diaspora. Lipka's reflections are inspired by Buchbinder's notion of "emergent masculinities": those masculinities that begin as marginalized or subordinate, but eventually rise to the position of hegemony. See David Buchbinder, *Studying Men and Masculinities* (London: Routledge, 2012), 158–79.

22. Roland Boer, "Of Fine Wine, Incense, and Spices: the Unstable Masculine Hegemony of the Books of Chronicles," in Creangă, *Men and Masculinity*, 20–33. Boer (ibid., 30) writes that Chronicles vacillates between a "comic machismo" that reflects an extreme version of the hegemonic masculine ideal and the less manly (at least from the perspective of hegemonic masculinity) pursuits of "interior design . . . temple organization and decoration."

23. The term "cultural performance" is Judith Butler's, who adds that gender is "an identity instituted through a stylized repetition of acts." See Butler, "Performative Acts and Gender Constitution: An Essay in Phenomenology and Feminist Theory," in *Performing Feminisms: Feminist Critical Theory and Theater* (ed. Sue-Ellen Case; Baltimore: Johns Hopkins University Press, 1990), 270.

24. By affirming that masculinity is constructed vis-à-vis femininity, scholars of biblical manhood echo a repeated claim in masculinity studies. Connell (*Masculinities*, 68) summarizes this thought succinctly: "masculinity does not exist except in contrast to femininity." Connell adds that subordinated masculinities are often rejected by hegemonic masculinity precisely because of their association with femininity, the binary opposite of true manhood in the view of the hegemonic ideal (ibid., 79). Brittan (*Masculinity and Power*, 3) similarly writes that "masculinity . . . does not exist in isolation from femininity—it will always be an expression of the current image that men have of themselves in relation to women." See also Whitehead, *Men and Masculinities*, 34.

25. Note, for example, that the most recent publication on the subject, Ovidiu Creangă and Peter-Ben Smit's 2014 edited volume *Biblical Masculinities Foregrounded*, begins with a quote from Björn Krondorfer arguing that "men become men by articulating their distinctiveness from women" (from Creangă's "Introduction," 3).

26. See the related work of Jessica Benjamin (*The Bonds of Love* [New York: Pantheon, 1984]), Dorothy Dinnerstein (*The Mermaid and the Minotaur* [New York: Harper and Row, 1977]),and Lilian Rubin (*Intimate Strangers* [New York: Harper and Row, 1983]).

27. This process is referred to by Margaret Mahler as "separation-individuation." See Margaret Mahler, Fred Pine, and Anni Bergman, *The Psychological Birth of the Human Infant: Symbiosis and Individuation* (New York: Basic Books, 1975), 3.

28. This understanding of male gender identity as a secondary event, following a primary female identification, contradicts Freud's claim that infant males possess male gender identity from birth, which results in the Oedipal attraction to the mother and fear of the father. Because of their conviction that the important work of gender identity happens in infancy, but their simultaneous rejection of Freud's analysis of this identity formation, Chodorow and others like her are referred to as "Neo-Freudians." See David D. Gilmore, *Manhood in the Making: Cultural Concepts of Masculinity* (New Haven: Yale University Press, 1990), 26–29.

29. Nancy Chodorow, "Family Structure and Feminine Personality" in *Woman, Culture, and Society* (ed. Michelle Z. Rosaldo and Louise Lamphere; Stanford: Stanford University Press, 1974), 50. See also Robert Stoller, "Facts and Fancies: An Examination of Freud's Concept of Bisexuality," in *Women and Analysis: Dialogues on Psychoanalytic Views of Femininity* (ed. Jean Strouse; New York: Dell, 1974), 358.

30. Roy Schafer, "Men Who Struggle Against Sentimentality," in *The Psychology of Men: New Psychoanalytic Perspectives* (ed. Gerald I. Fogel, Frederick M. Lane, and Roy S. Liebert; New York: Basic Books, 1986), 100.

31. Gilbert H. Herdt, *Guardians of the Flutes: Idioms of Masculinity* (New York: McGraw-Hill, 1981), 203–54.

32. Robert J. Stoller and Gilbert H. Herdt, "The Development of Masculinity: A Cross-Cultural Contribution," *Journal of the American Psychoanalytic Association* 30 (1982), 47.

33. Gilmore, *Manhood in the Making*, 29.

34. Arnold van Gennep, *The Rites of Passage* (trans. Monika B. Vizedom and Gabrielle L. Caffee; Chicago: University of Chicago Press, 1960).

35. Van Gennep emphasizes the distinction between *social* and *physiological* puberty. For example, rites of passage that initiate a boy into manhood only mark social puberty, and thus can take place well before or after actual physiological puberty. The rites simply emphasize that in his society's eyes the boy has become a man, regardless of whether he has, for instance, grown facial hair or developed a more defined musculature (ibid., 65–66).

36. Ibid., 65–115.

37. Van Gennep was particularly interested in male puberty rites, as can be seen in the high percentage of male-only puberty rites he discusses. Of the 25 examples of initiation rites, 19 are male-only; four are for both males and females; and only two are female-only.

38. Ibid., 11. Van Gennep originally conceived of this structure as describing three different kinds of rituals that together form the rites of passage. Since van Gennep's time it is more common to classify these three kinds of rites as elements of a single ritual, consisting of a separation phase, a marginal phase,

and a reintegration phase. See Alan Barnard and Jonathan Spencer, "Rites of Passage," in *The Routledge Encyclopedia of Social and Cultural Anthropology* (2d ed.; London and New York: Routledge, 2010), 616.

39. This describes a stereotypical coming-of-age rite. For specific examples, see van Gennep, *Rites*, 65–116. For a more recent collection of examples, see Glen Weisfield, "Puberty Rites as Clues to the Nature of Human Adolescence," *Cross-Cultural Research* 31 (1997), 32–45.

40. For a recent appraisal of van Gennep's enduring legacy, see Perrti J. Anttonen, "The Rites of Passage Revisited: A New Look at van Gennep's Theory of the Ritual Process and its Application in the Study of Finnish-Karelian Wedding Rituals," in *Folklore: Critical Concepts in Literary and Cultural Studies; Volume III: The Genres of Folklore* (ed. Alan Dundes; New York: Routledge, 2005), 178–92; repr. from *Temenos: Studies in Comparative Religion* 28 (1992): 15–52.

41. Turner observed that when conflicts erupted among the Ndembu, they were accompanied by a four-stage process that addressed and resolved these conflicts, a process he referred to as a "social drama." Throughout the four stages of the social drama (breach, crisis, redressive action, and reintegration), individual rituals moved the process along. See Victor W. Turner, Drama, Fields and Metaphors: Symbolic Action in Human Society (Ithaca: Cornell University Press, 1974), 33, 38–41. Turner recognized that not only did the rituals performed in each stage of these social dramas follow van Gennep's tripartite model of rites of passage, but also the entire social drama itself followed this schema. His "breach" stage coincided with van Gennep's "separation" phase; his "crisis" and "redressive action" stages paralleled van Gennep's "liminal" phase; and his "reintegration" stage reflected van Gennep's phase of the same name. See Langdon Elsbree, *Ritual Passages and Narrative Structures* (New York: Peter Lang, 1991), 156–57.

42. Victor W. Turner, *The Drums of Affliction: A Study of Religious Processes among the Ndembu of Zambia* (Oxford: Oxford University Press, 1968; repr. Ithaca: Cornell University Press, 1981), 2.

43. Robert A. Segal, "Victor Turner's Theory of Ritual," *Zygon: Journal of Religion and Science* 18 (1983): 330.

44. See, e.g., Victor W. Turner, "An Anthropological Approach to the Icelandic Saga," in *Translation of Culture: Essays to E. E. Evans-Pritchard* (ed. Thomas O. Beidelman; London: Tavistock Publications, 1971), 349–74. Here Turner applies the notions of social dramas and the rites-of-passage schema to the traditional sagas of Iceland.

45. Victor W. Turner, "African Ritual and Western Literature: Is a Comparative Symbology Possible?" in *The Literature of Fact: Selected Papers from the English Institute* (ed. Angus Fletcher; English Institute Series; New York: Columbia University Press, 1976), 45–81.

46. Victor W. Turner, "Social Dramas and the Stories about Them," *Critical Inquiry* 7 (1980): 158. See also the work of Langdon Elsbree (*Ritual Passages,* 1), who appeals to the shared biogenetic origins of ritual and narrative in the activity and structure of the human brain as grounds for using rite-of-passage analysis in his reading of narratives.

47. Victor W. Turner, *The Ritual Process: Structure and Anti-Structure* (Ithaca: Cornell University Press, 1969; repr. New Brunswick, NJ: AldineTransaction, 2007), 96–97.

48. Turner, *Ritual Process,* 106–7.

49. See Victor W. Turner, "Myth and Symbol," *International Encyclopedia of the Social Sciences* 10: 580–81.

50. See Victor W. Turner, "Variations on a Theme of Liminality," in *Secular Ritual* (ed. Sally Falk Moore and Barbara G. Myerhoff; Aasen, The Netherlands: Van Gorcum, 1977), 52.

51. Jacob Milgrom's study of the priestly consecration ritual of Lev 8 is one of the few examples of rite-of-passage analysis of a text connected to an actual ritual practiced in ancient Israel. See Milgrom, "The Priestly Consecration Ritual (Leviticus 8): A Rite of Passage," in *Bits of Honey: Essays for Samson H. Levey* (ed. Stanley F. Chyet and David H. Ellenson; South Florida Studies in the History of Judaism 74; Atlanta: Scholars Press, 1993), 57–61.

52. Gregory Mobley, *Samson and the Liminal Hero in the Ancient Near East* (Library of Hebrew Bible/Old Testament Studies 453; New York: T&T Clark, 2006), 28. Mobley's reading provides important grounding for the analysis of the Samson narrative in Chapter 5.

53. Susan Ackerman, *When Heroes Love: The Ambiguity of Eros in the Stories of Gilgamesh and David* (New York: Columbia University Press, 2005).

54. Jeremy Hutton, "The Left Bank of the Jordan and the Rites of Passage: an Anthropological Interpretation of 2 Samuel XIX," *VT* 56 (2006): 470–84.

55. Respectively: Ronald S. Hendel, *The Epic of the Patriarch: The Jacob Cycle and the Narrative Traditions of Canaan and Israel* (HSM 42; Atlanta: Scholars Press, 1987),159; William H. C. Propp, *Exodus 1–18: A New Translation with Introduction and Commentary* (AB 2; New York: Doubleday, 1998), 239–40; Susan Tower Hollis, "The Woman in Ancient Examples of the Potiphar's Wife Motif, K2111," in *Gender and Difference in Ancient Israel* (ed. Peggy L. Day; Minneapolis: Fortress, 1989), 28–42; D. Alan Aycock, "The Fate of Lot's Wife," in *Structuralist Interpretations of Biblical Myth* (ed. Edmund Leach and D. Alan Aycock; Cambridge: Cambridge University Press, 1983), 116–17.

56. Ronald S. Hendel, "Sacrifice as a Cultural System: The Ritual Symbolism of Exodus 24, 3–8," *ZAW* 101 (1989): 375; Robert L. Cohn, *The Shape of Sacred Space: Four Biblical Studies* (AAR Studies in Religion 23; Chico, CA: Scholars Press, 1981),13; Shemaryahu Talmon, "The 'Desert Motif' in the Bible and in

Qumran Literature," in *Biblical Motifs: Origins and Transformations* (ed. Alexander Altmann; Cambridge, MA: Harvard University Press, 1966), 50, 54; and Propp, *Exodus 1–18*, 35–36.

57. An exception to this oversight is Propp, who briefly notes that the rite of passage that Israel undergoes in the wilderness can be compared to rites of male initiation in tribal cultures (*Exodus 1–18*, 35–36). He uses the same approach in his reading of Moses' experiences in Midian. I discuss the latter case in more detail on pp. 18–19. Since my project is focused on individual characters, I will not treat Propp's reading of Israel's collective coming of age in the wilderness in detail.

58. Of the Israelites in the wilderness. See Cohn, *Sacred Space*, 13.

59. Of the wilderness experience. See Talmon, "Desert Motif," 54.

60. Describing David's exile and return to Jerusalem. See Hutton, "Left Bank," 480–82.

61. Of Jacob at Bethel (Gen 28:10–22) and at the Jabbok (Gen 32:22–32). See Hendel, *Epic of the Patriarch*, 149–50, 159.

62. See, e.g., the reading of the *Epic of Gilgamesh* as a coming-of-age story by Thorkild Jacobsen (*The Treasures of Darkness* [New Haven: Yale University Press, 1976], 193–220)and Rivkah Harris (*Gender and Aging in Mesopotamia: The* Gilgamesh Epic *and Other Ancient Literature* [Norman, OK: University of Oklahoma Press, 2000], 32—49). In classical studies, the effort to read narratives through the lens of the theme of initiation began in earnest with the publication in 1968 of Pierre Vidal-Naquet's "Le chasseur nor et l'origine de l'ephébie athénienne" (*Annales, Economies, Sociétés, Civilisations* 23 [1968]: 947–64), which argued that the Greek myth of the duel between Melanthos and Xanthos was an initiatory myth connected with the Athenian institution of ephebeia (an institution designed for the military and cultural training of young men). After Vidal-Naquet, classicists began to identify more myths with initiatory themes that they claimed were connected to coming-of-age rites. For a recent review of this literature, see Fritz Graf, "Initiation: A Concept with a Troubled History," in *Initiation in Ancient Greek Rituals and Narratives: New Critical Perspectives* (ed. David B. Dodd and Christopher A. Faraone; New York: Routledge, 2003), 3–24.

63. In so doing, this project follows up on a suggestion by Susan Niditch (*Underdogs and Tricksters: A Prelude to Biblical Folklore* [San Francisco: Harper & Row, 1987], 22) that the rite-of-passage schema "may well be applicable to tales about maturation."

64. This is not to suggest that a narrator would not intentionally structure a larger, multi-episodic narrative according to a rite-of-passage schema. Indeed, the case made by several scholars for viewing Israel's wilderness experience in Exodus–Deuteronomy as a rite of passage is a compelling one. The purpose for

limiting the rite-of-passage schema to one narrative episode or pericope in this book is instead to ensure against its over-application.

65. The relative ease with which this can be done is demonstrated by Joseph Campbell, whose *The Hero with a Thousand Faces* (3d ed., Novato, Calif.: New World Library, 2008) argues that *all* myths, hero tales, and folk legends can be considered a representation of a universal "monomyth" that follows the schema of a rite of passage (ibid., 1–32).

66. The case studies of the coming-of-age theme where the rite-of-passage schema is completely absent are: Solomon's coming of age in 1 Kgs 1–2 (discussed in Chapter 4); Moses's in Exod 2 (see Chapter 3); Samuel's in 1 Sam 3 (see Chapter 3); and Jether's in Judg 8 (see Chapter 5). Those that do contain a fully realized rite of passage are David's coming of age in 1 Sam 17 (see Chapter 4) and Solomon's in 1 Kgs 3 (see Chapter 4). Samson's story of failing to come of age in Judg 13–16 (discussed in Chapter 5) makes use of the concept of liminality derived from the discussion of rites of passage.

67. Edward E. Evans-Pritchard, *The Nuer: A Description of the Modes of Livelihood and Political Institutions of a Nilotic People* (Oxford: Clarendon Press, 1940), 254.

68. Charles Piot, *Remotely Global: Village Modernity in West Africa* (Chicago: University of Chicago Press, 1999), 89–90.

69. Jean Sybil La Fontaine, *Initiation* (Manchester: Manchester University Press, 1986), 124.

70. Gilmore, *Manhood in the Making*, 126.

71. Jennifer Rohrer-Walsh, "Coming of Age in *The Prince of Egypt*," in *Screening Scripture: Intertextual Connections between Scripture and Film* (ed. George Aichele and Richard Walsh; Harrisburg, PA: Trinity Press International, 2002), 78. Of course what is "culturally acceptable" and valued may change over time, but as it does, so too do coming-of-age stories. See also Sarah Iles Johnston, "'Initiation' in Myth, 'Initiation' in Practice: The Homeric *Hymn to Hermes* and its Performative Context," in Dodd and Faraone, *Initiation*, 160–61. Johnston argues that the qualities of bravery, initiative, and physical strength demonstrated by the divine initiatory hero in the *Hymn to Hermes* aligned with the expectations of manhood in ancient Greece. The initiatory hero Hermes expresses these qualities in the hymn by going on his first cattle raid; however, Iles Johnston argues that "even in groups where boys did not practice cattle-raiding as part of their maturation process . . . the *myth* of the cattle raid would have remained meaningful so long as the qualities the raiders demonstrated continued to be among those that constituted manliness" (ibid., 161).

72. The most thorough treatment of female coming of age is provided by Peggy L. Day ("From the Child Is Born the Woman: The Story of Jephthah's Daughter,"

in Day, *Gender and Difference*, 58–74). Day reads the story of Jephthah's daughter in Judg 11 as an etiology for a heretofore unrecognized life-cycle ritual among ancient Israelite girls. This ritual would have been designed to mark the transition of young women from childhood to the stage of בְּתוּלִים, or physical maturity (see ibid., 60). Additionally, the attention paid to the related topic of the female life cycle and the terminology employed to describe each stage of that cycle has resulted in greater attention to clarifying the contrasts between girlhood and womanhood in the HB. See, e.g., the review of the copious literature on just one of these life-cycle terms, בְּתוּלָה, in Hilary B. Lipka, *Sexual Transgression in the Hebrew Bible* (Sheffield: Sheffield Phoenix, 2006), 77–80, 92–97. For a discussion of the figurative coming of age of the collective group of Israelites in the wilderness, see pp. 15–16.

73. Lyn M. Bechtel's article ("Genesis 2.4B–3.24: A Myth about Human Maturation," JSOT 67 [1995]: 3–26) is not solely concerned with male coming of age since it describes the maturation of two characters: one male (Adam) and one female (Eve). Still, since it is one of the few examples of scholarly research that touches upon male coming of age, it is considered here.

74. Hugh C. White, "The Initiation Legend of Ishmael," *ZAW* 87 (1975): 267–306; "The Initiation Legend of Isaac," *ZAW* 91 (1979): 1–30.

75. White, "Initiation Legend of Ishmael," 268–76.

76. Ibid., 301–3. White relies here upon the work of Eliade, who especially emphasizes the significance of death imagery in a ritual's liminal phase. See Mircea Eliade, *Birth and Rebirth: The Religious Meanings of Initiation in Human Culture* (trans. Willard R. Trask; New York: Harper, 1958), 13–20.

77. White, "Initiation Legend of Ishmael," 303–4.

78. Ibid., 293–94.

79. White, "Initiation Legend of Isaac," 4–10.

80. Ibid., 14.

81. Ibid., 17.

82. Ibid., 28–29.

83. The movement in classical studies to identify the presence of initiatory rites in ancient Greece and to connect them to related myths reached its height in the 1960s and 1970s. In the last decade, however, many of the earlier conclusions on the question of initiatory rituals and myths have been challenged. In the introduction to a recent volume on Greek initiation, for example, Graf argues that with the exception of Sparta and Crete, "there is no institution in any Greek city that would fully conform to the anthropological definition of initiation" ("Initiation," 20). Moreover, Graf argues that a myth should only be considered an "initiation myth" connected to initiatory ritual in cases where it is clear that the myth serves as an etiology for a particular ritual (ibid.). He contends that these cases are "few," and the one example he gives—the Spartan

myth of Leukippe (ibid., 15)—is a myth that White does not reference in either of his articles.

This questioning of the connection between Greek initiation rituals and myths, however, has not resulted in an abandonment of the search for initiatory *themes* in Greek myth. Johnston's work ("'Initiation' in Myth," 155), for example, shows how initiatory themes could be present in a myth lacking a connection to initiation rituals.

84. See the examples discussed by Weisfield, "Puberty Rites," 32–36. See also Stoller and Herdt, "The Development of Masculinity," 29–59.

85. See Weisfield, "Puberty Rites," 38–39.

86. White argues based on the chronology provided by the P source in Gen 16:16, 17:25, and 21:5 that Ishmael would have been approximately 16 years old in this story, which would "make him the ideal age for . . . a puberty rite" ("Initiation Legend of Ishmael," 302). However, commentators generally agree that P's chronology does not apply to the story in Gen 21, which comes from a different source that contains many indications that Ishmael is a young child. See, e.g., Claus Westermann, *Genesis 12–36* (first Fortress Press ed.; trans. John J. Scullion; Minneapolis: Fortress, 1995), 341; Gerhard Von Rad, *Genesis: A Commentary* (trans. John H. Marks; OTL; Philadelphia: Westminster, 1961), 228; Ephraim A. Speiser, *Genesis: A New Translation with Introduction and Commentary* (AB 1; Garden City, NY: Doubleday, 1981), 155–57. Indicators that Ishmael is depicted as being much younger than 16 in Gen 21 include his helpless act of crying beneath the bush (Gen 21:16–17), his mother's ability to carry him on her shoulder (v. 14), cast him away (שלך; v. 15), and pick him up (נשא; v. 18), and that a term that is only applied to young boys is used to describe him (יֶלֶד; vv. 14, 15, 16; see Chapter 2 [p. 56–58] for a discussion of this term's use to describe only young boys).

87. See Chapter 2, pp. 51–52.

88. For helplessness and submission as characteristics of children in the HB, see Chapter 2, pp. 53–54, 58, 61, 63, 65.

89. Propp, *Exodus 1–18*, 239–40.

90. See the discussion of Moses's transition to manhood in Exod 2 in Chapter 3, pp. 77–84.

91. See Lyn M. Bechtel, "Genesis 2.4B–3.24," 11–12.

92. Ibid., 19–20.

93. See also Naomi Steinberg's informative recent study of biblical childhood, *The World of the Child in the Hebrew Bible* (Hebrew Bible Monographs 51; Sheffield: Sheffield Phoenix, 2013). Steinberg shows that the "contemporary idealization of childhood as a period of protected physical and emotional well-being" does not fit the biblical evidence (ibid., 20).

94. The Jewish coming-of-age rite of the bar mitzvah was not practiced in ancient Israel. In fact, it was only after the fourteenth century C.E. that the bar mitzvah

celebration became a permanent fixture in Jewish community life. See Ronald Eisenberg, *The JPS Guide to Jewish Traditions* (Philadelphia: Jewish Publication Society, 2004), 24.

95. Frank W. Young, *Initiation Ceremonies: A Cross-Cultural Study of Status Dramatization* (Indianapolis: Bobbs-Merrill, 1965), 42–62.For a discussion of the solidarity at the center of Israelite manhood, see Chapter 1, pp. 44–45.

96. See William H. C. Propp, "The Origins of Infant Circumcision in Israel," *HAR* 11 (1987):355–70; Nick Wyatt, "Circumcision and Circumstance: Male Genital Mutilation in Ancient Israel and Ugarit," JSOT 33 (2009): 411–12.

    It deserves mention that infant circumcision does not function as an effective coming-of-age ritual because the infant is too young to be considered a man after the procedure. Bilu argues that because this ceremony actually encourages mother–child bonding (the newly circumcised child being returned to its mother after the ritual for special care and affection), it actually functions in the opposite way to a typical male puberty rite, which distances boys from their mothers. See Yoram Bilu, "From *Milah* (Circumcision) to *Milah* (Word): Male Identity and Rituals of Childhood in the Jewish Ultraorthodox Community," *Ethos* 31 (2003): 180.

97. See Alice Schlegel and Herbert Barry III, "The Evolutionary Significance of Adolescent Initiation Ceremonies," *American Ethnologist* 7 (1980): 710–13. For the subsistence economy of early Israelite settlements, see, e.g., Amihai Mazar, "The Israelite Settlement," in *The Quest for the Historical Israel* (ed. Brian B. Schmidt; Atlanta: Society of Biblical Literature, 2007), 85–90.

98. For the connection between gender inequality and the presence of male coming-of-age rites, see Michael S. Kimmel, *Guyland: The Perilous World Where Boys Become Men; Understanding the Critical Years between 16 and 26* (New York: HarperCollins, 2008), 113. For the high levels of gender complementarity in ancient Israelite households, see Carol Meyers' *Rediscovering Eve: Ancient Israelite Women in Context* (Oxford: Oxford University Press, 2013). Meyers (ibid., 180–202, cf. 50–52, 121–22) argues that given the centrality of the household in the ancient Israelite economy, as well as the demands put on every member of a family by subsistence agriculture, women held a great deal of power in the agrarian households of ancient Israel.

99. For the lack of puberty rites in ancient Mesopotamia, see Harris, *Gender and Aging*, 3. For the absence of an initiatory ritual context for the recitation of the *Hymn to Hermes*, see Johnston, "'Initiation' in Myth,"155–57. The coming-of-age themes in *Gilgamesh* and the *Hymn to Hermes* are discussed above, n. 62; n. 71

100. David D. Gilmore, "Introduction: The Shame of Dishonor," in *Honor and Shame and the Unity of the Mediterranean* (ed. David D. Gilmore; Washington, DC: American Anthropological Association, 1987), 14–16.

101. Coming of age is reckoned as a "theme" in this study according to the definition of "theme" provided by Alter. A "theme" is "an idea which is part of the
value system of the narrative [that is] made evident in some recurring pattern"
(Robert Alter, *The Art of Biblical Narrative* [New York: Basic Books, 1981], 95).
Examples include the reversal of primogeniture in Genesis, obedience and rebellion in the wilderness narratives, and knowledge in the Joseph story (ibid.).
In contrast, coming of age does not fit the definition of a "type-scene" where
certain repeated elements are found together in a predictable pattern (ibid.,
50). As I will show in the following chapters, there are no such repeated elements in coming-of-age narratives. Nor can coming of age be described as a
motif (that is, a "concrete image, sensory quality, action, or object") because
coming of age is broader than a motif, which has no meaning of itself outside
the context of the larger narrative (see ibid., 95).

102. White ("Initiation Legend of Isaac," 17) argues that a significant change has
taken place in Isaac when he is called a נַעַר by the messenger of Yhwh in Gen
22:12; however, as I will show in Chapter 2, this term is associated with boyhood and not manhood (see pp. 48–56). Therefore its application to Isaac does
not signify an important transition out of boyhood for the character.

CHAPTER I

1. Clines, "David the Man," 212–43.
2. Scripture quotations from NRSV, unless otherwise noted.
3. Clines, "David the Man," 227.
4. Clines (ibid., 227–28) notes that David's skill in playing a stringed musical
instrument reflects an "essentially male trait" (228) in that of the more than
forty times that David's instrument of choice—the כִּנּוֹר or "lute" (see 1 Sam
16:23)—is mentioned in the Bible, only once (Isa 23:16) is a woman playing the
instrument. Still, Clines does not argue for musical talent as an essential in-
gredient of biblical masculinity *in general*; he merely argues that it enhances
David's masculinity. Also noteworthy is that Clines dismisses the text's acknowledgment that Yhwh was with David as "an accidental feature of his characterization, more dependent on his role in the narrative . . . than upon the
Hebrew construction of masculinity" (ibid., 227).
5. Ibid., 223–27.
6. Clines himself is among those that draw upon the description of manhood
presented in "David the Man" and use it to understand biblical manhood in
texts from different sources, such as the biblical legal corpus (David J. A.
Clines, "Being a Man in the Book of the Covenant," in *Reading the Law: Studies
in Honour of Gordon J. Wenham* [ed. J. G. McConville and Karl Möller; Library
of Hebrew Bible/Old Testament Studies 461; New York: T&T Clark, 2007],

3–9) and the narrative of the Israelites at Sinai (David J. A. Clines, "Dancing and Shining at Sinai: Playing the Man in Exodus 32–34," in Creangă, *Men and Masculinity*, 54–63). Clines notes that the characteristics he identified as important to masculinity in the David story are applicable throughout the HB, a conclusion that he attributes to either his failure to remove himself from "a grid of [his] own devising" or to the fact that "the image of masculinity in the biblical literature is really rather uniform" (ibid., 62).

7. Marcel V. Măcerlau, "Saul in the Company of Men: (De)Constructing Masculinity in 1 Samuel 9–31," in Creangă and Smit, *Biblical Masculinities Foregrounded*, 55.

8. Moreover, as Guest helpfully clarifies, it should be remembered that such ideal masculine characteristics are not performed by "a subject who preexists as an already-sexed 'man,'" but that the performance of these characteristics constitutes an artificial gender identity. See Deryn Guest, "From Gender Reversal to Genderfuck: Reading Jael through a Lesbian Lens," in *Bible Trouble: Queer Reading at the Boundaries of Biblical Scholarship* (ed. Teresa J. Hornsby and Ken Stone; Atlanta: Society of Biblical Literature, 2013), 12–13 n. 3.

9. Clines ("David the Man," 228–31) claims that especially during Absalom's rebellion David is revealed as emotionally weak (viz., his weeping over Absalom's death; 2 Sam 18:33) and cowardly (fleeing Jerusalem at the slightest hint of danger; 2 Sam 15:14). See also Ken Stone, "Queer Reading between Bible and Film: *Paris is Burning* and the 'Legendary Houses' of David and Saul," in Hornsby and Stone, *Bible Trouble*, 75–98. Stone shows that David's manhood is "potentially destabilized" by becoming feminized as the object of Jonathan's affections (ibid., 88).

10. Carol Meyers discusses the perspective of the urban men who composed and canonized the HB, as opposed to that of the 90 percent rural ancient Israelite society, in "Contesting the Notion of Patriarchy: Anthropology and the Theorizing of Gender in Ancient Israel," in *A Question of Sex? Gender and Difference in the Hebrew Bible and Beyond* (ed. Deborah W. Rooke; Hebrew Bible Monographs 14; Sheffield: Sheffield Phoenix, 2007), 85.

11. Clines, "David the Man," 216.

12. See Clines's extensive list of "strength language" in 1 and 2 Samuel (ibid., 218). Particularly convincing is Clines's case that "the 'hand' as the symbol of power" functions as a veritable "leitmotif of the David narrative," a claim in support of which he cites sixty-three individual verses.

13. Translation mine.

14. Harry A. Hoffner, "Symbols for Masculinity and Femininity: Their Use in Ancient Near Eastern Sympathetic Magic Rituals," *JBL* 85(1966): 327 n. 4. One is reminded here of the similar connection between the Hebrew יָד, meaning at times both "power" (as in Exod 13:3; Isa 10:32) and "penis" (Isa 57:8). See

Harold Washington, "Violence and the Construction of Gender in the Hebrew Bible: A New Historicist Approach," *BibInt* 5(1997): 330.

15. Hoffner, "Symbols," 329–30.

16. Cynthia R. Chapman, *The Gendered Language of Warfare in the Israelite–Assyrian Encounter* (HSM 62; Winona Lake, IN: Eisenbrauns, 2004), 20.

17. Ibid., 23–24.

18. Ibid., 47.

19. Ibid., 50–58. Again, biblical parallels are obvious. Yhwh is imaged breaking the bows of an army in Jer 49:35 and Hos 1:5, 2:20, which may draw upon this common image of emasculation to describe his complete victory.

20. Julia M. Asher-Greve, "The Essential Body: Mesopotamian Conceptions of the Gendered Body," *Gender and History* 9(1997): 444.

21. See David J. A. Clines, "He-Prophets: Masculinity as a Problem for the Hebrew Prophets and Their Interpreters," in *Sense and Sensitivity: Essays on Reading the Bible in Memory of Robert Carroll* (ed. Alastair G. Hunter and Philip R. Davies; JSOTSup 348; Sheffield: Sheffield Academic Press, 2002), 313. Clines singles out Isa 40 for special consideration, considering the prevalence of what he calls "language of strength" in this text, which features such terms as כֹּחַ, חָזָק, אַמִּיץ, אוֹנִים, רֹב, צָבָא, זְרוֹעַ, אָדֹנָי, and עָצְמָה.

   The prophet's individual power is emphasized in Mic 3:8, where Micah describes himself as being full of power (כֹּחַ), authority (מִשְׁפָּט), and might (גְּבוּרָה).

22. According to Clines, the slaughter by the Levites of their fellow Israelites and the military-style command structure presided over by Moses in these chapters contributes to an idealization of "the warrior male" in this passage ("Dancing and Shining," 55–56).

23. Haddox refers to this aspect of the hegemonic masculinity found in the Bible as "potency, including strength, virility, and skill as a warrior" ("Favoured Sons," 6).

24. Ovidiu Creangă, "Variations on the Theme of Masculinity: Joshua's Gender In/Stability in the Conquest Narrative," in Creangă, *Men and Masculinity*, 89–93.See also Măcerlau ("Saul in the Company of Men," 59–61), who shows how Saul's decreasing strength throughout 1 Samuel, particularly on the battlefield, is used to diminish Saul as a man.

25. Washington, "Violence," 330. See also Clines ("David the Man," 217), who defines strength in 1 and 2 Samuel as the capacity to commit "violence against other men." John Goldingay ("Hosea 1–3, Genesis 1–4, and Masculinist Interpretation," *HBT* 17[1995]: 39) similarly argues that violence is a major feature of the biblical depiction of masculinity in Gen 1–4, citing Cain's murder of Abel as an example.

26. For the connection between physical and psychological strength, see Lipka ("Masculinities in Proverbs," 90), who considers "inner-strength, demonstrated

by display of virtues such as courage, fortitude, self-discipline, and dignity" an important component of the manly strength so constitutive of hegemonic masculinity in the HB.

27. Clines, "David the Man," 219–21.

28. Note, for example, the frequency with which it is parallel to חָכָם "wise," as in Prov 1:5; 17:28; Isa 5:21; 29:14.

29. Clines ("David the Man," 219), referencing Ralph Klein, cites David's persuasiveness at convincing Saul to let him challenge Goliath in 1 Sam 17:34–26, his defense of his choice to spare Saul after their encounter in the cave in 24:10–15, and his words' effectiveness against Saul in 1 Sam 26 that cause the king to admit his wrongdoing (26:21), as examples of his persuasiveness and intelligence prior to ascending to the throne. Citing Norman Whybray, Clines (ibid., 220) identifies this characteristic after David's coronation in a number of places: his wisdom is recognized and praised by the wise woman of Tekoa in 2 Sam 14:20; it is on display in his sending Hushai to confuse Absalom with misleading counsel (15:33–35); and its dark side is seen when David cunningly tries to cover up his affair with Bathsheba (11:14–25).

30. Ibid., 219.

31. Ibid., 220. Clines here also identifies wisdom as "part of the repertory of the powerful male" in ancient Greece, as seen in the character of Odysseus.

32. The exception to the unanimous recognition that wisdom and persuasive speech are a significant component of biblical hegemonic masculinity is Lipka's claim that these qualities instead formed the core of an alternative masculinity dominant among the scribes of the wisdom school that authored Proverbs (see "Masculinities in Proverbs," 94–100). Ultimately, regardless of whether or not wisdom and rhetorical skill belong to a hegemonic or an alternative articulation of masculinity, they undeniably are understood as important parts of being an *adult* male, whether among one subgroup of biblical texts and authors or more generally.

While this debate is therefore largely tangential to the primary concerns of this study, it is worth noting that Lipka's argument that wisdom is only a significant feature of the alternative masculinity found in Proverbs does not stand up to closer criticism. Most significantly, it has no answer to the evidence from other areas in the canon where wisdom or persuasive speech seem to be important and valorized characteristics of masculinity, as Clines and others have shown. Lipka attempts to address this problem by acknowledging that there are texts that appear to prioritize persuasive speech, but that such speech seems to be only "important for leaders, military and otherwise," and that "there is little evidence that it was a quality expected of the general male population aspiring towards a successful performance of hegemonic masculinity. . . ." (ibid., 91 n. 17). The flaw in this claim is that by necessity all of the characteristics that can be identified as belonging to hegemonic masculinity in the HB are those garnered from texts about leaders, written and redacted by cultural elites. Our knowledge of the "general male population" and their views on manhood is woefully limited. We cannot, therefore, on the one hand acknowledge that strength is an important part of hegemonic masculinity, using as proof texts stories about heroes (as Lipka does, citing verses pertaining to David [1 Sam 16:18] and Samson [Judg 16:5], ibid., 89 n. 8), while on the other hand denying that wisdom and persuasive speech belong to hegemonic masculinity because these qualities seem important only to heroes and leaders.

Lipka's argument that the way of being a man presented in Proverbs eventually would be closer to the model of masculinity among colonized Jews is a good one, and is similar to many of the claims I make in the conclusion to this book. Her argument would be better served, however, by eliminating the claim that the emphasis on wisdom in Proverbs represents a new paradigm for masculinity. Instead, it seems that Proverbs emphasizes a certain feature of the preexistent hegemonic masculinity at the expense of others—such as physical strength—rather than creating a completely alternative paradigm.

33. Clines, "Dancing and Shining," 57.
34. DiPalma, "De/Constructing Masculinity," 49.
35. Măcerlau, "Saul in the Company of Men," 62–63.
36. Haddox, "Favoured Sons," 7–14. Haddox does note, however, that at times the patriarchs fail to live up to the mark, as seen in Abraham's inability to dissuade Sarah from her harsh actions against Hagar and Ishmael in Gen 16 and 21 (see ibid., 7).
37. Creangă, "Variations," 93–94. Examples include Joshua's persuasion of the Trans-Jordanian tribes to assist in the conquest west of the Jordan (Josh 1:13–18) and the use of the execution of the five kings of Makkedah (Josh 10:25, 42) "to convey, physically as well as verbally, the message of fearlessness and trust in the Divine Warrior fighting for Israel" (ibid., 94).
38. Clines, "David the Man," 221–23.
39. Two exceptions are Măcerlau and Alan Hooker. Măcerlau ("Saul in the Company of Men," 57–59) uses Saul's appearance as one of the categories by which he judges Saul's depiction as a man, while Hooker ("'Show Me Your Glory': The Kabod of Yahweh as Phallic Manifestation?" in Creangă and Smit, *Biblical Masculinities Foregrounded*, 24–27) discusses beauty as an essential feature of priestly masculinity in Exod 28, and of the masculinity of Yhwh in Exod 33.
40. Creangă, "Variations," 88.
41. Lipka, "Masculinities in Proverbs," 91 n. 17.
42. Note that the NIV concurs on this point, translating טוֹב in 1 Sam 9:2 as "impressive," as noted by Măcerlau, "Saul in the Company of Men," 57.
43. Absalom is not just called beautiful, but it is said that he was "praised" (הלל) for his beauty, and that "from the sole of his foot to the crown of his head there was no blemish in him" (1 Sam 14:25). Joseph is not just יְפֵה־תֹאַר (literally

"beautiful of form") but also יְפֵה מַרְאֶה ("beautiful of sight/beautiful to look at"). David's beauty, as seen above, is highlighted in three different passages in 1 Sam (16:12, 18; 17:42).

44. Stuart MacWilliam, "Ideologies of Male Beauty in the Hebrew Bible," *BibInt* 17(2009): 265–87.

45. MacWilliam, "Male Beauty," 283.

46. David famously refers to Absalom as a boy (נַעַר) in 2 Sam 18:5, 29, 32.

47. Stephen D. Moore, "Final Reflections on Biblical Masculinity," in Creangă, *Men and Masculinity*, 249–50.

48. Clines, "David the Man," 226–27.

49. Gregory Mobley (*Liminal Hero*, 85–108) sees women performing this function in the *Gilgamesh Epic*, where Shamhat initiates Enkidu into human culture and Siduri's reminder to Gilgamesh of the pleasures of life almost causes him to turn aside from his quest. He also notes that the practice of women greeting returning triumphant warriors from the battlefield outside the city, as in 1 Sam 18:6–7, shows that women had the responsibility "to convert [the men] from combatants to civilians" (ibid., 105).

50. For a discussion of the construction of masculinity in contrast to femininity, see Introduction, pp. 6–8. Interestingly, Clines himself is not of the opinion that biblical masculinity is constructed in stark opposition to all things feminine. He argues that while this may be the case in the modern world, in ancient Israel the social roles of males and females were so distinct that there was "no need for men to define themselves as masculine over against women" ("Dancing and Shining," 59).

51. Moore, "Final Reflections," 246. Additionally, Haddox ("Favoured Sons," 4) argues that one of the "norms of hegemonic masculinity" is "not to seem feminine." See also Creangă, "Introduction," 5; Stuart Macwilliam, "Athaliah: A Case of Illicit Masculinity," in Creangă and Smit, *Biblical Masculinities Foregrounded*, 81; and Ken Stone, "Gender Criticism: The Un-Manning of Abimelech," in *Judges and Method: New Approaches in Biblical Studies* (ed. Gale A. Yee; 2d ed.; Minneapolis: Fortress, 2007), 188–89.

52. See Hoffner, "Symbols," 331–32.

53. Chapman, *Gendered Language*, 160–63.

54. Karel van der Toorn, "Judges XVI 21 in the Light of Akkadian Sources," *VT* 36: 249, 252 n. 9.

55. Susan Niditch, *Judges: A Commentary* (OTL; Louisville: Westminster John Knox, 2008), 170.

56. See Carol Meyers, "The Family in Early Israel," in Leo G. Perdue et al., *Families in Ancient Israel* (Louisville: Westminster John Knox, 1997), 25.

57. Niditch, *Judges*, 166–67. Niditch also recognizes a double entendre in Samson's "sporting" before the Philistines (Judg 16:25), which further serves to feminize and sexually subjugate him.

58. Claudia D. Bergmann, " 'We Have Seen the Enemy, and He is Only a "She"': The Portrayal of Warriors as Women," in *Writing and Reading War: Rhetoric, Gender, and Ethics in Biblical and Modern Contexts* (ed. Brad E. Kelle and Brad Ritchel Ames; Atlanta: Society of Biblical Literature, 2008), 141–42.

59. Linda Day ("Wisdom and the Feminine in the Bible," in *Engaging the Bible in a Gendered World: An Introduction to Feminist Biblical Interpretation in Honor of Katharine Doob Sakenfeld* [ed. Linda Day and Carolyn Pressler; Louisville: Westminster John Knox, 2006], 114–27) has argued that the wisdom tradition itself is closely aligned with the feminine.

60. For an example of how Yhwh is depicted as the height of masculinity in Israel, see Susan E. Haddox, "(E)Masculinity in Hosea's Political Rhetoric," in *Israel's Prophets and Israel's Past: Essays on the Relationship of Prophetic Texts and Israelite History in Honor of John H. Hayes* (ed. Brad E. Kelle and Megan Bishop Moore; New York: T&T Clark, 2006), 174–200. Haddox argues that in Hosea the Israelite leaders breaking the treaty with Assyria have their masculinity challenged and are found severely deficient in the face of Yhwh's "ultimate" masculinity. It is Yhwh, not the leaders, who performs the quintessentially masculine tasks of acting as husband to the leaders' wives, breaking the bows of his foes, and exposing the cowardice and powerlessness of other men.

61. Carol Meyers ("Female Images of God in the Hebrew Bible," in *Women in Scripture: A Dictionary of Named and Unnamed Women in the Hebrew Bible, the Apocryphal/Deuterocanonical Books, and the New Testament* [ed. Carol Meyers with Toni Craven and Ross S. Kraemer; Grand Rapids, MI: Eerdmans, 2000], 525–28) points to several examples of feminine imagery applied to Yhwh in the HB. This imagery can at times be explicit (Yhwh is attributed with having birthed and suckled Israel in Num 11:12, will birth a new Israel in Isa 42:14, has maternal loyalty and compassion for Israel in Isa 49:15, and is famously described as רחום in the creedal statement accompanying his divine self-revelation in Exod 34:6 [a term deriving from the word for womb]) but is at other times more subtle (Yhwh is frequently shown doing such women's work as providing food and water, as in Neh 9:20–21).

62. See Stephen Moore and Janet Capel Anderson, "Taking it Like a Man: Masculinity in 4 Maccabees," *JBL* 117(1997): 250.

63. As Michael Satlow has shown ("'Try to be a Man:' The Rabbinic Construction of Masculinity," *HTR* 89[1996]: 19–40).

64. Mark K. George, "Masculinity and Its Regimentation in Deuteronomy," in Creangă, *Men and Masculinity*, 64–82.

65. More recent scholarship has also identified self-control as an important feature of biblical masculinity. Măcerlau argues that Saul's lack of self-mastery during his prophetic ravings (1 Sam 19:23–24) and when tormented by an evil spirit from Yhwh (1 Sam 16:14–16, 23; 18:10; 19:9) shows how he does not fit the hegemonic masculine ideal ("Saul in the Company of Men," 59). Lipka,

similarly, argues for the importance of manly self-control in Proverbs, citing Prov 19:11, 20:3, and 21:21 ("Masculinities in Proverbs," 98).

66. Ibid., 75.

67. Stone, "Queer Reading," 82.

68. Lipka, "Masculinities in Proverbs," 89.

69. Sandra Jacobs, "Divine Virility in Priestly Representation: Its Memory and Consummation in Rabbinic Midrash," in Creangă, *Men and Masculinities*, 146–70. Jacobs notes the prevalence of the concern for offspring in the ancestral narratives of Genesis (e.g,. Gen 13:16) and argues for the connection of circumcision with fertility given that Gen 17—the Priestly description of the inception of the rite among Israelites—couches the ceremony in multiple references to Abram's fertility and offspring (e.g., Gen 17:2, 6, 7, 8, 9, 10). Jacobs concludes that this Priestly concern with fertility shows that for this writer "the ideal conception of masculinity . . . is its ability to reproduce prolifically" (ibid., 150).

70. Hoffner, "Symbols," 397.

71. George, "Regimentation," 73. Illegitimacy is generally dissuaded outside of the Torah as well, as the Jephthah tale of Judg 11 shows.

72. See Victor P. Hamilton, "Marriage (OT and ANE)," *ABD* 4: 563–65.

73. Steinberg, *World of the Child*, 76, 91.

74. Ibid., 68–76.

75. See ibid., 79–81. See also Karel Van der Toorn, *From Her Cradle to Her Grave: The Role of Religion in the Life of the Israelite and the Babylonian Woman* (trans. Sara J. Denning-Bolle; Biblical Seminar 23; Sheffield: JSOT Press, 1994), 18.

76. Steinberg, *World of the Child*, 35, 39. This evidence leads her to argue that, for example, Isaac and Rebekah do not achieve "full adulthood" until Jacob and Esau are born, nor do Abraham and Sarah mature completely until Isaac's birth; see ibid., 76, 91, respectively.

77. See Edward F.Campbell, Jr. (*Ruth: A New Translation with Introduction, Notes, and Commentary* [AB 7; Garden City, NY: Doubleday, 1975], 56), who describes the use of the term here as "a very effective inclusio with 4:16, where Naomi takes a new *yeled* into her bosom." Kirsten Busch Nielsen (*Ruth* [OTL; trans. Edward Broadbridge; Louisville: Westminster John Knox, 1997], 44) concurs, believing that this "unusual" usage of the term only makes sense when considered in light of 4:16. See the further discussion of the use of יֶלֶד in Ruth 1:5 in Chapter 2, p. 57.

78. Note that Steinberg's argument also disregards the notion of "legal manhood" at age twenty (see p. 45).

79. Kenneth A. Stone, *Sex, Honor, and Power in the Deuteronomistic History* (JSOT-Sup 234; Sheffield: JSOT Press, 1996), 11.

80. Haddox, "(E)Masculinity," 174–200; Chapman, *Gendered Language*, 64. Chapman's book also discusses the honor-laden metaphor of Yhwh as a father

protecting daughter Zion (see ibid., 60–111). For a contrasting view on the significance of honor to the Yhwh–Israel marriage metaphor, see Carol Meyers,
"Rape or Remedy: Sex and Violence in Prophetic Marriage Metaphors," in *Prophetie in Israel* (Beiträge des Symposiums "Das Altes Testament und die Kultur
der Moderne," anlässlich des 100. Geburtstags Gerhard von Rads [1901–1971],
Heidelberg, 18.21 Oktober 2001; ed. Hugh Williamson, Konrad Schmid, and
Irmtraud Fischer; Münster: Lit-Verlag, 2003), 198. Meyers argues that what is
"at stake" in the case of an adulterous wife is not her husband's honor but instead "the possibility of a disruption of the biological continuity of the ownership of the family property and thus of survival."

81. Clines, "He-Prophets," 316.

82. Ela Lazarewicz-Wyrzykowska, "Samson: Masculinity Lost (and Regained?)" in
Creangă, *Men and Masculinity*, 171–88.

83. Lipka, "Masculinities in Proverbs," 92.

84. Note, e.g., that Stone (*Sex, Honor, and Power*, 27–49) devotes a chapter of his
book to summarizing this research. For an overview of the impact of research
into honor and shame on New Testament studies, see Halvor Moxnes, "Honor
and Shame," in *The Social Sciences and New Testament Interpretation* (ed. Richard L. Rohrbaugh; Peabody, MA: Hendrickson, 1996), 19–40.

85. See John G. Peristiany, ed., *Honour and Shame: The Values of Mediterranean
Society* (Chicago: University of Chicago Press, 1966). Peristiany's edited
volume was the first extended study of honor and shame in the field of cultural
anthropology.

86. This competition, however, must take place between social equals. For a man
of great honor with an exalted status in his society to accept the challenge of an
inferior would reflect poorly on him and would decrease his honor, even if he
emerged successful from the competition. See Pierre Bourdieu, "The Sentiment of Honour in Kayble Society," in Peristiany, *Honour and Shame*,
197–98.

87. Gilmore, "The Shame of Dishonor," 4.

88. Peristiany, *Honour and Shame*, 14.

89. Lazarewicz-Wyrzykowska, "Samson," 172.

90. David D. Gilmore, "Honor, Honesty, Shame: Male Status in Contemporary
Andalusia," in Gilmore, *Honor*, 90–103; Michael Herzfeld, "'As in Your Own
House': Hospitality, Ethnography, and the Stereotype of Mediterranean Soci-
ety," in Gilmore, *Honor*, 75–89.

91. John G. Peristiany and Julian Pitt-Rivers, eds., *Honour and Grace in Anthropology* (Cambridge: Cambridge University Press, 1992). See especially Julian Pitt-
Rivers, "Postscript: The Place of Grace in Anthropology," in ibid., 215–46.

92. An example of the inability to reconcile masculine honor with social cohesion
is found in Clines's "Being a Man in the Book of the Covenant." Here Clines
argues that because the goal of the Book of the Covenant is to build a

community centered on manly solidarity (i.e., a "band of brothers"), the text articulates a vision of society free of notions of honor and shame (ibid., 4). A notable exception to this tendency is Haddox's "Favoured Sons," which describes the importance of "positive" values like generosity and hospitality to honor in Genesis; see Haddox, "Favoured Sons," 16.

93. Abou A. M. Zeid, "Honour and Shame among the Bedouins of Egypt," in Peristiany, *Honour and Shame*, 250.

94. Clines, "He-Prophets," 317.

95. It is important to note, however, that ancient Israel need not be considered an "honor–shame culture" like those studied by modern anthropologists in order for honor to be considered an important masculine value found in its literature. See Clines, "He-Prophets," 316.

96. For a discussion of the kinship language employed to describe Israel as a whole, see Frank Moore Cross, *From Epic to Canon: History and Literature in Ancient Israel* (Baltimore: Johns Hopkins University Press, 1998), 3–21.

97. Clines, "David the Man," 223–25.

98. Clines, "Being a Man," 4–5.

99. Ibid., 4. Clines, "David the Man," 224–25.

100. Leo G. Perdue, "The Israelite and Early Jewish Family: Summary and Conclusions," in Perdue et al., *Families in Ancient Israel*, 167.

101. For the connection between covenant and kinship, see Cross, *From Epic to Canon*, 13.

102. Steinberg, *World of the Child*, 73.

103. The case of the rebellious son (בֵּן סוֹרֵר) in Deut 21:18–21—where a father and mother can bring their son to trial before the community's elders and have him executed for his rebelliousness, gluttony, and drunkenness—may seem to contradict this conclusion. However, most scholars believe that the son in question is an adult and thus over the age of twenty. See Lothar Ruppert, "סָרַר," *TDOT* 10: 355; Elizabeth Bellefontaine, "Deuteronomy 21:18–21: Reviewing the Case of the Rebellious Son," JSOT 4(1979): 15; Gerhard von Rad, *Deuteronomy: A Commentary* (trans. Dorothea Barton; OTL; Philadelphia: Westminster, 1966), 138.

104. Milton Eng, *The Days of our Years: A Lexical Semantic Study of the Life Cycle in Biblical Israel* (Library of Hebrew Bible/Old Testament Studies 464; New York: T&T Clark, 2011), 123. Eng adds that if a man lived beyond seventy, he was considered "extremely old" and would be described with terms like זָקֵן מְאֹד (1 Sam 2:22), or שֵׂיבָה טוֹבָה (Gen 15:5).

CHAPTER 2

1. Although presumably if a young man were to display the characteristics of masculinity before age twenty, including marriage and children, he would be

considered a man despite not having reached that age. However, since the HB rarely provides the ages of young male characters—and therefore it is impossible to present solid evidence of a man younger than twenty who is considered an adult man—this must remain speculation.

2. With the exception of נַעַר, which is considered at the end of this list despite its comparative frequency. As will be shown, נַעַר is not as frequently employed as a life-cycle term, and thus is appropriately considered separately.

3. Persons referred to as נְעָרוֹת/נְעָרִים range in age from the unborn Samson (Judg 13:5–12) to newborn infant Ichabod (1 Sam 4:21), three-month-old Moses (Exod 2:6), newly –weaned toddler Samuel (1 Sam 1:24), presumably young adolescent Jether (Judg 8:20–2) and David (1 Sam 16–17), sixteen-year-old Josiah (2 Chr 34:3), seventeen-year-old Joseph (Gen 37:2), of marriageable age (Shechem and Dinah in Gen 34), twenty-eight-year-old Joseph (Gen 41:12) to older adults like Gehazi (2 Kgs 4:12) and Ziba (2 Sam 9:9). They can be found in a servile status (Ziba, Gehazi, Abraham's servant in Gen 18:7), in military roles (as an armor bearer/personal attendant in Judg 7:10, 11; 9:14; 1 Sam 14:1, 6; 2 Sam 1:15; as errand boys for warriors in 1 Sam 20:35; 26:22; as a corps of [possibly elite] troops in 1 Sam 21:3–6; 30:17; 2 Sam 2:14, 21; 1 Kgs 20:14–15), or as participants in priestly and cultic duties (Exod 24:5; Judg 17:7–18:15; 1 Sam 2:11–17). Even a king can refer to himself (1 Kgs 3:7) or be referred to (2 Chr 13:7) as a נַעַר. They are primarily unmarried and childless, but can be married (the Levite's concubine in Jdg 19:3–9) or previously married (Ruth, see Ruth 2:5), and can have children (Ziba in 2 Sam 9:10 and Absalom, who is called a נַעַר throughout 2 Sam 18 but is depicted as having children in 2 Sam 14:27).

4. Hans Peter Stähli, *Knabe-Jüngling-Knecht: Untersuchungen zum Begriff* נער *im Alten Testament* (BBET 7; Frankfurt am Main: Peter Lang, 1978).

5. Carolyn S. Leeb, *Away from the Father's House: The Social Location of na'ar and na'arah in Ancient Israel* (JSOTSup 301; Sheffield: Sheffield Academic Press, 2000).

6. John MacDonald, "The Status and Role of the Na'ar in Israelite Society," *JNES* 35(1976): 147–70.

7. Lawrence E. Stager, "The Archaeology of the Family in Ancient Israel," *BASOR* 260(1985): 1–35.

8. Two noteworthy exceptions to this trend are Eng, *Days of Our Years*, and H. F. Fuhs' contribution on the term in *TDOT* ("נַעַר," *TDOT* 9: 474–85). Both scholars recognize the multivalence of the term, but recognize its primary connection to the notion of youth (Eng, *Days of Our Years*, 59–84; Fuhs, "נַעַר," 9: 480–82). Eng (ibid., 63) notes that the association of נַעַר with the definition "servant" reflects a common semantic drift—words denoting youth (such as the French garçon and in some contexts the English "boy") often come to be associated with servitude.

9. Cyrus H. Gordon, "*nʿr*," *UT*: 445 n. 1666.

10. Anson F. Rainey, "The Military Personnel of Ugarit," *JNES* 24(1965): 17–27.

11. Although, note that Gordon ("*nʿr*," *UT*: 445 n. 1666) also believed that the term was applied to young males.

12. MacDonald, "Status," 157.

13. As with Saul's steward Ziba (2 Sam 9:9), Joshua in his role as the "one ministering" to Moses (מְשָׁרֵת; Exod 33:11), Abraham's personal נַעַר, who helps him prepare food and drink for his visitors in Gen 18, and Gehazi the attendant of Elisha (2 Kgs 4:12). See ibid., 151–56.

14. Ibid., 147.

15. Ibid., 170.

16. Stähli, *Knabe*, 99.

17. Ibid., 100.

18. Ibid., 77–84.

19. Stager, "Archaeology," 25–28. Stager (28) hearkens back to a contention made by Albright in his *Archaeology and the Religion of Israel* that the tribe of Levites was composed of male children dedicated by their parents to priestly service to argue that levitical priesthood was nonhereditary and therefore an attractive option for a later-born son of a landholding family.

20. See above, n. 3, for examples.

21. Stager, "Archaeology," 26.

22. Leeb, *Away from the Father's House*, 41.

23. Stager ("Archaeology," 26), while believing that the term is "only indirectly related to age," still states that נְעָרִים are typically "youthful clients"(25). MacDonald's discussion is premised on the identification of the נַעַר as a "*young male* of high birth" ("Status," 147. emphasis mine). Stähli moves further away from the youthful connotations of the term than the others; however, one of the two groups that he argues are categorized under the term נַעַר are young and unmarried.

24. Fuhs, "נַעַר," 9: 480. Fuhs cites as evidence *b. Giṭ.* 70a; *Šabb.* 11a, and *Ber. Rab.* 48:19, 22 on Gen 18:11, 13.

25. Leeb, *Away from the Father's House*, 21. Leeb (165) even accepts that at certain very rare and late biblical texts, the abstract נְעוּרִים may connote youth, as in Ps 103:5.

26. Ibid., 187.

27. Of the 239 instances of נַעַר, 86 are found in 1–2 Samuel, 35 in 1–2 Kings, and 23 in Judges.

28. See Fuhs, "נַעַר," 9: 485.

29. Leeb, *Away from the Father's House*, 189.

30. Eng, *Days of Our Years*, 62.

31. Mayer I. Gruber, review of Carolyn S. Leeb, *Away from the Father's House: The Social Location of naʿar and naʿarah in Ancient Israel*, *JQR* 43 (2003): 615.

32. Note, for example, the frequency with which the word is used in parallel with יֶלֶד, which undeniably refers to young boys as discussed below. Examples of characters who are simultaneously named נַעַר and יֶלֶד include Ishmael (referred to as a נַעַר in Gen 21:12, 17 [two times], 18, 19, 20, and as a יֶלֶד in 21:14), Joseph (called נַעַר in Gen 37:2, and יֶלֶד in 37:30, although this may be due to source discrepancy), Benjamin (called a נַעַר in Gen 43:8; 44:22, 30, 31, 32, 33 [two times], and 34, and called a יֶלֶד in Gen 44:20), Moses (a נַעַר in Exod 2:6; a יֶלֶד in 2:3, 7, 8, 9, 10), David's ill-fated firstborn son by Bathsheba (a נַעַר in 2 Sam 12:16; a יֶלֶד in 12:15), Jeroboam's son (called נַעַר in 1 Kgs 14:3, 17, and a יֶלֶד in 14:12), and the group of boys who taunted the prophet Elijah (called נְעָרִים in 2 Kgs 2:23 and יְלָדִים in 2:24).

33. According to Eng's reckoning, of the 239 instances of the term, 120 are "age referential" (*Days of Our Years*, 31). Eng's review of the recent literature on the term concludes, in agreement with this study, that the term נַעַר "*does* describe a *lebensphase* (*pace* Stähli and others) and in particular that stage of life between infancy and full adulthood, incorporating the modern categories of childhood, adolescence, and early adulthood" (ibid., 81).

34. See Fuhs, "נַעַר," 9: 480, who rightly notes that "[a]lthough some terms refer to a specific age bracket or stage of development (*yônēq, ôlēl, yeled, 'elem, bāḥūr, zāqēn*), it is hardly possible to assign definite ages to them and associate them with other corresponding terms. . . ."

35. Leeb, *Away from the Father's House*, 13.

36. Absalom had three sons and a daughter and thus was presumably married (2 Sam 14:27). Also, his ability to sow the seeds of rebellion, lead an army, and have sex publicly with his father's concubines indicates his adulthood.

37. Fuhs, "נַעַר," 9: 481.

38. Note also that Joseph has been referred to in the text as a man (אִישׁ) by this point (Gen 39:2, 14). Presumably Joseph has aged sufficiently in the intervening years since he was sold into slavery so that, even though he is not yet married, he is still considered a "man."

39. Furthermore, as Eng argues (*Days of Our Years*, 73 n. 74), "the chronology of the patriarchal and Joseph narratives are notorious for their problems," therefore it is problematic to determine Joseph's age in this scene based only on the report of his age as a thirty-year-old in Gen 41:46. Eng also notes that by Gesenius's reckoning, Joseph is depicted in this scene as "a youth of nearly twenty years old" (ibid.).

40. For the unmarried status of נְעָרִים when understood as a life-cycle term, see also Victor Hamilton, "נַעַר," *NIDOTTE* 3: 125.

41. See Fuhs, "נַעַר," 9: 483.

42. Ibid.

43. It should be recognized, however, that while this lack of strength is a frequent feature of the description of נְעָרִים, "youthful energy" is not precluded by this

characteristic. See Isa 40:30–31, in which the seemingly inexhaustible energy of a boy is vital to the prophet's claim about the vitality that Yhwh will impart on those who rely on him; it will be even more inexhaustible than that of a נַעַר. Similarly, Lam 3:27 identifies youth as the proper time for exertion: "It is good for a man to bear a yoke in his youth" (נְעוּרָיו).

44. For the issue of Ishmael's age in Gen 21, see Introduction n. 86.

45. Note how the phrase is used in military contexts in Num 27:17; Josh 14:11; 1 Sam 18:16; 29:6; 2 Sam 11:1. See also Gregory Mobley, *The Empty Men: The Heroic Tradition of Ancient Israel* (ABRL; New York: Doubleday, 2005), 229; Anton Van Der Lingen, *"Bw'-Yṣ'* ('To Go Out and To Come In') as a Military Term," *VT* 42(1992): 59–66.

46. Note also the Roman application of the adjective *mollis* "soft" and *tener* "tender" to male children, usually to distinguish them from male adults. See Jonathan Walters, "'No More than a Boy:' The Shifting Construction of Masculinity from Ancient Greece to the Middle Ages," *Gender and History* 5(1993): 29.

47. For the distinction between authority and power, see Michelle Zimbalist Rosaldo, "Woman, Gender, and Society: A Theoretical Overview," in *Woman, Culture, and Society* (ed. Michelle Z. Rosaldo and Louise Lamphere; Stanford: Stanford University Press, 1974), 17–45.

48. However, despite the emphasis on this lack of wisdom, Brown shows that children in wisdom literature are "primarily educable" (William P. Brown, "To Discipline without Destruction: The Multifaceted Profile of the Child in Proverbs," in *The Child in the Bible* [ed. Marcia J. Bunge; Grand Rapids, MI: Eerdmans, 2008], 69). Indeed, the purpose of the collection of Proverbs, according to its prologue (1:4), is to impart knowledge (דַּעַת) and purpose/discretion (מְזִמָּה) to נְעָרִים.

49. See Hans Walter Wolff, *Anthropology of the Old Testament* (trans. Margaret Kohl; Philadelphia: Fortress, 1974), 40–53. Wolff argues that in the HB the heart (לֵבָב) performs cognitive functions rather than strictly emotional ones.

50. It is irrelevant here whether or not Jeremiah is actually of the age where he could be considered a נַעַר. Regardless of his age, his objection has no meaning unless the inability to speak effectively were not a known characteristic of נְעָרִים. See the Appendix for a discussion of why Jer 1 is not considered a coming-of-age tale for the purposes of this study.

51. Note that Edward F. Campbell, Jr., in *Ruth: A New Translation with Introduction, Notes, and Commentary* (AB 7; Garden City, NY: Doubleday, 1975), 85–86 translates נַעַר in Ruth 2:6 as "young man," and נְעָרִים in 2:9 as "young people," adding that the repetition of the term in both its masculine and feminines forms throughout the chapter adds a noteworthy "emphasis on youth" to this particular section of the text (ibid., 93). Tod Linafelt (*Ruth* [Berit Olam; Collegeville, MN: Liturgical Press, 1999], 31, 34–35)argues that the youth of the field hands should be emphasized in translation because of its connection with the

theme of sexual tension and power-plays in Ruth 2—particularly, Boaz's interest in ensuring his possession of Ruth over against the young men who are potential suitors.

52. Michael Carasik, "Ruth 2,7: Why the Overseer was Embarrassed," *ZAW* 107(1995): 493–94.

53. Among those who commented on the rash behavior of young males in the ancient world were Plato and Aristotle. Plato's Athenian argues that "Now of all wild young things a boy is the most difficult to handle. Just because he more than any other has a fount of intelligence in him which has not yet 'run clear,' he is the craftiest, most mischievous, and unruliest of brutes" (Plato, *Laws* [trans. A. E. Taylor] in *The Collected Dialogues of Plato* [ed. Edith Hamilton and Huntington Cairns; Princeton: Princeton University Press, 1961], bk. 7, 808d, 1379). Aristotle writes in his *Nichomachean Ethics* that the child lives "at the beck and call of his appetite" (Aristotle, *Nicomachean Ethics* [trans. W. D. Ross] in *The Complete Works of Aristotle* [ed. Jonathan Barnes; 2 vols.; Princeton: Princeton University Press, 1984], bk. 4, 1119b6, 2:1767), adding in his *Politics* that he is "imperfect" and his "excellence" is "not relative to himself alone, but to the perfect man and his teacher," and compares the two like a slave and a master (Aristotle, *Politics* [trans. B. Jowett] in Barnes, ed., bk. 2, 1260a31–33, 2:2000). These quotes were brought to my attention through Eric Ziolkowski, "Bad Boys of Bethel: Origin and Development of a Sacrilegious Type," *HR* 30(1991): 340–41.

54. That is, named characters. There is a passing reference to the beauty of an unnamed king in Ps 45:2 (MT 45:3).

55. Absalom is the only other named male character referred to as beautiful, but he is specifically called a beautiful *man* (אִישׁ־יָפֶה) in 2 Sam 14:25. However, when describing his beauty, his lack of blemish (מוּם) is emphasized, a characteristic of the young boys taken to Nebuchadnezzar's court in Dan 1:4. Furthermore, as argued above, the text's reference to Absalom's beauty may in fact be an attempt at reducing his rebellion to a youthful indiscretion, as David does by referring to him as a נַעַר throughout 2 Sam 18.

56. For a discussion of the aesthetic appreciation of young boys in the classical world, see Walters, "'No More than a Boy,'" 28–31.

57. See above, n. 32.

58. Malamat argues that the author used this term in a pejorative sense, dubbing Rehoboam's young contemporaries mere boys in juxtaposition to the learned elders whose counsel the king should have accepted "in order to emphasize the psychological and biological differentiations between both groups" (Abraham Malamat, "Organs of Statecraft in the Israelite Monarchy," *BA* 28[1965]: 45). He further argues that the council of young men was probably referred to by a different name like "king's sons" or "princelings" (ibid., 59). He also finds a parallel to the "bicameral" assembly of elders and younger men seen in 1 Kgs

12 in *Gilgamesh and Agga*, where the hero similarly rejects the advice of the assembly of elders in favor of an assembly of younger military men (see Abraham Malamat, "Kingship and Council in Israel and Sumer: A Parallel," *JNES* 22[1963]: 250–51).

59. See Chapter 1, p. 41.

60. An observation made by Ellen Davis (personal communication, July 2013).

61. See Claus Westermann, *Genesis 37–50* (first Fortress Press ed.; trans. John J. Scullion; Minneapolis: Fortress, 2002), 42. He identifies two variant sources at work in the chapter, one with Reuben as the hero empathetic to the suffering of his youngest brother, and the other casting Judah in this more positive light.

62. Note that Milton Eng's analysis of the term's usage similarly concludes that the best English term to translate the Hebrew יֶלֶד is "very young child" or "infant" (Eng, *Days of Our Years*, 84).

63. Malamat, "Kingship and Council," 249.

64. Robert Alter, *The Five Books of Moses: A Translation with Commentary* (New York: W. W. Norton, 2004), xxxv.

65. In the past, the last two terms were thought to have derived from a separate root עלל, meaning either "to be active" (so Franz Zorrel, *Lexicon hebraicum et aramaicum Veteris Testamenti* [Rome: Pontificium Institutum Biblicum, 1958], 579a) or having an unknown meaning (so BDB, "עלל II," 760). A recent consensus sees those two terms as *qatīl* constructions of the root עול; see Magne Sæbø, "עול," *TDOT* 10: 518–22.

66. See William R. Domeris, "עול"," *NIDOTTE* 3: 344.

67. Although note that the terms derived from עול are sometimes put into relationship with יוֹנֵק through the use of merism, as in 1 Sam 15:3; 22:19 and Jer 44:7. This would suggest that they are not interchangeable terms but rather have a difference of nuance, however slight. Sæbø refers to them as "closely related but different" terms (עול"," 10: 520).

68. Wolff (*Anthropology*, 121) cites 2 Macc 7:27 in support of this estimate, as does Eng (*Days of Our Years*, 53). Wolff (*Anthropology*, 243 n. 9) also refers to the Egyptian *Instruction of Ani*: "Her breast was in thy mouth for three years." See also 2 Chr 31:16.

69. Julia M. Asher-Greve ("Decisive Sex, Essential Gender," in *Sex and Gender in the Ancient Near East: Proceedings of the 47th Rencontre Assyriologique Internationale, Helsinki, July 2–6, 2001* [ed. S. Parpola and Robert M. Whiting; 2 vols.; Helsinki: The Neo-Assyrian Text Corpus Project, 2002], 1:15 shows that this was also the Sumerian conception of very young children: prior to their weaning at around age three both boys and girls are collectively referred to as *lú-tur* or "small people," only later being called boys (*dumu-nita*) and girls (*dumu-munus*).

70. Sæbø, "עול," 10: 521.

71. Trito-Isaiah writes that there will be no more עוּל יָמִים, or "infant of days," that is, a child who lives to see only a few days.

72. Reading with the LXX, suggesting the vocalization עָל as opposed to the MT עַל. Given the parallel term "orphan" in the first verset, this is the preferable vocalization. See Marvin H. Pope, *Job: A New Translation with Introduction and Commentary* (AB 15; Garden City, NY: Doubleday, 1965), 174–75; see also Norman C. Habel, *The Book of Job* (OTL; Philadelphia: Westminster, 1985), 345.

73. This second verset employs the term יֶלֶד, but given the Hebrew poetic principle of synonymous parallelism, what is said of the יְלָדִים in this verset may be applied to the parallel term עֲוִילִים in the first verset.

74. William R. Domeris, "ינק"," *NIDOTTE* 2: 473.

75. Helmer Ringgren, "יָנַק," *TDOT* 6: 107. Presumably Ringgren's reluctance to equate the terms completely stems from the use of the terms in merism constructions that would seem to imply their difference; see n. 67.

76. This verse, however, poses many difficulties for the interpreter, and it is possible that the meaning of the word derived from גמל in this verse may be related to the more common use of the verb, "to recompense," rather than to anything related to weaning. De Boer's translation of the verse reads "But on the contrary, I have made myself without resistance or movement, just as one does with his mother, thus have I made myself content." See Pieter A. H. de Boer, "Psalm 131:2," *VT* 16(1966): 292.

77. So BDB ("טַף," 382); see also the support for this limited understanding of the term in Wolff, *Anthropology*, 120, and Gesenius, *A Hebrew and English Lexicon of the Old Testament, Including the Biblical Chaldee: From the Latin of William Gesenius* (trans. Edward Robinson; Boston: Crocker and Brewster, 1854), s.v. טַף.

78. Gesenius, ibid.

79. C. Locher, "טַף," *TDOT* 5: 347.

80. John A. L. Lee, "ΑΠΟΣΚΕΥΗ in the Septuagint," *JTS* 23(1972): 430–37.

81. Locher, "טַף," 5: 348.

82. NEB and REB do so frequently, with NJPS (e.g., 2 Chr 31:18) and NRSV (e.g., Gen 47:12) doing so more selectively.

83. Eng, *Days of Our Years*, 93.

84. Michael P. O'Connor and John A. L. Lee, "A Problem in Biblical Lexicography: The Case of Hebrew *tap* and Greek *aposkeuē*," *ZAW* 119(2007): 406.

85. Locher ("טַף," 5: 349) claims that context can help the reader determine when children alone are the referent of the term, as in Num 14:31; Deut 1:39; and "possibly" Deut 29:10(11); 31:12; and Josh 8:35.

86. I do not include instances where these two terms are listed with other terms describing groups within the population, as in the stock phraseology "men, women, and children" meant to signify the entire population; see Deut 2:34; 3:6; 31:12; and Jer 43:6.

87. L. Koehler, W. Baumgartner, and J. J. Stamm ("בחר I," *HALOT* 1: 119) argue that בחר is related to the Akkadian *bahūlātu* found in Sargon and Sennacherib's inscriptions. See the arguments against the proposed alternative root made by Horst Seebass, "בָּחַר," *TDOT* 2: 73–87 and John H. Walton "בָּחוּר," *NIDOTTE* 1: 634–35.

88. Walton ("בָּחוּר," 1: 634) downplays this connection, claiming that "any aspect of 'choice quality' is subordinated, if not entirely absent from the connotation in the OT." However, in my judgment the frequency of association of בָּחוּר with positive evaluations of attractiveness and strength challenges Walton's assessment.

89. As noted above, the Sumerian term for "young man" (*guruš*) reflects a similar understanding, as it is written with the sign for "strong" (*kala*). See Asher-Greve, "The Essential Body," 444.

90. See 1 Sam 26:2; 2 Sam 6:1; 1 Kgs 12:21 = 2 Chr 11:1; Jer 51:3; 2 Chr 25:5; Ps 78:31.

91. Samson, in Judg 14:10, is depicted as having a feast before his wedding because that was the custom for בָּחוּרִים. Note, however, that this does not specifically state that Samson himself was a בָּחוּר.

92. Translation mine. This "goodness" may refer to his imposing physique, given that it is immediately followed by a report of Saul's impressive height. Still, the use of the term טוב indicates a positive evaluation of the בָּחוּר.

93. See Niditch, *Judges*, 156.

94. Translation mine.

95. See Deut 32:25; Isa 23:4; Jer 31:13; 51:22; Ezek 9:6; Amos 8:13; Zech 9:17; Ps 78:63; 148:12; Lam 1:18; 2:21; 2 Chr 36:17.

96. Tikva Frymer-Kensky, "Virginity in the Bible," in *Gender and Law in the Hebrew Bible and the Ancient Near East* (ed. Victor H. Matthews, Bernard M. Levinson, and Tikva Frymer-Kensky; JSOTSup 262; Sheffield: Sheffield Academic Press, 1998), 79–80.

97. Unlike with young women, the actual sexual experience of these young men is of no concern in the HB. There are no terms, in other words, that specifically denote male virginity, and sexual experience seems not to function as an important moment signifying a boy's transition to manhood as it often does in the modern West. See Steinberg (*World of the Child*, 59), who argues that "[virginity] does not appear to be essential in the construction of childhood for Israelite boys," which she claims to be the case partly because "there would be no physical means to track the virginity of a son."

98. See Niditch, *Judges*, 171, and van der Toorn, "Judges XVI," 249, 252 n. 9.

99. The seven occurrences of the feminine form exclude occurrences of the musical instruction עַל־עֲלָמוֹת before certain psalms (46:1; 48:15) and in 1 Chr 15:20, which BDB ("עַלְמָה," 761) suggests may refer to the "voice of young women," that is, soprano or falsetto.

100. For the early Christian equation of עַלְמָה and "virgin," see Adam Kamesar, "The Virgin of Isaiah 7:14: The Philological Argument From the Second to the Fifth Century," *JTS* 41(1990): 51–75. For a more recent attempt to make this connection, see Richard Niessen, "The Virginity of the עַלְמָה in Isaiah 7:14," *BSac* 137(1980): 133–50.

101. See, e.g., Christoph Dohmen and Helmer Ringgren, "עַלְמָה," *TDOT* 11: 160–63, and John H. Walton "עֲלוּמִים," *NIDOTTE* 3: 418.

102. L. Koehler, " עלם III," *HALOT* 2: 835.

103. See K. Beyer, *Die Aramäischen Texte vom Toten Meer* (Göttingen: Vandenhoek and Ruprecht, 1984), 508.

104. Walton, "עֲלוּמִים," 3:418.

105. Ibid., 417. Dohmen ("עַלְמָה," 11: 116) concurs, writing that these three form a "triad" expressing "the legal status of the various women belonging to the royal harem."

106. Walton, "עֲלוּמִים," 3£417.

107. Ibid., 418.

108. For an overview of the many suggestions made by scholars to explain the impenetrable MT, see Michael V. Fox, *Proverbs 10–31: A New Translation with Introduction and Commentary* (AB 18B; New Haven: Yale University Press, 2009), 870–71.

109. Note, however, that uniquely among the terms discussed above, נַעַר covers a broad age range. When those instances where נַעַר signifies "servant" are removed, the age range is from unborn child to seventeen. Thus a more physically developed young man in his late teens may be referred to with both terms נַעַר and עֶלֶם, provided he is at the upper end of the age spectrum of נַעַר.

110. Note also that abstract nouns derived from עלם and נער are paralleled in Job 33:25: "let his skin become fresher than in youth (מִנֹּעַר); let him return to the days of his virile youth (עֲלוּמָיו)." Here too the two words do not need to be considered as synonyms. Certainly Hebrew poetry has more techniques at its disposal than simple synonymous "thought rhymes," as Robert Alter puts it (*The Art of Biblical Poetry* [New York: Basic Books, 1985], 9). Indeed, this verse may be a classic example of Alter's "developmental impulse of biblical verse" (ibid., 17), where the move from the first verset to the second involves a move from the general (נַעַר, an abstract noun derived from a term with a rather large age window) to the more specific (עֲלוּמָיו, a term describing a more limited, and older, age range).

111. In proposing a two-stage schema of biblical boyhood ("young boys" and "older boys/young men") this analysis is in agreement with the work of other scholars who have addressed the matter of the male life cycle in the HB. Hans Walter Wolff's conception of the life cycle in the HB includes a similar two-stage childhood, consisting of "children" (in which he includes נְעָרִים alongside

יוֹנְקִים and טַף) and "young but fully grown men and grown up girls" (consisting of בַּחוּרִים and בְּתוּלוֹת). See Wolff, *Anthropology*, 120. Eng's schema is also similar, although he divides the larger group of younger children into two smaller groups: those who have been weaned and those who have not. The older group, consisting of בָּחוּרִים, he defines as "youth/young adulthood." See Eng, *Days of Our Years*, 57. Both Eng and Wolff appeal to such biblical passages as Ezek 9:6; Jer 6:11; and 51:22 to justify this separation because each distinguishes between older youths (described with the noun בָּחוּר) and young children (טַף in Ezek 9:6; עוֹלָל in Jer 6:11; נַעַר in Jer 51:22).

Indeed, this division of boyhood into two or three groups is remarkably consistent among ancient and even modern cultures. Johannes Louw and Eugene Nida, scholars of biblical Greek, emphasize that: "Languages employ a number of different terms for the age-grading of males. Some of the most common distinctions involve the following: (1) male baby boys up to the time of weaning; (2) boys from the age of weaning to the time of puberty rites, when they are recognized as being sexually capable; (3) from puberty to the time of marriage. . . ." See Johannes P. Louw and Eugene A. Nida, eds., *Greek-English English Lexicon of the New Testament: Based on Semantic Domains* (2d ed.; New York: United Bible Societies, 1989), 107–108. This quote was brought to my attention by Eng, *Days of Our Years*, 57.

Comparative evidence from the ancient Near East also shows this general separation of young males into subcategories. For example, John A. Brinkman's study of Middle Babylonian personnel rosters ("Sex, Age, and Physical Condition Designations for Servile Laborers in the Middle Babylonian Period: A Preliminary Survey," in *Zikir Šumim: Assyriological Studies Presented to F. R. Kraus* [ed. G. van Driel et al.; Leiden: Brill, 1982], 2) reveals three groups, adolescent (*guruš.tur*), weaned child (*pirsu*), and suckling child (*dumu gaba*). Interestingly, he also notes that adolescents are considered much closer to adults than to children in that they "often performed the same tasks as adults and were given correspondingly large rations" (ibid.). Sumerian ration lists, according to Marten Stol ("Private Life in Ancient Mesopotamia," *CANE* 1: 485), likewise separate children into three groups: birth to five years, five to ten years, and ten to thirteen years.

112. The term נַעַר cannot be fit into either of the proposed groups in this schema, as it encompasses such a large age window (birth to approximately twenty years of age). However, the characteristics that are ascribed to the term (physical weakness, lack of authority, impetuousness, lack of wisdom, beauty) would seem to put it in the first, younger group. Context is the only guide when attempting to recognize whether a character referred to as a נַעַר is better understood as belonging to this group of young children, or the latter group of older youths.

113. But note that both of these terms have comparably wide age ranges, and thus are not always used of older youths. Still, they can and do often describe older

boys, יֶלֶד having an age range that can extend to approximately twelve years of age, and נַעַר even reaching to approximately twenty.

114. Note that not all "fear" (ירא) is considered boyish in the HB. While the fear of going into battle—and particularly of killing in battle (Judg 8:20)—is associated with boys, a man can also fear. For example, Gideon's fear is a repeated theme in Judg 6–8 (e.g., Judg 6:27; 7:10), yet he is still considered a mighty man of valor (גִּבּוֹר; Judg 6:12). The key difference seems to be that boys are afraid of acting/killing, but men are afraid of being acted upon/killed.

115. Presumably the preference for depicting a young boy transitioning to manhood as opposed to older boyhood/young manhood in these stories would be a result of a desire for greater dramatic effect, since showing a transition from tender and inexperienced boyhood to virile manhood is a more exciting tale than just describing the boy transitioning from one phase of youth to another. Alternatively, this could be because in two cases (that of Moses in Exod 2 and Solomon in 1 Kgs 1–2), the coming-of-age stories end with marriage reports (thus older boyhood terminology would not apply), and in the other two (Solomon in 1 Kgs 3 and Samuel in 1 Sam 3) the stories conclude with the conferring of an important and authoritative vocation on the boy (king in Solomon's case, prophet in Samuel's), thus manhood terminology would be more appropriate than boyhood terminology.

CHAPTER 3

1. The overall unity of Exod 2:1–22, a foundational assumption of a reading like mine that divides the larger narrative into two scenes, has been demonstrated by a number of scholars. Carol Meyers (*Exodus* [New Cambridge Bible Commentary; Cambridge: Cambridge University Press, 2005], 46)identifies an *inclusio* formed by the reports of marriage and the birth of a son in v. 1 and v. 22, which serve to delimit the boundaries of the textual unit. John I. Durham (*Exodus* [WBC 3; Waco, TX: Word Books, 1987], 21) similarly argues for the unity of Exod 2:1–22. William H. C. Propp (*Exodus 1–18: A New Translation with Introduction and Commentary* [AB 2; New York: Doubleday, 1998], 145–46; 162) shows how thematic unity binds the narrative block together (although he asserts that the section begins one verse earlier, in Exod 1:22) and uses the sevenfold repetition of key words in certain portions of the narrative to identify the borders of the scenes within the story (see n. 7 and n. 9)

While precise identification of the initial source for Exod 2 is not essential for my argument, it is worth noting that most scholars consulted consider this block the work of J, who may have synthesized several earlier oral traditions in the composition. See e.g., Propp, *Exodus 1–18*, 146; Brevard S. Childs (*The Book of Exodus* [OTL; Louisville: Westminster, 1976], 28); Martin Noth (*Exodus* [trans. B.S. Bowden; OTL; Philadelphia: Westminster, 1962], 25; 34–35); George

W. Coats (*Exodus 1–18* [FOTL IIA; Grand Rapids, MI: Eerdmans, 1999], 7; 18–19). For the claim that these biographical traditions about Moses were known by the Deuteronomistic Historian(s) in the seventh century, see p. 94 and n. 58.

2. For the internal coherence of Scene II—as opposed to its being a random collection of unrelated traditions crudely joined by an editor—see Coats (*Exodus 1–18*, 30). Coats finds a similar structure in each episode of Scene II and identifies a unifying theme throughout the scene of Moses defending the oppressed.

3. The remaining verses in Exod 2 (vv. 23–25) are unrelated to the preceding pericope, being more of an "addendum" (Meyers, *Exodus*, 46) that likely comes originally from a separate source; see, e.g., Coats, *Exodus 1–18*, 33–34; Propp, *Exodus 1–18*, 170; 178.

4. Others who recognize that v. 11 begins a new narrative segment within the larger story of Exod 2:1–22 include: Meyers (*Exodus*, 44–46); Coats (*Exodus 1–18*, 18–19; 25); Nahum M. Sarna (*Exodus: The Traditional Hebrew Text with the New JPS Translation* [Philadelphia: Jewish Publication Society, 1991], 25); Terence E. Fretheim (*Exodus* [IBC; Louisville: John Knox, 1991], 41); Childs (*Book of Exodus*, 27); Propp (*Exodus 1–18*, 161); Moshe Greenberg (*Understanding Exodus* [New York: Behrman House, 1969], 44); and Jopie Siebert-Hommes ("But if She be a Daughter . . . She may Live! 'Daughters' and 'Sons' in Exodus 1–2," in *A Feminist Companion to Exodus to Deuteronomy* [ed. Athalya Brenner; FCB 6; Sheffield: Academic Press, 1994], 71–72).

5. See, for example, Childs (*Book of Exodus*, 21); Umberto Cassuto (*A Commentary on the Book of Exodus* [trans. Israel Abrahams; Jerusalem: Magnes Press, 1967], 21); and Greenberg (*Understanding Exodus*, 42). This reading is also supported by many translations (NRSV, NJPS, NAS, NJB) that render the second use of גדל in v. 11 as "grew up." The ambiguity of the verb גדל has generated much speculation concerning Moses's age in v. 11. Traditional and scribal conjecture on his age has run the gamut from forty (Acts 7:23–24) to twenty-one (*Jub.* 47:10; 48:11), twenty (*Exod. Rab* 5:2), eighteen, and twelve (for references, see Louis Ginzberg, *The Legends of the Jews* [Trans. by Henrietta Szold; 7 vols.; Philadelphia: Jewish Publication Society, 1911–36], 5.404). It is noteworthy that with the exception of Acts 7 many of these sources consider Moses to be approximately at the age of legal majority in the Torah (i.e., twenty; see Chapter 2), which supports a coming-of-age reading. According to Ginzberg (ibid.), the tradition of Moses being forty at this time (see Acts 7:23) has more to do with a desire for symmetry that anything else: Moses is said to have died at age 120 (Deut 34:7), and he lived forty years in the wilderness (Josh 5:6). Therefore, one strand of tradition assumes that he lived forty years in Midian and forty in Egypt.

6. Bryna Jocheved Levy, "Moshe: Portrait of the Leader as a Young Man," in *Torah of the Mothers: Contemporary Jewish Women Read Classical Jewish Texts* (ed. Ora

Wiskind Elper and Susan Handelman; New York: Urim Publications, 2000), 410. In this insightful article, Levy explores Exod 2:11–14 as Moses's "ethical coming of age," (ibid., 398) an argument with some similarities to mine. However, it is important to note that Levy does not treat the role of vv. 15–22 in Moses's maturation (as I do below), and her speculation is more concerned with Moses *ethical* development, not his transition from boyhood to manhood.

7. An observation made by Siebert-Hommes ("But if She be a Daughter," 71). Propp (*Exodus 1–18*, 146), as already noted, also recognizes this repetition; however, by adding Exod 1:22 to the scene the number of repetitions rises to eight (seven uses of the singular and one of the plural), which Propp compares to the frequent seven-plus-one motif in Hebrew and Ugaritic poetry.

8. See Siebert-Hommes, "But if She be a Daughter," 71.

9. Propp, *Exodus 1–18*, 146. Propp notes that the repetition of יֶלֶד and אִישׁ "may symbolize Moses's maturation and socialization" (ibid., 162), later speculating that the scene "tells the familiar story of a young man growing up" (ibid., 176). Even so, Propp does not give more attention to the coming-of-age theme in Exod 2 than these brief comments.

10. See George W. Coats, "Moses in Midian," *JBL* 92(1973): 3–10. Coats bases his contention not only on the paltry amount of attention paid to the courtship of Moses and Zipporah, but also on the return to the Jethro/Reuel tradition in Exod 18, in which the relationship of Moses to his father-in-law is stressed but where in contrast "[Moses's] wife and children are almost humorously ignored" (ibid., 6).

11. Those who prefer to view Moses's act of searching the area before slaying the Egyptian as a desire for secrecy include: Trent C. Butler ("An Anti-Moses Tradition," JSOT 12[1979]: 10); Childs (*Book of Exodus*, 30); and DiPalma ("De/Constructing Masculinity," 42).

12. See *Exod. Rab.* 1:29; *Lev. Rab.* 32:4. For parallels to the use of אֵין אִישׁ in Isa 59:16, see Isa 41:28 and 50:2. Among modern interpreters, this reading is favored by Cassuto (*Commentary on the Book of Exodus*, 22) and Benno Jacob (*The Second Book of the Bible: Exodus* [trans. W. Jacob; Hoboken, NJ: Ktav, 1992], 37–38). Propp (*Exodus 1–18*, 163) prefers a synthesis of this interpretation with that identifying a wish for secrecy in Moses's actions, writing that "the absence of bystanders both forces Moses to act and gives him hope of impunity."

13. Ari Zivotofsky ("The Leadership Qualities of Moses," *Judaism* 43[1994]: 260), in agreement with this midrashic interpretation, argues that by announcing that no "man" is present, the text means "a real man willing to take action." Zivotofsky's argument suffers, however, for equating all action with manhood, an equation belied by the notable instances in Exod 1–2 where women are the active agents of liberation (e.g., Shiphrah and Puah in Exod 1; Moses's mother and Pharaoh's daughter in the first scene of Exod 2). It is not that a

man is needed to act, but instead that the style of action demanded by the situation in Exod 2:11–12, physical force, is one more suited to a man in the worldview of the HB.

14. This interpretation of episode 1 is premised upon a positive view of Moses's action in this scene. Some readers, however, believe that the text is condemnatory of Moses's killing of the Egyptian (DiPalma ["De/Constructing Masculinity," 42–44]; Butler ["Anti-Moses," 10, 13]). Others believe that the text is neutral on the matter, leaving the final judgment of Moses's act to the audience (Childs, *Book of Exodus*, 44). Three features of the text militate against these readings. First, the fact that the same verb is used to describe Moses's killing of the Egyptian and the Egyptian's abuse of the Hebrew (נכה) suggests that the narrator views Moses's deed as justified proportional retribution. Second, Moses's act prefigures Yhwh's liberating work later in the narrative—where again the root נכה is employed to describe Yhwh's punishment of the Egyptians (Exod 3:20; 7:25; 12:12, 13, 29; 9:15). This further points to a positive assessment of Moses's actions. (The previous two points are made by Fretheim [*Exodus*, 43] and Cassuto [*Commentary on the Book of Exodus*, 22].) Third, this episode precedes two others in which Moses defends an oppressed group or individual, thereby leading the reader to view the episode similarly as an instance of Moses's concern for justice.

15. See Gordon F. Davies, *Israel in Egypt: Reading Exodus 1–2* (JSOTSup 135; Sheffield: Sheffield Academic Press, 1992), 133–34. See also Childs (*Book of Exodus*, 30) and Sarna (*Exodus*, 11).

16. See Clines, "Being a Man in the Book of the Covenant," 4.

17. For arguments in defense of this reading, see Childs (*Exodus*, 30) and Davies (*Israel in Egypt*, 119–22). See also the following translations, which provide minor variations but consistently translate the phrase אִישׁ שַׂר with one word in English: KJV, NAS, NJPS, NIV, ESV, NJB.

18. Scholars who advocate for this reading include: Alan D. Crown ("An Alternative Meaning for אִישׁ in the Old Testament," *VT* 24[1974]: 111); Durham (*Exodus*, 18); and Propp (*Exodus 1–18*, 4). Crown's article argues for viewing אִישׁ independently; however he contends that this term should occasionally be understood to imply "leader" or "king." I follow Crown's translation of אִישׁ as an independent term from שַׂר, but in my judgment אִישׁ should be taken at its most basic meaning: "man." Durham opts to translate the phrase אִישׁ שַׂר as "man-prince," representing a middle position between those arguing for apposition and those advocating the independence of the terms.

19. See Propp, *Exodus 1–18*, 4. Despite Propp's translation, he does not consider its exegetical implications.

20. Again, rabbinic interpreters seem to have recognized the importance of adult manhood to this objection. See *Exod. Rab.* 1.35 and *Yalkut Shimoni* 1:167, quoting *Midrash ʾAvkir* (cited by Zivotofsky, "Leadership," 261). Here the rabbis

speculate that the crux of the Hebrew's objection was that Moses was too young to be a judge.

21. See Fretheim (*Exodus*, 44), who recognizes how the guilty Hebrew functions to foreshadow the rebellious Israel in the wilderness.

22. For this reason, interpretations of the episode claiming that Moses is rightly criticized for overstepping his authority (e.g., DiPalma, "De/Constructing," 43–44; Davies, *Israel in Egypt*, 133–37; Butler, "Anti-Moses," 10) are mistaken. If this were the text's intention, why would the valid objection to Moses's presumptuousness be articulated by a character that the audience is led to distrust from the moment of his introduction because of his "guilt" (רָשָׁע) and abuse of a fellow Hebrew?

23. DiPalma ("De/Constructing Masculinity," 43) claims that Moses's fear of punishment stands as a critique of the link between masculinity and violence. His point is premised, however, on the belief that Moses's action of retaliation against the Egyptian is condemned by the narrator, a reading called into question above, n. 14.

24. See Chapter 2, pp. 53, 72 n. 114. Cf. Chapter 1, 31–32.

25. Whether or not Moses's intervention involved the use of physical force, his actions show a fearlessness in the face of potential harm from other men that is characteristically masculine. See Chapter 1, 00–00. Additionally, Chapman's study of the visual representation of war in Assyrian reliefs illuminates the importance of the defense of women to ancient Near Eastern masculinity (*Gendered Language*, 32).

26. The story of a male hero meeting his future wife at a well reflects a narrative betrothal type-scene in the Hebrew Bible; see, for example, Alter, *Art of Biblical Narrative*, 61–69. The story in Exod 2 is especially similar to that in Gen 29, where Jacob encounters Rachel. While Gen 29 may provide a model for this scene (see Davies [*Israel in Egypt*, 148] and John Van Seters, *The Life of Moses: The Yahwist as Historian in Exodus–Numbers* [Louisville: Westminster John Knox, 1994], 31–32), it significantly differs from Exod 2 in that it is apparently not influenced by the coming-of-age theme. See the Appendix for a more detailed treatment of the Jacob cycle, and its lack of a defined coming-of-age story for its central character.

27. Walter Brueggemann, *First and Second Samuel* (IBC; Louisville: Westminster John Knox, 1990), 23.

28. P. Kyle McCarter, Jr., *I Samuel: A New Translation with Introduction, Notes, and Commentary* (AB 8; Garden City, NY: Doubleday, 1980) 100. See also Bruce B. Birch ("The Books of First and Second Samuel: Introduction, Commentary and Reflections," *NIB* 2: 993), who claims that at the conclusion of 1 Sam 3 "Samuel has grown to adulthood." Hans Wilhelm Herzberg argues that "the closing verses [of 1 Sam 3] describe [Samuel's] growth to manhood" (*I & II Samuel: A Commentary* [OTL; Philadelphia: Westminster, 1964], 42); and

R. W. L. Moberly asserts that Josephus' reckoning of Samuel's age as twelve in 1 Sam 3 (see *AJ* V.10.4) is appropriate given that this is the traditional age of *bar mitzvah*. Just as in the *bar mitzvah* ceremony, the events in 1 Sam 3 effect "the transition . . . from a child's to an adult's standing before God," in Moberly's judgment ("To Hear the Master's Voice: Revelation and Spiritual Discernment in the Call of Samuel," *SJT* 48 [1995]: 459 n. 40).

29. Scholars are divided on the unity of composition in 1 Sam 1–3. On one end of the spectrum is John T. Willis ("An Anti-Elide Narrative Tradition from a Prophetic Circle at the Ramah Sanctuary," *JBL* 90[1971], 288–308; see also "Samuel versus Eli: 1 Samuel 1–7," *TZ* 35[1979]: 204–205), who argues for the overall unity not only of 1 Sam 1–3 but also for all of the first seven chapters of 1 Sam. Willis's position contradicts the majority viewpoint that sees 1 Sam 4–6 and 2 Sam 6 as a composition independent of the rest of 1–2 Sam, which has been known since Leonhard Rost's time as the "Ark Narrative." Patrick D. Miller and J. J. M. Roberts, on the other hand, view 1 Sam 1–3 as consisting of two originally separate sources, one concerned with story of Eli and the other with the rise to prominence of the young Samuel (*The Hand of the Lord: A Reassessment of the "Ark Narrative" of 1 Samuel* [JHNES; Baltimore: Johns Hopkins University Press, 1977], 114). For Miller and Roberts, the Elide material originally served as the introduction to the Ark Narrative that was only later edited together with the Samuel materials, and the many references to Samuel within the Elide materials in 1 Sam 2:12–36 are the creation of an editor who brought these disparate sources together. For a detailed discussion of the contours of the debate on the unity of 1 Sam 1–3 and its relationship to the Ark Narrative, see Robert Karl Gnuse, "The Dream Theophany of Samuel: Its Structure in Relation to Ancient Near Eastern Dreams and Its Theological Significance" (PhD diss., Vanderbilt University, 1980), 268–82. For a more recent discussion, see Erik Eynikel, "The Relation between the Eli Narrative and the Ark Narratives," in *Past, Present, Future: The Deuteronomistic History and the Prophets* (ed. Johannes C. de Moor and Herrie F. Van Rooy; Leiden: Brill, 2000), 88–106. The reading offered below of 1 Sam 3 as a coming-of-age story is not dependent upon any particular position regarding the source history behind 1 Sam 1–3, with the exception of what Gnuse recognizes as the scholarly consensus that 1 Sam 3 is a compositional unity and is from the same hand that included the many references to Samuel interspersed throughout the Elide materials ("Dream Theophany," 274–75).

30. See 1 Sam 1:22, 24 [two times], 25, 27; 2:11, 18, 21, 26; 3:1, 8. The only other character who is referred to as a נַעַר more than Samuel (twelve times versus Samuel's eleven) is Jonathan's unnamed assistant in 1 Sam 20. Moreover, it is important to mention that in each instance of the term's use to denote Samuel, a life-cycle meaning ("boy") is the most appropriate translation of this multivalent term. See NRSV, NJPS, NAS, NIV, KJV, etc., each of which unanimously

renders נַעַר as "boy," "child," or similar terms connoting youth when used in reference to Samuel. Alternative definitions such as "servant" do not fit the context. For example, one could hardly imagine Hannah presenting the newly weaned babe Samuel to Eli with the words "This is the servant that I prayed for" (1 Sam 1:27a).

31. Cf. the more common ways in which the term נַעַר is used to describe other characters: (1) the word may be used independently of the referent's name to designate him (e.g., Ishmael in Gen 21:17, 18; where the messenger of Yhwh calls him simply הַנַּעַר without any mention of his name); and (2) the term may follow a person's name (hereafter "PN"), either on its own (e.g., Joshua's appellation as "Joshua ben Nun, a lad/servant" [וִיהוֹשֻׁעַ בִּן־נוּן נַעַר] Exod 33:11), or in construct relationship with another PN indicating ownership (thus "Ziba the servant of Saul" [צִיבָא נַעַר שָׁאוּל], 2 Sam 9:9).

32. See also Nathan (2 Sam 7:2; 12:25; 1 Kgs 1:8, 10, 22, 23, 32, 34, 38, 44, 45), Ahijah (1 Kgs 11:29; 14:2, 18), Jehu ben Hanani (1 Kgs 16:7, 12), Elijah (1 Kgs 18:36), Elisha (2 Kgs 6:12; 9:1), and Isaiah (2 Kgs 19:2; 20:1, 11, 14), all of whom are referred to as "PN the prophet" rather than "the prophet PN."

33. LXX[B] and 4QSam[a] differ significantly from the MT in v. 24. The MT at 1:24–25 reads "She brought him to the house of the Lord at Shiloh; and the child was young. Then they slaughtered the bull, and they brought the child to Eli." (so NRSV). LXX, in contrast, here reads: "And she came to the house of Yahweh in Shiloh, and the child was with them. And they went before Yahweh, and his father slaughtered the sacrifice as he did regularly to Yahweh. And she took the child, and he slaughtered the calf. And Hannah, the mother of the child, went to Eli" (translation McCarter, *I Samuel*, 57). McCarter (ibid.), wishing to explain away what he finds to be the awkward phrasing at the end of 1:24 in MT, argues that the MT originally more resembled the LXX, but now it contains a haplography resulting from homoioteleuton when it was transcribed from the *Vorlage* of the LXX, which he reconstructs. However, many scholars find the MT perfectly comprehensible and view McCarter's reconstruction of the *Vorlage* artificial and overly speculative. These include: Herzberg (*I & II Samuel*, 27); Anthony F. Campbell, S. J., *1 Samuel* (FOTL 7; Grand Rapids, MI: Eerdmans, 2003), 38; Stephen Pisano, *Additions or Omissions in the Books of Samuel* (OBO 57; Freiburg: Universitätsverlag, 1984), 157–63; and David Toshio Tsumura, *The First Book of Samuel* (NICOT; Grand Rapids, MI: Eerdmans, 2007), 131. See also Carol Meyers ("Hannah and Her Sacrifice: Reclaiming Female Agency," in *A Feminist Companion to Samuel and Kings* [ed. Athalya Brenner; FCB 5; Sheffield: Sheffield Academic Press, 1994], 100–101), who argues that the MT is preferable because it highlights Hannah's agency in the sacrifice of 1 Sam 1:24 and therefore reflects an earlier time in the history of Israel's religion when women had a more active role in cultic and ceremonial practices. The LXX and 4QSam[a] altered the MT to remove Hannah's agency in the

sacrifice to have the text reflect the limited cultic participation of women in later times.

34. See Chapter 2, 53–54, 58. Samuel's fear to speak because of his lack of social power compared to his elder Eli is analogous to Jether's fear to act in battle because of his physical weakness and emotional fortitude in comparison to the veteran warriors around him.

35. Moberly, "Master's Voice," 459–60.

36. Most scholars end 1 Sam 3 at 1 Sam 4:1a. See, e.g., McCarter (*I Samuel*, 97–103) and Campbell (*1 Samuel*, 52).

37. While this structural feature of the text is noted by several commentators, no one discusses it with more depth than Campbell (ibid., 47–49) and Tsumura (*First Book of Samuel*, 132). Tsumura differs from the popular reading, which identifies six reports, and instead argues for seven reports. According to his formulation, 1:24 is Report 1, and Scene 1 consists primarily of Samuel's arrival at Shiloh and Hannah's prayer. Each of the subsequent reports then shifts one place. Report 6, the concluding report, becomes Report 7 in this template. While Tsumura offers an attractive alternative, the vocabulary similarities shared by the six generally recognized reports, as well as their clear structural purpose demarcating scene breaks, are not as evident in 1:24. Consequently, lacking any reference to Samuel's growth or ministry, 1:24 should not be viewed as the initial report.

38. This interpretation is favored by McCarter (*I Samuel*, 99); Gnuse ("Dream Theophany," 164); Robert P. Gordon, *I & II Samuel: A Commentary* (Grand Rapids, MI: Zondervan, 1988), 91; and Birch ("First and Second Books of Samuel," 993). Rather than Yhwh's words, Samuel's words are not allowed to fall to the ground. Even though the referent of דְּבָרָיו is unclear, it is doubtful that the subject of the verb and the referent of the 3 ms suffix in this clause, which is clear in the preceding clause (Yhwh is the subject, Samuel the referent of the 3 ms suffix), would change in the following clause without indication by the narrator. For a contrary opinion, see Ralph W. Klein (*1 Samuel* [WBC 10; Waco, TX: Word Books, 1983], 30) and Hans Joachim Stoebe (*Das Erste Buch Samuelis* [KAT 8/1; Gütersloh: Mohn, 1973], 126).

39. See K. M. Beyse ("שָׁלֵשׁ," *TDOT* 5: 124), who notes the prevalence of the threefold repetition of actions as a narrative motif in biblical literature.

40. McCarter (*I Samuel*, 82) argues that the participle מְשָׁרֵת when used in this context connotes priestly activity (see also K. Engelken, "שׁרת," *TDOT* 5: 507). Taken together with the reports of Samuel wearing an ephod (2:18), it is apparent that Samuel is being described as a priest.

41. This is not to argue that Samuel no longer functions in the role of priest after this point. Indeed, he continues the priestly activity of offering sacrifices on behalf of the people throughout the following narrative (see, e.g., 1 Sam 7:9–10). The third report of Samuel's priestly ministry instead marks the completion of

his priestly service at Shiloh. After this point, Samuel's role at Shiloh is more prophetic than priestly since Yhwh appears to him there (3:21).

42. Note that the use of the verb גדל in 3:19 can best be translated with the English "to grow up," but this is not the usual meaning of the verb. Most often the English "to grow" more accurately reflects the meaning of the verb, and does so when describing Samuel prior to 3:19 (2:21, 26), despite McCarter's translation of גדל in 2:21 as "grew up" (McCarter, *I Samuel*, 77). In English, "to grow up" suggests a completed process—the final transition from childhood to adulthood—while "to grow" simply denotes physical development. On one hand, since Samuel is said to גדל in 2:21b, and is later still referred to as a boy (נַעַר; see 2:26; 3:1, 8), translating the verb as "grow up" in 2:21, 26 is inappropriate. In 3:19, on the other hand, the context dictates that here גדל may rightly be translated as "grow up" because it serves as the third repetition of the verb in the parallel reports, marking the completion of the growth process. See also the discussion of the use of גדל in Exod 2:11 above (n. 5), as well as in the Samson cycle (see Chapter 5, p. 134).

43. See, for example, McCarter (*I Samuel*, 85), Campbell (*1 Samuel*, 47–49), and Klein (*1 Samuel*, 26).

44. McCarter, *I Samuel*, 85.

45. The central issue in the debate about the identity of the אֲנָשִׁים and נְעָרִים in 2:17 is whether the נְעָרִים in this verse are to be identified with the נַעַר הַכֹּהֵן mentioned in 2:13 and 15. Most believe these two uses of נַעַר refer to different characters—the נַעַר הַכֹּהֵן being a priest's servant and the נְעָרִים of v. 17 being Eli's sons (see, e.g., NRSV, NAS, NJPS, KJV—all of which translate נַעַר הַכֹּהֵן as "the priest's servant" but then translate נְעָרִים as "young men"). Tsumura's translation (*First Book of Samuel*, 157–58), however, allows for both the נַעַר הַכֹּהֵן and the נְעָרִים of v. 17 to refer to Eli's sons, since he translates נַעַר הַכֹּהֵן as "the young priest." McCarter also equates the נְעָרִים and the נַעַר הַכֹּהֵן, but he believes both refer to temple servants, not Eli's sons. Thus he stands alone among commentators for asserting that 2:17 does not refer to Eli's sons at all. Unlike Tsumura's argument that equates the two expressions, McCarter's argument is unconvincing because it has no regard for the larger narrative context. It would be curious indeed for this section of the narrative (2:12–17) to be introduced with a statement about the evil of Eli's sons (referred to as בְּנֵי בְלִיָּעַל in 2:12) and then to proceed in the ensuing story to make no mention of them at all—and instead to criticize the temple servants.

46. LXX dispenses with the ambiguity in this verse by reckoning the young men/boys (παιδαρίον) as the subject of both clauses, thereby having no parallel to the MT אֲנָשִׁים. Again, presumably these youths are Eli's sons; therefore LXX offers a less nuanced assessment of the two in 1 Sam 2:12–17, referring to them throughout the passage as boys. Thus the contrast between the priests (1:3) who act like boys and Samuel, the boy who becomes a man (1 Sam 3), is even

more starkly drawn in LXX. Additionally, 4Q Sam^a follows the LXX and reproduces none of the MT's ambiguity.

47. Reading with NJPS at 2:13–16 and *contra* NRSV. NJPS accepts that the "potluck" approach through which the priests would randomly select their portion of the sacrificed meat described in vv. 13–14 was the standard, and that Eli's sons had altered it by taking whatever piece they wanted before the meat was boiled in a cauldron (v. 16). According to NRSV, both the "potluck" system and the direct confiscation of meat by the priests represented an alteration of the proper procedure.

48. Reading with Tsumura (*First Book of Samuel*, 152), who identifies the נַעַר הַכֹּהֵן mentioned in 2:13, 15 as "the young priest," that is, one of Eli's sons.

49. Note that especially the Deuteronomic tradition views legitimate male offspring as essential to "perpetuating a name in Israel"—a vital task for Israelite men in this tradition. See the further discussion of this feature of Israelite masculinity in Chapter 1, 40–41, and Chapter 5, 135–36.

50. Moberly, "Master's Voice," 459–60.

51. See Gordon, *I & II Samuel*, 91. The explanation of the statement is McCarter's (*I Samuel*, 99). Stoebe concurs (*Samuelis*, 122), with reference to evidence from Josh 21:45; 23:14; 1 Kgs 8:56; 2 Kgs 10:10.

52. Despite Moberly's insightful reading of the story suggesting that recognizing God's voice as distinctive from one's parent or mentor's voice is a marker of spiritual maturation ("Master's Voice," 459–60), this aspect of maturation is not explicitly found as a characteristic of manhood in the HB according to the study of the components of biblical masculinity in Chapter 2.

53. The question of whether 1 Sam 3 should be considered a prophetic call narrative has elicited much debate. Through a strict form-critical lens, the story should not be considered a prophetic call narrative because it does not conform exactly to the recognized elements of this *gattung* (see Norman C. Habel, "The Form and Significance of the Call Narratives," *ZAW* 77[1965]: 297–323). However, scholars like Savran and Simon have a different perspective. For them, form criticism entails an artificial imposition of certain rigid schemata onto literature (and especially narratives) in an effort to categorize traditions into genres (see George Savran, "Theophany as Type Scene," *Proof* 23[2003]: 119–49; Uriel Simon, *Reading Prophetic Narratives* [trans. ; Bloomington, IN: Indiana University Press, 1997], 51–72. See also Uriel Simon, "Samuel's Call to Prophecy: Form Criticism with Close Reading," *Proof* 1[1981]: 119–32). Indeed, it is curious that a story like 1 Sam 3 in which a prophet encounters Yhwh for the first time and delivers a prophetic message is considered separately from other stories of a prophet's vocation.

Whether or not 1 Sam 3 belongs to the call narrative genre, it is clearly concerned with both Samuel's inauguration as a prophet and his maturation as a man. For this reason the description of the change in Samuel in 1 Sam 3 focuses on his acquisition of the characteristics of a prophet alongside his display of manly social power.

54. It is interesting to note that in Exod 2 the *Leitwort* stressing Moses's youth is יֶלֶד, but in 1 Sam the word נַעַר functions in this way. The former term is used of younger boys from birth to approximately age twelve (see Chapter 2, 56–58), therefore it is appropriately employed in scene I of Exod 2, in which Moses is an infant. The term נַעַר covers a wider age range (from before birth to approximately age twenty; see Chapter 2, 51–52). This range is evident in the "childhood narrative" of 1 Sam 1–3 where נַעַר is used to describe Samuel as an infant who has not yet been weaned (1 Sam 1:22) and as an older boy on the verge of maturation (1 Sam 3:8). Note also that נַעַר is used once in reference to the infant Moses in Exod 2:6.

No satisfactory explanation can be provided for why the two narratives choose different *Leitworte* to denote youthfulness. However, since DtrH uses נַעַר more often than any other term to connote boyhood (seventy-five times with the definition "boy" versus only twenty-six occurrences of יֶלֶד), it is possible that the choice of נַעַר as a *Leitwort* in 1 Sam 3 reflects DtrH's general preference for this term.

55. The critique of Moses's right to be a judge and political leader (the other two elements of the guilty Hebrew's challenge to Moses) is of less concern to Exod 2. However, it is the major theme of the subsequent scene in the Moses story: the call narrative at the burning bush in Exod 3–4, in which Moses's authority is granted to him directly by Yhwh.

56. For the recognition of the idyllic nature of much of the childhood narrative of Samuel, see Brueggemann (*First and Second Samuel*, 25) and Gnuse ("Dream Theophany," 288).

57. An observation made by Rolf Rendtdorff, "Samuel the Prophet: A Link between Moses and the Kings," in *The Quest for Context and Meaning: Studies in Biblical Intertextuality in Honor of James A. Sanders* (ed. Craig A. Evans and Shemaryahu Talmon; Leiden: Brill, 1997), 30–31; for more on Samuel as an inheritor to Moses, see A. P. B. Breytenbach ("Who is Behind the Samuel Narrative?" in de Moor and Van Rooy, *Past, Present, Future*, 53–54) and Gnuse ("Dream Theophany," 320–21).

58. For the most recent discussion of the compositional history of the Deuteronomistic History, see Thomas C. Römer, *The So-Called Deuteronomistic History: A Sociological, Historical and Literary Introduction* (New York: T&T Clark, 2007). According to Römer, citing primarily the work of Otto and Blum, the biography of Moses found in Exod 2 would have been a foundational document for the earliest Deuteronomists (ibid., 72). Referencing Schmid, Römer also suggests that Exod 2 may have served as the introduction to the Deuteronomistic History in its earliest form (ibid., 34). In contrast, 1 Sam 3 is reckoned as having a later date of composition than the Moses material. Römer

argues that 1 Sam 3 belongs to a later stratum of the Deuteronomistic History composed in the Neo-Babylonian period, since all of 1 Sam 1–6 seems to presuppose the destruction of the Jerusalem temple in 587 B.C.E. and the concomitant "replacement of the temple by the prophetic word as a medium of access to the divine will." (ibid., 94).

59. See McCarter, *I Samuel*, 59, 89.

60. See Römer, *So-Called Deuteronomistic History*, 93–94. For concurring opinions on the late date and the influence of DtrH on this composition, see Gnuse, "Dream Theophany," 289; Joseph Bourke, "Samuel and the Ark," *Dominican Studies* 7(1954): 73–103; Arthur E. Zannoni, "An Investigation of the Call and Dedication of the Prophet Samuel: I Samuel 1:1–4:1a" (PhD diss., Marquette University, 1975), 153–60.

61. The textual reconstruction I propose for understanding 1 Sam 1–3 envisions this narrative block added, likely during the Neo-Babylonian period, to preexistent traditions about Samuel pertaining to his judgeship and his relationships with Saul and David. Therefore, the more passive depiction of Samuel sketched in his coming-of-age and prophetic call narrative need not be consistent throughout 1 Samuel. It is worth noting, however, that even the most ostensibly violent act attributed to Samuel—his execution of Agag the Amalekite king in 1 Sam 15:33—is viewed less as an agonistic struggle between two men in which Samuel prevails than as a sacrifice akin to the slaying of a large animal, in that Agag is brought to Samuel as a prisoner, perhaps even in shackles depending on the translation of מַעֲדַנֹּת (1 Sam 15:32).

CHAPTER 4

1. See Introduction, 13–15.

2. "1 Sam 17" and "the David and Goliath story" are used interchangeably throughout this chapter. In addition, I will argue later that the story actually concludes in 1 Sam 18:9. Thus, "1 Sam 17" or "the David and Goliath story" is equivalent to "1 Sam 17–18:9."

3. Berquist argues that while David experiences a "moment of borrowed adulthood" after defeating Goliath, he regresses to adolescence afterwards and does not become a man once and for all until he is crowned king (Jon L. Berquist, "Childhood and Age in the Bible," *Pastoral Psychology* 58[2009]: 526). *Pace* Berquist, I argue below that David demonstrates all of the characteristics of biblical masculinity by the end of the David and Goliath narrative and the text never reverts to describing him as a boy.

4. Campbell is among the most vocal critics of the traditional interpretation that views David as a youth in 1 Sam 17. He contends that this reading has "bedeviled" interpretation throughout the years (Campbell, *1 Samuel*, 171). Moreover, Campbell argues that in David's fight with Goliath, he "is no little boy" but is

instead "portrayed as fast, tough and strong, with excellent reflexes" (ibid., 181). For similar views, see also McKenzie (Steven L. McKenzie, *King David: A Biography* [Oxford: Oxford University Press, 2000], 50–51) and Halpern (Baruch Halpern, *David's Secret Demons: Messiah, Murderer, Traitor, King* [Grand Rapids, MI: Eerdmans, 2001], 12–13).

5. See the discussion of the many uses of נַעַר in Chapter 2, n. 3. The association of the term with the military rank of squire is apparent in certain texts, as shown by MacDonald ("Status," 147–70). However, I demonstrated in Chapter 2 that besides this meaning, the noun's more common use is as a life-cycle term denoting youth. In addition, I will show in the subsequent discussion that this latter meaning better fits the context of the term's use in 1 Sam 17.

6. Halpern emphasizes that in ancient Near Eastern warfare, light infantry— defined by its speed, maneuverability, and the use of ranged weapons like the slingshot—was often the perfect answer to heavy infantry unaided by cavalry. David's choice to fight the heavily armored Philistine armed only with a slingshot and without protective armor makes sense in light of this knowledge and is therefore indicative of David's tactical brilliance (Halpern, *Secret Demons*, 11–13).

7. An observation first made by Folker Willesen ("The Yalid in Hebrew Society," *ST* 12[1958]: 202).

8. See Chapter 2.

9. Translation mine.

10. It is important to note here that David never refers to himself as a נַעַר in the text; thus his belief that a man will dispatch Goliath can be read as the cocksure declaration of an adolescent male who already considers himself a man.

11. N.B. also the similar tension between the Hebrew adjectives גָּדוֹל and קָטָן ("large" and "small," respectively) in vv. 13–14.

12. See Chapter 2.

13. The significance of Saul's terminological shift from referring to David as a נַעַר to later calling him an עֶלֶם has largely gone unnoticed by scholars. Even as attentive a reader as Fokkelman simply equates the two terms as synonymous for "young man," without recognizing the important differences in connotation (J. P. Fokkelman, *Narrative Art and Poetry in the Books of Samuel: A Full Interpretation Based on Stylistic and Structural Analyses. Volume II: The Crossing Fates [I Sam. 13–31 & II Sam. 1]* [SSN 23; Aasen/Maastricht, The Netherlands: Van Gorcum, 1986], 194). To my knowledge, the only scholar who has commented on the significance of this shift is Edelman, who argues that Saul's use of עֶלֶם "tends to emphasize his promise that Goliath's slayer would marry a princess, since the word designates a sexually ripe young man" (Diana Vikander Edelman, *King Saul in the Historiography of Judah* [Sheffield: Sheffield Academic Press, 1991], 134).

14. See the discussion of the relationship between strength demonstrated on the battlefield, masculinity, and the feminization of the enemy in Chapter 1.

15. For a more general discussion regarding why masculinity so often requires defense in battle or competition, and is often demonstrated by feminizing other men, see Alan Dundes, "Traditional Male Combat: From Game to War," in *From Game to War, and Other Psychoanalytic Essays on Folklore* (ed. Alan Dundes; Lexington: University Press of Kentucky, 1997), 25–45. Dundes draws upon both anthropological and psychological resources to argue that "male competitive attempts to feminize one's opponent in games and war [are] a means of demonstrating masculinity as a reaction to the female-centered conditioning experience from birth through early childhood until adolescence" (ibid., 42).

16. Goliath's emasculation by David also advances the rhetoric of Philistine feminization recognized by Jobling as a recurring theme in 1 Samuel. See David Jobling, *1 Samuel* (Berit Olam; Collegeville, Minn.: Liturgical Press, 1998), 216, 231.

17. Translation mine.

18. Ariella Deem, "And the Stone Sank Into His Forehead: A Note on 1 Samuel 17:49," *VT* 28(1978): 349–51.

19. See Jack M. Sasson, "Reflections on an Unusual Practice Reported in ARM X:4," *Or* 93(1974): 409–10.

20. By relying on such unconventional tactics in his duel with Goliath, David's actions here also reflect the "wisdom" incumbent upon an ideal biblical man, if that "wisdom" is understood as "savvy" or "cunning."

21. The root is often translated inadequately as "to defy" (see NRSV, NAS, NJPS of 1 Sam 17:10), when a translational choice that reflects its connection to the culture of honor and shame is more appropriate. Alter, noting the inadequacy of "defy" in this verse, proposes instead to translate the root with words like "insult," "disgrace," or "shame." (Robert Alter, *The David Story: A Translation with Commentary of 1 and 2 Samuel* [New York: Norton, 1999], 102).

22. See the discussion of the importance of defending honor to biblical masculinity in Chapter 1. For the connection between reputation and honor (כָּבוֹד), see Moshe Weinfeld, "כָּבוֹד," *TDOT* 7: 26–27.

23. See Chapter 1.

24. Damrosch similarly argues for viewing the David–Jonathan relationship as a metaphorical marriage (David Damrosch, *The Narrative Covenant: Transformation of Genre in the Growth of Biblical Literature* [San Francisco: Harper and Row, 1987], 206).

25. Ackerman, *When Heroes Love*, 218–27.

26. Ibid., 200–218.

27. It is not my contention that since 1 Sam 17–18:9 appears to be a coming-of-age story, it follows that a rite-of-passage exegesis must be applied to it. I am instead articulating a desideratum in biblical studies: maturation rites are the most frequently mentioned rites of passage in van Gennep's work; therefore it

is curious that scholars only rarely have applied a rite-of-passage exegesis to a biblical story in order to illuminate a coming-of-age theme. My reading attempts to fill this lacuna.

28. For the identification of 1 Sam 17 as a folktale, see Alexander Rofé ("The Battle of David and Goliath: Folklore, Theology, Eschatology," in *Judaic Perspectives on Ancient Israel* [ed. Jacob Neusner, Baruch A. Levine, and Ernest S. Frerichs; Philadelphia: Fortress, 1987], 118), who argues that the original story of David and Goliath was a "popular fairy tale" that was later reworked to include an explicitly theological message. This opinion is also shared by Jason, who refers to the tale as a folkloric "romantic epic" (Heda Jason, "The Story of David and Goliath: A Folk Epic?," *Bib* 60 [1979]: 36–90). Lust also labels one of the two sources he identifies within the chapter a "fairy tale" (Johan Lust, "The Story of David and Goliath in Hebrew and in Greek," in *The Story of David and Goliath: Textual and Literary Criticism. Papers of a Joint Research Venture* [ed. Dominique Barthélemy et al.; OBO 73; Göttingen: Vandenhoeck & Ruprecht/ Freiburg: Éditions Universitaires, 1986], 13). De Vries likewise identifies the early version of the story as a "simple hero-saga" told among the common folk (Simon J. De Vries, "David's Victory over the Philistine as Saga and as Legend," *JBL* 92[1973]: 31). Isser stresses the folkoric origins of the story and considers it a "popular heroic legend" (Stanley Isser, *The Sword of Goliath: David in Heroic Literature* [SBLStBl 6; Atlanta: Society of Biblical Literature, 2003], 28–34).

29. Mircea Eliade, *Myth and Reality* (New York: Harper Torchbook, 1968), 202.

30. Vladimir I. Propp, *Morphology of the Folktale* (trans. L. Scott; 2d ed.; Austin: University of Texas Press, 1968), 114.

31. N. J. Girardot, "Initiation and Meaning in the Tale of Snow White and the Seven Dwarfs," *Journal of American Folklore* 90(1977): 275.

32. See Turner, *Ritual Process*, 95.

33. According to Anttonen ("Rites," 178), among van Gennep's unique insights is that "movement in social space is accompanied and identified with movement in territorial space." Thus, an initiate's movement through a rite of passage is not merely a psychological journey, but involves actual bodily movement to accompany the phases of separation, liminality, and reincorporation.

34. Van Gennep, *Rites*, 18.

35. John A. Beck, "David and Goliath, A Story of Place: The Narrative-Geographical Shaping of 1 Samuel 17," *WTJ* 68(2006): 326.

36. Following de Vaux, who understands בֵּנַיִם to be the preposition בֵּין with a dual ending (Roland de Vaux, "Single Combat in the Old Testament," in *The Bible and the Ancient Near East* [trans. Damian McHugh; ed. Roland de Vaux; Garden City, NY:1971], 124).

37. For the argument that the term denotes a "champion," see de Vaux (ibid., 124). Jeffrey Zorn claims that the term refers to a chariot warrior ("Reconsidering Goliath: An Iron Age I Philistine Chariot Warrior," *BASOR* 360[2010]: 1–22).

Using comparative evidence from Qumran, both Serge Frolov and Allen Wright ("Homeric and Ancient Near Eastern Intertextuality in 1 Samuel 17," *JBL* 130[2011]: 460 n. 36) and McCarter (*I Samuel*, 291) argue that the proper understanding of the term is "skirmisher."

38. Goliath's embodiment of liminality may also extend to his status as someone caught between the divine and human worlds since in the worldview of the biblical writers giants descended from the union of human women and divine beings (Gen 6:1–4; Num 13:33).

39. Turner shows that during the liminal phase the typical conventions and norms of the initiate's society are often reversed, thus making the liminal phase a "world turned upside down" (see Turner, *Ritual Process*, 96–97). Vidal-Naquet's discussion of the liminality of boys in ancient Greece during their maturation rites stresses how this aspect of liminality was often actualized by the explicit overturning of the typical military rules of conduct and engagement. The Greek ephebes (initiatory boys) represented an "anti-hoplite" ethos, fighting contrary to the hoplite's warrior code (Pierre Vidal-Naquet, "The Black Hunter and the Origin of the Athenian *Ephebia*," in *The Black Hunter: Forms of Thought and Forms of Society in the Greek World* [trans. A. Szegedy-Maszak; Baltimore: The Johns Hopkins University Press, 1986], 120). In a similar way, David's unorthodox choice of weapons and his somewhat underhanded targeting of Goliath's groin should perhaps be understood in light of the typical convention-reversal common to the liminal phase of a rite of passage.

40. Male puberty rites, as discussed previously (see Introduction), require the separation of the boy from the feminine space of the home. These rites end, however, with the boy's return to that same space, now as a man. See, e.g., Piot, *Remotely Global*, 80–82. For a discussion of the celebrations common to the conclusion of rites of passage, see Weisfield, "Puberty Rites," 38–39. See also Claude Calame, *Choruses of Young Women in Ancient Greece: Their Morphology, Religious Role and Social Functions* (trans. D. Collins and J. Orion; Lanham, MD: Rowman and Littlefield, 2001), 13.

41. See the discussion of this point in the Introduction.

42. I use the abbreviation MT as shorthand designating the text tradition that served as the textual predecessor to the much later (ninth century c.e.) Masoretic Text.

43. Evidence from the Qumran Samuel scroll (4QSam^a) has typically not been considered in this debate because it is fragmentary throughout 1 Sam 17–18 and the extant fragments seem to support MT at some points and LXXB at others. Recently Benjamin J. A. Johnson ("Reconsidering 4QSam^a and the Textual Support for the Long and Short Versions of the David and Goliath Story," *VT* 62[2012]) has argued that 4QSam^a "likely contained the longer version as found in MT" (ibid., 538) although it remains a *"codex mixtus"* (ibid., 548) containing elements of both traditions.

44. For an extensive discussion of the contours of this debate, see most recently John Van Seters, *The Biblical Saga of King David* (Winona Lake, IN: Eisenbrauns, 2009), 137–57.

45. Of course, minor divergences are found between the scholarly works grouped together under these categories. My purpose, however, is not to discuss at length the intricacies of this debate but instead to show that the coming-of-age reading I have offered above is not contradicted by any of the major positions in this discussion.

46. See Jason, "Folk Epic," 37–40.

47. See Robert Polzin (*Samuel and the Deuteronomist: A Literary Study of the Deuteronomistic History. Part Two: 1 Samuel* [Bloomington, IN: University of Indiana Press, 1993], 172–74) and Fokkelman (*Narrative Art Vol. 2*, 143–208), both of whom argue that the text only *appears* to have contradictions.

48. Scholars that hold this position include: Dominque Barthélemy ("Troi Niveaux d'Analyse," in Barthélemy et al., *The Story of David and Goliath*, 47–54); Pisano (*Additions or Omissions*, 83–86); and D. W. Gooding ("An Approach to the Literary and Textual Problems in the David–Goliath Story," in Barthélemy et al., *The Story of David and Goliath*, 55–86).

49. See, e.g., McCarter (*I Samuel*, 298; 306–309); Emmanuel Tov ("The Nature of the Differences between MT and the LXX," in Barthélemy et al., *The Story of David and Goliath*, 19–46); McKenzie (*Biography*, 73); and Lust ("Story," 5–18).

50. See Rofé ("Battle," 117–51) and Van Seters (*Saga*, 154–62).

51. The possible exception being my remarks on the defense-of-honor motif, which may overlap with the proposed "theological edit" of the text, given that much of the indignity at Goliath's insult stems from the Philistine having reproached "the armies of the living God" (v. 26, 36). Furthermore, David's statement of faith in Yhwh in v. 45, which would belong to this theological stratum, also mentions Goliath's shaming insult against Israel and its god.

52. The LXXB, however, does put more emphasis on the emasculation of the Philistine (vv. 49, 50).

53. Still, as I have previously demonstrated, the theme also is readily evident in the LXXB.

54. See above, p. 97.

55. See, e.g., DeVries ("Victory," 30–33), Lust ("Story," 11–14), Ackerman (*When Heroes Love*, 201) and McCarter (*I Samuel*, 296, 307–308).

56. It is important to note that even if נַעַר is understood as "squire" here, and not as a life-cycle term denoting youthfulness as I have argued, the contradiction with 1 Sam 16:14–23 is still glaring. A mighty man of valor/man of war is clearly a far cry from a lowly squire.

57. A possible exception to the claim that 1 Sam 17 is totally unaware of 1 Sam 16:14–23 is found in 17:15, which belongs to the non-LXXB. Most scholars, however, identify this verse (which tells how David would shuttle between his

father's house in Bethlehem and Saul's army) as an awkward and late editorial addition. See McCarter, *I Samuel*, 303, 308 and Gordon, *I & II Samuel*, 65.

58. Campbell, *1 Samuel*, 183.

59. This quality, of course, is also associated with women in the HB. See Chapter 1.

60. Indeed, Lasine recently has argued that Solomon is quite exceptional among important biblical figures in that the text provides no information about his formative childhood years (Stuart Lasine, *Knowing Kings: Knowledge, Power and Narcissism in the Hebrew Bible* [SemeiaSt 40; Atlanta: Society of Biblical Literature, 2001], 133). I will challenge Lasine on this point below.

61. In both instances where David refers to Solomon in this way, it is to persuade the people to assist Solomon in the daunting task of building the Jerusalem temple. Given the context, then, it is most likely that the multivalent term נַעַר is employed to emphasize Solomon's youthfulness. Most modern translations agree with this assessment (see NRSV, NAS, NJPS of 1 Chr 22:5; 29:1).

62. According to *S. 'Olam Rab.* 14, Solomon was twelve at his accession. For other rabbinic sources suggesting that Solomon was thirteen at this time, see Louis Ginzberg, *The Legends of the Jews* (Philadelphia: Jewish Publication Society, 1928), 6.277 n. 1.

63. Translation mine.

64. Leonhard Rost, *Die Überlieferung von der Thronnachfolge Davids* (BWANT 3/6; Stuttgart: Kohlhammer, 1926). For a recent discussion of the *status quaestionis* of Rost's proposed Succession Narrative, see John Barton, "Dating the 'Succession Narrative,'" in *In Search of Pre-exilic Israel* (ed. John Day; JSOTSup 406; New York: T&T Clark, 2004), 95–106.

65. See Mordechai Cogan, *1 Kings: A New Translation with Introduction and Commentary* (AB 10; New York: Doubleday, 2000), 190. See also Burke Long, *I Kings: With an Introduction to Historical Literature* (FOTL 9; Grand Rapids, MI: Eerdmans, 1984), 66; Jean-Marie Husser, *Dreams and Dream Narratives in the Biblical World* (trans. J. Munro; Sheffield: Sheffield Academic Press, 1999), 124–28; David McLain Carr, "Royal Ideology and the Technology of Faith: A Comparative Midrash Study of 1 Kgs 3:2–15" (PhD diss., The Claremont Graduate School, 1988), 140–77.

66. Others have noticed Solomon's strange lack of involvement in the events of this chapter. For example, Walsh notes that throughout 1 Kgs 1, Solomon is "utterly passive," adding that he is "the subject of no verbs, the speaker of no words, [and] the performer of no actions" (Jerome T. Walsh, "The Characterization of Solomon in First Kings 1–5," *CBQ* 57[1995]: 474). Long similarly describes Solomon here as "something of a shadow, pictured only in what people do for and to him" (*I Kings*, 38).

67. See Chapter 2.

68. See Introduction.

69. For the right hand of the king as the position of honor, see Ps 45:9 (MT 45:10); 110:1.

70. According to Preuss, when the root חוה is used in a secular context, it indicates "respect" and "honor" for the person towards whom the gesture is directed and serves as a way to acknowledge one of "higher rank" (Horst Dietrich Preuss, "חוה," *TDOT* 4: 251).

71. The exceptional nature of this act possibly explains why the LXX here translates that Solomon did not bow to his mother but instead "kissed her" (κατεφίλησεν αὐτήν).

72. Translation mine.

73. Sweeney's translation ("you must be strong and be a man") is closer to mine, and therefore differs from NRSV (Marvin Sweeney, *I & II Kings: A Commentary* [OTL; Louisville: Westminster John Knox, 2007], 51). See also the translations by Cogan ("be strong and be a man!" [*I Kings*, 5]) and Jerome T. Walsh ("Be strong! Be a man!" *I Kings* [Berit Olam; Collegeville, MN: Liturgical Press, 1996], 39).

74. L. Koehler, W. Baumgartner, J. J. Stamm, "היה," *HALOT* 1: 244. Other cited examples include Gen 2:7—where the human becomes a living being (חַיָּה נֶפֶשׁ) after Yhwh breathes into its nostrils—and Num 10:31, where Hobab is asked to become Israel's eyes in the wilderness.

75. A potential objection to this reading can be raised by noticing that David's encouragement to Solomon echoes the rallying cry of the Philistines in 1 Sam 4:9: "Be strong, and be men, O Philistines!" (הִתְחַזְּקוּ וִהְיוּ לַאֲנָשִׁים פְּלִשְׁתִּים). Surely here the Philistine army is not identifying itself literally as boys who need to mature to battle the Israelites. The use here is apparently a figure of speech meaning "act like men," spoken in response to the unmanly fear that had taken hold of the Philistines. In this view, then, contra *HALOT*, the use of the construction in 1 Kgs 2:2 also may mean more "to act like a man" than "to become a man."

   While this reading is just as defensible as that proposed by *HALOT*, which I have followed above, the consequences of accepting it as an alternative are relatively minor for my argument. No matter which reading one prefers, it is clear that David does not believe that Solomon is currently acting like a man. Therefore, the advice David gives in his final testament to Solomon enumerates how his son can begin to enact his masculinity. Furthermore, if David's exhortation is understood as "act like a man" instead of "become a man," one wonders how Solomon's previous actions are viewed as less than manly and in need of change in David's eyes. The simplest answer to this question begins by recognizing the prevalence of youthful imagery in the description of Solomon in the preceding chapter. David's demand that his son act like a man is most likely given in light of Solomon's previous immature behavior; indeed no other answer to this query is readily apparent. Thus, even if the alternative reading is accepted, David's command that Solomon "act like a man" essentially means that he "stop acting like a child" as he had up to this point. The difference between the two readings, therefore, is relatively minor. Either David tells Solomon to "grow up" (*HALOT* reading) or to "act like a man (and stop acting like a boy)" (alternative reading).

76. See Chapter 1, 31–33. Note, however, that the display of strength through physical and violent force is not to be equated with unbridled aggression or bloodlust but is instead to be controlled and only expressed in appropriate and limited ways (see Chapter 1, 32–33, 39–40).

77. J. P. Fokkelman, *Narrative Art and Poetry in the Books of Samuel: A Full Interpretation Based on Stylistic and Structural Analyses. Volume I: King David (II Sam. 9–20 & I Kings 1–2)* (SSN 20; Aasen/Maastricht, The Netherlands: Van Gorcum, 1981), 389. Fokkelman also notices the "cynical ring" that is recognizable in the application of the term "wisdom" to the violent deeds Solomon is to perform (ibid.).

78. In fact, David here refers to Solomon as a "wise man" (אִישׁ חָכָם). In light of his earlier declaration in v. 2 that Solomon needs to become/act more like a man, David's use of the term אִישׁ here in reference to Solomon should be interpreted as either an affectionate title (as when a modern father refers to his young son as a "man"), a foreshadowing of the future (that is, "if you do these things, you will be a man"), or an attempt to stroke the ego of his boyish son by rhetorically elevating him to manhood.

79. H. P. Müller, "חכם" *TDOT* 4: 373. Fokkelman similarly refers to the "wisdom" on display in 1 Kgs 2 as "practical and tactical intelligence, cleverness" (*Narrative Art Vol. 1*, 408), while Walsh (*I Kings*, 38) prefers the adjective "shrewd" to "wise" when describing Solomon's actions in this chapter. I have adopted Fokkelman's suggestion and use "cleverness" to translate חָכְמָה in 1 Kgs 2.

80. See Chapter 1, 39–40.

81. David's words of advice directing Solomon to follow Yhwh's statutes in v. 3, therefore, are not simply "Deuteronomistic platitudes," as Walsh argues (*I Kings*, 38; see also Alter, *David Story*, xiii). The motivation for Solomon's obedience of Yhwh are considerations of realpolitik and therefore fit with the practical and calculating tone of the remainder of David's deathbed speech. This does not completely discount the possibility that vv. 3–4 are additions by DtrH; indeed, David's request reflects the same desire to "have a name in Israel" so common in Deuteronomy. However, if they are additions, DtrH has effectively inserted his theological message in a way that respects and mimics the content of the surrounding speech. See also below, n. 110.

82. This request reflects the frequent connection between hospitality and honor noted by several scholars of the honor-shame system in Mediterranean cultures. See Gilmore, "Honor, Honesty, Shame," 101. See also Michael Herzfeld,

"'As in Your Own House,'" 75–89. For a discussion of hospitality and its association with honor in ancient Israel, see T. R. Hobbs, "Hospitality in the First Testament and the 'Teleological Fallacy,'" JSOT 95(2001): 3–30. Hobbs argues that too often in biblical studies the modern conceptions of hospitality centered on entertaining and feeding one's guests are projected upon the biblical texts. Ancient Israelite hospitality operated within a system of give-and-take, where failing to return a favor (like the loyalty shown by Barzillai to David) detracted from one's honor (see ibid., 28–29).

83. For the importance of defending the honor of one's kinsmen in an honor–shame system, see Zeid, "Honour and Shame among the Bedouins," 243–59.

84. The frequency with which the verb פגע ("to strike") is used in 1 Kgs 2 (vv. 25, 29, 31, 32, 34, 46) indicates the emphasis on the violent use of force in this portion of the narrative. See Jung Ju Kang (*The Persuasive Portrayal of Solomon in 1 Kings 1–11* [Bern: Peter Lang, 2003], 138) and Walsh (*I Kings*, 55), both of whom argue for פגע as the *Leitwort* of 1 Kgs 2.

85. In fact, this indirect use of force—Solomon's ordering others to carry out the killings of his enemies—is the more common way that kings display their manly bellicosity. Note that before David's coronation in 1 Sam 5, he frequently triumphs over his enemies through his own power (his slaying of Goliath in 1 Sam 17; his slaughter of two hundred Philistines in 1 Sam 18). However, after that point others fight and kill on his behalf (e.g., he arranges Uriah's death in 2 Sam 11, and his warrior Abishai defends him from the threat of death at the hands of the Philistine champion Ishbi-benob in 2 Sam 21:16–17).

86. This contrast is emphasized further if "in the hand of Solomon" is understood to mean "through Solomon's agency" instead of "under Solomon's control." Both translations of the Hebrew בְּיַד are possible. See J. Bergman, W. von Soden, P. R. Ackroyd, "יָד," TDOT 5: 410.

87. Whether or not Solomon is correct in assuming that Bathsheba is oblivious to Adonijah's intentions depends on one's interpretation of the text. It is, of course, possible that Bathsheba has masterminded the entire scenario to achieve the desired result of Adonijah's execution (see, e.g., Terence E. Fretheim, *First and Second Kings* [Westminster Bible Companion; Louisville: Westminster John Knox Press, 1999], 26).

88. See Albert Šanda, *Die Bucher der Könige* (EHAT 9; Münster: Aschendorffsche Verlagsbuchhandlung, 1911), 53–54; James A. Montgomery, *A Critical and Exegetical Commentary on the Books of Kings* (ICC 10; New York: Scribner's, 1951), 102.

89. The presence of the adjective קָטֹן ("little" or "young") here provides all the context necessary to conclude that נַעַר in this instance should be translated with a life-cycle noun denoting youth (i.e., "boy"). Note also the similarities between Solomon's claim to be a small boy and the Egyptian Stele of Thutmose IV, in which the Pharaoh similarly identifies himself before a deity as a child. See

Siegfried Hermann, "Die Königsnovelle in Ägypten und Israel," *Wissenschaftliche Zeitscrhift der Karl-Marx Universität* 3 (1953–54): 51–62. Long, noting that since this Egyptian inscription describes the Pharaoh's gifts to the gods in exchange for a long reign and afterlife, dismisses these similarities as "remote from 1 Kings 3, both in content and general intention" (*I Kings*, 65).

90. W. Malcolm Clark, "A Legal Background to the Yahwist's Use of 'Good and Evil' in Genesis 2–3," *JBL* 88(1969): 274.

91. Steven Weitzman, *Solomon: The Lure of Wisdom* (New Haven: Yale University Press, 2011), 26. For the view that the phrase refers to military endeavors, see n. 102.

92. Weitzman himself does not notice the exceptional nature of the phrase "to know good and evil," nor does he highlight the sexual overtones of the verb ידע, even though these observations would significantly advance his case.

93. For a discussion of the scholarly consensus on this question, including an extensive bibliography, see Carr, *Royal Ideology*, 24–30. See also Long, *I Kings*, 61–63. It is also important to note that even Kenik—who alone among scholars in considering the Gibeon dream narrative to be a compositional unity written by DtrH—views 1 Kgs 3:1–3 as "entirely distinct from the narrative [of vv. 4–15]" that was only added later as an introduction to the story (Helen A. Kenik, *Design for Kingship: The Deuteronomistic Narrative Technique in 1 Kings 3:4–15* [SBLDS 15; Chico, CA: Scholars Press, 1983], 179 n. 8).

94. See, e.g., 1 Kgs 22:41–43 (22:41–44 MT); 2 Kgs 14:1–4; 15:1–4.

95. Carr, *Royal Ideology*, 24.

96. See Connell, *Masculinities*, 29.

97. For the connection between riches and Yhwh's blessing, see, for example, Prov 10:22.

98. Since Yhwh has already given Solomon the gifts that transform him from a boy into a man by v. 13, the obedience to Yhwh's statutes and commandments recommended to Solomon in v. 14 is not a constituent component of his masculine maturation in this narrative. This is not to argue that Torah obedience is unimportant in the masculinity described in this story, but simply to note that it is not emphasized as essential to *becoming* a man. Note also that the motivation for obedience to Yhwh in this narrative is a long life (v. 14), not the perpetuation of the Davidic line as in 1 Kgs 1–2.

99. See Victor W. Turner, *The Forest of Symbols: Aspects of Ndembu Ritual* (Ithaca, NY: Cornell University Press, 1967), 98–101.

100. Gibeon lies in the heart of the Israelite kingdom, yet is peopled by foreigners (Hivites). Geographically, it sits on contested borderland between the tribes of Benjamin and Judah. These observations on Gibeon's liminality were brought to my attention by Dale Loepp (personal communication, February 2012).

101. See Introduction, 22–23.

102. See Van Der Lingen, "*Bw'-Yṣ'*," 59–66. Van Der Lingen considers each use of the term separately and finds that the vast majority of its uses have a military context (see, e.g., Josh 14:10–11). Of 1 Kgs 3:7, he suggests the following translation: ". . . I do not know how to go to war successfully as a commander" (ibid., 66).

103. See in particular Ps 21, where the king is given "splendor and majesty" (v. 5), "rich blessings" (v. 3), and "long life" (v. 4) but is also given victory over his enemies (vv. 9–12).

104. The similarities between 1 Kgs 1–2 and David's coming of age in 1 Sam 17 should perhaps come as no surprise from a literary perspective, because David himself defines what constitutes masculinity and "becoming a man" with his deathbed speech (1 Kgs 2:2–9) in this version of Solomon's coming of age. David, understandably, advises his son to mature in the same way that he did.

105. Shimei, similarly, is executed to avenge David (v. 44).

106. The presence of a farewell speech in this chapter further emphasizes this retrospective quality. Long argues that such speeches are important to the larger literary context because they provide a "definitive theological perspective" on the era or life that is coming to a close with the death of the speaker (Long, *I Kings*, 45).

107. This conclusion holds despite the fact that 1 Sam 17 and 1 Kgs 3 employ the same formal narrative technique of using the rite-of-passage structure to tell their respective tales of maturation. However, the contrasts between the two tales' use of this structural technique are noteworthy: in David's liminal stage, he proves himself physically by defeating the embodiment of the ordeals typically endured by initiates; in Solomon's, the imparting of special knowledge—also characteristic of tribal rites of passage—is emphasized. Given the common association of rites of passage with coming of age, it should be expected that different stories describing maturation would employ the structure independently of one another.

108. For Carr's extensive discussion of the DtrH editing of 1 Kgs 3, see *Royal Ideology*, 178–207. Carr assumes a Josianic DtrH but this is not central to his argument. My suggestions below assume an exilic or post-exilic DtrH. For bibliography of others who note the "many marks of deuteronomistic editing" in 1 Kgs 3, see Gary N. Knoppers, *Two Nations Under God: The Deuteronomistic History of Solomon and the Dual Monarchies Volume 1: The Reign of Solomon and the Rise of Jeroboam* (HSM 52; Atlanta: Scholars Press, 1993), 81.

109. See Carr, *Royal Ideology*, 127. Note also that Carr believes that the addition of 1 Kgs 3:1 (the report of Solomon's wedding to Pharaoh's daughter) comes from a post-DtrH redactor. See ibid., 203–205.

110. Knoppers (*Two Nations Under God*, 61) notes that scholars "almost unanimously agree that the Deuteronomist drew extensively from an older source in

composing 1 Kings 1–2." See ibid., 61 n. 6 and 63 n. 14 for bibliography supporting this claim. David's final words to Solomon in 1 Kgs 2:2–9, however, were
considered by Noth as entirely the work of DtrH, since Noth argued that
lengthy speeches at the end of a major character's life were DtrH's preferred
way of marking structural transitions in the historical narrative (Martin Noth,
The Deuteronomistic History [JSOTSup 15; Sheffield: JSOT Press, 1981], 4–11).
However, David's farewell speech contains far fewer references to the characteristic theology of DtrH than other farewell speeches Noth identifies as
DtrH's handiwork, such as Joshua's in Josh 23 or Samuel's in 1 Sam 12. Instead,
David's speech is primarily concerned, as I have shown, with sealing the fate
of David's enemies and ensuring that the kingdom is in capable hands. DtrH's
theology is perhaps evident in vv. 3–4, where David recommends Torah obedience to Solomon. Still, even here this typical feature of DtrH thought is appropriately altered to fit the context of the rest of the speech, as it is solely linked
to the continued perpetuation of the Davidic line. See above, n. 81.

111. The conclusions here challenge Mobley's claim that the Israel's "heroic age,"
where men displayed their masculinity through military exploits and the display of might through violence, ended with Solomon (see *Empty Men*, 229–34).
Pace Mobley, I argue that the connection between Israelite manhood and violence is broken with *DtrH's retelling* of the Solomon coming-of-age narrative in
1 Kgs 3 but is still present in the earlier version of that tale in 1 Kgs 1–2.

CHAPTER 5

1. Indeed, Josephus eliminates any mention of this section of the Gideon cycle in
his *Antiquities* (see *A.J.* 5:6). The limited attention that modern scholars have
devoted to the Jether story is discussed throughout this section.

2. In accordance with the obligation of male next of kin to act as blood avenger for
a murdered relative. See S. David Sperling, "Blood, Avenger Of," *ABD* 1:
763–64.

3. Stanley Isser (*Sword of Goliath*, 22–25) suggests that brief allusions to otherwise unknown characters such as this in the biblical text often point to a larger
corpus of legend, no longer extant, wherein the character may have a larger
role. In other words, the biblical text does not refer to a figure like Jether unless
traditions existed in which he is more prominent. This possibility further establishes the need to examine this short passage and minor character.

4. Scholars disagree on the motive for Gideon's order to Jether. On one hand,
Niditch (*Judges*, 105) speculates that the intent may have been to dishonor the
kings by having someone who is not their equal execute them, drawing parallels to Goliath's anger at being challenged by the boy David in 1 Sam 17:42–43.
On the other hand, Soggin claims that Gideon's order coheres with the "law of

chivalry," and therefore is a proper and proportionate act not meant as an insult to the kings (J. Alberto Soggin, *Judges: A Commentary* [trans. John S. Bowden; OTL; Philadelphia: Westminster John Knox, 1981], 157). Angel believes the purpose to be Gideon's training of his eldest son as a possible successor (Hayyim Angel,"The Positive and Negative Traits of Gideon: As Reflected in his Sons Jotham and Abimelech," *JBQ* 34[2006]: 165).

5. For the proverbial nature of this phrase, see Soggin, *Judges*, 155; Susan Niditch, *War in the Hebrew Bible: A Study in the Ethics of Violence* (New York: Oxford University Press, 1993), 104. The translation of the proverb is mine. The Hebrew גבורה is translated "manly strength" to highlight the noun's relationship with the related terms "man" (גֶּבֶר) and "mighty warrior" (גִּבּוֹר).

6. Tammi J. Schneider, *Judges* (Berit Olam; Collegeville, MN: Liturgical Press, 2000), 126. Emphasis mine.

7. See Macdonald, "Status," 158. Moreover, it is difficult to imagine a military code of conduct where such conventions would outweigh the duty of a soldier to carry out a commander's orders—especially if the commander is also one's father!

8. See Yaira Amit, *The Book of Judges: The Art of Editing* (trans. Jonathan Chipman; Leiden: Brill, 1999), 238; Barry G. Webb, *The Book of Judges: An Integrated Reading* (JSOTSup 46; Sheffield: Sheffield Academic Press, 1987), 151; J. Paul Tanner, "The Gideon Narrative as the Focal Point of Judges," *BSac* 149(1992): 158–60; E. T. A. Davidson, *Intricacy, Design, and Cunning in the Book of Judges* (Philadelphia: Xlibris, 2008), 119; Dennis T. Olson "The Book of Judges: Introduction, Commentary, and Reflections," *NIB* 2: 808.

9. Quoted in Greg Jaffe, "War Wounds: Breaking a Taboo, Army Confronts Guilt After Combat," *Wall Street Journal*, August 17, 2005. Cited January 11, 2012. Online: http://online.wsj.com/article/0SB112424442541515220,00.html.

10. Auld argues that the Gideon cycle is a late retelling of several biblical stories, based on the many echoes of other texts in the HB found in the cycle; see A. Graeme Auld, "Gideon: Hacking at the Heart of the Old Testament," *VT* 39[1989]: 257–67. If Auld is correct, this contrast between the story of David's coming of age and that of Jether's failure to do so may be intentional.

11. See the discussion of the term עֶלֶם in Chapter 2, 68–71.

12. Mobley, *Liminal Hero*.

13. Mobley compares Samson to other ancient Near Eastern "liminal heroes" like Enkidu (ibid., 31–33). Susan Ackerman (*When Heroes Love*) similarly applies the concept of liminality to other heroes of ancient Near Eastern literature, including Enkidu, Gilgamesh, David, and Jonathan.

14. See Hermann Gunkel, *Reden und Aufsätze* (ed. Hermann Gunkel; Göttingen: Vandenhoeck & Ruprecht, 1913), 38–64. For an argument that Gunkel's characterization of Samson as a "wild man" is too simplistic, particularly in its

disregard for Samson's more cultured and urbane qualities, see James Crenshaw, *Samson: A Secret Betrayed, A Vow Ignored* (Atlanta: John Knox, 1978), 17–18.

15. See Susan Niditch, "Samson as Culture Hero, Trickster, and Bandit: The Empowerment of the Weak," *CBQ* 52 (1990): 616–17. Samson's feminization at the hands of the Philistines, according to Niditch, is seen in the symbolic castration of having his hair cut, being forced to do work traditionally associated with women (grinding grain), and "making sport" (שחק) before the Philistines (which Niditch identifies as language of a woman's sexual subjugation to a man).

16. Mobley, *Liminal Hero*, 14.

17. Ibid., 37–65.

18. Ibid., 66–84.

19. Ibid., 85–108.

20. Contra Mobley, who refers to Samson's actions in Judg 14–16 as his "adult adventures" (ibid., 1) and rejects the concept that any "youthful crisis" is on display in the story of this fully grown man (ibid., 13). See also Amit, *Art of Editing* (274–75; 297), who argues that Samson has "grown up" and completed his maturation by the end of Judg 13. Niditch, in contrast, identifies Samson as an example of the social bandit typology in traditional literature, a character that significantly is typically a "young [man] between puberty and marriage" ("Culture Hero," 622). Still, while Niditch recognizes Samson's young age, she does not draw attention to the importance of Samson's liminal status on the spectrum from boyhood to manhood.

21. Susan Niditch, *My Brother Esau is a Hairy Man: Hair and Identity in Ancient Israel* (New York: Oxford University Press, 2008), 50. Niditch cites Irene Winter ("Art in Empire: The Royal Image and the Visual Dimensions of Assyrian Ideology" in *Assyria 1995: Proceedings of the 10th Anniversary Symposium of the Neo-Assyrian Text Corpus Project, Helsinki September 7–11, 1995* [ed. Simo Parpola and Robert M. Whiting; Helsinki: Neo-Assyrian Text Corpus Project, 1997], 371), who compares the long facial hair common to the depiction of Assyrian monarchs to the long mane of a dominant male in a pride of lions.

22. The connection between the linguistic play characteristic of riddles and the demonstration of special knowledge (both cultural and sexual) is made by Crenshaw in his discussion of Samson's wit and intelligence (*Secret Betrayed*, 99–120). See also my discussion of the connection between intelligence, rhetorical skill, and wisdom in Chapter 1, 33–34.

23. Certainly Mobley and Amit would agree with this translational choice, as they believe that the text passes over Samson's adolescence, only revisiting the character as a fully grown adult (see n. 20). See also Niditch (*Judges*, 141), who translates the verb as "grew up."

24. Bal, however, argues that none of Samson's relationships with women were consummated sexually. See Mieke Bal, *Lethal Love: Feminist Literary Readings of Biblical Love Stories* (Bloomington, IN: Indiana University Press, 1987), 41–64.

25. See Chapter 2, n. 97.

26. Niditch, *Esau*, 79.

27. For the expectation that an Israelite man "perpetuate a name in Israel," see George ("Regimentation," 75).

28. The Jephthah narrative (Judg 11:1–12:7), wherein the protagonist is excluded by his fellow Israelites for being the product of an illegitimate union between his Israelite father and a prostitute, demonstrates legitimacy's enduring importance in the Deuteronomistic History, and specifically in Judges.

29. Within the legal code of Deuteronomy, note the prohibition of marriage to Canaanites (7:3) and the apparent moratorium of three generations placed on intermarriage with Edomites and Egyptians (23:7–8) and of ten generations in the case of Ammonites and Moabites (23:2–6). Also indicative of this general disapproval of exogamy in the Dtn legal code is the elaborate procedure in Deut 21:10–14 that must accompany an Israelite man's marriage to a foreign woman captured in war; see Hamilton, "Marriage [OT and ANE]," 564. The most obvious example of the dangers of exogamy to ideal Israelite manhood in the Deuteronomistic History is that of Solomon (1 Kgs 11:1–8), whose foreign wives turn the king away from his devotion to Yhwh. Finally, and most relevantly to the present discussion, Samson's parents voice the Dtn disapproval of exogamy in Judg 14:3, pleading with their son to reconsider his choice of a Philistine bride.

30. Samson's ill-fated wedding in Judg 14 hardly constitutes a marriage, especially considering that it is unlikely that the marriage was ever consummated; see Mieke Bal, "The Rhetoric of Subjectivity," *Poetics Today* 5[1984]: 354; Soggin, *Judges*, 242. This may explain the ease with which the Timnite's father can give her away to Samson's "best man" (Judg 15:2). Consequently, when Samson and the Timnite woman are referred to as "husband" and "wife" with the terms אִישׁ (Judg 14:15) and אִשָּׁה (Judg 14:15, 16, 20; 15:1, 6), this signifies a potential status more than an actual one.

31. See the discussion of this crucial difference between boyhood and manhood in the HB on pp. 39–40, 54–55, 58–59, 72–73.

32. In illustrating the dangers of rash and unrestrained violence, the Samson narrative reflects a repeated theme in Judges, one that reaches its horrific culmination in the cycle of intra-Israelite vengeance and sexual violence found in Judg 19–21.

33. Crenshaw, *Secret Betrayed*, 65.

34. For the relationship between honey and fertility, see Niditch, *Judges*, 156, and Bal, "Rhetoric of Subjectivity," 352.

35. The humor of this scene likely was not lost on an ancient audience. James Crenshaw ("Samson," *ABD* 5: 953) claims that the tale of the lion and the found honey would have elicited "raucous laughter" from listeners.

36. This is not meant to suggest that Samson must completely separate himself *spatially* from his parents in order to mature. The modern notion that "leaving home" is essential to maturation does not fit the patrilocal ancient Israelite context, in which multiple generations would live together in the same domicile (see, e.g., Meyers, "Family in Early Israel," 16–19). I contend that Samson's tendency to return repeatedly to his parents—frequently after facing difficulty or rejection in the outer world—metaphorically represents his lack of *emotional* detachment from his parents.

37. Note, however, that it is unclear whether Samson is considered a בָּחוּר in Judg 14:10 because the text only states that Samson had a feast before his wedding because that was the custom for בַּחוּרִים. Presumably Samson is reckoned among these בַּחוּרִים; but this is not certain.

38. Samson is never identified as a גֶּבֶר, and the single reference to him as an אִישׁ (Judg 14:15) ironically ends up highlighting his inability to attain the status of manhood. Here the Philistines urge the Timnite woman to coax Samson into revealing the answer to his riddle, referring to Samson as "your husband" (אִישֵׁךְ). Given that Samson's marriage is ultimately a failure and was likely never consummated (see n. 30), this term's application to Samson by the Philistines—and, notably, not by the narrator—does not constitute a narrative acknowledgement of Samson's manhood. In fact, it seems more to mock the would-be groom for his unsuccessful attempt at marriage.

39. Mobley (*Empty Men*, 35) shows that גִּבּוֹר functions etymologically as an intensive form of גֶּבֶר, and therefore denotes an emphasized masculinity—or "masculinity squared"—and is best translated with the English "he-man." Note also that in the opening line of the Samson cycle, his father Manoah is called a "man" (אִישׁ; 13:1), and the narrative that immediately follows the Samson cycle similarly begins by identifying one of its main characters—Micah—as a "man" (אִישׁ; 17:1).

40. Following Robert G. Boling's translation (*Judges: A New Translation with Introduction and Commentary* [AB 6A; Garden City, NY: Doubleday, 1975], 245–46). Emphasis mine.

41. See, e.g., Ludwig Koehler, Walter Baumgartner, and Johann Jakob Stamm (אדם" I," *HALOT* 1: 14).

42. See Othniel Margalith, "Samson's Riddle and Samson's Magic Locks," *VT* 36(1986): 229.

43. See Boling (*Judges*, 82–83) for a description of Othniel's career notice in Judg 3:7–11 as "exemplary" and paradigmatic for the tales of judges that follow. That Othniel's career as judge lasted forty years, therefore, establishes the ideal model for the careers of future Judges. While other minor judges like Izban

(Judg 12:9), Elon (12:11), and Abdon (12:14) judge Israel for less than forty years, no judge whose deeds are recounted at length besides Jephtah (12:7) rules for less than the ideal forty years.

44. Some scholars see this repetition as evidence for different sources comprising the Samson cycle. See Amit (*Art of Editing*, 274–75 n. 54) for an extensive bibliography of scholars making this claim. Opposed to this position is Martin Noth (*Deuteronomistic History*, 52) who argues that the notices of Samson's rule as judge in Judg 15:20 and 16:31 are from the same hand. Joseph Blenkinsopp also argues for a "principle of unity in the Samson cycle" ("Structure and Style in Judges 13–16," *JBL* 82[1963]:69). Furthermore, the strong case made by Cheryl Exum for the careful symmetry of the cycle ("Aspects of Symmetry and Balance in the Samson Saga," JSOT 19[1981]: 3–29) as well as Robert Alter's convincing illumination of the cycle's use of key terms like פעם and אשָׁה ("Samson Without Folklore," in *Text and Tradition: The Hebrew Bible and Folklore* [ed. Susan Niditch; SBL Semeia Studies; Atlanta: Scholars Press, 1990], 47–56) argue for the unity of the text.

45. Such anointing of a charismatic individual for a special office or role from the time of his birth or before is not uncommon in the HB. Jeremiah, for example, is informed by God that he was appointed a prophet to the nations from the womb (Jer 1:5). Note also that, as I argue is the case for Samson, Samuel too judges Israel "all the days of his life" according to 1 Sam 7:15.

46. Note the frequency with which the root ישע is employed to describe a judge's action for Israel, just as it is used of Samson in Judg 13:5. See Judg 2:16, 18 (the opening précis of the cycle of sin–forgiveness–redemption in Judges, which describes how Yhwh would raise up judges to "deliver" Israel), and the following examples of judges said to have "delivered" Israel with this root: Judg 3:9 (Othniel); 3:15 (Ehud); 3:31 (Shamgar); 6:14–15, 36–37; 8:22 (Gideon); 10:1 (Tola).

47. See Chapter 1, p. 45.

48. The importance to a boy's maturation of a cooperative relationship with the adult males of his society is shown by anthropologist Frank W. Young. In his examination of fifty-four communities on six continents from the mid-nineteenth century to the mid-twentieth century, Young demonstrates that particularly in societies with high levels of adult male solidarity (like that described in the HB), a boy must be accepted into the social group of elder males in his culture to be considered a man. This is often accomplished through rites of passage that ensure the continuation of adult male solidarity, while also enabling boys to "view the world from the adult male standpoint", a necessity if they are adequately to embody the male sex role (*Initiation Ceremonies*, 30).

According to this view, if a boy or young man has no evidence of acceptance by the adult males of his society, he has no evidence of his manhood. He is instead likely to remain stuck in boyhood—a case of arrested development—and cross into manhood only with great difficulty. Looking at Samson in light of Young's research, therefore, adds another, deeper layer to the depiction of his liminality with regard to his development as an adult man.

49. Samson's failure to find acceptance among the Philistine men is obvious in light of the disastrous and mutually destructive consequences that result whenever Samson and Philistine men mix.

50. Applying research from folklore studies to the Samson cycle is appropriate in light of the general scholarly agreement on the folkloric and presumably oral origins of the Samson cycle. See, e.g., Everett Fox, "The Samson Cycle in an Oral Setting," *Alcheringa: Ethnopoetics* 4(1978): 52; David Bynum, "Samson as a Biblical φὴρ ὀρεσκῷς," in Niditch, *Text and Tradition*, 57–73; Albert B. Lord, "Patterns of the Lives of the Patriarchs from Abraham to Samson and Samuel," in ibid., 7–18. However, perhaps no better argument exists for the likelihood of an oral, folkloric context for the cycle's original composition than the fact that even Robert Alter's study of Samson, with its express purpose of showing how carefully composed the final form of the story is as written literature, admits that it would be "foolish to ignore [the] abundance of folkloric elements" in the story ("Samson Without Folklore," in ibid., 48).

In the case of the Jether narrative, applying folklore research is appropriate because, as Isser argues (see above, n. 3), it is likely that characters like Jether who are only briefly mentioned in the HB were well known in the folklore of ancient Israel (hence they do not require extensive introduction in the HB).

51. David E. Bynum, "Themes of the Young Hero in Serbocroatian Oral Epic Tradition," *Proceedings of the Modern Language Association* 83(1968): 1296–1303.

52. Margaret H. Beissinger, "Rites of Passage and Oral Storytelling in Romanian Epic and the New Testament," *Oral Tradition* 17(2002): 236–58.

53. Bynum, "Young Hero," 1296.

54. See Beissinger, "Romanian Epic," 242–43; Bynum, "Young Hero," 1299–1300.

55. For Bynum's recognition of the failure-to-come-of-age theme in Homer, see "Young Hero," 1300. Bynum compares the tales of the Slavic initiatory heroes with those of Telemachus, Odysseus's young son. Telemachus similarly goes on a quest to find his father, a quest that Charles Eckert shows to be filled with initiation themes ("Initiatory Motifs in the Story of Telemachus," *Classical Journal* 59[1963]: 49–57). Telemachus ultimately fails and is later freed from his tenuous fate as stepson to the potential new ruler of Ithaca by his father.

56. Beissinger writes that ". . . the Romanian initiation epics and their heroes articulate a variety of concerns relating to the traditional family and the succession of generations" ("Romanian Epic," 237). Bynum similarly argues that the tale of failed maturation that he heard in his research in Yugoslavia "is quite overtly about the problems and process of 'socializing' a male child and about

the crucial moments of 'role-transference' between father and sons" ("Young Hero," 1297).

57. The biblical stories do, however, share some similarities with the stories of Gruia, Mehmed Smailagić, and Omer Hrnijca. Like the Balkan novice heroes, Samson and Jether attempt to perform certain manly deeds (marriage in the case of the former, a display of battlefield prowess with the latter), but ultimately fail. Moreover, Jether's story depicts him needing his father's assistance to complete his task, a frequent feature in the Balkan tales. Samson further resembles the Balkan novice heroes because both have attracted to themselves a number of separate vignettes reflecting the arrested development theme, and do not appear in their respective narrative traditions as full-fledged men.

However, differences between the biblical stories and the Balkan tales are also apparent. Note that Samson is never rescued by a father figure in the course of his adventures (unlike the Balkan novice heroes and Jether). Similarly, if a cycle of Jether narratives existed consisting of many stories in which he fails to achieve manhood (as with the Balkan novice heroes and Samson), these are no longer extant.

58. See Childs, *Book of Exodus*, 418; see also William H. C. Propp, *Exodus 19–40: A New Translation with Introduction and Commentary* (AB 2A; New York: Doubleday, 2006), 178. Both emphasize that this commandment is targeted at adult children, enjoining them to take care of their aging parents. The modern interpretation of this commandment—that young children obey their parents—may also have been implied, but was not as significant in the original context of the law (see also Exod 21:15, 17; Lev 20:9; Deut 27:16).

59. Meyers, "Family in Early Israel," 35.

60. Jon Berquist, *Controlling Corporeality: The Body and the Household in Ancient Israel* (New Brunswick, NJ: Rutgers University Press, 2002), 127.

61. Michael J. Smith's claim that Samson's characterization fits the description of the rebellious son in Deut 21:18–21 ("Failure of the Family in Judges, Part 2: Samson," *BSac* 162[2005], 430) lends support to this proposal.

62. In this view, the Samson cycle would bear similarities with texts from the wisdom tradition such as Prov 7. Indeed, the similarity between the Samson cycle and wisdom literature is demonstrated by Brettler, who argues that the polemic against marriage to foreign women and the use of riddles in the Samson cycle are evidence of wisdom's influence on the composition. See Marc Zvi Brettler, *The Book of Judges* (Old Testament Readings; London/New York: Routledge, 2002), 51–52.

63. Niditch, *Judges*, 9–10. The Jether pericope indicates its place in this tradition for its use of bardic conventions like proverbs, and its concern with codes of military conduct (ibid., 105). The use of epic language and style in the Samson

story (ibid., 15, 142), as well as the similarity of Samson to other epic heroes like Hercules (ibid., 9), provides evidence for the "epic bardic" origins of the Samson cycle.

64. See Susan Niditch, *Oral World and Written Word: Ancient Israelite Literature* (Louisville: Westminster John Knox, 1996), 113; see also Niditch, *War*, 90–105.

65. Niditch, *War*, 105; see also Niditch, *Oral World*, 113.

66. Others who argue that Samson stands in as a metaphorical representation of all Israel include: Crenshaw (*Secret Betrayed*, 134); Brevard S. Childs (*Old Testament Theology in a Canonical Context* [Philadelphia: Fortress, 1985] 114–15); and Everett Fox ("Samson Cycle," 53). More generally, Jeremy Schipper shows that in the Deuteronomistic History the historical predicament of Israel is often inscribed on the bodies of the history's characters, since characters with disabilities appear at moments of political transition in the historical narrative, reflecting the deterioration of the old political order ("Disabling Israelite Leadership: 2 Samuel 6:23 and Other Images of Disability in the Deuteronomistic History," in *This Abled Body: Rethinking Disabilities in Biblical Studies* [ed. Hector Avalos, Sarah J. Melcher, and Jeremy Schipper; SemeiaSt 55; Atlanta: Society of Biblical Literature, 2007], 103–13).

67. Dennis T. Olson, "Judges," 860–62.

68. Edward L. Greenstein, "The Riddle of Samson," *Proof* 1(1981): 247–55.

69. For the first and most succinct of the six instances of this cycle, see Judg 3:7–11.

70. The observation that many of the major judges possess a crucial flaw that makes them unlikely heroes is that of Carol Meyers (personal communication, December 2011).

71. For a discussion of this deterioration, see, for example, Tanner, "Gideon Narrative," 152.

CONCLUSION

1. See Chapter 3, p. 94; Chapter 4, p. 127. In the case of 1 Kgs 3, DtrH could be the author of the story outright, or, as Carr argues (*Royal Ideology*, 178–207) DtrH could have heavily edited and rewritten a pre-existent legend to bring it in line with his ideology.

2. For a recent summary of the status of the question of the Deuteronomistic History and the editors/authors responsible for its compilation, see Römer, *So-Called Deuteronomistic History*, 13–43.

3. See ibid., 34, 72.

4. Ibid., 94.

5. Ibid., 105.

6. Whether or not this hypothesis concerning textual reconstruction is ultimately convincing, the relevance of the present study to scholarship on biblical masculinity is still evident. The texts of 1 Sam 3 and 1 Kgs 3, even if they are not from the same hand and therefore do not provide evidence of a diachronic development in views of normative masculinity in Israel, still stand as representations of an alternative masculinity to the hegemonic form that is found in much of the HB.

APPENDIX

1. Note also that in Hosea's description of Jacob's encounter with God at the Jabbok he describes Jacob in this scene as already "in his manhood" (בְּאוֹנ֑וֹ; Hosea 12:3 [MT 12:4]).

Bibliography

Ackerman, Susan. *When Heroes Love: The Ambiguity of Eros in the Stories of Gilgamesh and David*. New York: Columbia University Press, 2005.

Adams, Rachel, and David Savran, eds. *The Masculinity Studies Reader*. Malden, MA: Blackwell, 2002.

Alter, Robert. *The Art of Biblical Narrative*. New York: Basic Books, 1981.

———. *The Art of Biblical Poetry*. New York: Basic Books, 1985.

———. "Samson Without Folklore." Pages 47–56 in *Text and Tradition: The Hebrew Bible and Folklore*. Edited by Susan Niditch. Society of Biblical Literature Semeia Studies. Atlanta: Scholars Press, 1990.

———. *The David Story: A Translation with Commentary of 1 and 2 Samuel*. New York: Norton, 1999.

———. *The Five Books of Moses: A Translation with Commentary*. New York: Norton, 2004.

Amit, Yaira. *The Book of Judges: The Art of Editing*. Translated by Jonathan Chipman. Leiden: Brill, 1999.

Angel, Hayyim. "The Positive and Negative Traits of Gideon: As Reflected in His Sons Jotham and Abimelech." *Jewish Bible Quarterly* 34(2006): 159–67.

Anttonen, Perrti J. "The Rites of Passage Revisited: A New Look at van Gennep's Theory of the Ritual Process and Its Application in the Study of Finnish-Karelian Wedding Rituals." Pages 178–211 in *Folklore: Critical Concepts in Literary and Cultural Studies; Volume III: The Genres of Folklore*. Edited by Alan Dundes. New York: Routledge, 2005. Repr. from *Temenos: Studies in Comparative Religion* 28(1992): 15–52.

Asher-Greve, Julia M. "The Essential Body: Mesopotamian Conceptions of the Gendered Body." *Gender and History* 9(1997): 432–61.

———. "Decisive Sex, Essential Gender." Pages 11–26 in *Sex and Gender in the Ancient Near East: Proceedings of the 47th Rencontre Assyriologique Internationale, Helsinki, July 2–6, 2001*. Edited by S. Parpola and Robert M. Whiting. 2 vols. Helsinki: The Neo-Assyrian Text Corpus Project, 2002.

Auld, A. Graeme. "Gideon: Hacking at the Heart of the Old Testament." *Vetus Testamentum* 39(1989): 257–67.

Aycock, D. Alan. "The Fate of Lot's Wife." Pages 113–19 in *Structuralist Interpretations of Biblical Myth*. Edited by Edmund Leach and D. Alan Aycock. Cambridge: Cambridge University Press, 1983.

Bal, Mieke. "The Rhetoric of Subjectivity." *Poetics Today* 5(1984): 337–76.

———. *Lethal Love: Feminist Literary Readings of Biblical Love Stories*. Bloomington, IN: Indiana University Press, 1987.

Barnard, Alan, and Jonathan Spencer. "Rites of Passage." Pages 616–17 in *The Routledge Encyclopedia of Social and Cultural Anthropology*. Edited by Alan Barnard and Jonathan Spencer. 2d ed. London and New York: Routledge, 2010.

Barnes, Jonathan, ed. *The Complete Works of Aristotle*. 2 vols. Princeton, NJ: Princeton University Press, 1984.

Barthélemy, Dominique. "Troi Niveaux d'Analyse." Pages 47–54 in *The Story of David and Goliath: Textual and Literary Criticism. Papers of a Joint Research Venture*. Edited by Dominique Barthélemy, David W. Gooding, Emanuel Tov, and Johan Lust. Orbis biblicus et orientalis 73. Göttingen: Vandenhoeck & Ruprecht/Freiburg: Éditions Universitaires, 1986.

Barton, John. "Dating the 'Succession Narrative.'" Pages 95–106 in *In Search of Pre-exilic Israel*. Edited by John Day. Journal for the Study of the Old Testament: Supplement Series 406. New York: T&T Clark, 2004.

Bechtel, Lyn M. "Genesis 2.4B–3.24: A Myth about Human Maturation." *Journal for the Study of the Old Testament* 67(1995): 3–26.

Beck, John A. "David and Goliath, A Story of Place: The Narrative-Geographical Shaping of 1 Samuel 17." *Westminster Theological Journal* 68 (2006): 321–30.

Beissinger, Margaret H. "Rites of Passage and Oral Storytelling in Romanian Epic and the New Testament." *Oral Tradition* 17(2002): 236–58.

Bellefontaine, Elizabeth. "Deuteronomy 21:18–21: Reviewing the Case of the Rebellious Son." *Journal for the Study of the Old Testament* 4(1979): 13–31.

Benjamin, Jessica. *The Bonds of Love*. New York: Pantheon, 1984.

Bergmann, Claudia D. "'We Have Seen the Enemy, and He is Only a "She"': The Portrayal of Warriors as Women." Pages 129–42 in *Writing and Reading War: Rhetoric, Gender, and Ethics in Biblical and Modern Contexts*. Edited by Brad E. Kelle and Brad Ritchel Ames. Atlanta: Society of Biblical Literature, 2008.

Berquist, Jon L. *Controlling Corporeality: The Body and the Household in Ancient Israel*. New Brunswick, NJ: Rutgers University Press, 2002.

———. "Childhood and Age in the Bible." *Pastoral Psychology* 58(2009): 521–30.

Beyer, K. *Die Aramäischen Texte vom Toten Meer: samt den Inschriften aus Palästina, dem Testament Levis aus der Kairoer Genisa, der Fastenrolle und den alten talmudischen Zitaten: aramaistische Einleitung, Text, Übersetzung, Deutung, Grammatik/Wörterbuch, deutsch-aramäische Wortliste, Register*. Göttingen: Vandenhoek and Ruprecht, 1984.

Bilu, Yoram. "From *Milah* (Circumcision) to *Milah* (Word): Male Identity and Rituals of Childhood in the Jewish Ultraorthadox Community." *Ethos* 31(2003): 172–203.

Birch, Bruce B. "The Books of First and Second Samuel: Introduction, Commentary and Reflections." Pages 947–1383 in *The New Interpreter's Bible* vol. 2. Edited by Leander E. Keck et al. 12 vols. Nashville: Abingdon, 1994.

Blenkinsopp, Joseph. "Structure and Style in Judges 13–16." *Journal of Biblical Literature* 82(1963): 65–76.

Boer, Roland. "Of Fine Wine, Incense, and Spices: the Unstable Masculine Hegemony of the Books of Chronicles." Pages 20–33 in *Men and Masculinity in the Hebrew Bible and Beyond*. Edited by Ovidiu Creangă. The Bible in the Modern World 33. Sheffield: Sheffield Phoenix, 2010.

Boling, Robert G. *Judges: A New Translation with Introduction and Commentary*. Anchor Bible 6A. Garden City, NY: Doubleday, 1975.

Botterweck, G. Johannes, Helmer Ringgren, and Heinz-Josef Fabry, eds. *Theological Dictionary of the Old Testament*. Translated by John T. Willis, Geoffrey W. Bromiley, David E. Green, and Douglas W. Stott. 15 vols. Grand Rapids, MI: Eerdmans, 1974–2006.

Bourdieu, Pierre. "The Sentiment of Honour in Kayble Society." Pages 171–90 in *Honour and Shame: The Values of Mediterranean Society*. Edited by John G. Peristiany. Chicago: University of Chicago Press, 1966.

Bourke, Joseph. "Samuel and the Ark." *Dominican Studies* 7(1954): 73–103.

Brettler, Marc Zvi. *The Book of Judges*. Old Testament Readings. London and New York: Routledge, 2002.

Breytenbach, Andries P. B. "Who is Behind the Samuel Narrative?" Pages 50–61 in *Past, Present, Future: The Deuteronomistic History and the Prophets*. Edited by Johannes C. de Moor and Herrie F. Van Rooy. Leiden: Brill, 2000.

Brinkman, John A. "Sex, Age, and Physical Condition Designations for Servile Laborers in the Middle Babylonian Period: A Preliminary Survey." Pages 1–8 in *Zikir Šumim: Assyriological Studies Presented to F. R. Kraus*. Edited by G. van Driel et al. Leiden: Brill, 1982.

Brittan, Arthur. *Masculinity and Power*. Oxford and New York: Blackwell, 1989.

Brown, Francis, S. R. Driver, and Charles A. Briggs, eds. *The Brown-Driver-Briggs Hebrew and English Lexicon, with an appendix containing the Biblical Aramaic*. Based on the lexicon of Wilhelm Gesenius and reprinted from the 1906 edition originally published by Houghton, Mifflin and Company, Boston. 6th printing. Peabody, MA: Hendrickson, 2001.

Brown, William P. "To Discipline without Destruction: The Multifaceted Profile of the Child in Proverbs." Pages 63–81 in *The Child in the Bible*. Edited by Marcia J. Bunge. Grand Rapids, MI: Eerdmans, 2008.

Brueggemann, Walter. *First and Second Samuel*. Interpretation: A Biblical Commentary for Teaching and Preaching. Louisville: Westminster John Knox, 1990.

Buchbinder, David. *Studying Men and Masculinities*. London: Routledge, 2012.

Butler, Judith. "Performative Acts and Gender Constitution: An Essay in Phenomenology and Feminist Theory." Pages 270–82 in *Performing Feminisms: Feminist Critical Theory and Theater*. Edited by Sue-Ellen Case. Baltimore: Johns Hopkins University Press, 1990.

———. *Gender Trouble: Feminism and the Subversion of Identity*. 2d ed. New York and London: Routledge, 1999.

Butler, Trent C. "An Anti-Moses Tradition." Journal for the Study of the Old Testament 12(1979): 9–15.

Bynum, David E. "Themes of the Young Hero in Serbocroatian Oral Epic Tradition." *Proceedings of the Modern Language Association* 83(1968): 1296–303.

———. "Samson as a Biblical φὴρ ὀρεσκῷς." Pages 57–73 in *Text and Tradition: The Hebrew Bible and Folklore*. Edited by Susan Niditch. Society of Biblical Literature Semeia Studies. Atlanta: Scholars Press, 1990.

Calame, Claude. *Choruses of Young Women in Ancient Greece: Their Morphology, Religious Role and Social Functions*. Translated by D. Collins and J. Orion. Lanham, MD: Rowman and Littlefield, 2001.

Campbell, Anthony F., S. J. *1 Samuel*. Forms of the Old Testament Literature 7. Grand Rapids, MI: Eerdmans, 2003.

Campbell, Edward F., Jr. *Ruth: A New Translation with Introduction, Notes, and Commentary*. Anchor Bible 7. Garden City, NY: Doubleday, 1975.

Campbell, Joseph. *The Hero with a Thousand Faces*. 3d ed. Novato, CA: New World Library, 2008.

Carasik, Michael. "Ruth 2,7: Why the Overseer was Embarrassed." *Zeitschrift für die alttestamentliche Wissenschaft* 107(1995): 493–94.

Carr, David McLain. "Royal Ideology and the Technology of Faith: A Comparative Midrash Study of 1 Kgs 3:2–15." PhD diss. The Claremont Graduate School, 1988.

Carrigan, Tim, Bob Connell, and John Lee. "Toward a New Sociology of Masculinity." Pages 99–118 in *The Masculinity Studies Reader*. Edited by Rachel Adams and David Savran. Malden, MA: Blackwell, 2002. Repr. from *Theory and Society* 14(1985): 551–604.

Cassuto, Umberto. *A Commentary on the Book of Exodus*. Translated by Israel Abrahams. Jerusalem: Magnes Press, 1967.

Chapman, Cynthia R. *The Gendered Language of Warfare in the Israelite–Assyrian Encounter*. Harvard Semitic Monographs 62. Winona Lake, IN: Eisenbrauns, 2004.

Childs, Brevard S. *The Book of Exodus*. Old Testament Library. Louisville: Westminster, 1976.

———. *Old Testament Theology in a Canonical Context*. Philadelphia, Fortress, 1985.

Chodorow, Nancy. "Family Structure and Feminine Personality." Pages 43–66 in *Woman, Culture, and Society*. Edited by Michelle Z. Rosaldo and Louise Lamphere. Stanford: Stanford University Press, 1974.

Clark, W. Malcolm. "A Legal Background to the Yahwist's Use of 'Good and Evil' in Genesis 2–3." *Journal of Biblical Literature* 88(1969): 266–78.

Clines, David J. A. "David the Man: The Construction of Masculinity in the Hebrew Bible." Pages 212–43 in *Interested Parties: The Ideology of Writers and Readers of the Hebrew Bible*. Edited by David J. A. Clines. Journal for the Study of the Old Testament Supplement Series 205. Sheffield: Sheffield Academic Press, 1995.

———. "He-Prophets: Masculinity as a Problem for the Hebrew Prophets and Their Interpreters." Pages 311–28 in *Sense and Sensitivity: Essays on Reading the Bible in Memory of Robert Carroll*. Edited by Alastair G. Hunter and Philip R. Davies. Journal for the Study of the Old Testament Supplement Series 348. Sheffield: Sheffield Academic Press, 2002.

———. "Being a Man in the Book of the Covenant." Pages 3–9 in *Reading the Law: Studies in Honour of Gordon J. Wenham*. Edited by J. G. McConville and Karl Möller. Library of Hebrew Bible/Old Testament Studies 461. New York: T&T Clark, 2007.

———. "Dancing and Shining at Sinai: Playing the Man in Exodus 32–34." Pages 54–63 in *Men and Masculinity in the Hebrew Bible and Beyond*. Edited by Ovidiu Creangă. The Bible in the Modern World 33. Sheffield: Sheffield Phoenix, 2010.

Coats, George W. "Moses in Midian." *Journal of Biblical Literature* 92(1973): 3–10.

———. *Exodus 1–18*. Forms of the Old Testament Literature IIA. Grand Rapids, MI: Eerdmans, 1999.

Cogan, Mordechai. *1 Kings: A New Translation with Introduction and Commentary*. Anchor Bible 10. New York: Doubleday, 2000.

Cohn, Robert L. *The Shape of Sacred Space: Four Biblical Studies*. American Academy of Religion Studies in Religion 23. Chico, CA: Scholars Press, 1981.

Connell, R. W. *Masculinities*. Cambridge and Oxford: Polity Press, 1995.

——— and James W. Messerschmidt. "Hegemonic Masculinity: Rethinking the Concept." *Gender and Society* 19(2005): 829–59.

Creangă, Ovidiu. "Variations on the Theme of Masculinity: Joshua's Gender In/Stability in the Conquest Narrative." Pages 83–109 in *Men and Masculinity in the Hebrew Bible and Beyond*. Edited by Ovidiu Creangă. The Bible in the Modern World, 33. Sheffield: Sheffield Phoenix, 2010.

———. "Introduction." Pages 3–14 in *Biblical Masculinities Foregrounded*. Edited by Ovidiu Creangă and Peter-Ben Smit. Hebrew Bible Monographs 62. Sheffield: Sheffield Phoenix, 2014.

Crenshaw, James. *Samson: A Secret Betrayed, A Vow Ignored*. Atlanta: John Knox, 1978.

———. "Samson." Pages 950–54 in vol. 5 of *The Anchor Bible Dictionary*. Edited by David Noel Freedman. 6 vols. New York: Doubleday, 1992.

Cross, Frank Moore. *From Epic to Canon: History and Literature in Ancient Israel*. Baltimore: Johns Hopkins University Press, 1998.

Crown, Alan D. "An Alternative Meaning for אִישׁ in the Old Testament." *Vetus Testamentum* 24(1974): 110–12.

Damrosch, David. *The Narrative Covenant: Transformation of Genre in the Growth of Biblical Literature*. San Francisco: Harper and Row, 1987.

Davidson, E. T. A. *Intricacy, Design, and Cunning in the Book of Judges*. Philadelphia: Xlibris, 2008.

Davies, Gordon F. *Israel in Egypt: Reading Exodus 1–2*. Journal for the Study of the Old Testament: Supplement Series 135. Sheffield: Sheffield Academic Press, 1992.

Day, Linda. "Wisdom and the Feminine in the Bible." Pages 114–27 in *Engaging the Bible in a Gendered World: An Introduction to Feminist Biblical Interpretation in Honor of Katharine Doob Sakenfeld*. Edited by Linda Day and Carolyn Pressler. Louisville: Westminster John Knox, 2006.

Day, Peggy L. "From the Child is Born the Woman: The Story of Jephthah's Daughter." Pages 58–74 in *Gender and Difference in Ancient Israel*. Edited by Peggy L. Day. Minneapolis: Fortress, 1989.

De Boer, Pieter A. H. "Psalm 131:2." *Vetus Testamentum* 16(1966): 287–92.

Deem, Ariella. "And the Stone Sank Into His Forehead: A Note on 1 Samuel 17:49." *Vetus Testamentum* 28(1978): 349–51.

Demetriou, Demetrakis Z. "Connell's Concept of Hegemonic Masculinity: A Critique." *Theory and Society* 30(2001): 337–61.

De Vaux, Roland. "Single Combat in the Old Testament." Pages 122–35 in *The Bible and the Ancient Near East*. Translated by Damian McHugh. Edited by Roland de Vaux. Garden City, NY: Doubleday, 1971.

De Vries, Simon J. "David's Victory over the Philistine as Saga and as Legend." *Journal of Biblical Literature* 92(1973): 23–36.

Dinnerstein, Dorothy. *The Mermaid and the Minotaur*. New York: Harper and Row, 1977.

DiPalma, Brian Charles. "De/Constructing Masculinity in Exodus 1–4." Pages 36–53 in *Men and Masculinity in the Hebrew Bible and Beyond*. Edited by Ovidiu Creangă. The Bible in the Modern World 33. Sheffield: Sheffield Phoenix, 2010.

Dundes, Alan. "Traditional Male Combat: From Game to War." Pages 25–45 in *From Game to War, and Other Psychoanalytic Essays on Folklore*. Edited by Alan Dundes. Lexington: University Press of Kentucky, 1997.

Durham, John I. *Exodus*. Word Biblical Commentary 3. Waco, TX: Word Books, 1987.

Eckert, Charles. "Initiatory Motifs in the Story of Telemachus." *Classical Journal* 59(1963): 49–57.

Edelman, Diana Vikander. *King Saul in the Historiography of Judah*. Sheffield: Sheffield Academic Press, 1991.

Eisenberg, Ronald. *The JPS Guide to Jewish Traditions*. Philadelphia: Jewish Publication Society, 2004.

Eliade, Mircea. *Birth and Rebirth: The Religious Meanings of Initiation in Human Culture*. Translated by Willard R. Trask. New York: Harper, 1958.

————. *Myth and Reality*. New York: Harper Torchbook, 1968.

Elsbree, Langdon. *Ritual Passages and Narrative Structures*. New York: Peter Lang, 1991.

Eng, Milton. *The Days of Our Years: A Lexical Semantic Study of the Life Cycle in Biblical Israel*. Library of Hebrew Bible/Old Testament Studies 464. New York: T&T Clark, 2011.

Evans-Pritchard, Edward E. *The Nuer: A Description of the Modes of Livelihood and Political Institutions of a Nilotic People*. Oxford: Clarendon Press, 1940.

Exum, Cheryl J. "Aspects of Symmetry and Balance in the Samson Saga." *Journal for the Study of the Old Testament* 19(1981): 3–29.

Eynikel, Erik. "The Relation between the Eli Narrative and the Ark Narratives." Pages 88–106 in *Past, Present, Future: The Deuteronomistic History and the Prophets*. Edited by Johannes C. de Moor and Herrie F. Van Rooy. Leiden: Brill, 2000.

Fausto-Sterling, Anne. *Sexing the Body: Gender Politics and the Construction of Sexuality*. New York: Basic Books, 2000.

Fokkelman, J. P. *Narrative Art and Poetry in the Books of Samuel: A Full Interpretation Based on Stylistic and Structural Analyses. Volume I: King David (II Sam. 9–20 & I Kings 1–2)*. Studia semitica neerlandica 20. Aasen/Maastricht, The Netherlands: Van Gorcum, 1981.

————. *Narrative Art and Poetry in the Books of Samuel: A Full Interpretation Based on Stylistic and Structural Analyses. Volume II: The Crossing Fates (I Sam. 13–31 & II Sam. 1)*. Studia semitica neerlandica 23. Aasen/Maastricht, The Netherlands: Van Gorcum, 1986.

Fox, Everett. "The Samson Cycle in an Oral Setting." *Alcheringa: Ethnopoetics* 4(1978): 51–68.

Fox, Michael V. *Proverbs 10–31: A New Translation with Introduction and Commentary*. Anchor Bible 18B. New Haven: Yale University Press, 2009.

Fretheim, Terence E. *Exodus*. Interpretation: A Biblical Commentary for Teaching and Preaching. Louisville: John Knox, 1991.

————. *First and Second Kings*. Westminster Bible Companion. Louisville: Westminster John Knox Press, 1999.

Frolov, Serge, and Allen Wright. "Homeric and Ancient Near Eastern Intertextuality in 1 Samuel 17." *Journal of Biblical Literature* 130(2011): 451–71.

Frymer-Kensky, Tikva. "Virginity in the Bible." Pages 79–96 in *Gender and Law in the Hebrew Bible and the Ancient Near East*. Edited by Victor H. Matthews, Bernard M. Levinson, and Tikva Frymer-Kensky. Journal for the Study of the Old Testament Supplement Series 262. Sheffield: Sheffield Academic Press, 1998.

George, Mark K. "Masculinity and Its Regimentation in Deuteronomy." Pages 64–82 in *Men and Masculinity in the Hebrew Bible and Beyond*. Edited by Ovidiu Creangă. The Bible in the Modern World 33. Sheffield: Sheffield Phoenix, 2010.

Gesenius, Wilhelm. *A Hebrew and English Lexicon of the Old Testament, Including the Biblical Chaldee: From the Latin of William Gesenius.* Translated by Edward Robinson. Boston: Crocker and Brewster, 1854.

Gilmore, David D. "Honor, Honesty, Shame: Male Status in Contemporary Andalusia." Pages 90–103 in *Honor and Shame and the Unity of the Mediterranean.* Edited by David D. Gilmore. Washington, DC: American Anthropological Association, 1987.

———. "Introduction: The Shame of Dishonor." Pages 2–21 in *Honor and Shame and the Unity of the Mediterranean.* Edited by David D. Gilmore. Washington DC: American Anthropological Association, 1987.

———. *Manhood in the Making: Cultural Concepts of Masculinity.* New Haven: Yale University Press, 1990.

Ginzberg, Louis. *The Legends of the Jews.* Translated by Henrietta Szold. 7 vols. Philadelphia: Jewish Publication Society, 1911–1936.

Girardot, N. J. "Initiation and Meaning in the Tale of Snow White and the Seven Dwarfs." *Journal of American Folklore* 90(1977): 274–300.

Gnuse, Robert Karl. "The Dream Theophany of Samuel: Its Structure in Relation to Ancient Near Eastern Dreams and Its Theological Significance." PhD diss. Vanderbilt University, 1980.

Goldingay, John. "Hosea 1–3, Genesis 1–4, and Masculinist Interpretation." *Horizons in Biblical Theology* 17 (1995): 37–44.

Gooding, David W. "An Approach to the Literary and Textual Problems in the David–Goliath Story." Pages 55–86 in *The Story of David and Goliath: Textual and Literary Criticism. Papers of a Joint Research Venture.* Edited by Dominique Barthélemy, David W. Gooding, Emanuel Tov, and Johan Lust. Orbis biblicus et orientalis 73. Göttingen: Vandenhoeck & Ruprecht/Freiburg: Éditions Universitaires, 1986.

Gordon, Cyrus H. *"n'r." Ugaritic Textbook.* C. H. Gordon. Analecta Orientalia 38. Rome, 1965.

Gordon, Robert P. *I & II Samuel: A Commentary.* Library of Biblical Interpretation. Grand Rapids, MI: Zondervan, 1988.

Graf, Fritz. "Initiation: A Concept with a Troubled History." Pages 3–24 in *Initiation in Ancient Greek Rituals and Narratives: New Critical Perspectives.* Edited by David B. Dodd and Christopher A. Faraone. New York: Routledge, 2003.

Greenberg, Moshe. *Understanding Exodus.* New York: Behrman House, 1969.

Greenstein, Edward L. "The Riddle of Samson." *Prooftexts: A Journal of Jewish Literary History* 1(1981): 237–60.

Gruber, Mayer I. Review of Carolyn S. Leeb, *Away from the Father's House: The Social Location of na'ar and na'arah in Ancient Israel. Jewish Quarterly Review* 43(2003): 612–15.

Guest, Deryn. "From Gender Reversal to Genderfuck: Reading Jael through a Lesbian Lens." Pages 9–43 in *Bible Trouble: Queer Reading at the Boundaries of*

Biblical Scholarship. Edited by Teresa J. Hornsby and Ken Stone. Atlanta: Society of Biblical Literature, 2013.

Gunkel, Hermann. *Reden und Aufsätze.* Edited by Hermann Gunkel. Göttingen: Vandenhoeck & Ruprecht, 1913.

Habel, Norman C. "The Form and Significance of the Call Narratives." *Zeitschrift für die alttestamentliche Wissenschaft* 77(1965): 297–323.

———. *The Book of Job.* Old Testament Library. Philadelphia: Westminster, 1985.

Haddox, Susan E. "(E)Masculinity in Hosea's Political Rhetoric." Pages 174–200 in *Israel's Prophets and Israel's Past: Essays on the Relationship of Prophetic Texts and Israelite History in Honor of John H. Hayes.* Edited by Brad E. Kelle and Megan Bishop Moore. New York: T&T Clark, 2006.

———. "Favoured Sons and Subordinate Masculinities." Pages 2–19 in *Men and Masculinity in the Hebrew Bible and Beyond.* Edited by Ovidiu Creangă. The Bible in the Modern World 33. Sheffield: Sheffield Phoenix, 2010.

Halpern, Baruch. *David's Secret Demons: Messiah, Murderer, Traitor, King.* Grand Rapids, MI: Eerdmans, 2001.

Hamilton, Edith, and Huntington Cairns, eds. *The Collected Dialogues of Plato.* Princeton: Princeton University Press, 1961.

Hamilton, Mark W. *The Body Royal: The Social Poetics of Kingship in Ancient Israel.* Leiden: Brill, 2005.

Hamilton, Victor P. "Marriage (OT and ANE)." Pages 559–69 in vol. 4 of *The Anchor Bible Dictionary.* Edited by David Noel Freedman. 6 vols. New York: Doubleday, 1992.

Harris, Rivkah. *Gender and Aging in Mesopotamia: The Gilgamesh Epic and Other Ancient Literature.* Norman, OK: University of Oklahoma Press, 2000.

Hendel, Ronald S. *The Epic of the Patriarch: The Jacob Cycle and the Narrative Traditions of Canaan and Israel.* Harvard Semitic Monographs 42. Atlanta: Scholars Press, 1987.

———. "Sacrifice as a Cultural System: The Ritual Symbolism of Exodus 24,3–8." *Zeitschrift für die alttestamentliche Wissenschaft* 101(1989): 366–90.

Herdt, Gilbert H. *Guardians of the Flutes: Idioms of Masculinity.* New York: McGraw-Hill, 1981.

Hermann, Siegfried. "Die Königsnovelle in Ägypten und Israel." *Wissenschaftliche Zeitscrhift der Karl-Marx Universität* 3(1953–1954): 51–62.

Herzberg, Hans Wilhelm. *I & II Samuel: A Commentary.* Old Testament Library. Philadelphia: Westminster, 1964.

Herzfeld, Michael. "'As in Your Own House': Hospitality, Ethnography, and the Stereotype of Mediterranean Society." Pages 75–89 in *Honor and Shame and the Unity of the Mediterranean.* Edited by David D. Gilmore. Washington, DC: American Anthropological Association, 1987.

Hobbs, T. R. "Hospitality in the First Testament and the 'Teleological Fallacy.'" *Journal for the Study of the Old Testament* 95(2001): 3–30.

Hoffner, Harry A. "Symbols for Masculinity and Femininity: Their Use in Ancient Near Eastern Sympathetic Magic Rituals." *Journal of Biblical Literature* 85(1966): 326–34.

Hollis, Susan Tower. "The Woman in Ancient Examples of the Potiphar's Wife Motif, K2111." Pages 28–42 in *Gender and Difference in Ancient Israel*. Edited by Peggy L. Day. Minneapolis: Fortress, 1989.

Hooker, Alan. "'Show Me Your Glory': The Kabod of Yahweh as Phallic Manifestation?" Pages 17–34 in *Biblical Masculinities Foregrounded*. Edited by Ovidiu Creangă and Peter-Ben Smit. Hebrew Bible Monographs 62. Sheffield: Sheffield Phoenix, 2014.

Husser, Jean-Marie. *Dreams and Dream Narratives in the Biblical World*. Translated by J. Munro. Sheffield: Sheffield Academic Press, 1999.

Hutton, Jeremy. "The Left Bank of the Jordan and the Rites of Passage: An Anthropological Interpretation of 2 Samuel XIX." *Vetus Testamentum* 56(2006): 470–84.

Isser, Stanley. *The Sword of Goliath: David in Heroic Literature*. Society of Biblical Literature Studies in Biblical Literature 6. Atlanta: Society of Biblical Literature, 2003.

Jacob, Benno. *The Second Book of the Bible: Exodus*. Translated by W. Jacob. Hoboken, NJ: Ktav, 1992.

Jacobsen, Thorkild. *The Treasures of Darkness*. New Haven: Yale University Press, 1976.

Jaffe, Greg. "War Wounds: Breaking a Taboo, Army Confronts Guilt After Combat." *Wall Street Journal*, August 17, 2005. Cited January 11, 2012. Online: http://online.wsj.com/article/0SB112424442541515220,00.html.

Jason, Heda. "The Story of David and Goliath: A Folk Epic?" *Biblica* 60(1979): 36–90.

Jefferson, Tony. "Subordinating Hegemonic Masculinity." *Theoretical Criminology* 6(2002): 63–88.

Johnson, Benjamin J. A. "Reconsidering 4QSamᵃ and the Textual Support for the Long and Short Versions of the David and Goliath Story." *Vetus Testamentum* 62(2012): 534–49.

Johnston, Sarah Iles. "'Initiation' in Myth, 'Initiation' in Practice: The Homeric *Hymn to Hermes* and its Performative Context." Pages 155–80 in *Initiation in Ancient Greek Rituals and Narratives: New Critical Perspectives*. Edited by David B. Dodd and Christopher A. Faraone. New York: Routledge, 2003.

Kamesar, Adam. "The Virgin of Isaiah 7:14: The Philological Argument From the Second to the Fifth Century." *Journal of Theological Studies* 41(1990): 51–75.

Kang, Jung Ju. *The Persuasive Portrayal of Solomon in 1 Kings 1–11*. Bern: Peter Lang, 2003.

Kenik, Helen A. *Design for Kingship: The Deuteronomistic Narrative Technique in 1 Kings 3:4–15*. Society of Biblical Literature Dissertation Series 15. Chico, CA: Scholars Press, 1983.

Kimmel, Michael S. *The Gendered Society*. 3d ed. Oxford: Oxford University Press, 2008.

———. *Guyland: The Perilous World Where Boys Become Men; Understanding the Critical Years between 16 and 26*. New York: HarperCollins, 2008.

Klein, Ralph W. *1 Samuel*. Word Bible Commentary 10. Waco, TX: Word Books, 1983.

Knoppers, Gary N. *Two Nations Under God: The Deuteronomistic History of Solomon and the Dual Monarchies. Volume 1: The Reign of Solomon and the Rise of Jeroboam*. Harvard Semitic Monographs 52. Atlanta, Scholars Press, 1993.

Koehler, L., W. Baumgartner, and J. J. Stamm. *The Hebrew and Aramaic Lexicon of the Old Testament*. Translated and edited under the supervision of M. E. J. Richardson. 4 vols. Leiden: Brill, 1994–2000.

La Fontaine, Jean Sybil. *Initiation*. Manchester: Manchester University Press, 1986.

Lasine, Stuart. *Knowing Kings: Knowledge, Power and Narcissism in the Hebrew Bible*. Semeia Studies 40. Atlanta: Society of Biblical Literature, 2001.

Lazarewicz-Wyrzykowska, Ela. "Samson: Masculinity Lost (and Regained?)" Pages 171–88 in *Men and Masculinity in the Hebrew Bible and Beyond*. Edited by Ovidiu Creangă. The Bible in the Modern World 33. Sheffield: Sheffield Phoenix, 2010.

Lee, John A. L. "*ΑΠΟΣΚΕΥΗ* in the Septuagint." *Journal of Theological Studies* 23(1972): 430–37.

Leeb, Carolyn S. *Away from the Father's House: The Social Location of na'ar and na'arah in Ancient Israel*. Journal for the Study of the Old Testament: Supplement Series 301. Sheffield: Sheffield Academic Press, 2000.

Levy, Bryna Jocheved. "Moshe: Portrait of the Leader as a Young Man." Pages 398–429 in *Torah of the Mothers: Contemporary Jewish Women Read Classical Jewish Texts*. Edited by Ora Wiskind Elper and Susan Handelman. New York: Urim Publications, 2000.

Linafelt, Tod. *Ruth*. Berit Olam. Collegeville, MI: Liturgical Press, 1999.

Lincoln, Bruce. *Emerging from the Chrysalis: Rituals of Women's Initiation*. Oxford: Oxford University Press, 1991.

Lipka, Hilary B. *Sexual Transgression in the Hebrew Bible*. Sheffield: Sheffield Phoenix, 2006.

———. "Masculinities in Proverbs: An Alternative to the Hegemonic Ideal." Pages 86–103 in *Biblical Masculinities Foregrounded*. Edited by Ovidiu Creangă and Peter-Ben Smit. Hebrew Bible Monographs 62. Sheffield: Sheffield Phoenix, 2014.

Long, Burke. *I Kings: With an Introduction to Historical Literature*. Forms of the Old Testament Literature 9. Grand Rapids, MI: Eerdmans, 1984.

Lord, Albert B. "Patterns of the Lives of the Patriarchs from Abraham to Samson and Samuel." Pages 7–18 in *Text and Tradition: The Hebrew Bible and Folklore*. Edited by Susan Niditch. Society of Biblical Literature Semeia Studies. Atlanta: Scholars Press, 1990.

Louw, Johannes P., and Eugene A. Nida, eds. *Greek-English Lexicon of the New Testament: Based on Semantic Domains.* 2d ed. New York: United Bible Societies, 1989.

Lust, Johan. "The Story of David and Goliath in Hebrew and in Greek." Pages 5–18 in *The Story of David and Goliath: Textual and Literary Criticism. Papers of a Joint Research Venture.* Edited by Dominique Barthélemy, David W. Gooding, Emanuel Tov, and Johan Lust. Orbis biblicus et orientalis 73. Göttingen: Vandenhoeck & Ruprecht/Freiburg: Éditions Universitaires, 1986.

MacDonald, John. "The Status and Role of the Naʻar in Israelite Society." *Journal of Near Eastern Studies* 35(1976): 147–70.

Măcerlau, Marcel V. "Saul in the Company of Men: (De)Constructing Masculinity in 1 Samuel 9–31." Pages 51–68 in *Biblical Masculinities Foregrounded.* Edited by Ovidiu Creangă and Peter-Ben Smit. Hebrew Bible Monographs 62. Sheffield: Sheffield Phoenix, 2014.

Macwilliam, Stuart. "Ideologies of Male Beauty in the Hebrew Bible." *Biblical Interpretation* 17(2009): 265–87.

———. "Athaliah: A Case of Illicit Masculinity." Pages 69–85 in *Biblical Masculinities Foregrounded.* Edited by Ovidiu Creangă and Peter-Ben Smit. Hebrew Bible Monographs 62. Sheffield: Sheffield Phoenix, 2014.

Mahler, Margaret, Fred Pine, and Anni Bergman. *The Psychological Birth of the Human Infant: Symbiosis and Individuation.* New York: Basic Books, 1975.

Malamat, Abraham. "Kingship and Council in Israel and Sumer: A Parallel." *Journal of Near Eastern Studies* 22(1963): 247–53.

———. "Organs of Statecraft in the Israelite Monarchy." *Biblical Archaeologist* 28(1965): 35–65.

Margalith, Othniel. "Samson's Riddle and Samson's Magic Locks." *Vetus Testamentum* 36(1986): 225–34.

Mazar, Amihai. "The Israelite Settlement." Pages 85–98 in *The Quest for the Historical Israel.* Edited by Brian B. Schmidt. Atlanta: Society of Biblical Literature, 2007.

McCarter, P. Kyle, Jr. *I Samuel: A New Translation with Introduction, Notes, and Commentary.* Anchor Bible 8; Garden City, NY: Doubleday, 1980.

McKenzie, Steven L. *King David: A Biography.* Oxford: Oxford University Press, 2000.

Meyers, Carol. "Hannah and Her Sacrifice: Reclaiming Female Agency." Pages 93–104 in *A Feminist Companion to Samuel and Kings.* Edited by Athalya Brenner. Feminist Companion to the Bible 5. Sheffield: Sheffield Academic Press, 1994.

———. "The Family in Early Israel." Pages 1–47 in Perdue, Leo G., Joseph Blenkinsopp, John J. Collins, and Carol Meyers, *Families in Ancient Israel.* Louisville: Westminster John Knox, 1997.

———. "Female Images of God in the Hebrew Bible." Pages 525–28 in *Women in Scripture: A Dictionary of Named and Unnamed Women in the Hebrew Bible, the Apocryphal/Deuterocanonical Books, and the New Testament.* Edited by Carol Meyers, Toni Craven, and Ross S. Kraemer. Grand Rapids, MI: Eerdmans, 2000.

————. "Rape or Remedy: Sex and Violence in Prophetic Marriage Metaphors." Pages 185–98 in *Prophetie in Israel.* Beiträge des Symposiums "Das Altes Testament und die Kultur der Moderne," anlässlich des 100. Geburtstags Gerhard von Rads (1901–1971), Heidelberg, 18.21 Oktober 2001. Edited by Hugh Williamson, Konrad Schmid, and Irmtraud Fischer. Münster: Lit-Verlag, 2003.

————. *Exodus.* New Cambridge Bible Commentary. Cambridge: Cambridge University Press, 2005.

————. "Contesting the Notion of Patriarchy: Anthropology and the Theorizing of Gender in Ancient Israel." Pages 83–105 in *A Question of Sex? Gender and Difference in the Hebrew Bible and Beyond.* Edited by Deborah W. Rooke. Hebrew Bible Monographs 14. Sheffield: Sheffield Phoenix, 2007.

————. *Rediscovering Eve: Ancient Israelite Women in Context.* Oxford: Oxford University Press, 2013.

Milgrom, Jacob. "The Priestly Consecration Ritual (Leviticus 8): A Rite of Passage." Pages 57–61 in *Bits of Honey: Essays for Samson H. Levey.* Edited by Stanley F. Chyet and David H. Ellenson. South Florida Studies in the History of Judaism 74. Atlanta: Scholars Press, 1993.

Miller, Patrick D. and J. J. M. Roberts. *The Hand of the Lord: A Reassessment of the "Ark Narrative" of 1 Samuel.* Johns Hopkins Near Eastern Studies. Baltimore: Johns Hopkins University Press, 1977.

Moberly, R. W. L. "To Hear the Master's Voice: Revelation and Spiritual Discernment in the Call of Samuel." *Scottish Journal of Theology* 48(1995): 443–68.

Mobley, Gregory. *The Empty Men: The Heroic Tradition of Ancient Israel.* Anchor Bible Reference Library. New York: Doubleday, 2005.

————. *Samson and the Liminal Hero in the Ancient Near East.* Library of Hebrew Bible/Old Testament Studies 453. New York: T&T Clark, 2006.

Montgomery, James A. *A Critical and Exegetical Commentary on the Books of Kings.* International Critical Commentary 10. New York: Scribner, 1951.

Moore, Stephen D. "Final Reflections on Biblical Masculinity." Pages 240–55 in *Men and Masculinity in the Hebrew Bible and Beyond.* Edited by Ovidiu Creangă. The Bible in the Modern World 33. Sheffield: Sheffield Phoenix, 2010.

———— and Janet Capel Anderson. "Taking it Like a Man: Masculinity in 4 Maccabees." *Journal of Biblical Literature* 117(1997): 249–73.

————, eds. *New Testament Masculinities.* Semeia Studies 45. Atlanta: Society of Biblical Literature, 2003.

Moxnes, Halvor. "Honor and Shame." Pages 19–40 in *The Social Sciences and New Testament Interpretation.* Edited by Richard L. Rohrbaugh. Peabody, MA: Hendrickson, 1996.

Niditch, Susan. *Underdogs and Tricksters: A Prelude to Biblical Folklore*. San Francisco: Harper & Row, 1987.

———. "Samson as Culture Hero, Trickster, and Bandit: The Empowerment of the Weak." *Catholic Biblical Quarterly* 52(1990): 608–24.

———. *War in the Hebrew Bible: A Study in the Ethics of Violence*. New York: Oxford University Press, 1993.

———. *Oral World and Written Word: Ancient Israelite Literature*. Louisville: Westminster John Knox, 1996.

———. *Judges: A Commentary*. Old Testament Library. Louisville: Westminster John Knox, 2008.

———. *My Brother Esau Is a Hairy Man: Hair and Identity in Ancient Israel*. New York: Oxford University Press, 2008.

Nielsen, Kirsten Busch. *Ruth*. Old Testament Library. Translated by Edward Broadbridge. Louisville: Westminster John Knox, 1997.

Niessen, Richard. "The Virginity of the עַלְמָה in Isaiah 7:14." *Bibliotheca sacra* 137(1980): 133–50.

Noth, Martin. *Exodus*. Old Testament Library. Translated by B. S. Bowden. Philadelphia: Westminster, 1962.

———. *The Deuteronomistic History*. Journal for the Study of the Old Testament: Supplement Series 15. Sheffield: JSOT Press, 1981.

O'Connor, Michael P., and John A. L. Lee. "A Problem in Biblical Lexicography: The Case of Hebrew *tap* and Greek *aposkeuē*." *Zeitschrift für die alttestamentliche Wissenschaft* 119(2007): 403–409.

Olson, Dennis T. "The Book of Judges: Introduction, Commentary, and Reflections." Pages 721–888 in *The New Interpreter's Bible* vol. 2. Edited by Leander E. Keck, et al. 12 vols. Nashville: Abingdon, 1994.

Perdue, Leo G. "The Israelite and Early Jewish Family: Summary and Conclusions." Pages 163–222 in Perdue, Leo G., Joseph Blenkinsopp, John J. Collins, and Carol Meyers, *Families in Ancient Israel*. Louisville: Westminster John Knox, 1997.

Piot, Charles. *Remotely Global: Village Modernity in West Africa*. Chicago: University of Chicago Press, 1999.

Pisano, Stephen. *Additions or Omissions in the Books of Samuel*. Orbis biblicus et orientalis 57; Freiburg: Universitätsverlag, 1984.

Pitt-Rivers, Julian. "Postscript: The Place of Grace in Anthropology." Pages 215–46 in *Honour and Grace in Anthropology*. Edited by John G. Peristiany and Julian Pitt-Rivers. Cambridge: Cambridge University Press, 1992.

Polzin, Robert. *Samuel and the Deuteronomist: A Literary Study of the Deuteronomistic History. Part Two: 1 Samuel*. Bloomington, IN: Indiana University Press, 1993.

Pope, Marvin H. *Job: A New Translation with Introduction and Commentary*. Anchor Bible 15. Garden City, NY: Doubleday, 1965.

Propp, Vladimir I. *Morphology of the Folktale*. Translated by L. Scott. 2d ed. Austin: University of Texas Press, 1968.

Propp, William H. C. "The Origins of Infant Circumcision in Israel." *Hebrew Annual Review* 11(1987): 355–70.

———. *Exodus 1–18: A New Translation with Introduction and Commentary*. Anchor Bible 2. New York: Doubleday, 1998.

———. *Exodus 19–40: A New Translation with Introduction and Commentary*. Anchor Bible 2A. New York: Doubleday, 2006.

Rainey, Anson F. "The Military Personnel of Ugarit." *Journal of Near Eastern Studies* 24(1965): 17–27.

Rendtdorff, Rolf. "Samuel the Prophet: A Link between Moses and the Kings." Pages 27–36 in *The Quest for Context and Meaning: Studies in Biblical Intertextuality in Honor of James A. Sanders*. Edited by Craig A. Evans and Shemaryahu Talmon. Leiden: Brill, 1997.

Rofé, Alexander. "The Battle of David and Goliath: Folklore, Theology, Eschatology." Pages 117–51 in *Judaic Perspectives on Ancient Israel*. Edited by Jacob Neusner, Baruch A. Levine, and Ernest S. Frerichs. Philadelphia: Fortress, 1987.

Rohrer-Walsh, Jennifer. "Coming of Age in *The Prince of Egypt*." Pages 77–99 in *Screening Scripture: Intertextual Connections between Scripture and Film*. Edited by George Aichele and Richard Walsh. Harrisburg, PA: Trinity Press International, 2002.

Römer, Thomas C. *The So-Called Deuteronomistic History: A Sociological, Historical and Literary Introduction*. New York: T&T Clark, 2007.

Rosaldo, Michelle Zimbalist. "Woman, Gender, and Society: A Theoretical Overview." Pages 17–45 in *Woman, Culture, and Society*. Edited by Michelle Z. Rosaldo and Louise Lamphere. Stanford: Stanford University Press, 1974.

Rost, Leonhard. *Die Überlieferung von der Thronnachfolge Davids*. Beiträge zur Wissenschaft vom Alten und Neuen Testament 3/6. Stuttgart: Kohlhammer, 1926.

Rubin, Lilian. *Intimate Strangers*. New York: Harper and Row, 1983.

Šanda, Albert. *Die Bucher der Könige*. Exegetisches Handbuch zum Alten Testament 9. Münster: Aschendorffsche Verlagsbuchhandlung, 1911.

Sarna, Nahum M. *Exodus: The Traditional Hebrew Text with the New JPS Translation*. Philadelphia: Jewish Publication Society, 1991.

Sasson, Jack M. "Reflections on an Unusual Practice Reported in ARM X:4." *Orientalia* 93(1974): 404–10.

Satlow, Michael. "'Try to be a Man:' The Rabbinic Construction of Masculinity." *Harvard Theological Review* 89(1996): 19–40.

Savran, George. "Theophany as Type Scene." *Prooftexts: A Journal of Jewish Literary History* 23(2003): 119–49.

Schafer, Roy. "Men Who Struggle Against Sentimentality." Pages 95–110 in *The Psychology of Men: New Psychoanalytic Perspectives*. Edited by Gerald I. Fogel, Frederick M. Lane, and Robert S. Liebert. New York: Basic Books, 1986.

Schipper, Jeremy. "Disabling Israelite Leadership: 2 Samuel 6:23 and Other Images of Disability in the Deuteronomistic History." Pages 103–13 in *This Abled Body: Rethinking Disabilities in Biblical Studies.* Edited by Hector Avalos, Sarah J. Melcher, and Jeremy Schipper. Semeia Studies 55. Atlanta: Society of Biblical Literature, 2007.

Schlegel, Alice, and Herbert Barry III. "The Evolutionary Significance of Adolescent Initiation Ceremonies." *American Ethnologist* 7(1980): 696–715.

Schneider, Tammi J. *Judges.* Berit Olam. Collegeville, MN: Liturgical Press, 2000.

Segal, Robert A. "Victor Turner's Theory of Ritual." *Zygon: Journal of Religion and Science* 18(1983): 327–35.

Siebert-Hommes, Jopie. "But if She Be a Daughter . . . She May Live! 'Daughters' and 'Sons' in Exodus 1–2." Pages 62–74 in *A Feminist Companion to Exodus to Deuteronomy.* Edited by Athalya Brenner. Feminist Companion to the Bible 6. Sheffield: Academic Press, 1994.

Simon, Uriel. "Samuel's Call to Prophecy: Form Criticism with Close Reading." *Prooftexts: A Journal of Jewish Literary History* 1(1981): 119–32.

———. *Reading Prophetic Narratives.* Translated by Lenn J. Schramm. Bloomington, IN: Indiana University Press, 1997.

Smith, Michael J. "Failure of the Family in Judges, Part 2: Samson." *Bibliotheca sacra* 162(2005): 424–36.

Soggin, J. Alberto. *Judges: A Commentary.* Translated by John S. Bowden. Old Testament Library. Philadelphia: Westminster John Knox, 1981.

Speiser, Ephraim A. *Genesis: A New Translation with Introduction and Commentary.* 3d ed. Anchor Bible 1. Garden City, NY: Doubleday, 1981.

Sperling, S. David. "Blood, Avenger Of." Pages 763–64 in vol. 1 of *The Anchor Bible Dictionary.* Edited by David Noel Freedman. 6 vols. New York: Doubleday, 1992.

Stager, Lawrence E. "The Archaeology of the Family in Ancient Israel." *Bulletin of the American Schools of Oriental Research* 260(1985): 1–35.

Stähli, Hans Peter. *Knabe-Jüngling-Knecht: Untersuchungen zum Begriff* נער *im Alten Testament.* Beiträge zur biblischen Exegese und Theologie 7. Frankfurt am Main: Peter Lang, 1978.

Steinberg, Naomi. *The World of the Child in the Hebrew Bible.* Hebrew Bible Monographs 51. Sheffield: Sheffield Phoenix, 2013.

Stoebe, Hans Joachim. *Das Erste Buch Samuelis.* Kommentar zum Alten Testament 8/1. Gütersloh: Mohn, 1973.

Stol, Marten. "Private Life in Ancient Mesopotamia." Pages 485–501 of vol. 1 in *Civilizations of the Ancient Near East.* Edited by Jack M. Sasson. 4 vols. New York: Scribner, 1995.

Stoller, Robert J. "Facts and Fancies: An Examination of Freud's Concept of Bisexuality." Pages 343–64 in *Women and Analysis: Dialogues on Psychoanalytic Views of Femininity.* Edited by Jean Strouse. New York: Dell, 1974.

———— and Gilbert H. Herdt. "The Development of Masculinity: A Cross-Cultural Contribution." *Journal of the American Psychoanalytic Association* 30(1982): 29–59.

Stone, Ken. "Gender Criticism: The Un-Manning of Abimelech." Pages 183–201 in *Judges and Method: New Approaches in Biblical Studies*. Edited by Gale A. Yee. 2d ed. Minneapolis: Fortress, 2007.

————. "Queer Reading between Bible and Film: *Paris is Burning* and the 'Legendary Houses' of David and Saul." Pages 75–98 in *Bible Trouble: Queer Reading at the Boundaries of Biblical Scholarship*. Edited by Teresa J. Hornsby and Ken Stone. Atlanta: Society of Biblical Literature, 2013.

Stone, Kenneth A. *Sex, Honor, and Power in the Deuteronomistic History*. Journal for the Study of the Old Testament: Supplement Series 234. Sheffield: JSOT Press, 1996.

Sweeney, Marvin. *I & II Kings: A Commentary*. Old Testament Library. Louisville: Westminster John Knox, 2007.

Talmon, Shemaryahu. "The 'Desert Motif' in the Bible and in Qumran Literature." Pages 31–63 in *Biblical Motifs: Origins and Transformations*. Edited by Alexander Altmann. Cambridge: Harvard University Press, 1966.

Tanner, J. Paul. "The Gideon Narrative as the Focal Point of Judges." *Bibliotheca sacra* 149(1992): 146–61.

Tov, Emmanuel. "The Nature of the Differences between MT and the LXX." Pages 19–46 in *The Story of David and Goliath: Textual and Literary Criticism. Papers of a Joint Research Venture*. Edited by Dominique Barthélemy, David W. Gooding, Emanuel Tov, and Johan Lust. Orbis biblicus et orientalis 73. Göttingen: Vandenhoeck & Ruprecht/Freiburg: Éditions Universitaires, 1986.

Tsumura, David Toshio. *The First Book of Samuel*. New International Commentary on the Old Testament. Grand Rapids, MI: Eerdmans, 2007.

Turner, Victor W. *The Forest of Symbols: Aspects of Ndembu Ritual*. Ithaca, NY: Cornell University Press, 1967.

————. *The Drums of Affliction: A Study of Religious Processes among the Ndembu of Zambia*. Oxford: Oxford University Press, 1968. Repr., Ithaca: Cornell University Press, 1981.

————. *The Ritual Process: Structure and Anti-Structure*. Ithaca: Cornell University Press, 1969. Repr., New Brunswick, NJ: AldineTransaction, 2007.

————. "An Anthropological Approach to the Icelandic Saga." Pages 349–74 in *Translation of Culture: Essays to E. E. Evans-Pritchard*. Edited by Thomas O. Beidelman. London: Tavistock Publications, 1971.

————. "Myth and Symbol." Pages 576–82 in *International Encyclopedia of the Social Sciences* 10. Edited by David Sills. New York: Macmillan, 1972.

————. *Drama, Fields and Metaphors: Symbolic Action in Human Society*. Ithaca: Cornell University Press, 1974.

Turner, Victor W. "African Ritual and Western Literature: Is a Comparative Symbology Possible?" Pages 45–81 in *The Literature of Fact: Selected Papers from the English Institute*. Edited by Angus Fletcher. English Institute Series. New York: Columbia University Press, 1976.

———. "Variations on a Theme of Liminality." Pages 36–52 in *Secular Ritual*. Edited by Sally Falk Moore and Barbara G. Myerhoff. Aasen, The Netherlands: Van Gorcum, 1977.

———. "Social Dramas and the Stories about Them." *Critical Inquiry* 7(1980): 141–68.

Van Der Lingen, Anton. *"Bw'-Yṣ'* ('To Go Out and To Come In') as a Military Term." *Vetus Testamentum* 42(1992): 59–66.

Van der Toorn, Karel. "Judges XVI 21 in the Light of Akkadian Sources." *Vetus Testamentum* 36(1986): 248–53.

———. *From Her Cradle to Her Grave: The Role of Religion in the Life of the Israelite and the Babylonian Woman*. Translated by Sara J. Denning-Bolle. Biblical Seminar 23. Sheffield: JSOT Press, 1994.

VanGemeren, Willem A., ed. *New International Dictionary of Old Testament Theology and Exegesis*. 5 vols. Grand Rapids, MI: Zondervan, 1997.

Van Gennep, Arnold. *The Rites of Passage*. Translated by Monika B. Vizedom and Gabrielle L. Caffee. Chicago: University of Chicago Press, 1960.

Van Seters, John. *The Life of Moses: The Yahwist as Historian in Exodus–Numbers*. Louisville: Westminster John Knox, 1994.

———. *The Biblical Saga of King David*. Winona Lake, IN: Eisenbrauns, 2009.

Vidal-Naquet, Pierre. "The Black Hunter and the Origin of the Athenian *Ephebia*." Pages 106–28 in *The Black Hunter: Forms of Thought and Forms of Society in the Greek World*. Translated by A. Szegedy-Maszak. Baltimore: The Johns Hopkins University Press, 1986. Repr. of "Le chasseur noir et l'origine de l'ephébie athénienne." *Annales, Economies, Sociétés, Civilisations* 23(1968): 947–64.

Von Rad, Gerhard. *Genesis: A Commentary*. Translated by John H. Marks. Old Testament Library. Philadelphia: Westminster, 1961.

———. *Deuteronomy: A Commentary*. Translated by Dorothea Barton. Old Testament Library. Philadelphia: Westminster, 1966.

Walsh, Jerome T. "The Characterization of Solomon in First Kings 1–5." *Catholic Biblical Quarterly* 57(1995): 471–93.

———. *I Kings*. Berit Olam. Collegeville, MN: Liturgical Press, 1996.

Walters, Jonathan. "'No More than a Boy': The Shifting Construction of Masculinity from Ancient Greece to the Middle Ages." *Gender and History* 5(1993): 20–33.

Washington, Harold. "Violence and the Construction of Gender in the Hebrew Bible: A New Historicist Approach." *Biblical Interpretation* 5(1997): 324–63.

Webb, Barry G. *The Book of Judges: An Integrated Reading*. Journal for the Study of the Old Testament: Supplement Series 46. Sheffield: Sheffield Academic Press, 1987.

Weisfield, Glen "Puberty Rites as Clues to the Nature of Human Adolescence." *Cross-Cultural Research* 31(1997): 27–54.

Weitzman, Steven. *Solomon: The Lure of Wisdom*. New Haven: Yale University Press, 2011.

Westermann, Claus. *Genesis 12–36*. Translated by John J. Scullion. First Fortress Press ed. Minneapolis: Fortress, 1995.

———. *Genesis 37–50*. Translated by John J. Scullion. First Fortress Press ed. Minneapolis: Fortress, 2002.

Wetherell, Margaret and Nigel Edley. "Negotiating Hegemonic Masculinity: Imaginary Positions and Psycho-Discursive Practices." *Feminism and Psychology* 9(1999): 335–56.

White, Hugh C. "The Initiation Legend of Ishmael." *Zeitschrift für die alttestamentliche Wissenschaft* 87(1975): 267–306.

———. "The Initiation Legend of Isaac." *Zeitschrift für die alttestamentliche Wissenschaft* 91(1979): 1–30.

Whitehead, Stephen M. *Men and Masculinities: Key Themes and New Directions*. Cambridge and Oxford: Polity Press, 2002.

Willesen, Folker. "The Yalid in Hebrew Society." *Studia theologica* 12(1958): 192–210.

Willis, John T. "An Anti-Elide Narrative Tradition from a Prophetic Circle at the Ramah Sanctuary." *Journal of Biblical Literature* 90(1971): 288–308.

———. "Samuel versus Eli: 1 Samuel 1–7." *Theologische Zeitschrift* 35(1979): 201–12.

Wilson, Brittany E. *Unmanly Men: Refigurations of Masculinity in Luke–Acts*. Oxford: Oxford University Press, 2015.

Winter, Irene J. "Art in Empire: The Royal Image and the Visual Dimensions of Assyrian Ideology." Pages 359–81 in *Assyria 1995: Proceedings of the 10th Anniversary Symposium of the Neo-Assyrian Text Corpus Project, Helsinki September 7–11, 1995*. Edited by Simo Parpola and Robert M. Whiting. Helsinki: Neo-Assyrian Text Corpus Project, 1997.

Wolff, Hans Walter. *Anthropology of the Old Testament*. Translated by Margaret Kohl. Philadelphia: Fortress, 1974.

Wyatt, Nick. "Circumcision and Circumstance: Male Genital Mutilation in Ancient Israel and Ugarit." *Journal for the Study of the Old Testament* 33(2009): 405–31.

Young, Frank W. *Initiation Ceremonies: A Cross-Cultural Study of Status Dramatization*. Indianapolis: Bobbs-Merrill, 1965.

Zannoni, Arthur E. "An Investigation of the Call and Dedication of the Prophet Samuel: I Samuel 1:1–4:1a." PhD diss., Marquette University, 1975.

Zeid, Abou A. M. "Honour and Shame among the Bedouins of Egypt." Pages 243–59 in *Honour and Shame: The Values of Mediterranean Society*. Edited by John G. Peristiany. Chicago: University of Chicago Press, 1966.

Ziolkowski, Eric. "Bad Boys of Bethel: Origin and Development of a Sacrilegious Type." *History of Religions* 30(1991): 331–58.

Zivotofsky, Ari. "The Leadership Qualities of Moses." *Judaism* 43(1994): 258–69.

Zorn, Jeffrey. "Reconsidering Goliath: An Iron Age I Philistine Chariot Warrior." *Bulletin of the American Schools of Oriental Research* 360(2010): 1–22.

Zorrel, Franz, ed. *Lexicon hebraicum et aramaicum Veteris Testamenti.* Rome: Pontificium Institutum Biblicum, 1958.

Index

majority, age of, 45, 47, 121, 138–39
marriage
    absence of, among HB boys, 68, 71
    connection to HB manhood, 41–42, 83
    in Exod 2, 83
    in Jacob cycle, 156
    in Judg 13–16, 135–36, 138
    in 1 Kgs 1–2, 119
    in 1 Sam 17, 103
masculinity studies
    history of field, 3–4
    lack of discussion of boyhood and
        coming of age, 6
    See also hegemonic masculinity

parents
    excessive connection with (quality of
        HB boyhood), 114–15, 137–38,
        220 n. 36
    powerlessness (quality of HB boyhood),
        53–54, 58, 61, 63, 65, 185–86 n. 43
    defined including lack of strength
        and authority, 53–54
    in Joseph novella, 156
    in 1 Kgs 1–2, 113–14
    See also fear, timidity.
puberty rites, female, 161 n. 1
    evidence in HB, 169–70 n. 72
puberty rites, male 1, 9
    in ancient Greece, 16, 21, 168 n. 62,
        169 n. 71, 170–71 n. 83, 172
        n. 99, 208 n. 39
    in ancient Israel, 20
    in ancient Mesopotamia, 21, 168 n. 62
    characteristics, 17
    and coming-of-age stories, 20–21
    and society's masculine ideal, 13–15

repetition
    threefold, 87–88
    sevenfold, 79, 195 n. 7

rites of passage
    application to literature by Turner,
        9–11
    in biblical coming-of-age stories, 22,
        103–6, 122–23, 215 n. 107
    in biblical exegesis, 11–12
    definition by van Gennep, 8–9, 165
        n. 35, 207 n. 33
    original emphasis on coming
        of age, 9 (*see also* puberty
        rites, male)
    principles for application in present
        study, 12–13
    schema misidentified in Gen 2–3,
        19
    structure defined, 9, 165–66 n. 38

self-control (quality of HB manhood),
        39–40, 179–80 n. 65
    relation to Torah obedience
        in 1 Kgs 1–2, 116–17
strength (quality of HB manhood),
        31–33
    in ancient Near East, 31–32
    equation with violence challenged,
        32–33
    in Exod 2, 80–81, 83
    in Jer 1, 158
    in Judg 8, 130–31
    in Judg 13–16, 134
    in 1 Kgs 1–2, 115, 116, 117–18
    and older boys/young men, 66
    in 1 Sam 17, 101
    See also authority
Succession Narrative, 33, 152, 210 n. 64
    conclusion in 1 Kgs 1–2, 113

theme
    definition, 172 n. 101
timidity/social fear (quality of HB
        boyhood), 85–86, 90, 200 n. 34